PART OBJECT

PART SCULPTURE

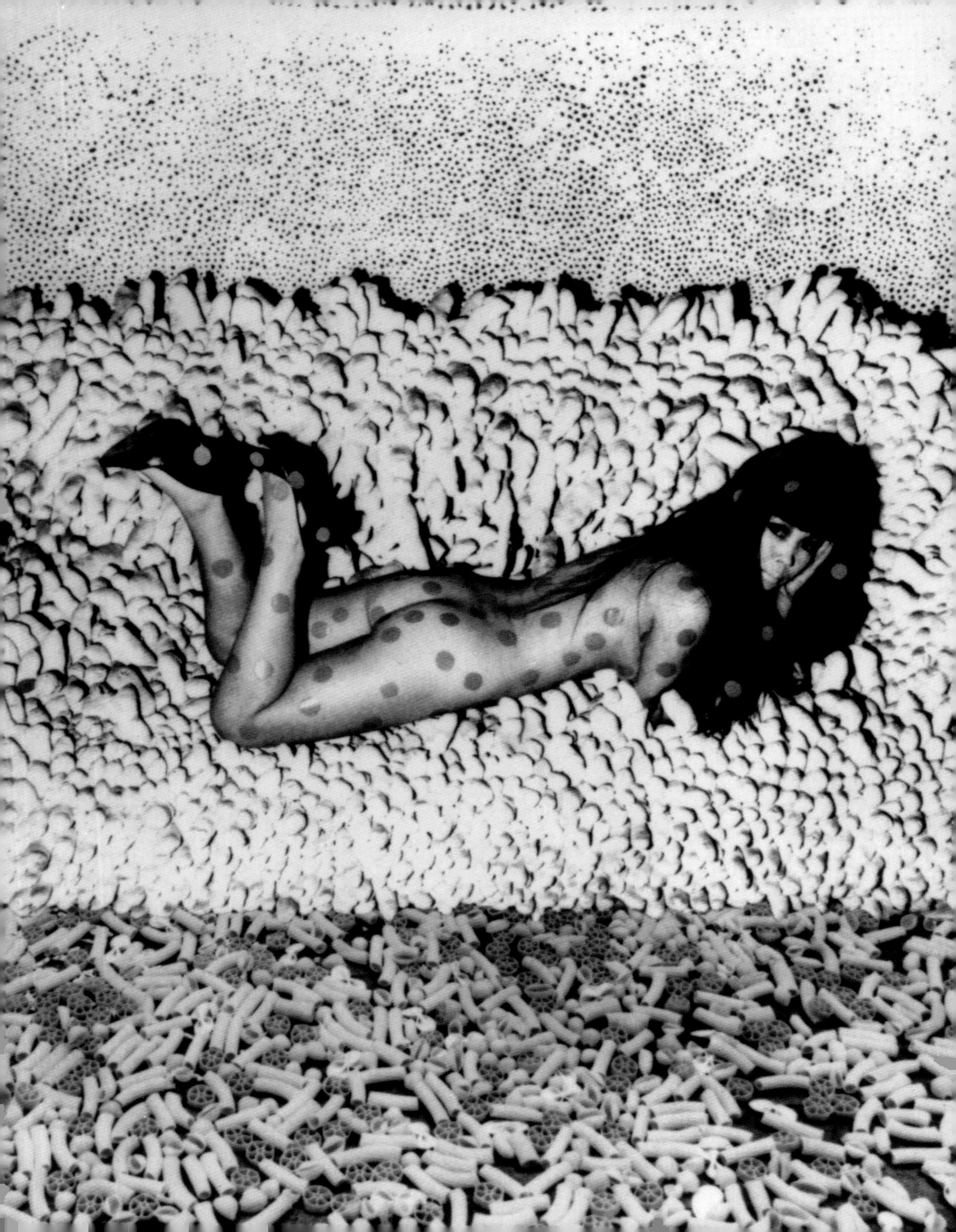

PART OBJECT

PART SCULPTURE

HELEN MOLESWORTH

WEXNER CENTER FOR THE ARTS | THE OHIO STATE UNIVERSITY
THE PENNSYLVANIA STATE UNIVERSITY PRESS

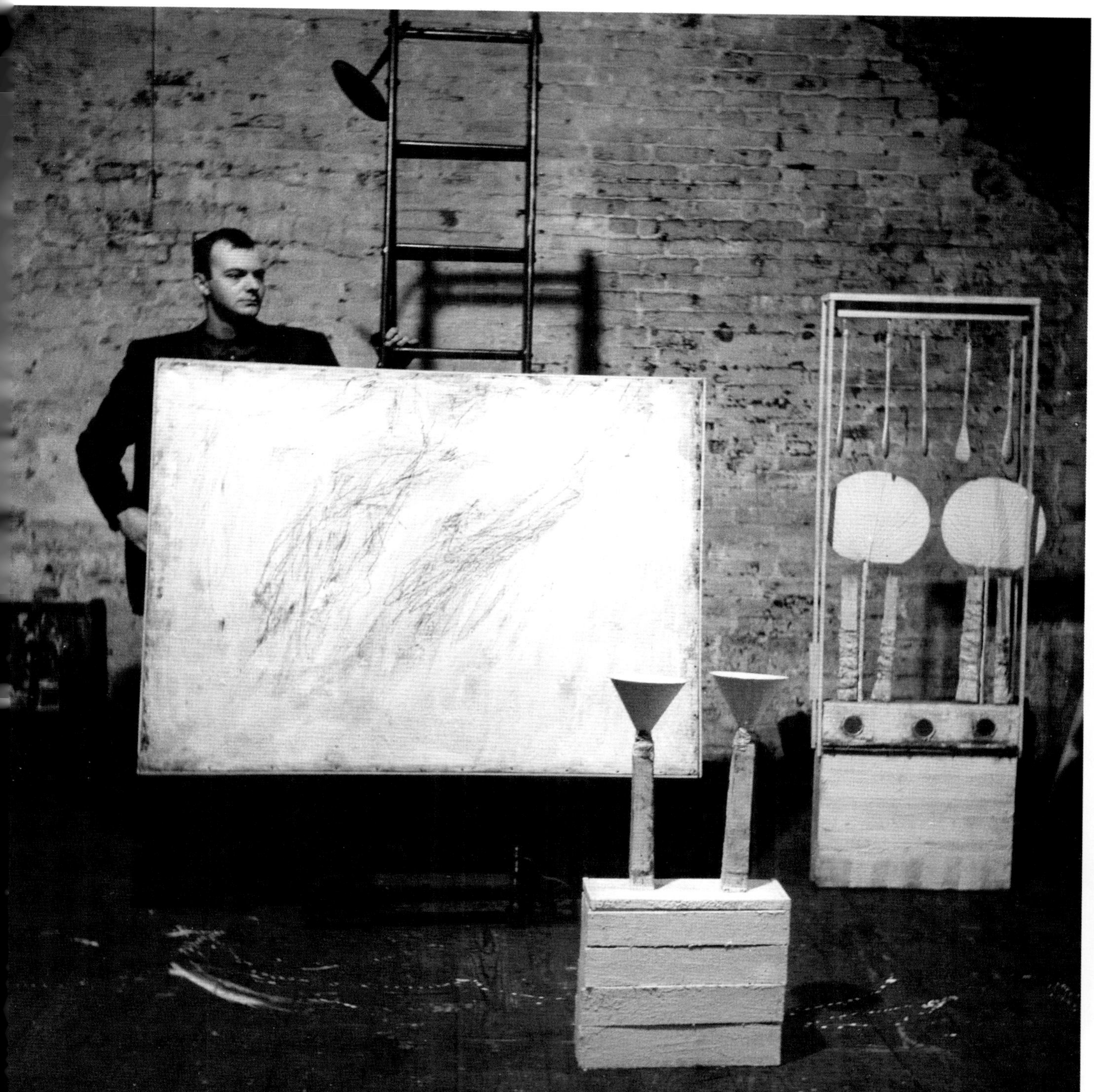

Catalogue entries by
Helen Molesworth and Lisa Florman

previous spread: left Yayoi Kusama
Collage, 1966
with photograph by Hal Reiff of Kusama reclining on *Accumulation No. 2*

previous spread: right Robert Rauschenberg
Cy Twombly with sculptures and a painting in Robert Rauschenberg's studio, Fulton Street, New York, 1954

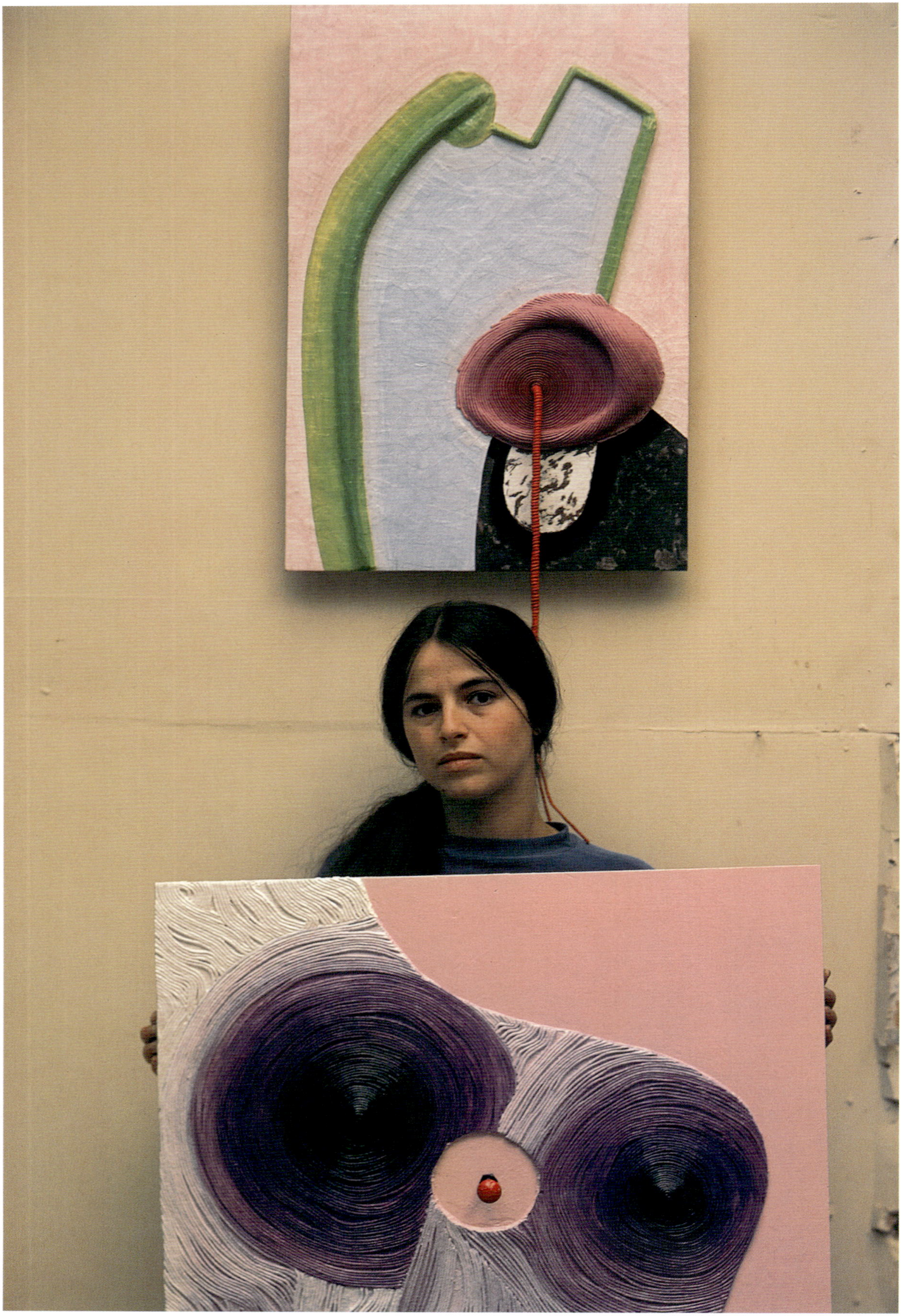

LENDERS TO THE EXHIBITION

Becht Collection, Naarden, The Netherlands

Lynda Benglis

The Berardo Collection – Sintra Museum of Modern Art

Louise Bourgeois

Marie Puck Broodthaers

Collection of Peggy and Ralph Burnet

Constance Caplan

Carnegie Museum of Art, Pittsburgh

Cheim & Read, New York

Des Moines Art Center

Detroit Institute of Arts

Stefan T. Edlis Collection

Fogg Art Museum, Harvard University Art Museums

Fondazione Palazzo Albizzini "Collezione Burri," Città di Castello, Italy

Maxine and Stuart Frankel

Friedrich Petzel Gallery, New York

Kathy and Richard S. Fuld, Jr.

Robert Gober

Collection Jerry Gorovoy

Hauser and Wirth Collection, Switzerland

Hauser & Wirth Zürich London

Henry Art Gallery, University of Washington

Herbert F. Johnson Museum, Cornell University

Hirshhorn Museum and Sculpture Garden, Smithsonian Institution

Hood Museum of Art, Dartmouth College, Hanover, New Hampshire

Collection of Jasper Johns

Leeum Samsung Museum of Art

Barbara and Aaron Levine

The Lucio Fontana Foundation, Milan

Magasin 3 Stockholm Konsthall

Maxine and Stuart Frankel Foundation for Art

Allan McCollum

Michael Werner Gallery, New York and Cologne

Moderna Museet, Stockholm

Musées royaux des Beaux-Arts de Belgique, Bruxelles – Koninklijke Musea voor Schone Kunsten van België, Brussel

Museum of Contemporary Art, Chicago

The Museum of Fine Arts, Houston

The Museum of Modern Art, New York

Museum Wiesbaden, Germany

The National Gallery of Art, Washington DC

National Gallery of Canada, Ottawa

New Orleans Museum of Art

Gabriel Orozco

Philadelphia Museum of Art

Ron and Ann Pizzuti

Collection of Robert Rauschenberg

Collection of Howard Read

Darwin and Geri Reedy

Collection of Ruth and Donald Saff

San Francisco Museum of Modern Art

Sonnabend Collection, New York

Sperone Westwater, New York

Stedelijk Museum voor Actuele Kunst (Municipal Museum of Contemporary Art), Ghent

Cy Twombly

Walker Art Center, Minneapolis

Private collections

Manfred Tischer, Düsseldorf
Eva Hesse with her 1965 reliefs
An Ear in a Pond and *2 in 1*

DIRECTOR'S FOREWORD

"He has changed the condition of being here."

So went the last line of Jasper John's poignant obituary for Marcel Duchamp in the November 1968 issue of *Artforum*. Johns observed that Duchamp's "persistent attempt to destroy frames of reference altered our thinking, established new units of thought, 'a new thought for that object.'" Artists, and architects for that matter, have been sparring with Duchamp's legacy for nearly a century, staking their own claims on that "field where language, thought and vision act upon one another." The ripples and reverberations of his work are legion; cultural production in the twentieth century is simply unimaginable without him. Indeed, the very existence of a Wexner Center is argument for his enduring influence: the "cross-references of sight and thought, the changing focus of the eyes and mind, give fresh sense to the time and space we occupy...."

And what of that space? Not unlike such architectural landmarks as Mies van der Rohe's Neue Nationalgalerie in Berlin, Frank Lloyd Wright's Guggenheim Museum in New York, and Renzo Piano and Richard Rogers's Centre Georges Pompidou in Paris, the Wexner Center erupted on the cultural landscape when it first opened – not just as a bold and daring building dedicated to the art of the present, but as a building that dared art to be bold. Peter Eisenman and Richard Trott created what the late Spalding Gray, a pioneer of vanguard theater who appeared many times on Wexner Center stages, called the "spaceship that crash landed on the prairies."

To everyone's surprise, the unlikely experiment of such a multidisciplinary center in the heartland garnered unprecedented support from its inception, primarily through the generosity of a visionary benefactor, Leslie H. Wexner, and an equally visionary institution of learning, The Ohio State University. Together, they placed considerable resources at the service of this nascent institution, enabling it to grow into a laboratory that today sustains research, development, and interpretation of contemporary cultural practices in virtually every creative guise and across all media.

The Wexner Center thrives on the dizzying diversity and complexity of contemporary life, and the Eisenman/Trott design for the center is the very embodiment of that confluence and cacophony. There is no mistaking it; the design emphatically declares its commitment to provide a dynamic setting for contemporary art that intrigues, invigorates, and engages the university and the city around it. Not despite but *because* of its architectural idiosyncrasies, the

Wexner Center building turns out to be a remarkably generous and generative space in which to work. In fact, it may be most exhilarating in its very refusal to comport to traditional notions of gallery space, thereby catalyzing collisions and juxtapositions as memorable as they are unpredictable.

Within that challenging context, Helen Molesworth, our chief curator of exhibitions, has embraced the momentous task of organizing the reopening exhibition for the center following its extensive renovation. This curatorial undertaking also marks Helen's initiation into the pleasures and paradoxes of installing in the Eisenman galleries, a daunting rite of passage by any measure. Nonetheless, thanks to her fearless spirit and acute curatorial mind, *Part Object Part Sculpture* aptly and exquisitely engages both the physical territory of the building and the conceptual territory of the center's mission: to celebrate watershed moments of artistic expression over the last half century and draw vital connections between such historic innovations and more recent breakthroughs.

Helen reawakens our long-dormant galleries with cunning and savvy as she fills Eisenman's experiment in "part object part architecture" with *Part Object Part Sculpture,* parlaying the building itself into her curatorial scheme. With an installation free of temporary walls, she choreographs a duet between gallery and exhibition that dazzles in its rigor and luminance.

She takes as her point of departure the potent mythology that arises from Marcel Duchamp's readymades, which underlies and propels so much of twentieth-century art. Deftly dodging the plethora of industrially replicated machinations known as Minimalism, Helen follows the more sensuous, tactile, and handmade impulse that simultaneously coursed through sculptural production over the last fifty years.

Intrepid curatorial sleuth that she is, Helen uncovers intriguing connections among artists of several generations, selecting sumptuous, rarely seen works that trace a particularly organic and fertile artistic lineage from Duchamp to the present. Provocative, poignant, humorous, and irreverent, the exhibition aspires to nothing short of casting sculptural practice of the last half-century in a new light as it fills the center's galleries with spectacular work by twenty artists, including three former Wexner Prize recipients (Louise Bourgeois, Robert Rauschenberg, and Bruce Nauman).

The capstone of the exhibition is surely *An End to Modernity*, a spectacular blown-glass sculpture by artist-in-residence Josiah McElheny, commissioned by the center for its reopening. Created with the assistance of Ohio State's

departments of astronomy, mechanical engineering, electrical engineering, and others, it joins so many artist projects commissioned by the center over the years that have engaged and enriched the intellectual capital of this university. We thank Josiah and his partners across campus for so avidly pursuing this remarkable opportunity for cross-disciplinary research.

We are enormously grateful for the generosity of our colleagues in public institutions around the world, as we are to the private collectors who have so graciously parted with precious works in order to make them available to us for this exhibition. Their encouragement and participation are all the more gratifying in that the Wexner Center is not a collecting institution that can readily reciprocate such remarkable loans.

I join Helen in expressing my thanks to the brilliant essayists included in this publication – Briony Fer, Rosalind Krauss, Rachel Haidu, David Joselit, and Molly Nesbit. Their respective contributions join with Helen's essay to cultivate a fresh conversation about truly seminal moments in contemporary art history. Designer Lorraine Wild of Green Dragon Office has deftly created a publication that captures and conveys the pulse and spirit of the exhibition. Although the exhibition cannot travel because of the fragility of several works, we trust this catalogue will propel its intellectual force across the miles and the decades.

An enterprise such as *Part Object Part Sculpture* would not be possible without the support of numerous individuals, corporations, and foundations that I am deeply honored to recognize here. Early and generous support was provided by The Andy Warhol Foundation for the Visual Arts, and I express my utmost gratitude to President Joel Wachs, Chairman Wynn Kramarsky, and the entire Warhol foundation board. We are also enormously grateful to Bill and Sheila Lambert, Agnes Gund and Daniel Shapiro, and the Trueman family, all of whom have been exemplary in their largesse.

The center is proud and fortunate to have also enlisted significant support from Mary and Bob Kidder, Joyce and Chuck Shenk, Triumph International Spiesshofer & Braun Kommanditgesellschaft, the Altria Group Inc., the Nimoy Foundation, The Judith Rothschild Foundation, and Nancy and David Gill. Each has been an enthusiastic partner and patron over the years—particularly in support of vanguard ideas and projects. Additional support was provided by Constance Caplan, the Greater Columbus Arts Council, the National Endowment for the Arts, and the Art Alliance for Contemporary Glass.

As ever, I remain profoundly grateful to the leadership of the Ohio State University, the board of trustees of the Wexner Center Foundation, and donors to the foundation's Corporate Annual Fund, whose unstinting moral and financial support makes so many remarkable things possible. Finally, it is my honor and privilege to recognize the unparalleled generosity of Leslie and Abigail Wexner, without whom the center would be simply unimaginable.

While I would like to individually name all the staff members at the center who have made *Part Object Part Sculpture* possible, space limitations require that I refrain. But I heartily echo Helen's expression of gratitude to the extended exhibition team, whose dedication to this project has been phenomenal. Likewise, I am profoundly grateful to each and every member of the Wexner Center staff, who have been simply remarkable in their steadfast commitment to this institution and its mission, even during the unsettling period of renovation and off-site programs. So, too, we thank our many volunteers, members, and patrons who have remained loyal to the center throughout this ambitious undertaking. We all look forward that unique creative combustion that comes of reuniting all the center's programs under one roof. It will be pure pleasure to welcome everyone back to "home base" at last.

In closing, let me note that, while I may hail from a so-called cultural capital on the coast, I have come to recognize that the innate modesty and openness of the Midwest makes some very surprising things possible, culturally and otherwise. With abundant thanks to my peerless board of trustees – and also to the exceptional leadership of The Ohio State University – the center has taken its place as a truly unique institution that continues to evolve and grow.

Perhaps its greatest potential lies in the very conviction that a place like the Wexner Center is more important than ever to a civil and enlightened society in our complex and increasingly intolerant times. Obviously, physical and financial resources are crucial, but the real fuel for this place is imagination. I like to think that Duchamp himself would have been at home here. And for everyone who might have wondered if this unusual experiment in the heartland would survive, even flourish, we believe that the array of astounding events on stage, on screen, and in our galleries to celebrate the reopening of the Wexner Center deliver a resounding *yes.*

SHERRI GELDIN, *Director*

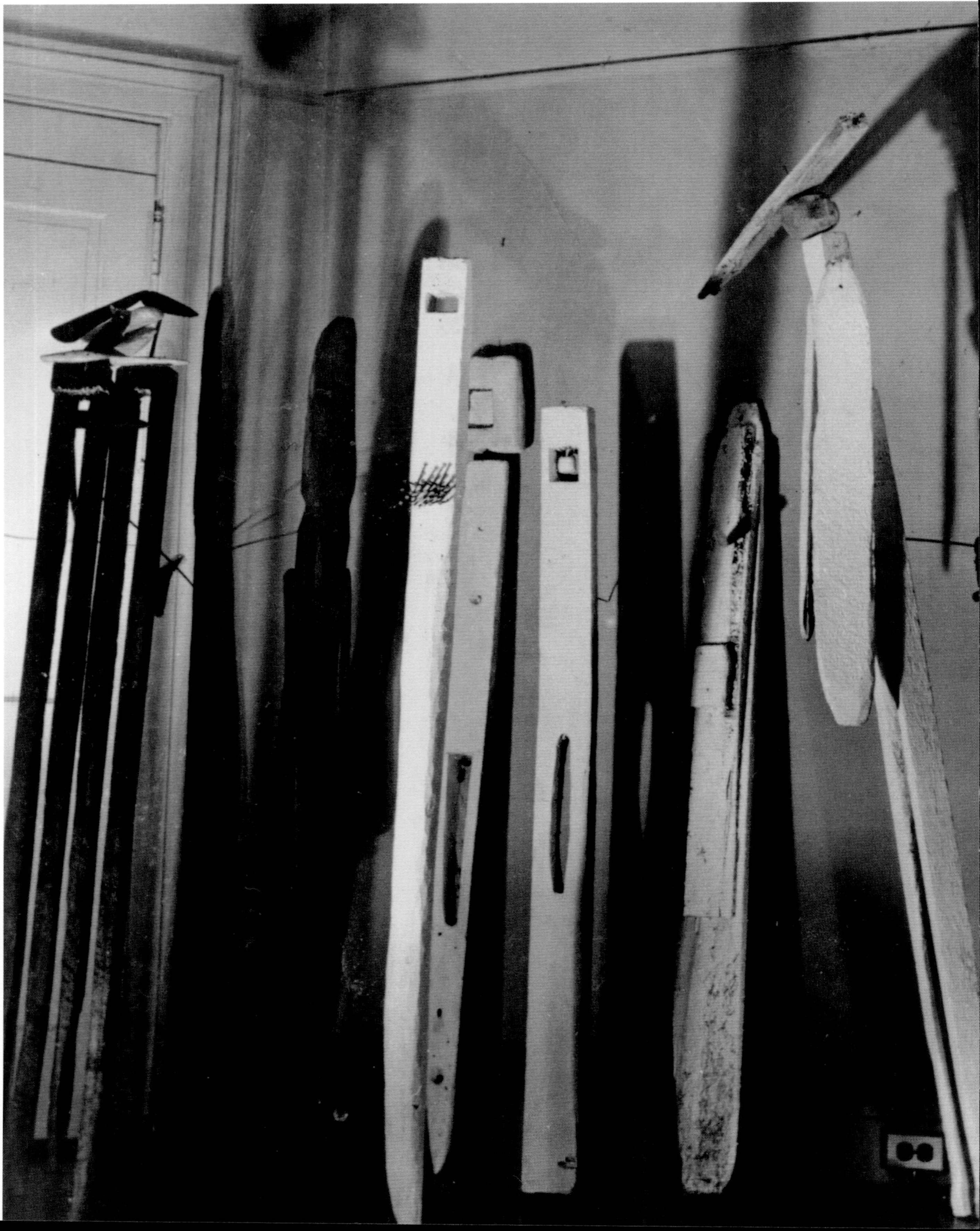

ACKNOWLEDGMENTS

As always, exhibitions and catalogues of this scale are utterly dependent on a vast network of individuals, all of whom dedicate themselves in various ways to aiding and abetting the vision of the curator. It is particularly humbling to register my gratitude in this instance. I am truly fortunate to work at an institution where everyone who labored on *Part Object Part Sculpture* did so with consummate grace under pressure. My first and most abiding thanks go to two people: Director Sherri Geldin and Curatorial Assistant Megan Cavanaugh Novak. Sherri believed in this project from its very first utterance, and her support made her an incisive critic who strengthened the overall project. If her ambition and tenacity are contagious, then this exhibition is a symptom. Megan is a consummate perfectionist whose high standards of work and daily good humor made the exhibition possible, as well as a pleasure to work on. The entire staff of the exhibitions department labored in ways large and small to make this venture come to fruition. Many thanks to Exhibitions Manager, Jill Davis; Preparator, Will Fugman; Assistant Exhibitions Designer, Larry Heller; Head Registrar, Joan Hendricks; Exhibition Department Assistant, Cara Hering; Associate Curator, Claudine Isé; Assistant Registrar, Jennifer Roy; Graduate Assistant Maruta Vitols; and Preparator, Patrick Weber. Others played key roles as well: Editor Ann Bremner; Director of Development, Jeff Byars; Grant Writer, Brigid Flynn; Deputy Director, Jack Jackson; Director of Design, Chris Jones; Design Engineer, Steve Jones; Assistant to the Director, James Petsche; Communications Manager, Karen Simonian; and Senior Graphic Designer, Myung Jin Song. In addition, I join Sherri in my heartfelt thanks to our Board of Trustees for their exemplary support of contemporary culture.

There is no such thing as an art exhibition without the art. I convey my deepest gratitude to the artists for making it and to the lenders, both private and institutional, who entrusted us with these marvelous and precious objects. Additionally, this exhibition would not have been possible without the many foundations, corporations, and private individuals who generously lent their financial support. Many colleagues helped to track down elusive works, thanks to: Marian Goodman, Leslie Nolen, and Andrew Richards, Marian Goodman Gallery; Ann Goldstein and Paul Schimmel, LA MOCA; Charles Wylie, Dallas Museum of Art; Carla Chammas and Glenn McMillan, CRG Gallery; Peter Freeman, Peter Freeman Gallery; Simon Lee, Sprüth Magers and Lee; Roland Augustine and

Sculptures in progress in Louise Bourgeois's studio in New York, circa 1947

Claudia Altman-Siegel, Luhring Augustine; Michelle Reyes, Estate of Felix Gonzalez-Torres; Andrea Rosen, Andrea Rosen Gallery; Florian Berktold, Hauser & Wirth; Tina Kim, Tina Kim Fine Art; Antonio Homen, Sonnabend Gallery; and Friedrich Petzel and Zach Miner, Friedrich Petzel Gallery.

Three years in the making, *Part Object Part Sculpture* is the result of numerous conversations with friends and colleagues, many of whom I hope will see themselves reflected in either the catalogue texts or the exhibition proper. Jacqueline Matisse Monnier opened her home to me, shared her reminisces and intimate knowledge of Marcel Duchamp, and then graciously supported the project in every way. I was lucky enough to have a long conversation with Walter Hopps before his sad passing. It was revelatory; he had forgotten more about Duchamp than I will ever know. A day in London with Briony Fer shaped the project in ineffable ways. Her sense that the art and the writing really matter have been very sustaining. So too, her book *The Infinite Line* has been a wonderful interlocutor. Carolyn Christov Bakargiev not only cured me of terrible jet lag but insisted, rightly so, on the importance of Alberto Burri to this project. Molly Nesbit's generosity, warmth, and subtle criticism have meant a great deal to me. Stephen Melville gave me an opportunity to try out some of these ideas in public at the Sterling and Francine Clark Art Institute, which in turn allowed him, along with Emily Apter and George Baker, to respond in ways I readily incorporated. I've also learned a great deal about how complicated the art-historical venture is from Steve at many a convivial gathering in Columbus. Lisa Florman incisively read a draft of the lead essay, critiquing it in the best sense of the word. Exchanges with Gregg Bordowitz helped to clarify my thoughts in instrumental ways. Tom Eccles, Agnes Gund, Jason Simon, Maruta Vitols, Joe Volpe, and David Weinberg were indispensable in their help with Josiah McElheny's work. Lorraine Wild and Green Dragon Office designed a beautiful volume, and Gloria Kury and Cherene Holland gracefully edited it. And special thanks to Barry Rosen, my cherished ally and friend.

I have talked about art in general, and this exhibition specifically, with Marie Puck Broodthaers, Connie Butler, William Camfield, Helen Hesse Charash, Moyra Davey, Leah Dickerman, Brigid Doherty, Matthew Drutt, Maria Gilissen, Robert Gober, Alison de Lima Greene, John Elderfield, Andrea Fraser, Jason Fusco, Rachel Haidu, Rachel Harrison, David Joselit, Rosalind Krauss, Ulf Linde,

Catherina Machanda, Allan McCollum, Josiah McElheny, Carol and Charles Molesworth, Karen Nielsen, Diana Nemiroff, Gabriel Orozco, Renate Petzinger, Arturo Schwarz, Amy Sillman, Elisabeth Sussman, Michael Taylor, Ann Temkin, Jeffery Weiss, and Iris Müller Westerman. All were generous with their time and insights. Life in Columbus, Ohio, is wonderfully agreeable, largely due to a network of friends who make my day-to-day quite pleasurable. For all the dinners, lunches, coffees, and drinks, I want to thank Jill Davis and Fred Dirkse, Steve and Ruthie Melville, Lisa Florman and David Weinberg, Bill Horrigan, Dave Filipi, Catherine Evans and Ted Inbusch, Nancy and Dave Gill, and Jan and Ben Maiden.

I especially want to thank the two people whose teaching shaped the beginning of my interest in Marcel Duchamp: Rosalind Krauss and Hal Foster, both of whom presided over my graduate studies. Rosalind taught me how to look at art and to trust what I saw and thought when I did. Hal taught me that any argument with only two sides isn't worth having. It is a true pleasure to be able to thank them publicly. There is Susan, about whom I feel very lucky, and whose example I endeavor to follow. Finally, this volume is dedicated to the memory of my grandmother, Anne Molesworth (January 22, 1910–February 10, 2005), with gratitude for all of the happiness offered by her long life.

HELEN ANNE MOLESWORTH, *Chief Curator of Exhibitions*

HELEN MOLESWORTH

INTRODUCTION

PART OBJECT PART SCULPTURE

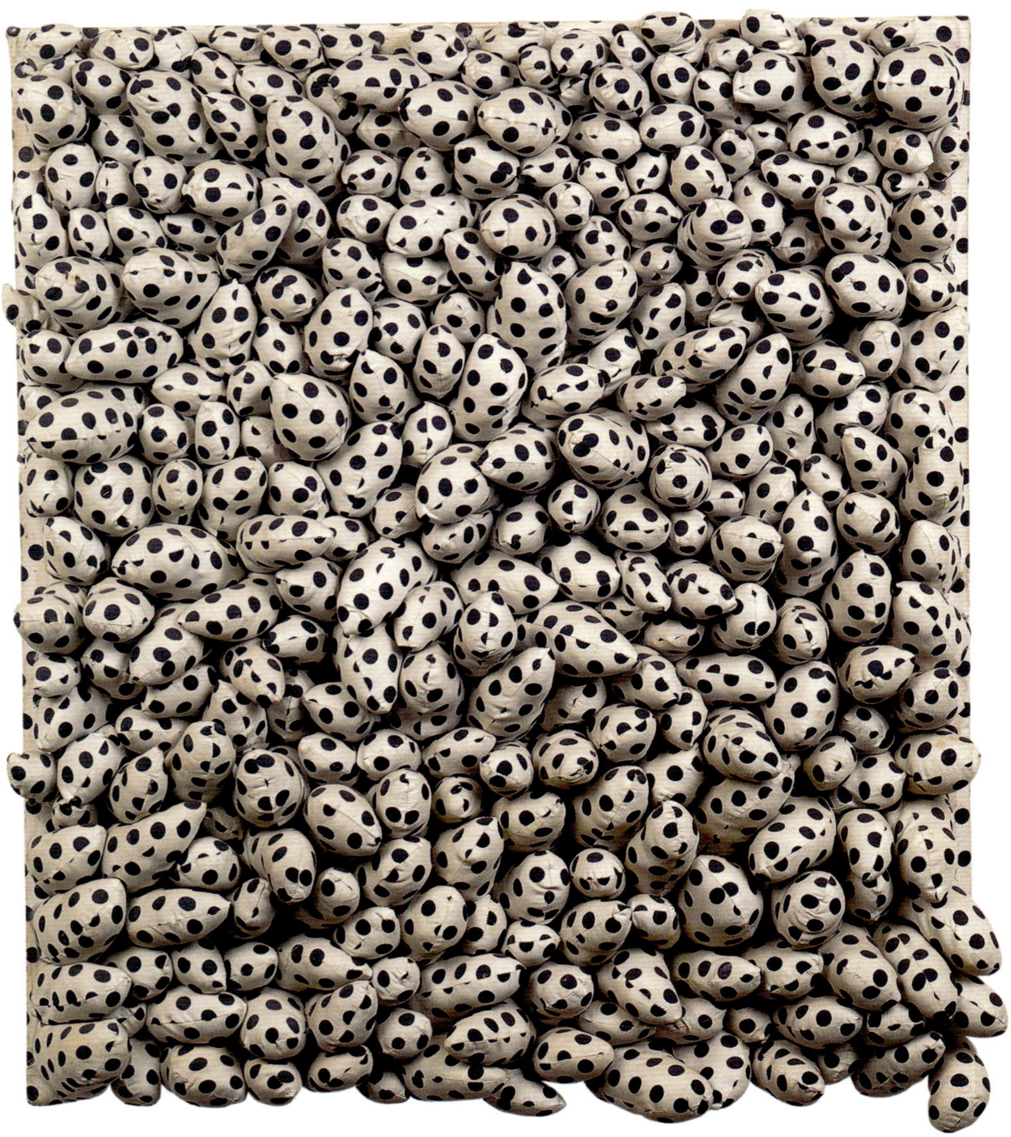

Part Object Part Sculpture brings together the sculpture of a select group of European and American artists to propose a new way of looking at the history of postwar art. The prolific achievements of Minimalism have long dominated accounts of the scope and aim of late twentieth-century sculpture, an orthodoxy that takes no small part of its authority from an interpretation of Marcel Duchamp that treats his early readymades as radical, yet foundational, works of postwar sculpture. This narrative insists, to the point of exclusivity, on the mass-produced nature of Duchamp's readymades. However, for nearly three decades after World War II, Duchamp was making art by hand. The combination of a strictly machine-made Duchampian paradigm and the industrial materials and repetitious procedures of much Minimalist art has consolidated as well the notion that the widespread practice of repetition in postwar art largely follows the logic of industrial production. In turn, the dominant but blinkered account of the readymade tends to unfold in a rather neat art-historical progression that begins with Pop art, leads into Minimalism, enters Conceptualism, and exits finally with the challenges of both Pictures generation photographic-based work and Institutional Critique.

Part Object Part Sculpture tells another story, one that shifts attention away from the Dada-inflected Duchamp of the teens to the Duchamp of the 1950s, who spent the final decades of his career pursuing an abiding interest in the ties binding desire to the body and to things. This narrative shift means that *Part Object Part Sculpture* stakes out new territories in which repetition involves the body, not the machine; materials harbor traces of human touch; and the viewer is often caught in a web where the threads of the psychic and the phenomenological intertwine. By bridging the gap that has separated Duchamp's readymades from the major works of his postwar years – the *Boîte-en-Valise*, the three erotic objects, and *Etant donnés* – Duchamp emerges less as a proto-Conceptualist or critic of art's claims to transcendent meaning, and more, far more, as an artist absorbed in the pleasures and problems of the body and all those energies known as eros.

During the early 1950s, Duchamp made three enigmatic, diminutive, and clearly erotic sculptures. They were subsequently reproduced in editions and, in time, it became clear that they were preambles to his last, and most mysterious, work, *Etant donnés*. In 1964, several years after he had made and editioned the three erotic objects, Duchamp authorized Arturo Schwarz to fabricate a set of his, then, mostly lost readymades. Although the original readymades had been mass-produced objects, purchased by the artist and transformed into art through the artist's choice, the readymades of the 1960s were anything but mass produced. These replicas were laboriously crafted by Italian artisans whose work was subject to Duchamp's approval. The temporal proximity of the intimate, handmade erotic sculptures and the replicas of the readymades suggests that the erotics of the body and the allure of the commodity are connected in Duchamp's practice. Such doubled stagings of desire would have far-reaching implications for postwar sculpture. Duchamp's triumvirate of concerns: the problem of the

Yayoi Kusama
Blue Spots, 1965

object, the most predominant form of which is the commodity; the situation of desire – and the inevitability of the displacement of erotic desire onto the desire for objects; and a continual play with various forms of reproduction, replication, and repetition create a field of aesthetic play for artists of the postwar period. In the work of the artists who explore this tripartite field of play, one often finds the emotional, psychological, and physical effects of shattering, a kind of wild dispersal of the erotic, as everywhere the presence of the body is felt but nowhere is it imaged. This genealogical strain of sculpture is bound together by several shared formal attributes, such that one often finds an exploration of sculptural practices that are diminutive in scale and sculpture made through the process of casting. So too this genealogy traffics in objects that are bound together by their shared indeterminacy – paintings may behave like sculptures, sculptures like objects, and repetition generates the unique. *Part Object Part Sculpture* charts this volatile aesthetic and psychic terrain.

Duchamp was by no means alone in his preoccupation with eros and objects: the examples of Louise Bourgeois and Alberto Burri are undeniable. Bourgeois's Personages animate the inanimate, bestowing upon objects the psychic energy of the human world. Burri's inclusion of readymade objects into the picture plane created a series of excruciating and ravishing analogues for skins and bodies. Lucio Fontana's ejaculatory spray of gemstones and crushed glass onto punctured canvases establishes the erotic dimension of both the art object and artistic activity. Other artists had their ear to the ground, so to speak. Marcel Broodthaers was quick to grasp the erotic dimension of Duchamp's work, as his accumulations of mussel and eggshells offer a humorous and erotic version of Karl Marx's notion of reification: soft interiors protected by calcified exteriors. Jasper Johns was alert to the handmadeness of Duchamp's erotic objects: his light bulbs and flashlights of the late 1950s offer the commodity object as an exercise in bodily tactility. And the phallic encrusted objects of Yayoi Kusama revel in an everyday domesticity gone deeply awry.

Part Object Part Sculpture does not include sculpture dependent upon the serial logic of Pop art's parodies of consumerism, nor does it feature examples of Minimalism's fusion of industrial materials and geometric principles or instances of Conceptualism's logarithmic logic. The decision to resist the impulse to survey postwar sculpture as such goes hand in hand with the choice to run the risk of assembling an exhibition of heterogeneous objects that have in common a Duchampian genealogy and the use of repetition to yield difference and provoke embodied responses. This is why the art in *Part Object Part Sculpture* so often makes the hairs on the beholder's neck stand on end, summoning unconscious thoughts of the hidden recesses and pleasures of the body. Think of Lynda Benglis's wax lozenges: all are roughly the same size and made with the same materials, yet each is utterly different. The unsettled identity of the wax objects plays directly into their erotic pull; they seem both phallic and vaginal, disturbing and pleasurable. The seductive interweaving, which occurs in much of the art in this exhibition, lends support to the supposition that

right Lucio Fontana
Concetto spaziale (Spatial Concept), 1956

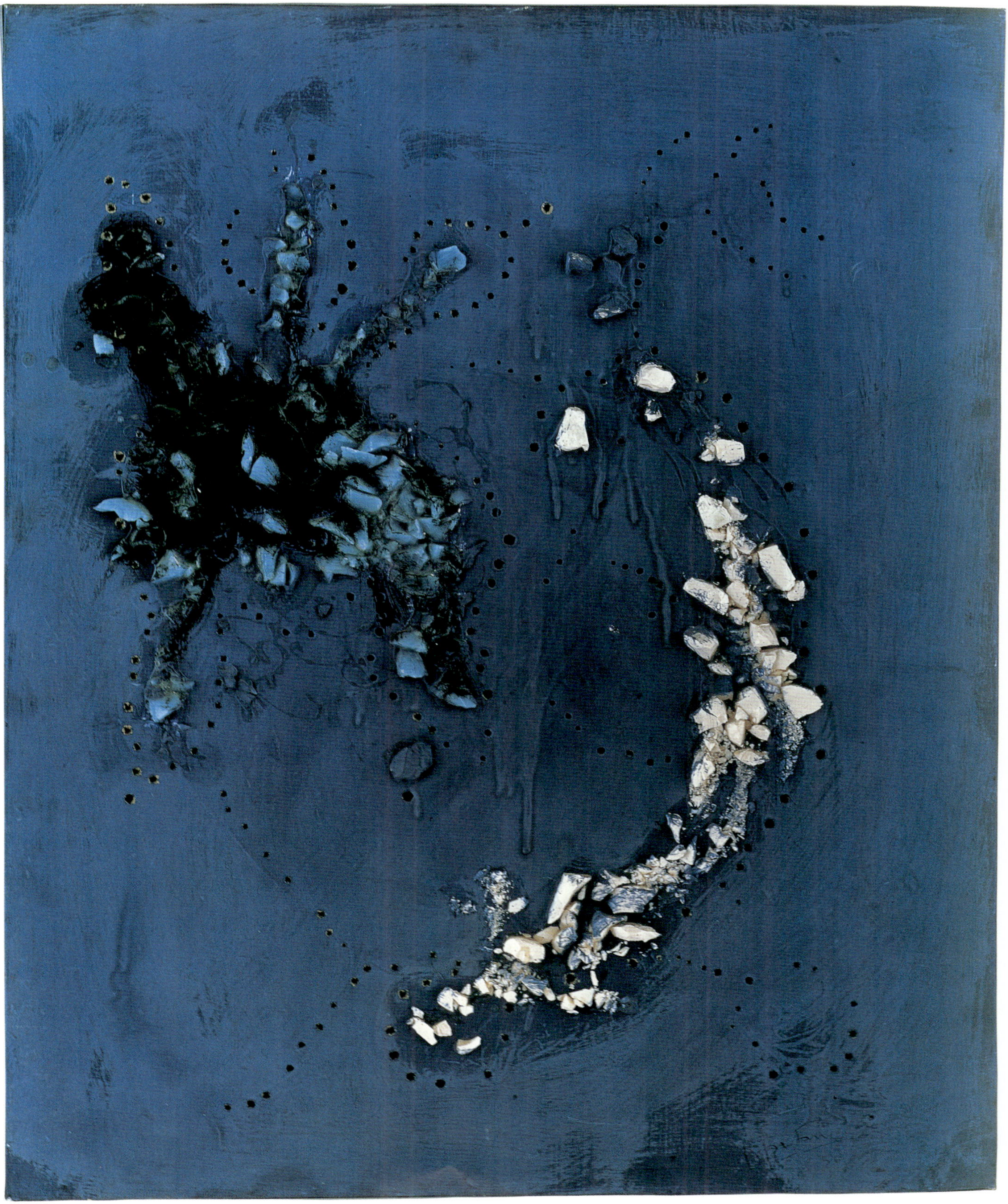

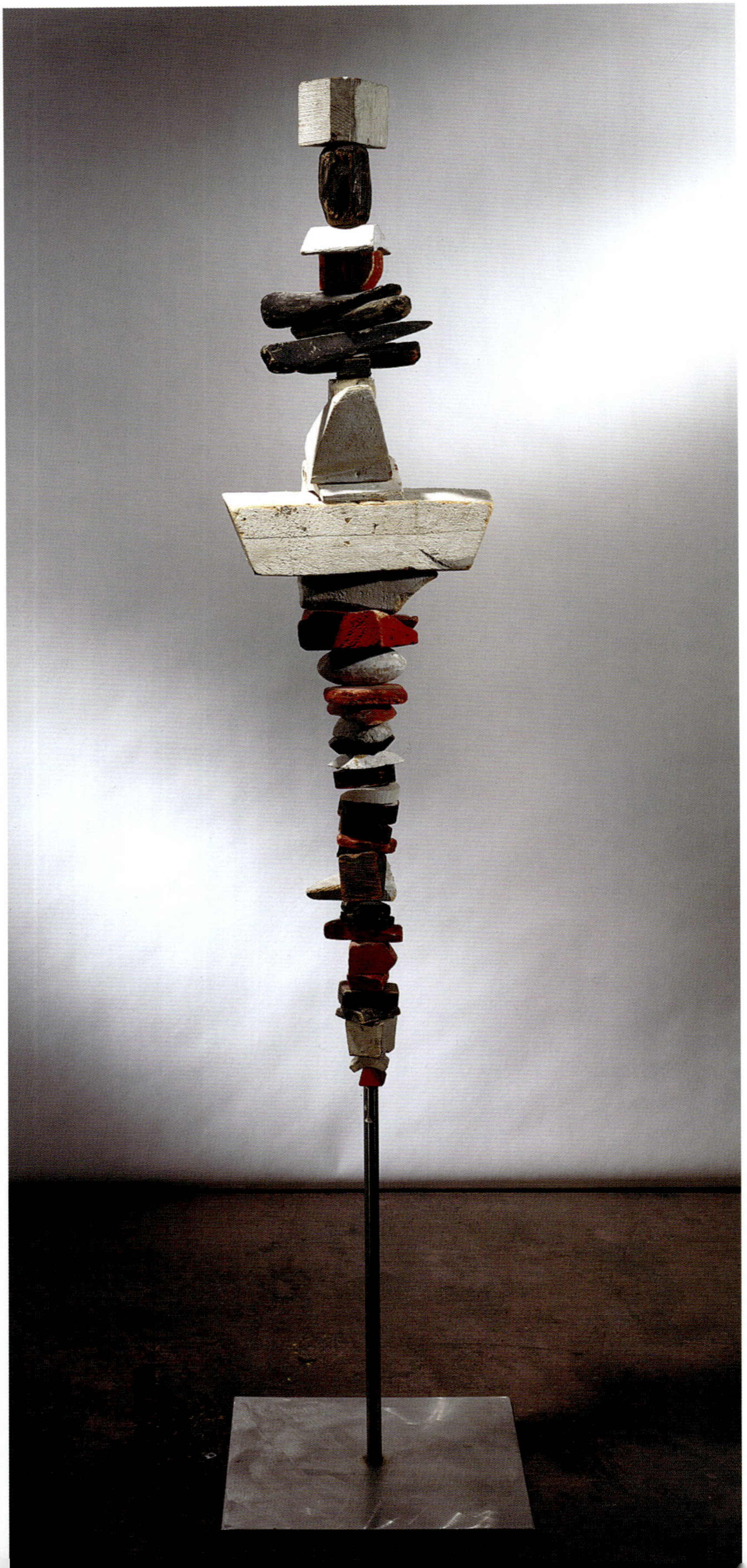

left Louise Bourgeois
Untitled, 1950

right Lynda Benglis
Karen, 1972

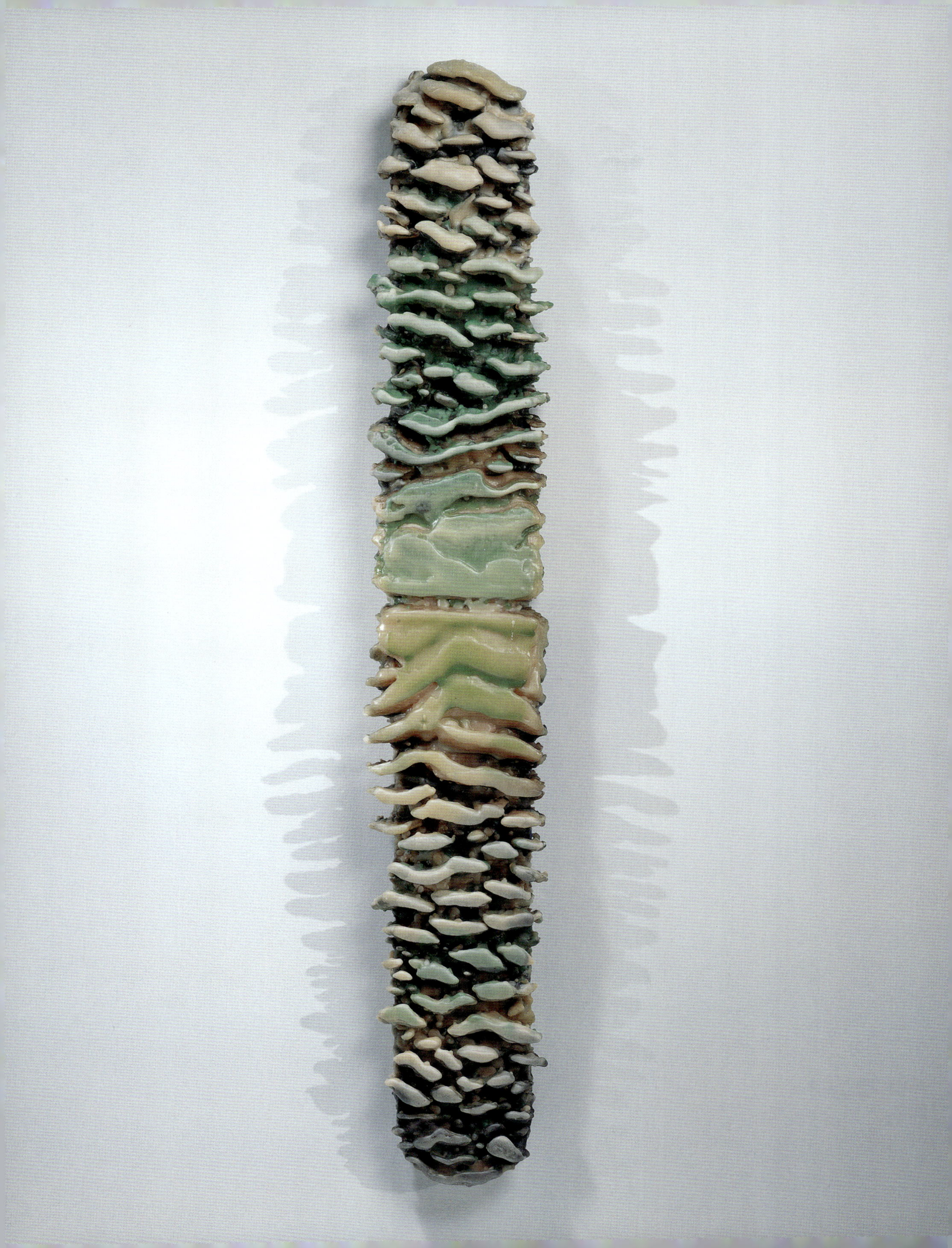

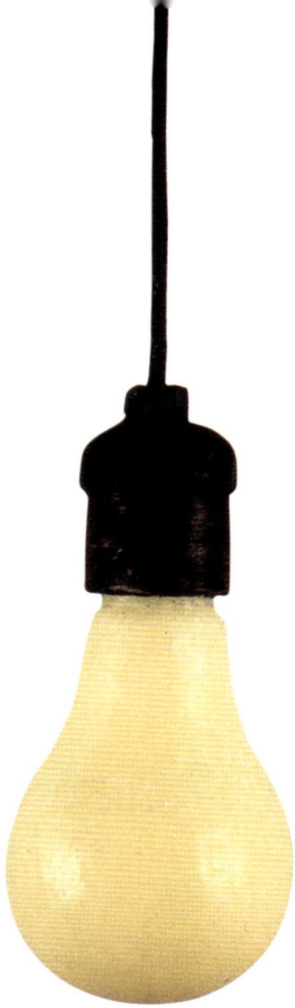

Robert Gober & Sherrie Levine
Untitled, Lightbulb, 1990

left Eva Hesse
Compass, 1967

biological and industrial models of production and repetition are porous to one another. Repetition, here, is not a negative term; rather, it serves as a vehicle for sorting out the human condition. As Briony Fer has recently argued, without it we are lost.

Bodily repetitions both emanate from and are governed by the space of fantasy and desire, regions of consciousness that are particularly resistant to language. While eros is lived and felt, it is also recalcitrant to rational description and linear narration. Much of the work in *Part Object Part Sculpture* rides in the slipstream of such ideas. Definitively eschewing straightforward narrative, figuration, or content, the very abstraction of the works in *Part Object Part Sculpture* gestures over and over again to the obdurate failure of language to articulate the sensory realms of the body – think of the stubborn quietude of Rachel Whiteread's casts of everyday objects, and the strong bodily presence left by the laborious and loving traces of the hand in Robert Gober's objects. Both Gober's and Whiteread's work seems, at the very least, skeptical of language's ability to contain our bodily experiences of the world. Instead, their work offers a series of imperfect vessels, cast objects filled with the matter of their own making, surfaces resistant to words.

Those accustomed to regarding Duchamp's legacy through the readymade may be surprised at the importance of the process of casting in *Part Object Part Sculpture*. The cast objects of Allan McCollum's *Over 10,000 Individual Works,* in which we see ten thousand objects that appear similar but are in fact each different from the other, suggest that bodily, psychic, and industrial modes of repetition are mutually contingent upon one another as the desire to repeat the pleasurableness of the erotic encounter transmogrifies into the repetition of the workday. The adaptation of the tradition of casting could be fast, loose, and fiendishly clever. Piero Manzoni used kaolin, a compound of porcelain powder and pigment, much as if it were the clay covering the wax model in bronze casting. He poured it over an array of low-grade industrial materials – polystyrene pellets, cotton batting, or canvas. The coating or casting, since it is permanent, produces amorphous things subsisting in an in-between state in which one plus one never quite equals two.

To move from Manzoni's *Achromes* to Lee Bontecou's massive wall reliefs supplies a lesson in the multifarious potential of industrial materials for the making of corporeal surrogates. Within this framework one can see the protruding velvety voids of Lee Bontecou as monster machines, intrauterine spaces, as well as an abyss that lay at the threshold of consciousness and the unconscious. So too we can consider Eva Hesse's *Accession II,* an industrially fabricated cube, laboriously threaded by hand with hundreds of mass-produced plastic tubes, that is so strangely animated, so human, that it arouses desire for entry into its ticklish interior.

These artists are obsessed with returning, with repetition, like machines and like creatures ruled by the contradictory laws of eros. In each instance they return to a particular gesture, working over the permutations of materials, scale,

color, and texture, repeating the gesture as a way of making a thing that is as much about repetition as it is about anything else. These gestures and series generate scatters, dispersed fields of aesthetic, physical, and psychic apprehension that are similar to the endless repetitions of the ego's search for pleasure and the body's experience of it. The liminality of the objects in *Part Object Part Sculpture* – their uneasy place between art and something else, between sculpture and painting, between commodity and art object, between objects and *objets d'art*, between language and its failures – in the end offers an art so suffused with eros, and objects so redolent with desire, that they fail to be purely one or the other, and remain instead part object, part sculpture.

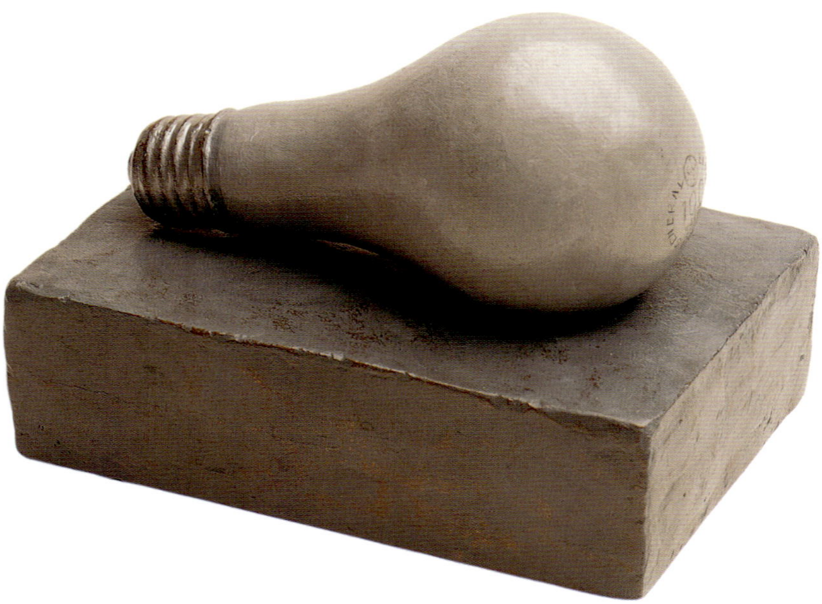

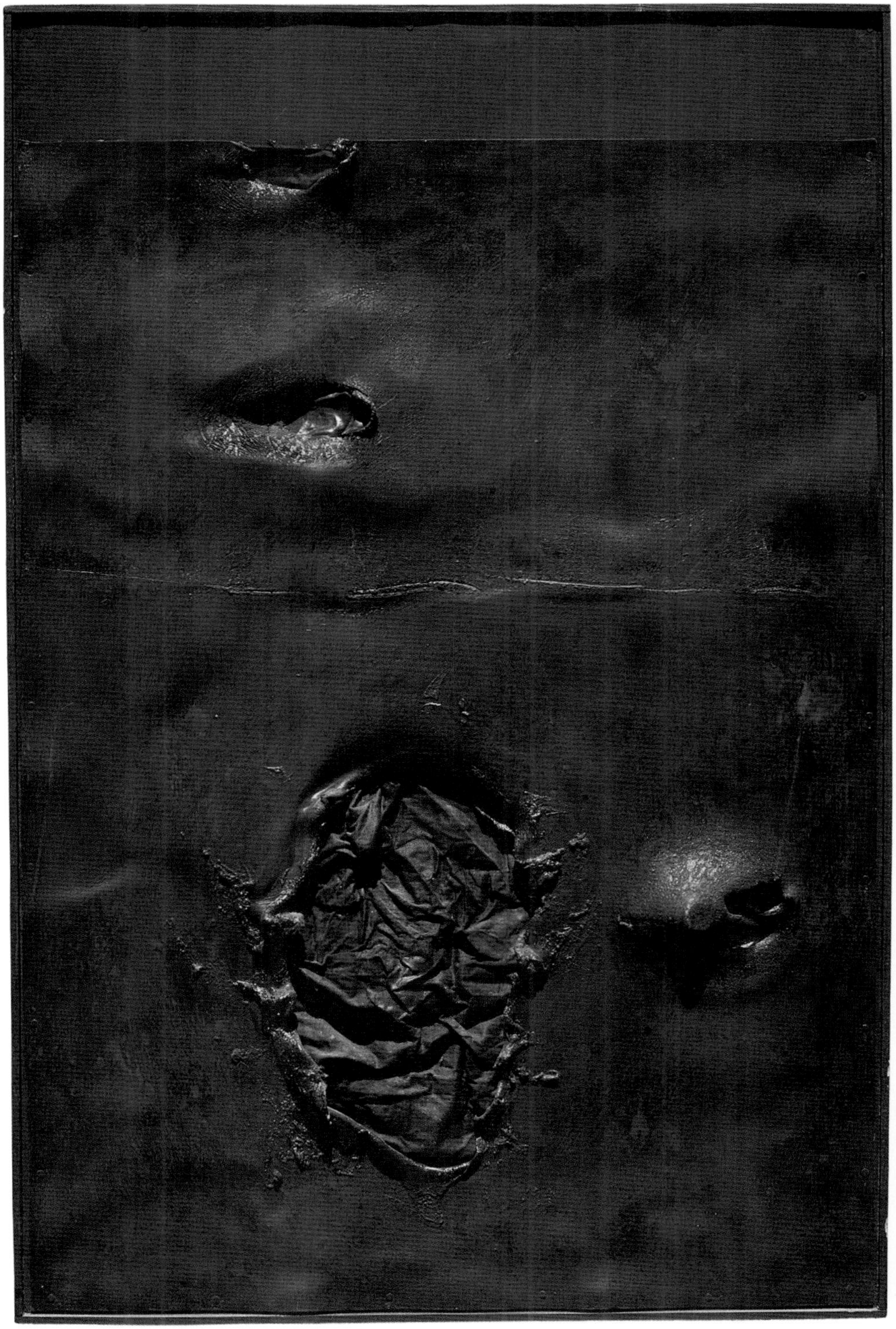

Alberto Burri
Nero Plastica, 1961

left Jasper Johns
Light Bulb, 1960

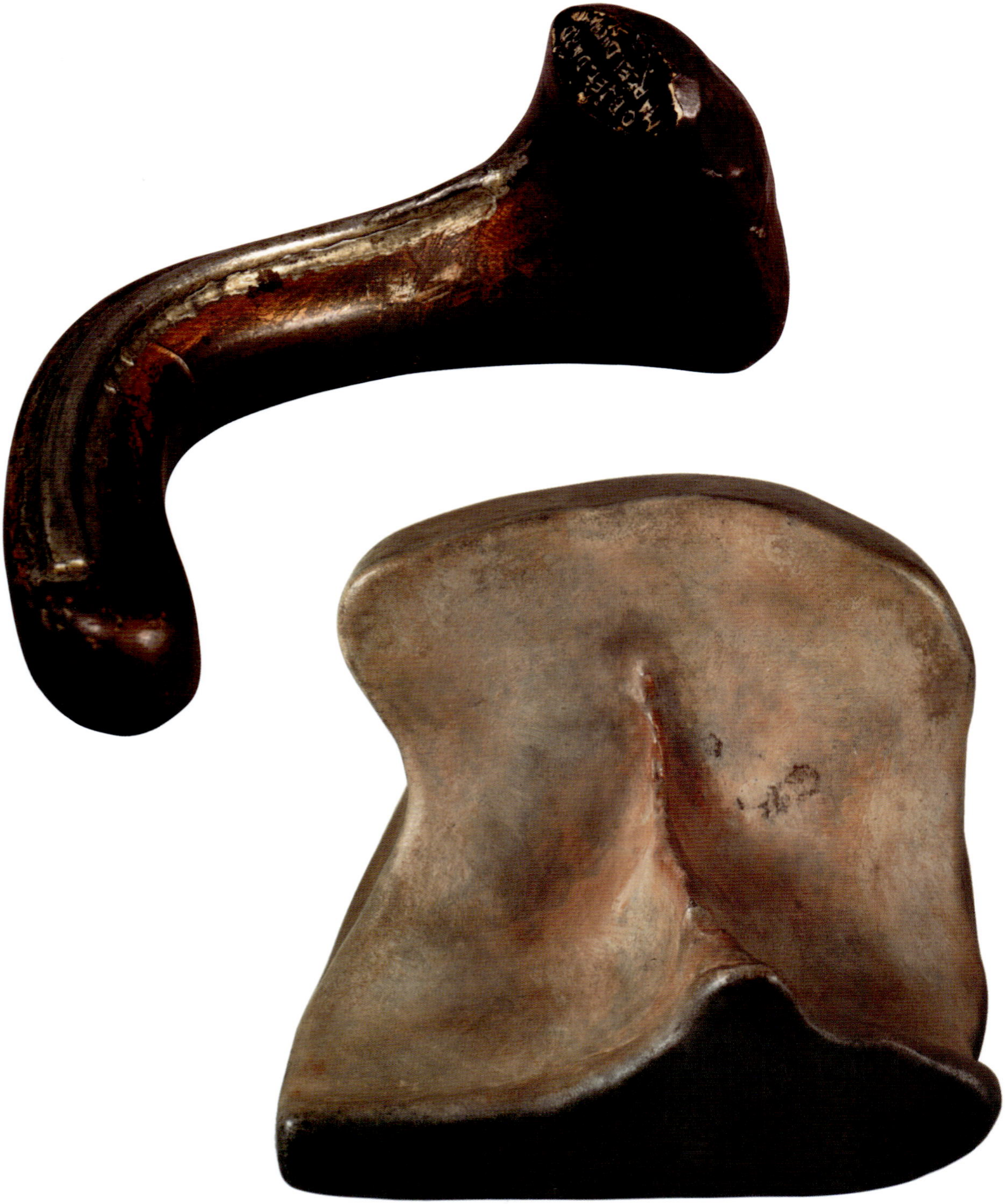

MARCEL DUCHAMP 1887–1968

Despite Marcel Duchamp's self-proclaimed abandonment in the 1920s of making art, by the mid-1940s he was quite busy making things. During the war he began fabricating the *Boîte-en-Valise* ("Box in a Valise"), first in a deluxe edition, each housed in a red leather suitcase. The open suitcase reveals an extraordinary array of reproductions, in miniature, of sixty-nine of Duchamp's most important works. Rendered in loving detail, using a variety of methods from color lithography, to *pouchoir,* to hand-built miniature models of three readymades, to a reproduction of *The Large Glass* on a piece of acetate, the *Boîte* is comprised of mechanical reproductions that are paradoxically laborious. So too the assembly of the boxes, with their moving components and multiple compartments (and the labeling of each work as if it is in a museum), constitutes an extraordinary degree of hand labor.

The *Boîte* is a miniature museum, a portable retrospective of works by Duchamp. The first twenty *Boîtes* were made for friends and patrons (from his longtime companion, Mary Reynolds, to gallery owner Sidney Janis), and each included a unique object fabricated for that *Boîte*. They were gifts, tokens of affection. Quickly thereafter, the *Boîte* was reproduced in several editions, which were compiled by friends and family over a period of twenty years. By the end of his life, approximately three hundred *Boîtes-en-Valise* had been produced, rivaling and reminiscent of the boxlike constructions of Joseph Cornell, in both their number and handicraft.

While the *Boîte-en-Valise* fully initiated Duchamp's interest in reproduction as an artistic idea and activity in and of itself, his sculptural work of the late 1950s continued it. Each of the three erotic objects was made by hand before it was reproduced in editions of eight. *Female Fig Leaf* and *Objet-Dard,* both at the scale of the human hand, are oblique in their relation to sexuality and eros. *Female Fig Leaf* appears to be cast from a woman's genitals, and *Objet-Dard* seems simultaneously phallic and scatological. In retrospect, it would come to light that both objects were related to Duchamp's magnum opus, *Etant donnés*, a work he also labored on in secret during the postwar period. *Female Fig Leaf* was cast from the female body that forms the centerpiece of *Etant donnés*, and *Objet-Dard* was a fragment of the cast that made that body.

The third of the erotic objects was *Wedge of Chastity*, an object first made as a wedding present for Duchamp's wife, Teeny Matisse. The work is comprised of two parts, a plaster wedge that sits ensconced in an unformed lump of dental plaster. When the wedge is lifted, a fleshy, erotic, and surprisingly lifelike rendition of a woman's pussy is revealed. This work, despite its most intimate of origins, was also editioned. All three works were included in Duchamp's major postwar exhibitions, and hence constituted an important part of his reception for artists, who readily assimilated the lessons these three diminutive works offered. Critics and art historians have been slower to pay attention to these works, focusing instead on Duchamp's prewar work.

Wedge of Chastity was also the physical introduction to Duchamp's neologistic invention of the "infra mince," or the "infra thin." The "infra thin" is a moment of intense liminality, an in-betweeness so ineluctable that it exists as a state in which its component parts are inseparable. Duchamp described it thus: "When the smoke of the tobacco smells also of the mouth from which it comes the 2 smells marry by infra thin."[1] It is telling that the concept of marriage and intimacy is the engine of connection in Duchamp's most famous statement of this concept. Yet, as we will see again and again in Duchamp, where we find eros and intimacy we also find the readymade and reproduction. Another example of "infra thin" is "the difference (dimensional) between 2 mass-produced objects from the same mold is an infra thin when the maximum precision is obtained."[2] "Infra thin," then, is yet another vehicle through which Duchamp can think of the relations between models of repetition and objects offered by sexuality and eros and those offered by the commodity and art.

After the three erotic objects were editioned, Duchamp was approached by two separate individuals about the possibility of reproducing the then mostly lost or discarded readymades. The first was Ulf Linde, a Swedish curator, who produced a complete set of readymades, with the help of Swedish craftsmen, as well as a copy of *The Large Glass.* Duchamp went to Stockholm and signed both the readymades and *The Large Glass* "copie conforme" and requested that they all be donated to the modern art museum in Stockholm (the Moderna Museet). The second was the Italian art dealer Arturo Schwarz. Working closely with Duchamp, Schwarz had blueprints made, based on photographs of the mostly lost or discarded readymades from the teens and twenties. Duchamp reviewed these drawings, giving them a handwritten OK and a signature. The blueprints were subsequently sent to various Italian craftsmen, who fabricated the readymades with a variety of artisanal methods. The fabrication ultimately resulted in the 1964 set of readymades in an edition of eight available for sale, two sets for exhibition only, and one set each for Duchamp and Schwarz to keep for themselves.

Historically, the handmade reality of the 1964 readymades has been somewhat swept under the rug. While no one denies it, no one has dealt with it head on. *Part Object Part Sculpture* takes the intensity of Duchamp's postwar practice as its starting point by articulating his oeuvre as ironically handmade, profoundly erotic, and surprisingly prolific. To see Duchamp's late work in this way is to see it as emblematic of a strain in postwar art that deals with the problems of repetition and reproduction and the reciprocity between bodies and things and vision and tactility.

MARCEL DUCHAMP 1887–1968

Despite Marcel Duchamp's self-proclaimed abandonment in the 1920s of making art, by the mid-1940s he was quite busy making things. During the war he began fabricating the *Boîte-en-Valise* ("Box in a Valise"), first in a deluxe edition, each housed in a red leather suitcase. The open suitcase reveals an extraordinary array of reproductions, in miniature, of sixty-nine of Duchamp's most important works. Rendered in loving detail, using a variety of methods from color lithography, to pouchoir, to hand-built miniature models of three readymades, to a reproduction of *The Large Glass* on a piece of acetate, the *Boîte* is composed of mechanical reproductions that are paradoxically laborious. So too the assembly of the boxes, with their moving components and multiple compartments (and the labeling of each work as if it is in a museum), constitutes an extraordinary degree of hand labor.

The *Boîte* is a miniature museum, a portable retrospective of works by Duchamp. The first twenty *Boîtes* were made for friends and patrons (from his longtime companion, Mary Reynolds, to gallery owner Sidney Janis), and each included a unique object fabricated for that *Boîte*. They were gifts, tokens of affection. Quickly thereafter, the *Boîte* was reproduced in several editions, which were compiled by friends and family over a period of twenty years. By the end of his life, approximately three hundred *Boîtes-en-Valise* had been produced, rivaling and reminiscent of the boxlike constructions of Joseph Cornell, in both their number and handicraft.

While the *Boîte-en-Valise* fully initiated Duchamp's interest in reproduction as an artistic idea and activity in and of itself, his sculptural work of the late 1950s continued it. Each of the three erotic objects was made by hand before it was reproduced in editions of eight. *Female Fig Leaf* and *Objet-Dard*, both at the scale of the human hand, are oblique in their relation to sexuality and eros. *Female Fig Leaf* appears to be cast from a woman's genitals; and *Objet-Dard* seems simultaneously phallic and scatological. In retrospect, it would come to light that both objects were related to Duchamp's magnum opus, *Étant donnés*, a work he also labored on in secret during the postwar period. *Female Fig Leaf* was cast from the female body that forms the centerpiece of *Étant donnés*, and *Objet-Dard* was a fragment of the cast that made that body.

The third of the erotic objects was *Wedge of Chastity*, an object first made as a wedding present for Duchamp's wife, Teeny Matisse. The work is comprised of two parts, a plaster wedge that sits ensconced in an unformed lump of dental plaster. When the wedge is lifted, a fleshy, erotic, and surprisingly lifelike rendition of a woman's pussy is revealed. This work, despite its most intimate of origins, was also editioned. All three works were included in Duchamp's major postwar exhibitions, and hence constituted an important part of his reception for artists, who readily assimilated the lessons these three diminutive works offered. Critics and art historians have been slower to pay attention to these works, focusing instead on Duchamp's prewar work.

Wedge of Chastity was also the physical introduction to Duchamp's neologistic invention of the "infra mince," or the "infra thin." The "infra thin" is a moment of intense liminality, an in-betweenness so ineluctable that it exists as a state in which its component parts are inseparable. Duchamp described it thus: "When the smoke of the tobacco smells also of the mouth from which it comes the 2 smells marry by infra thin."[1] It is telling that the concept of marriage and intimacy is the engine of connection in Duchamp's most famous statement of this concept. Yet, as we will see again and again in Duchamp, where we find eros and intimacy we also find the readymade and reproduction. Another example of "infra thin" is "the difference (dimensional) between 2 mass-produced objects from the same mold is an infra thin when the maximum precision is obtained."[2] "Infra thin," then, is yet another vehicle through which Duchamp can think of the relations between models of repetition and objects offered by sexuality and eros and those offered by the commodity and art.

After the three erotic objects were editioned, Duchamp was approached by two separate individuals about the possibility of reproducing the then mostly lost or discarded readymades. The first was Ulf Linde, a Swedish curator, who produced a complete set of readymades, with the help of Swedish craftsmen, as well as a copy of *The Large Glass*. Duchamp went to Stockholm and signed both the readymades and *The Large Glass* "copie conforme" and requested that they all be donated to the modern art museum in Stockholm (the Moderna Museet). The second was the Italian art dealer Arturo Schwarz. Working closely with Duchamp, Schwarz had blueprints made, based on photographs of the mostly lost or discarded readymades from the teens and twenties. Duchamp reviewed these drawings, giving them a handwritten OK and a signature. The blueprints were subsequently sent to various Italian craftsmen, who fabricated the readymades with a variety of artisanal methods. The fabrication ultimately resulted in the 1964 set of readymades in an edition of eight available for sale, two sets for exhibition only, and one set each for Duchamp and Schwarz to keep for themselves.

Historically, the handmade reality of the 1964 readymades has been somewhat swept under the rug. While no one denies it, no one has dealt with it head on. *Part Object/Part Sculpture* takes the intensity of Duchamp's postwar practice as its starting point by articulating his oeuvre as ironically handmade, profoundly erotic, and surprisingly prolific. To see Duchamp's late work in this way is to see it as emblematic of a strain in postwar art that deals with the problems of repetition and reproduction and the reciprocity between bodies and things and vision and tactility.

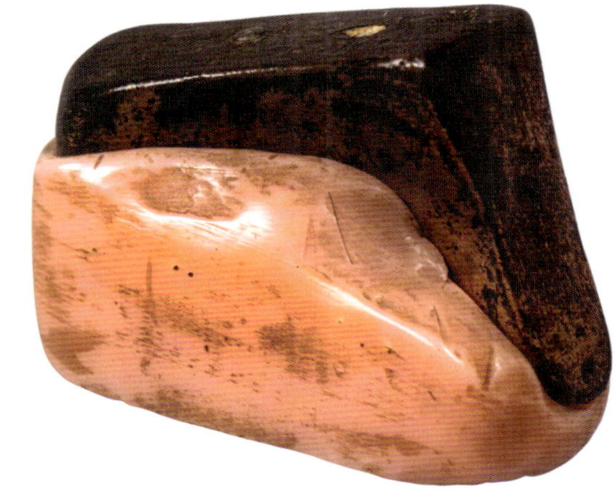

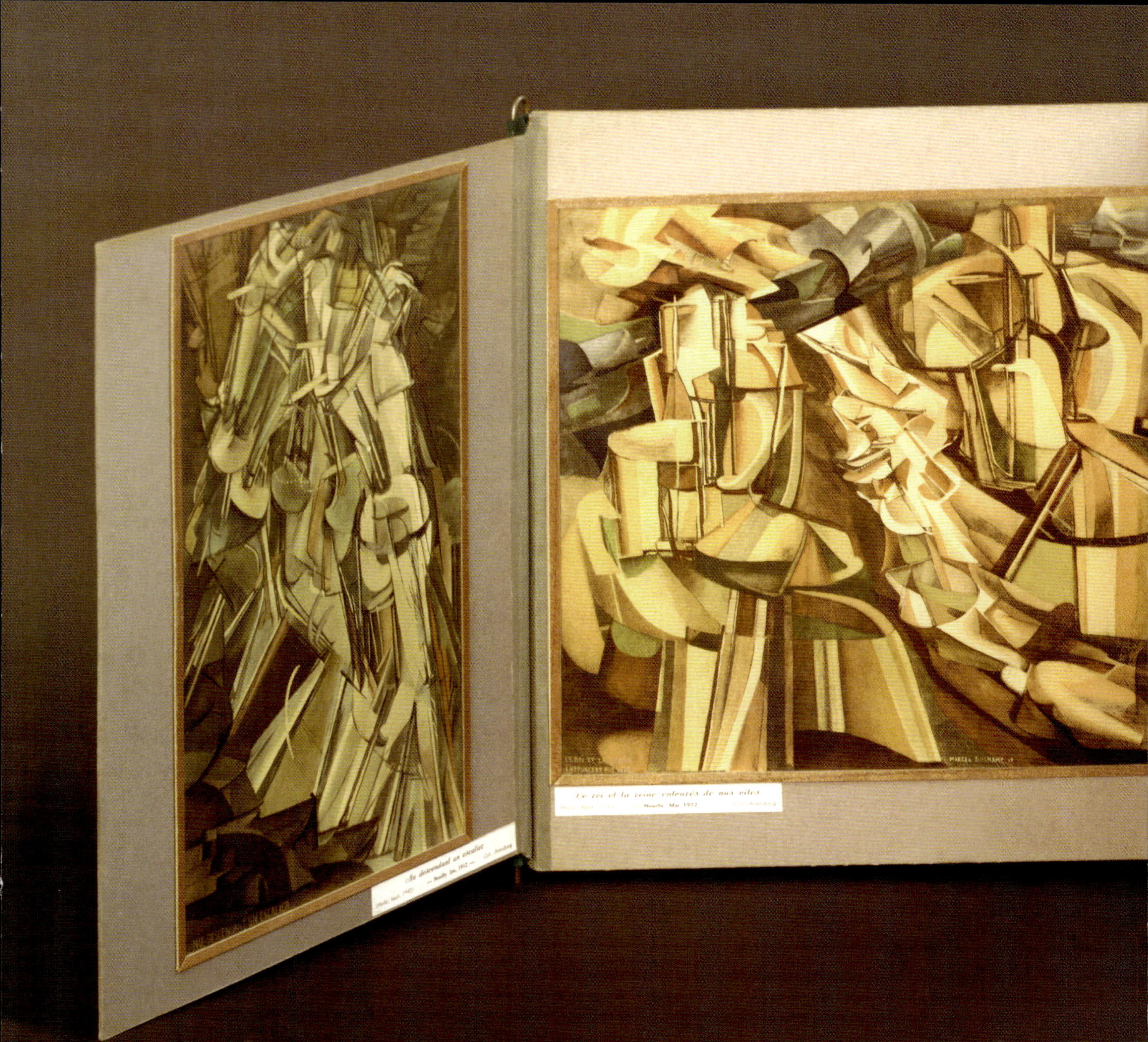

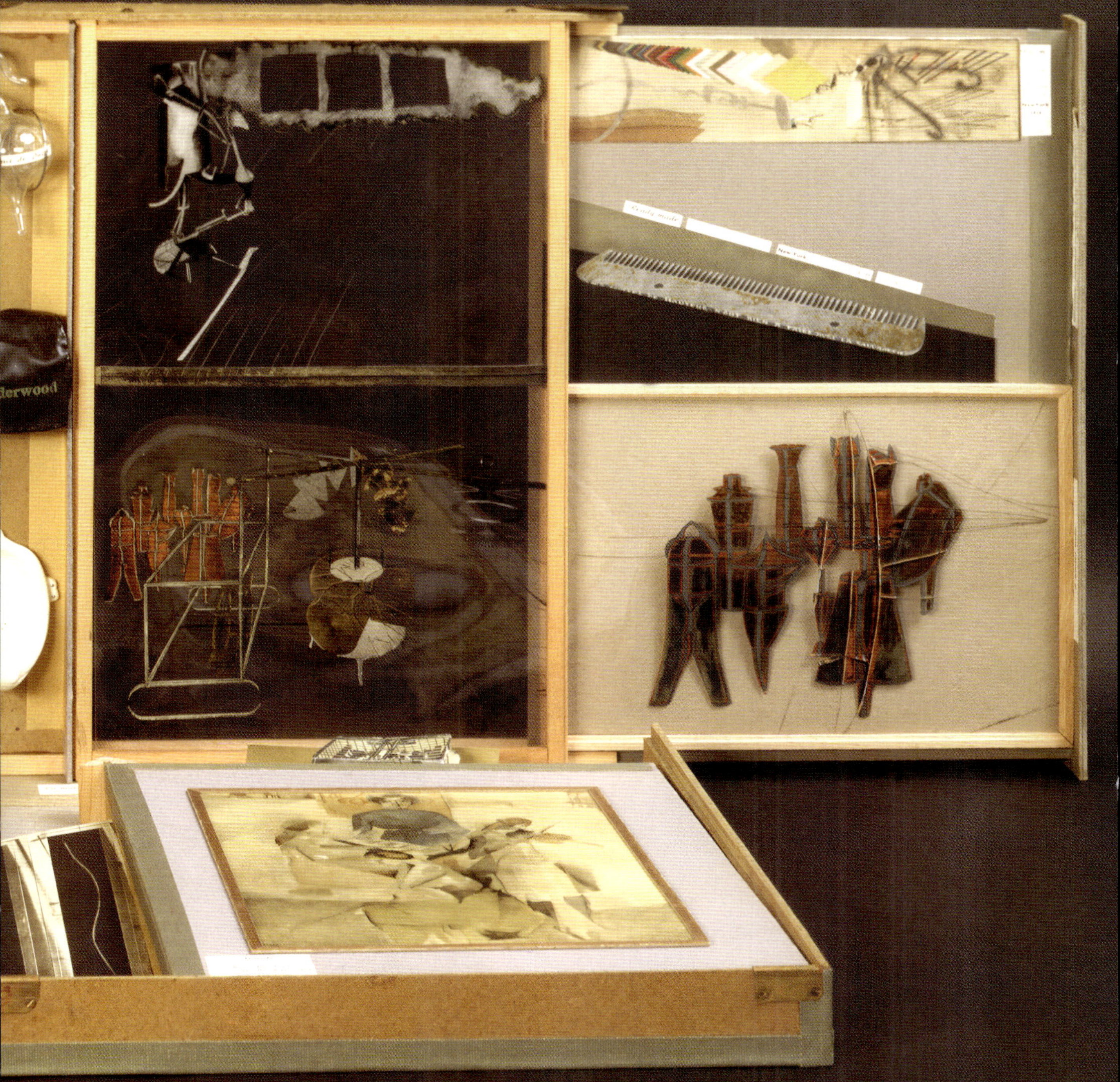

Boîte-en-Valise
(The Box in a Valise), 1935–41

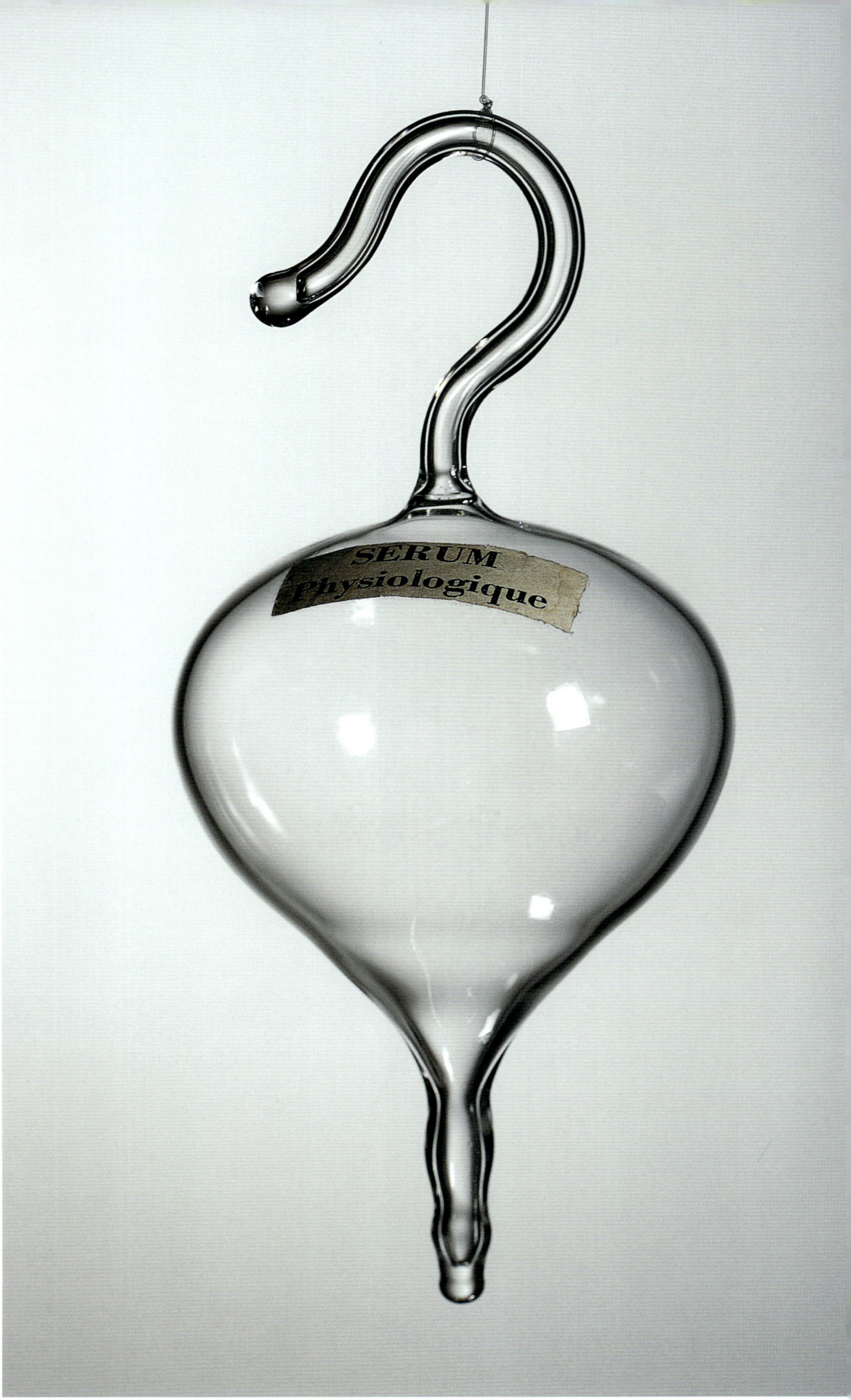
SERUM
Physiologique

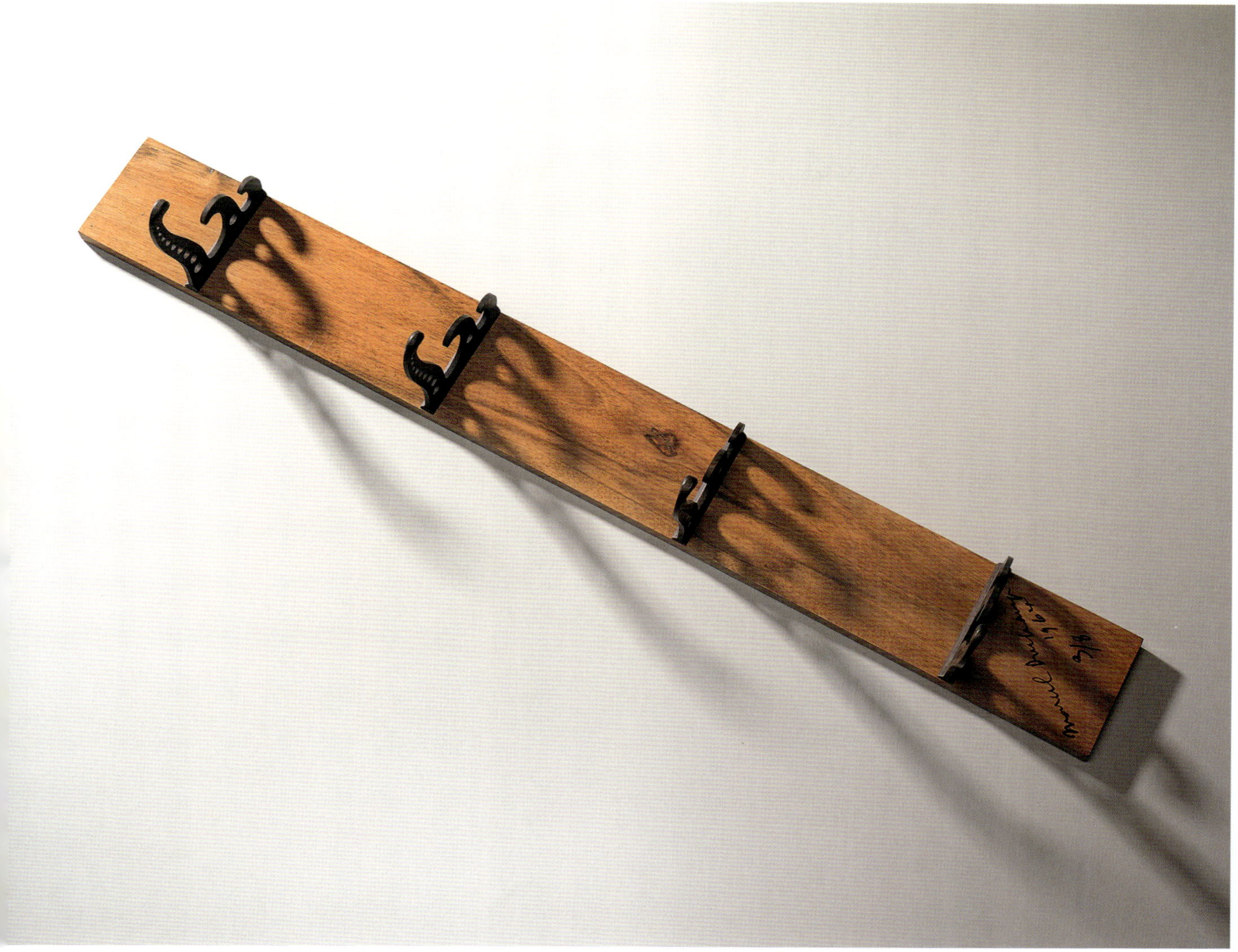

Trébuchet (Trap), 1917, 2nd version 1964

left **Air de Paris** (Paris Air), 1919 / 1974

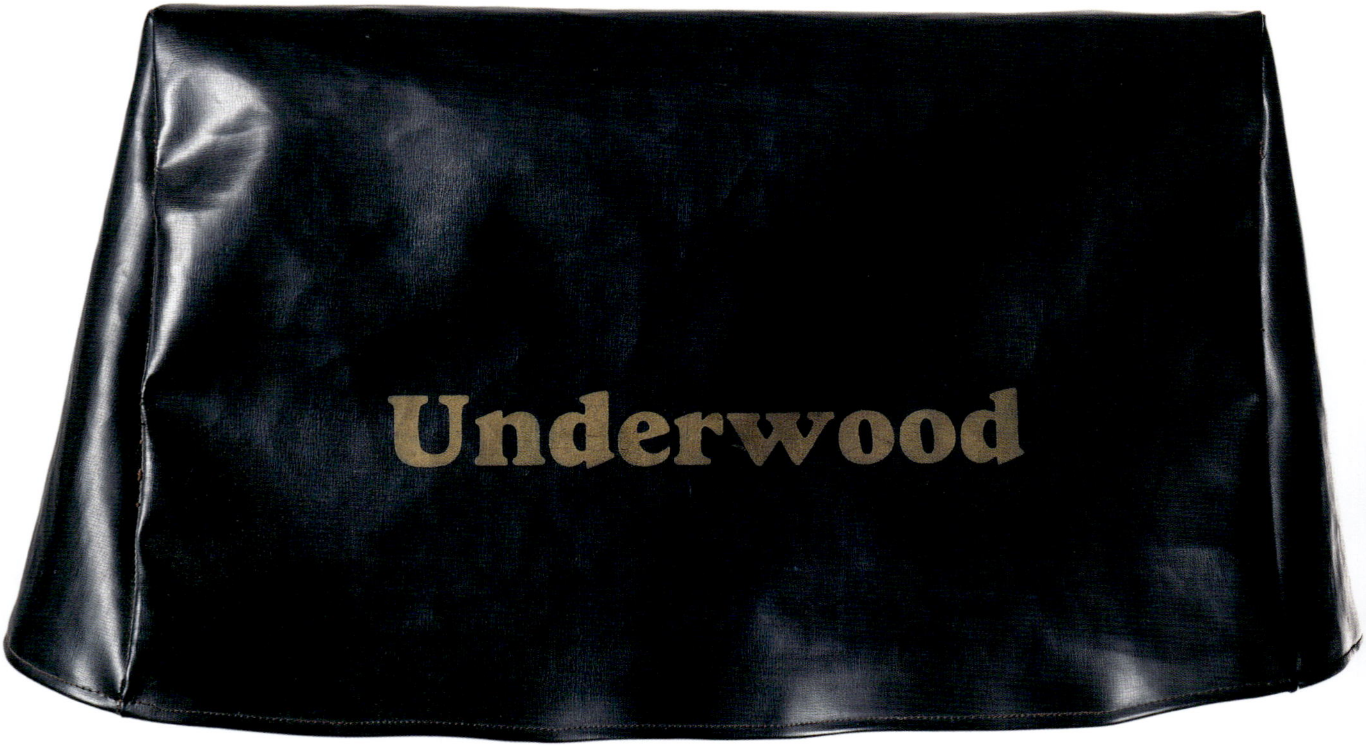

...pliant...de voyage
(Traveler's Folding Item), 1917/1963

right **Porte-chapeaux** (Hat Rack), 1917,
2nd version 1964

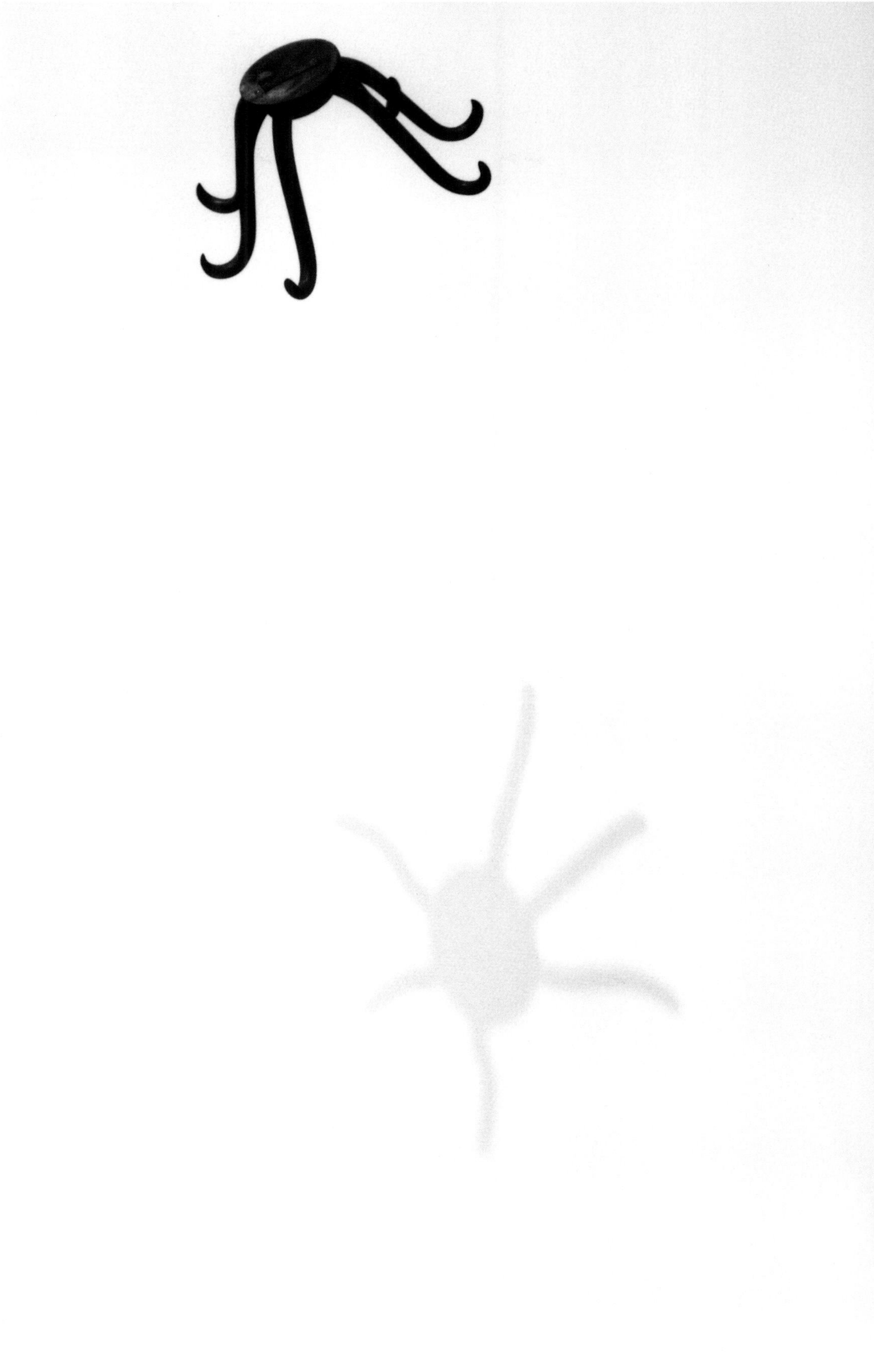

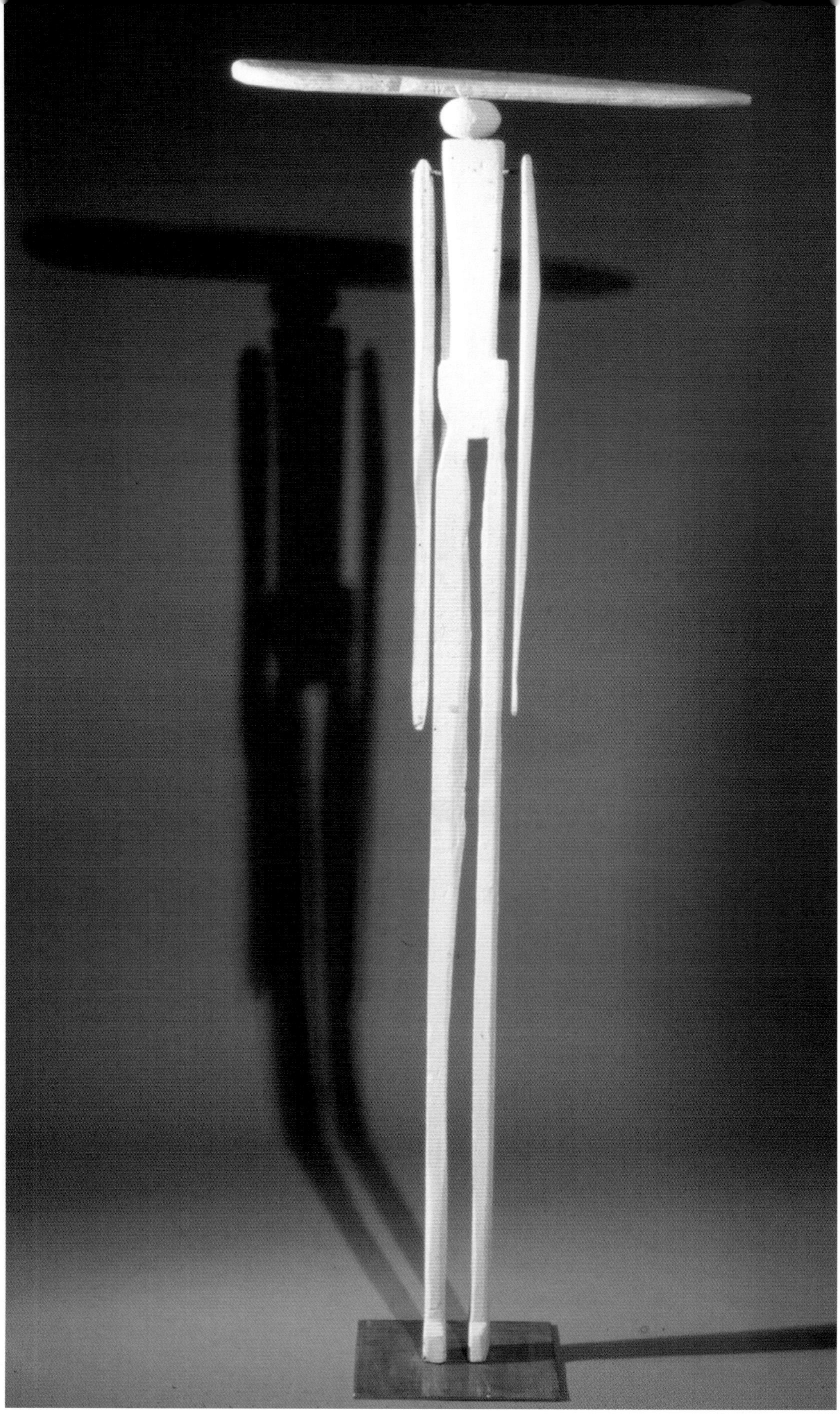

LOUISE BOURGEOIS 1911–

In 1938, Louise Bourgeois moved to New York from her native Paris. In just under a year, she began to exhibit work, and by 1949 she had her first solo exhibition of sculpture at the Peridot Gallery in New York, followed quickly in 1950 by another solo sculpture show. Exhibited both times was a then-growing body of work entitled Personages, a group that comprises the approximately eighty wood sculptures that Bourgeois maintains was her first mature body of work. The works were uniformly vertical in nature, all cobbled together from carved pieces of wood. They share a human scale as well, both mimicking and addressing the human torso. Each work displays the same tenuous sense of balance, as they grow increasingly slender toward the bottom, and seem precariously placed on flat metal bases. While many of the works were painted, they retain the rough-hewn quality of the carved wood, so much so that often the individual wood pieces appear as scraps or discards, found objects put together in the tradition of assemblage, although in fact Bourgeois crafted each work herself. In addition to the life-size scale of the works, each piece has a kind of anthropomorphic quality, a tilting or leaning, a bulbousness amid the angularity, an ineffable sense of internal proportions (the long ovoid cut out of the right-hand figure in *Listening One* or the larger piece of rectangular white wood underneath the rounder piece in *Untitled*) that connotes the human form. And yet the human is not all that is there. As Jeremy Strick notes, the works "recall the mechanthropomorphic inventions of Marcel Duchamp and Francis Picabia."[1]

The exhibition met with mixed reviews. Most critics had a tin ear to the emotional, even interpersonal, intensity of the pieces and saw primarily what they understood to be the influence of tribal sculpture from Africa and Oceania, a response typical of the concerns of the moment. Even within this readily available context, one reviewer offered another frame of reference, deciding that "these attenuated creatures actually belong to a nostalgic sky scraper world."[2] It was the *New York Times* reviewer who really seems to have hit the nail on the head, although unintentionally (the review is largely negative), when he opined: "Louise Bourgeois has fashioned three-dimensional wooden forms – they cannot correctly be called sculpture."[3]

It is telling that Personages, upon their first outing, were likened to skyscrapers and were seen to have a somewhat problematic relationship to sculpture, for architecture and an ambiguous hold on the identity of these objects do appear to be at the heart of the matter. Bourgeois worked on the sculptures in a variety of venues – in her New York apartment and on the roof of her building. Further, she traveled with Personages, transporting them back and forth, along with her young children and husband, to a weekend house in Connecticut.

Thinking of Personages propped along the roof of a New York apartment building, a space marked by an expanse of sky and the shadows of fellow tall buildings, is telling. Here the sculptures must have seemed more objectlike than ever, mirroring not only the logic of the buildings but also their inhabitants: everywhere the gridded sameness of the city's buildings, and everywhere its wild heterogeneity, both in the architecture and the people – no two buildings or people are alike in New York. Bourgeois herself thought of Personages as actual people, and her positioning of them in groups tended to emphasize their humanoid quality. Oddly, the emotional intensity of Bourgeois's cathexsis onto these objects is evident in our inability to think of them fully as sculpture, as if their retention of object status is also in some way part of their purchase on an anthropomorphic one. This blurring of subject and object was not lost on Bourgeois. Looking back on her two exhibitions, she said, "The sculptures in the first show were objects, those in the second show were subjects."[4] So too in her 1954 artist's statement, she never refers to them as sculptures, but either as objects or figures. Or describing the situation on the roof, she said: "The figures on the roof had nothing to do with sculpture, they meant physical presences."[5] Perhaps they had nothing to do with sculpture because until the late 1950s, when Bourgeois began to cast the works in bronze, Personages had no adequate bases; instead, they were routinely propped up against walls, or stored in a closet and a dumbwaiter, furthering their ambiguous identity.[6] This mobility has led one art historian to argue that "by integrating them into her daily life and moving them back and forth from one private environment to another, Bourgeois brought them closer to life, appropriating them as her personal objects."[7] It was only when Bourgeois cast these fragile wood objects in the durable, venerable, and properly sculptural material of bronze, that the works fully entered the realm of sculpture. One set of repetitions allowed Bourgeois to explore the proliferation of difference in Personages, while another form of reproduction allowed them to become works of art proper.

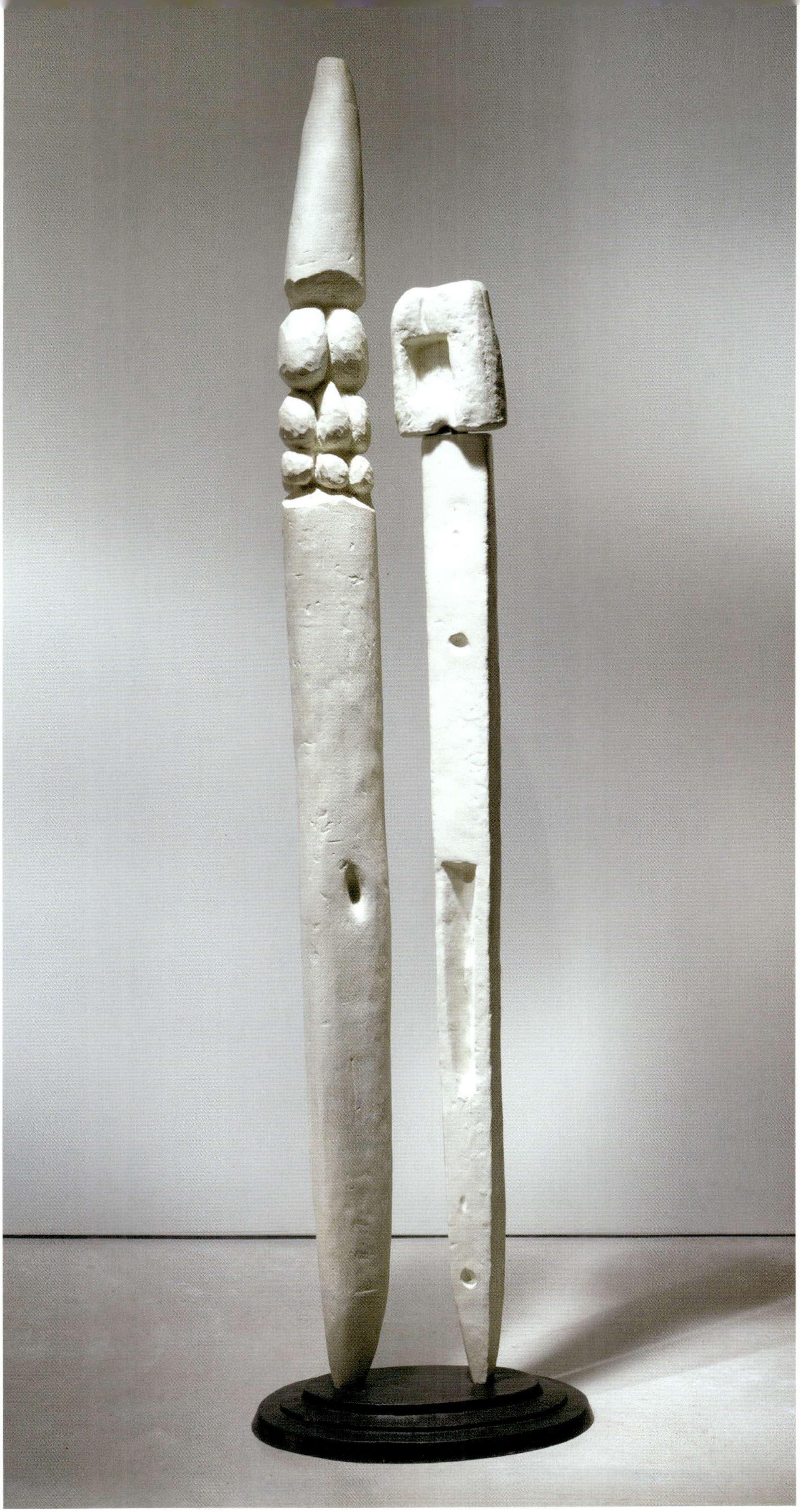

previous spread: left
Observer, 1947–49

previous spread: right
Listening One, 1947–49

right **Janus Fleuri**, 1968

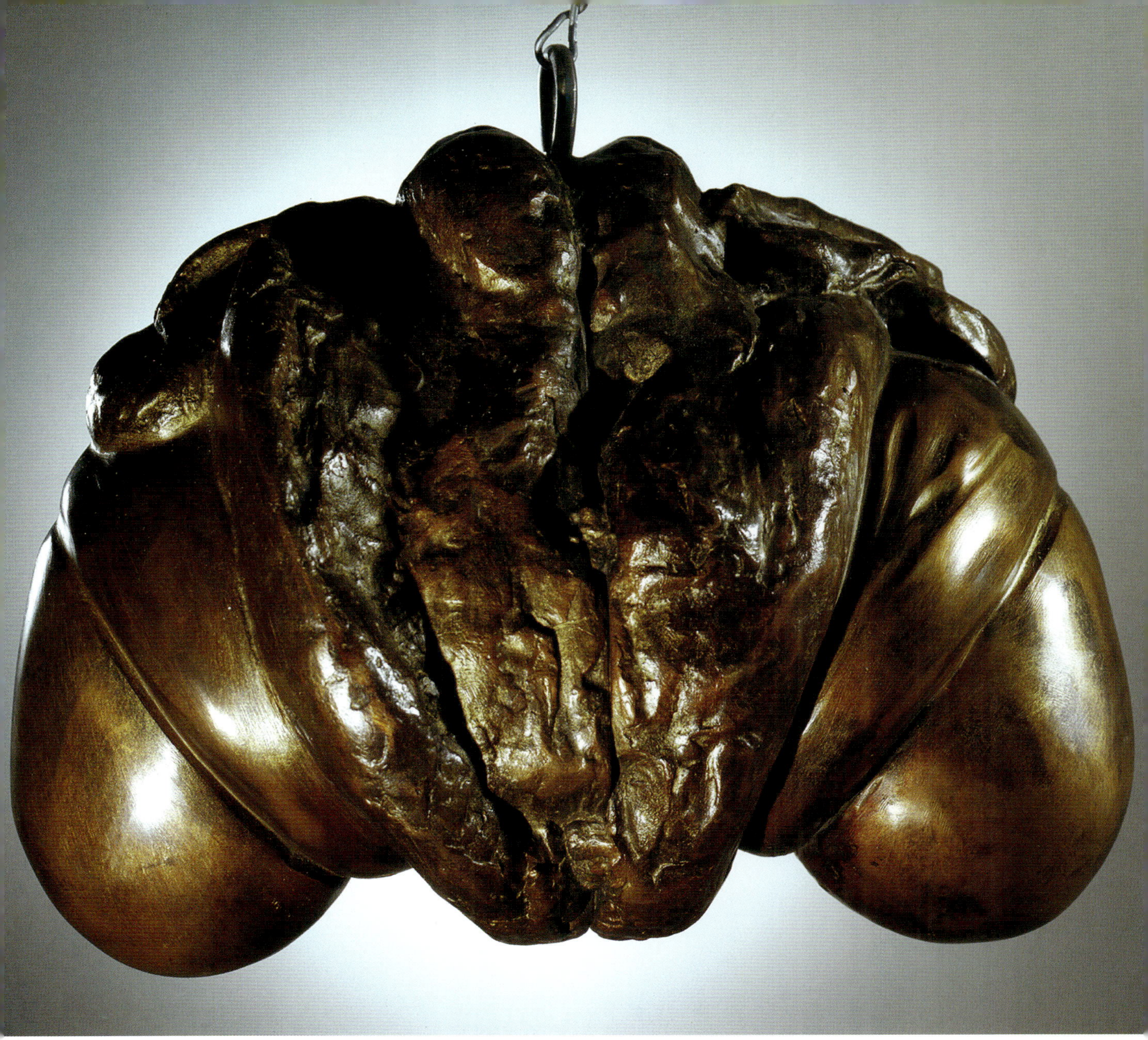

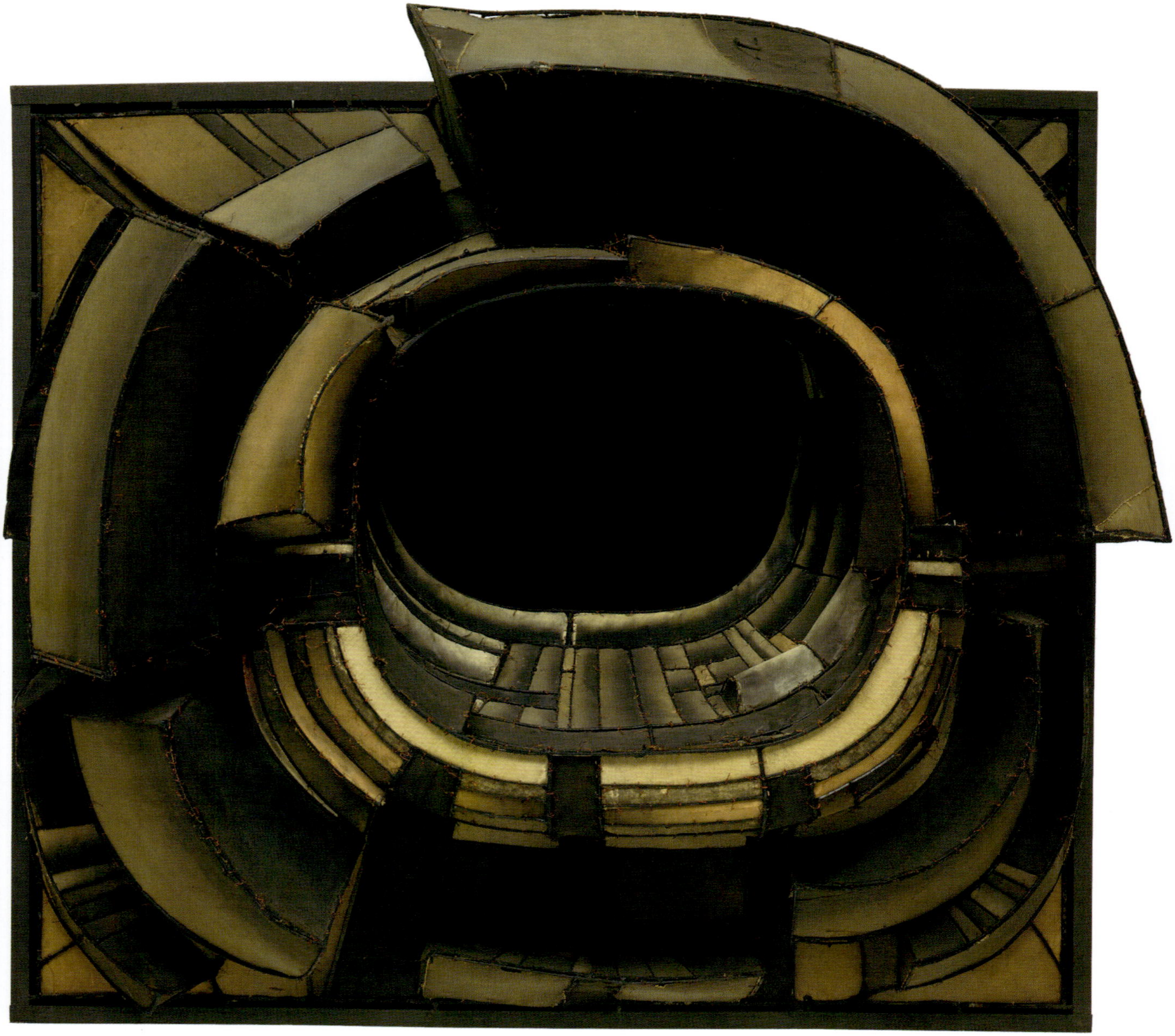

Untitled, 1961

right **Flit**, 1959

LEE BONTECOU 1931–

Lee Bontecou burst onto the New York art scene in 1960 with an exhibition at the Leo Castelli Gallery showing a group of stunningly innovative wall reliefs. Neither painting nor sculpture, the works hung on the wall in painterly rectangles but also projected off the wall, sometimes as much as a foot and a half. They are all similarly fashioned; patches of burlap and rough canvas are assembled over a metal armature. The fabric is attached to itself and to the armature with small pieces of rusty wire that have been twisted together, their sharp ends sticking out in an orderly row, revealing a trace of the skeleton underneath. The effect is one of suturing, a poor woman's sewing, a rudimentary form of attachment, devoid of inherent skill but diligently achieved nonetheless. More often than not, this burlap and metal patchwork forms concentric circles or ovoids that culminate in a large void or hole that dominates the piece. This hole is invariably an inky midnight black, sometimes crafted out of sumptuous black velvet, sometimes from the soot that came from Bontecou's use of a blowtorch for welding the metal armatures together, and sometimes comprised of black paint.

Bontecou's reliefs were fabricated from a wide variety of scavenged and cheaply bought materials, such as "laundry bags and canvas conveyor belts acquired from the owner of the laundry directly under her loft, metal bolts, gears, war helmets, shrapnel, knapsacks, and an abundance of army surplus items, rope, and various other detritus found on Canal Street."[1] Yet despite this heterogeneous list of ingredients, the intensity of these protruding voids made Bontecou's work very immediate, a total gestalt, felt all at once. Singling out Bontecou for an in-depth look in his now-seminal article, "Specific Objects," Donald Judd described the immediacy of her work: "Each of Bontecou's reliefs is an image. The image, all of the parts and the whole shape are coextensive. The parts are either part of the hole or part of the mound that forms the hole. The hole and the mound are only two things, which, after all, are the same thing. The parts and the divisions are either radical or concentric in regard to the hole, leading in and out and enclosing."[2] Judd opts for language steeped in the formal attributes of the work, and yet even he cannot help but register that Bontecou's reliefs are also redolent with associations around sexuality and death. Within this framework, the hole and the mound that are one and the same generate instead a metonymic chain: breasts turn into mouths, which become anuses, which are also vaginas and eyes. The intense tactility creates a space in which the viewer is either aggressively devoured by the object or engulfed by it in ecstatic abandon and voluptuousness. This is a version of sexuality and the body offered by psychoanalysis; it is the body before it has been properly mapped and formed by language and the mandates of society. This polymorphous perverse body is a site of intense pleasure and also a space of fear, for it is a zone of experience that lies at the very threshold of language. This might explain why Bontecou's works are relatively easy to describe, if what is at stake is a matter of enumerating their parts, and even, as we have seen in Judd's text, their gestalt. What almost always escapes the literary turn, however, is the phenomenological and psychic effect they produce – often the hairs on the back of one's neck stand on edge.

For all of Bontecou's internal repetition, the work possesses an intense singularity of vision. In short, it doesn't look "like" anyone else's work of the period. This is only true, however, when she is seen within an exclusively American context. Like her fellow artists Cy Twombly and Robert Rauschenberg, Bontecou was most likely aware of European artists, notably Italian Alberto Burri, who was working and exhibiting in Rome when all three were there.[3] In addition to his position in the artistic community of Rome, Burri had numerous exhibitions in New York and was shown at the most important galleries (Betty Parsons) and exhibitions (*Art of Assemblage*) of the day. Burri's nonillusionistic use of found and cheap materials to create highly textured relief works formed a context in which Bontecou's dramatic reliefs of 1959 could emerge. Burri also deployed repetition, working through the same core ideas in bodies of work that evoke skins and wounds and partake in the culture of rationing and scarcity that defined postwar Europe.

If Burri's work shows us the salving nature of skin – no matter the wound, no matter the scar, the body tends to heal, skin renews itself – then Bontecou is concerned with the openings of the body, as her sculptures offer voids through which one enters or is expelled. Both artists explore this liminal territory through the use of relief and through a sparse economy of means. Their repetitious recourse to "real" materials permits a psychic opening that reveals the nature of bodily space. Where language pauses, tactility fills the void.

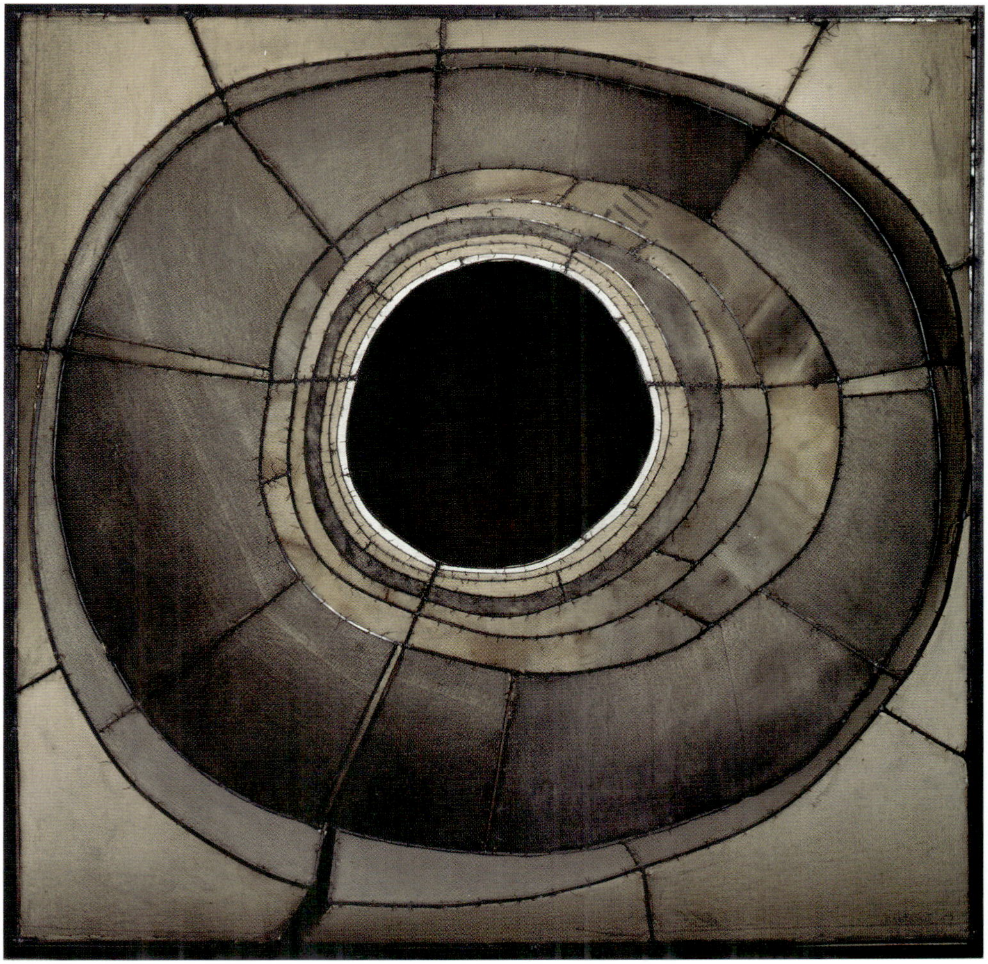

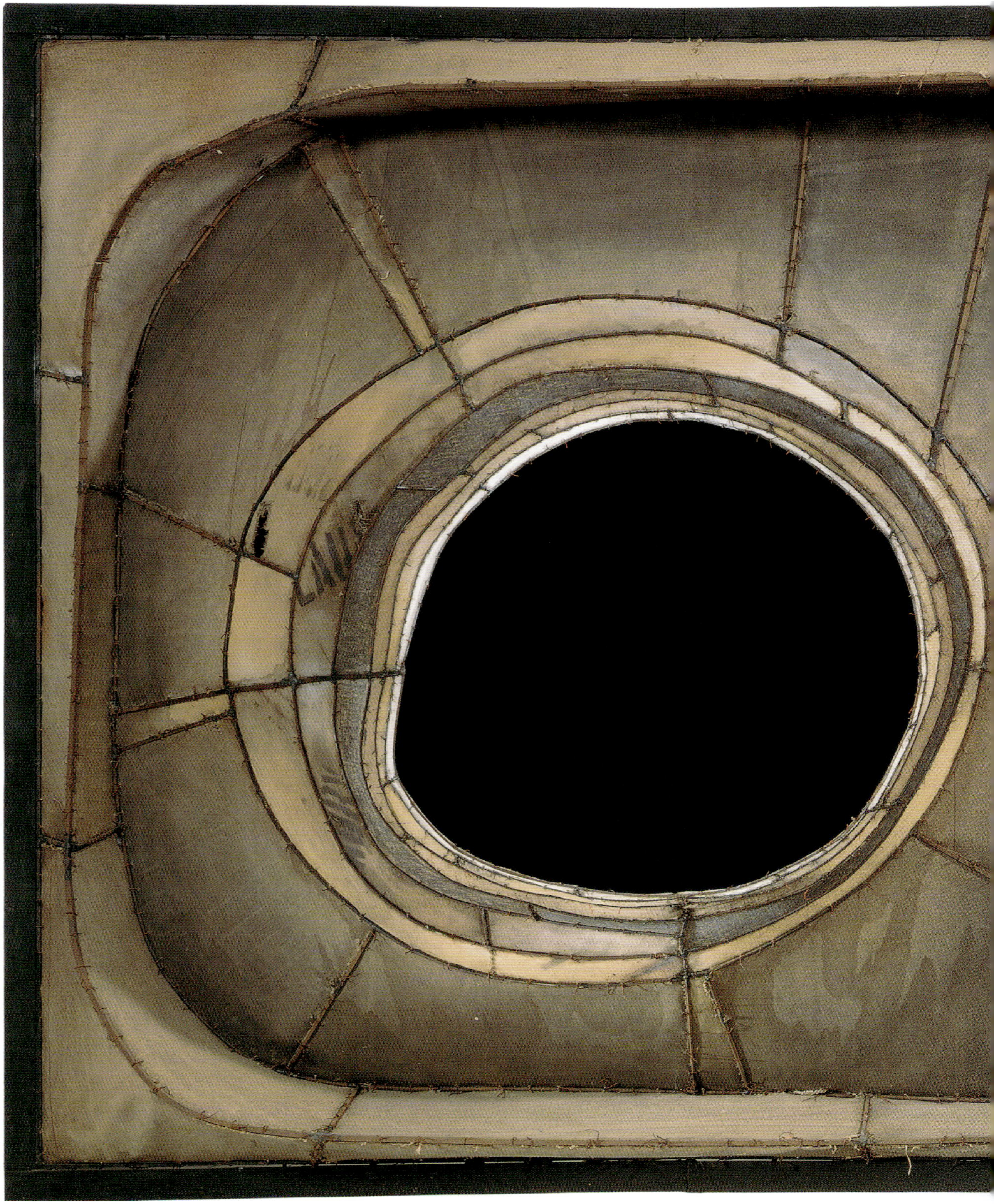

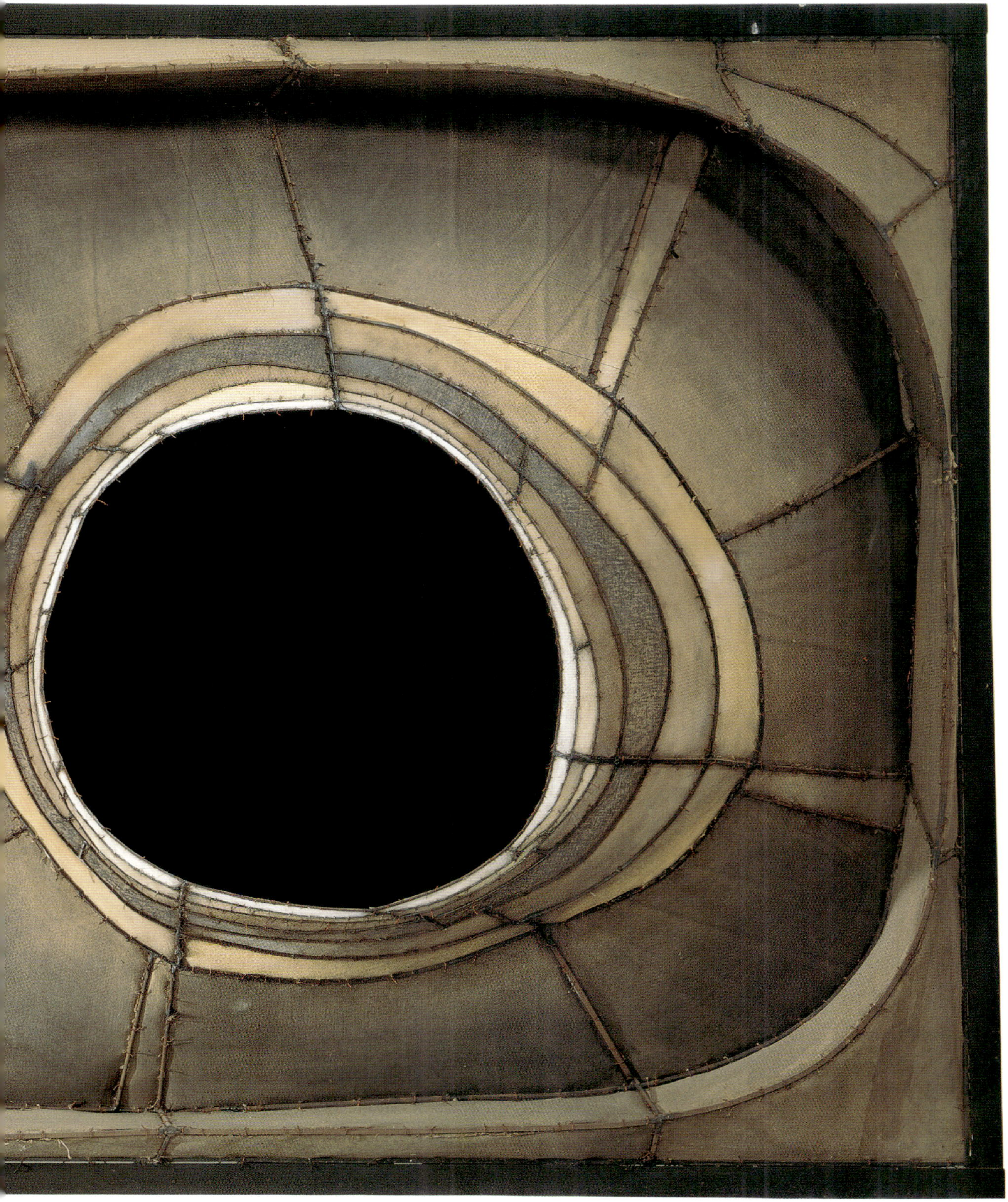

Untitled, 1959–60

BRIONY FER

COLOR-IN-PIECES: THE ITALIAN NEO-AVANT-GARDE

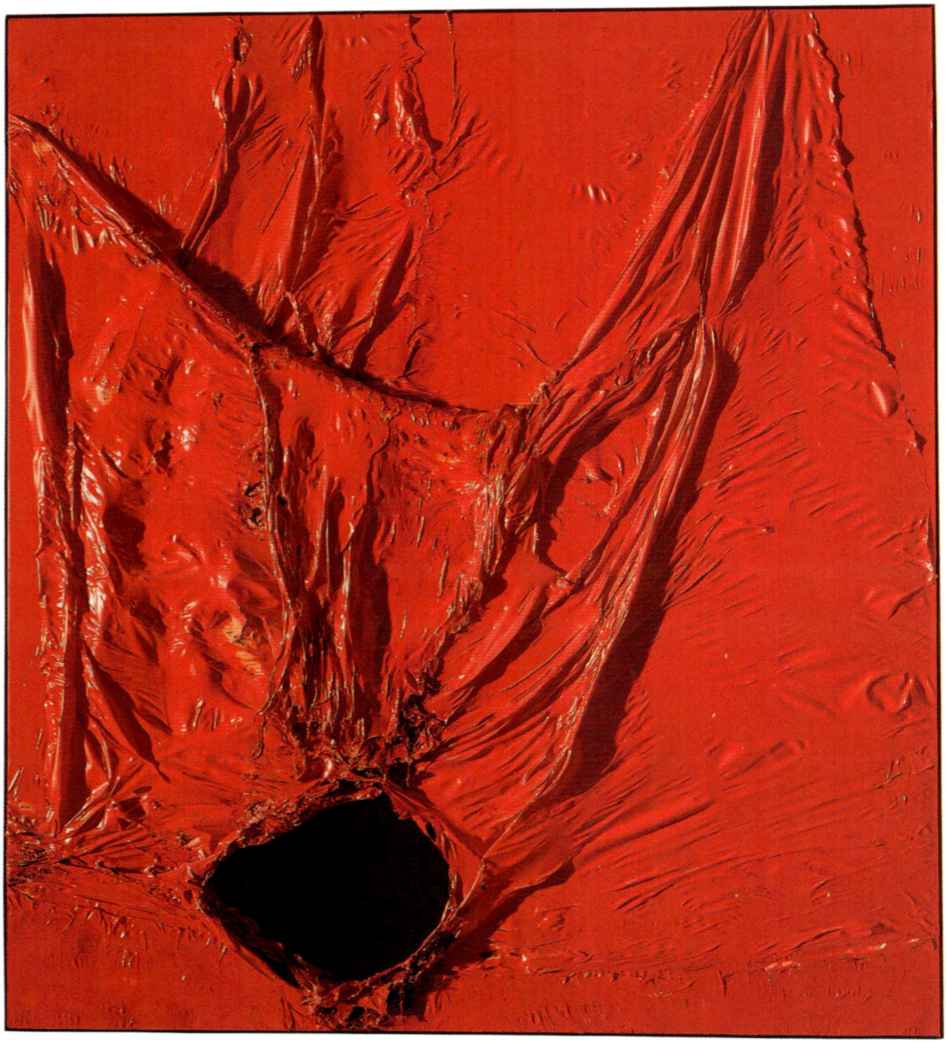

There is a type of artwork that hangs on the wall like a picture but acts more like an object. Conventions of pictorial composition, even abstract composition, are ignored in favor of the literal materiality of a thing that refuses to behave as a picture should even though it is attached to a wall. Unconventional materials might literally jut out from the wall into the viewer's space, but not necessarily. Monochrome paintings can fit into this category too – once you stop thinking of a monochrome as an abstract painting but instead see it simply as a flat colored object. This move from picture to object was enacted once by the historic avant-garde (the Russian Constructivists Vladimir Tatlin and Alexander Rodchenko, for example) and then again in Italy in the 1950s by the neo-avant-garde, in particular by the artists Alberto Burri, Lucio Fontana, and Piero Manzoni. When Donald Judd formalized his thinking on what he named a "specific object," that is, an object that was "neither painting nor sculpture," he studiously avoided reference to all three Italian artists. Instead he singled out Yves Klein as the only interesting European and relegated the others, we can presume, to the "stagnant pond" that, for Judd, was recent European art.[1] Although Burri and Fontana had both been given exhibitions at the Museum of Modern Art in New York in 1966, from Judd's perspective both stood for something incurably pictorial, still tied to European traditions of compositional painting. Even aside from Judd's particular prescriptions for the new art, their work fit neither high modernist ideals for painting nor the logic of the readymade as it was internalized in Pop and Minimalism. In retrospect, however, and in the light of the many revisions to that history, the situation looks rather different. Here I want to consider the radical reconfiguration of the art object that was worked through by the Italian neo-avant-garde of the 1950s, as a phenomenon distinct from yet parallel to the shifts that occurred at roughly the same time in the United States.[2] The work of Burri and Fontana forms a cusp, in some ways still tied to older models but at the same time turning those models on their heads. Surprisingly, color became the site of the most dramatic of these inversions. Color, after all, has been thoroughly caught up in expressive models of art, acting almost as a measure of pictorial sensibilities and yet, with the monochrome, had also precipitated their downfall. It is this twin impulse in Italian art of the 1950s both to intensify the effects of color *and* to empty color out of the art work, culminating in Manzoni's all-white *Achromes*, that I focus on here. The push and pull of the chromatic and the achromatic obey no predetermined rules of color theory but conform instead to a bodily system of drives.

COLLAGE

First, let me backtrack to a slightly earlier moment and replace Donald Judd, who liked cadmium red but also *saw* red when he saw European-type painting, with Robert Rauschenberg. It is 1952, and Rauschenberg is in Rome with Cy Twombly. He admires Burri's work and visits his studio twice. Then, after traveling in North Africa for a while, he returned to Rome and gave Burri, who was ill at the time, a "healing fetish" – one of the small boxes he named *scatole personali.*

Alberto Burri
Rosso Plastica, 1964

Burri gave him a work in return. This was not only an exchange of gifts, but also a small token of a more telling exchange. It is not Burri's "influence" that interests me, but the temporary connection. Maybe Rauschenberg saw in Burri not just old-fashioned European abstraction but something like he was interested in at the time: the way things stick to a surface, how scraps might collect in the container that is a monochrome painting, how debris can be recycled and salvaged. In the work that Rauschenberg produced when he was in Rome – the little fetish objects, the photographs of fleamarkets, the shirtboard collages – we can detect an intensely tactile imagination.[3] It is as if the city revealed itself not just in the throwaway, but in the throwaway textures of torn fabrics or stones picked out of the dirt and strung together.

The French artist Jean Fautrier had powerfully rendered texture traumatic in his notion of *texturologie,* where thick encrustations of paint acted as repositories of psychic trauma in the aftermath of war. Burri's work has also been seen as traumatic, even though he replaces painterly texture with that of ready-made materials. Burri is best known for his *Sacci,* which he began to make in 1950 using the burlap sacks imported under the Marshall Plan. His surfaces have been read as wounds, cut and torn, then stitched and sutured. The fact that Burri had trained as a doctor has fueled this dynamic of wounding and repair. This is persuasive up to a point, but it is worth saying that it also marks something of a swansong. The artwork is both in thrall to and transformed by a metaphorics of surface as skin – to be rent and punctured and sewn up again – but it is also transformed by the sheer materiality of rough burlap. Burri makes remarkably intricate material and tactual worlds inside his collages. Tiny spirals of machine stitching may cover over a crater or hole in the fabric; elsewhere a tear gently opens the surface to another layer that can be glimpsed behind it. Aside from the sacks, Burri used a staggering array of materials, including pumice to encrust the surface like a mineral deposit or an uneven layer of ash. This is about as far away as you can get from the kind of monochrome that stares blankly back at the viewer. Instead, Burri is like a miniaturist let loose on a surface. His friend the poet and critic Emilio Villa once wrote of Burri's "terrifying panoramas: ash in the eyes, blood in the eyes"[4] – making the ash-gray and the patches of red paint a function of traumatized vision. Despite Villa's lacerated gaze, Burri's color is rarely talked about, yet it is hard to see what he does with material that is distinctive – especially what separates him from other Informel artists like Nicolas de Staël or Antoni Tàpies – without attending to it. For a start, the burlap is not neutral or colorless. A whole range of dirt-brown tones offers an almost tragic burlesque of painterly "tone." In between, or glimpsed behind, there are patches not just of added hessian but of gold paint and vivid cadmium red, sometimes spread out as a ground, sometimes applied in a crack between two pieces of sacking, sometimes congealing as a small pool.

What this is not is a subtle color accent or "touch" of color. A touch of color can accentuate a part of a compositional whole, but Burri's red tends to puncture and so destroy the whole surface structure (as Barthes would write of Cy Twombly's use of color and its capacity to puncture and lacerate).[5] Burri works with color as if it were a collage material like hessian, which he can cut up into pieces and stitch together again. In the *Sacci* color is separated into two main registers: the browns and grays of the sacks, on one hand, and then the red, gold, white, and black of the painted sections, on the other. This is Burri's color chart. Rather than touches of color, Burri explores the color of touch in the thick, haptic surface of collage. To look at it is to become imaginatively involved in what it feels like to touch the world of everyday experience. The color chart is not so different from Rauschenberg's, who, on his return to the United States, would embark on his red and gold and dirt series of paintings. A logic of cutting up color into separate and singular blocks underlies the monochrome. If the first time around Kasimir Malevich had equated white (treated as a noncolor) with space, Burri's white monochromes are anything but voids. His earliest white monochromes, for example, were painted with white lead (which we now know to be highly toxic) in which the color is drained out but the palpable materiality is left in. Then in a later series he took old white linen shirts and other clothing, cut the sleeves out, and spread them flat across the surface. This is very far from the "purity" of white as it had been part of an earlier rhetoric of utopian abstraction.

SPATIAL CONCEPTS, COLOR CONCEPTS

The famous photographs of Fontana by Ugo Mulas heighten the sense that the performative act of making the work is almost a crime scene to which the spectator is a guilty witness, the overdramatic shadows and grainy black-and-white tones having the patina of *film noir.* Like the allegory of the surgeon-artist applied to Burri, it is tempting to see in Fontana the opposite: the perverse erotics of the artist-as-violator. However, as some commentators have suggested, Fontana's work has also been overdetermined by the Mulas photos. What they obviously do not show is the color, which has a perverse erotics all its own. They also staged Fontana's working process in a particular way. Sarah Whitfield has discussed how Fontana would not let Mulas photograph him actually cutting into the canvas of his *Attesi* series, but only pretending to after the fact. The actual process was more elaborate: Fontana first painted the monochrome surface in emulsion and then, while the paint was still slightly wet, made the cut. With great care, he next slightly furled back the sides of the slit. Finally he applied tapes to secure the cuts at the back like a bandage.[6] One of the insights that the artist Richard Tuttle brings to our thinking about Fontana is his remark that he first understood his work only when he happened to see one of the backs of one of the *Attesi* in Marilena Bonomo's collection.[7] As a dynamic of process, this is far closer to Burri than one might have imagined.

The photographs of Fontana at work dramatize the hand of the artist – caught in the act of creation, although at a fictitious and reenacted moment of origin. Sometimes the hand is cropped or sometimes as it moves swiftly to the act of cutting it is caught by the camera as a blur. Unlike Burri, who came to collage from painting, Fontana had already had one career as a sculptor before

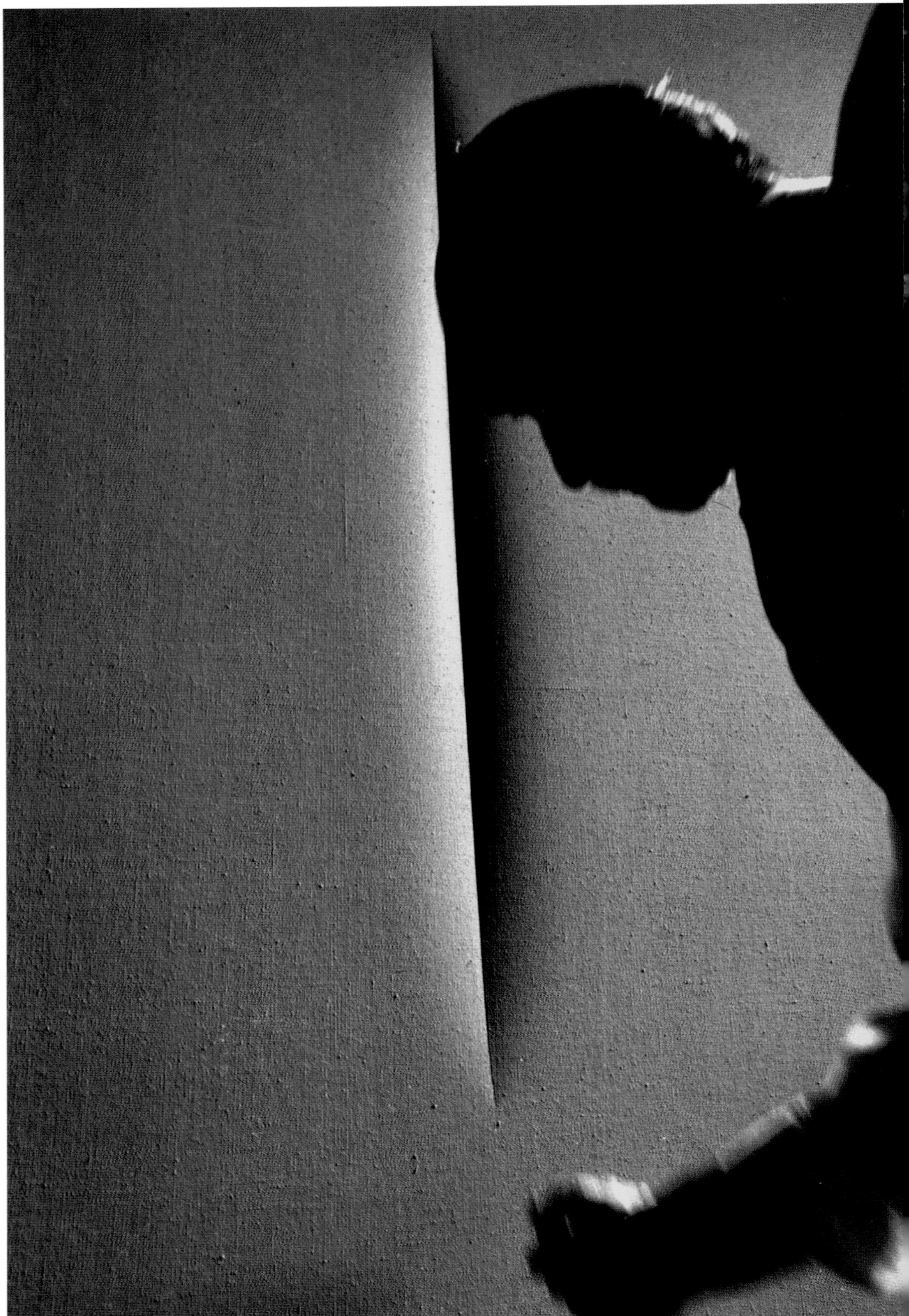

he began to produce his first *Buchi* (*Holes*) in 1949. It is very much *as* a sculptor that he attacks painting. It is a sculptor's hand that comes to cut into the monochrome surface of painting *as if it were* a sculptural mass. Yet at the end of his life, Fontana recalled, "From the outset I never called the work I was doing in 1946 painting. I called it a 'spatial concept.'"[8] Nor would the word "sculpture" accommodate his project. To call something as material as this a "spatial concept" introduced a new dimension as well, in addition to what Fontana seems to have intended. There is surely something contradictory in the claims for infinity – and the infinite space beyond the cuts and holes – and the sheer materiality of the surface. Utopian images of space exploration pervade Fontana's writing, as if the cuts and holes could open onto a vast cosmic experience. Yet where the experience really lies, and where the shadow hands and bodies of Mulas's photographs are not mistaken, is in the space in front of the work – in the corridor of space between the canvas and the spectator, the space where the phantasmatic projection of a bodily surface is enacted (and each time reenacted) in viewing the *Spatial Concepts.*

Although the sculptures that Fontana produced at Albisola in 1959 have been seen as the antitheses of the cut monochromes, they carry through this logic, expanding the vocabulary of cuts and holes into the whole space of a room. The Nature series was comprised of large round terracotta sculptures that sat directly on the floor in various arrangements. They were later cast in bronze, but the terracotta ones have a rawness to them that the bronze ones can only mimic. Some have slits; others have holes gouged out of them. In the openings and cavities are sexual allusions, but there is also a radical disorganization of an iconography of the body (orifices, balls, eyeballs intermingle). If this is a spatial concept, as Fontana titled them, then the proposition must be: not what body parts are these, male or female, but that *nothing* falls *outside* of the body. These uneven lumps of clay are not large sculptures, but because of their awkwardness and weight, they seem oversize. The disproportion of scale echoes in Fontana's writing, where he invokes the infinite space of the cosmos: even a lunar landscape could be a libidinal landscape, gaping open, lips of clay oozing at the opening crevice – and vice versa.

Traditionally, color is the preserve of painting, not sculpture, unless we count the color of clay and bronze (which we should). But in Fontana's background as a sculptor in the 1930s and 1940s, this was not the case, in particular in his work as a ceramicist, where he used vivid colored glazes in his small-scale sculptural objects, as well as in his use of colored and black or ultraviolet neon light in his light installations. From 1952 he embarked on a series of spatial concepts called "stones," in which he added little bits of colored Murano glass, which is dispersed across a surface, with the glue still evident. This surface is tacky from every point of view. Tacky in the sense of sticky and glutinous *and* in the sense of kitsch, in which, as Yve-Alain Bois has discussed, Fontana was thoroughly immersed.[9] Here, at this point, fantasies of bodily fluids mingle with those of an ersatz culture. Fontana's fake gems reflect the light and occupy an almost

Ugo Mulas
Photograph of Fontana at work

hallucinatory zone between a jeweled surface and a phantasmagoric mess. The way Fontana used color seems to me to be the most interesting aspect of his work, particularly from the late 1950s on, when he uses more and more stridently artificial, even lurid, colors: bright candy pink, lime green, blue, orange. Increasingly, in the 1960s he mixes glitter with his colors to make the gaudy, ravaged surfaces of his egg-shaped series entitled *La Fine di Dio* (The End of God). In a large pink monochrome in bright lipstick pink from 1968, paint oozes voluptuously from the furled edges of the gouged-out holes. Even "hot" colors, like the shocking pink, are cold in Fontana's hands, reminiscent of Robert Smithson's comment that Frank Stella's metallic paintings of the early 1960s disclose a "cold scintillation."[10] They are the colors of commodities, not the color of bodies; the colors of makeup and cosmetics, not the color of nature. The colors are toxic and the gesture is extreme, repellent as much as seductive, as if Fontana is mimicking precisely the lure of the color of a culture of spectacle. The possibility for sensual experience exists, but only as an experience that is at times perverse and fetishistic and always – quite literally in Fontana's case – riven.

Burri's *Plastici,* begun in 1960, are also synthetic. Burri took sheets of plastic, transparent, black or red, and used a blowtorch to melt and mold them into complex and convoluted arrangements. Scorching the edges and patches that he had systematically used through the 1950s, the effects on plastic are spectacular and different. *Rosso plastica* is like looking inside a body and wondering at the intricate structures to be found there (as alien and mysterious as the surface of the moon, which Fontana found so seductive). Far from inchoate or accidental, they show Burri's extraordinary control of the medium. But the nature of the material and the way it behaves when heated suggests an uncanny wetness. It is not just that the liquidity of wet paint is parodied in the process, but that it is transformed into glistening viscera. When Eva Hesse first made her latex works, they also had a shine, but latex goes matte with age. In Burri's red plastics, the body's interior is splayed out and opened to view – and it turns out to be full of holes, like a spectacular ruin. Shiny red plastic has the lure, like Fontana's colors, of contemporary colors and fetishistic materials. Color may be in ruins, it may be sham, but it also becomes the site of fantastic bodily projections.

PLEASE TOUCH

When Manzoni began to make art in the mid-1950s, he used a number of materials that seem almost predictable: oil paint, tar, glue, even the safety pins imprinted onto a surface. Each one can be understood within the realm of materials that Burri, Fontana, and a host of others artists were working with at that time. But in 1957, Manzoni took a stance: he proclaimed the advent of the *Achrome* and the exhaustion of color that was irredeemably tied to a pictorial sensibility. In part this was a gesture of one-upmanship, beating Yves Klein at his own blue monochrome game by declaring the victory of colorlessness. But in practice the tactic grew steadily out of recent developments. The first tentative moves to the *Achrome* were achieved through draping white fabric in complex arrangements, echoing Burri's textile vocabulary. The white monochrome was already well established as a site for experiment by the early 1950s, linked to the aesthetics of crumbling white walls as much as to Burri's aesthetics of debris. Manzoni began soaking pieces of canvas in materials like kaolin or gesso; then he moved on to a wide array of ready-made white materials. Calling them "Achromes" was to bring them all together under a single title – just as Fontana had done by calling his work, however varied, "Spatial Concepts." Fontana had sometimes marked his monochromes with a thumbprint instead of signing them, just as Manzoni, in July 1960, would imprint eggs for his audience to eat in the live performance *The Consumption of art by the art-devouring public.* Most important, Manzoni recognized in Fontana that, for all the talk of infinity beyond the surface, the most significant and productive site of action was going to be in front of it, in the space of the spectator. The palpable material, the tactile, the bodily – all this would seem to contradict the rhetoric of infinite space that concerned Italian artists in the 1950s and 1960s. But on the contrary, this was a way of registering the messy lining of the utopian vision that could not be. As Samuel Beckett wrote: "To find a form that accommodates the mess, that is the task of the artist now."[11]

White seems the least likely color to accommodate the mess. Yet both Burri and Fontana had demonstrated how even a white monochrome can verge on repulsion in the glutinous agglomeration of materials, playing out a dialectics of matte and shiny, of wet and dry. White turned out to be the ideal ground for scatological fantasy, and Manzoni, for one, quickly gave up the sticky morass of tar that he had started out using: too obvious and, oddly enough, just far too pictorial, too much like the textural composition of so much Informel art. Manzoni seemed to have understood Duchamp's invitation to "Please touch" in the cover he made for the catalogue of the 1947 Surrealist exhibition in Paris,[12] which consisted of a pink rubber prosthetic breast sitting on velvet. It is not very big, and the invitation is edged with the irresistibility of transgression (*prière* in French means both "please" and "prayer"). It is interesting that when Manzoni occasionally does use colors other than white in his *Achromes* it is often as a blue velvet ground. Maybe for Manzoni color itself has the feel of a relic, so it is well suited to his purpose. There is no need for his *Achromes* to take the form of specific body parts for them to create bodily affect. The glossy shine of the small and absurdly crimped shanks of white fiberglass does it simply and effortlessly. You can think of the achromatic strategy in terms of a desire to void the object of color and then proceed to fill it with matter, or – the word that seems most appropriate for Manzoni – *stuff.* What is this if not itself part and parcel of a fantasy that is as excremental as it is libidinal?

Manzoni died prematurely at the age of twenty-nine in February 1963, but his project left a lasting legacy. One can see clearly in his achromatic position a proto-Conceptual refusal of a pictorial aesthetic. The generation that would follow, the younger artists associated with Arte Povera, would, on initial reflection at least, share something of the necessary repression of color that

occurred at the moment of Conceptualism. But in the light of the way color functioned in the work of the neo-avant-garde of the 1950s, at least as I have tried to characterize it here, that claim falls well short. The disintegration of color that I have described is not the same as the death of color. As David Batchelor has put it, "Chromophobia might not really have its opposite in chromophilia; chromophobia might be seen as simply chromophilia's weak form."[13] White, rather than not being a color, is perhaps the most seductive color of all. And in the context of Arte Povera, so were the colors of sackcloth and ashes. Far from neutral, Burri's sacks would provide a key word in the vocabulary of "poor art"; Jannis Kounellis would take the sacks off the wall and fill them with grain and put them on the gallery floor, or fill a gallery with gold leaf; Michelangelo Pistoletto would take the discarded clothes off the wall and place them in piles on the floor or make a rose out of corrugated cardboard; and at the other end of the chromatic scale, Alighiero Boetti and Pino Pascale would work with industrial and kitsch color; Boetti's sprayed monochromes would take color into new realms. Far from exhausting itself, the dynamic between the chromatic and the achromatic continues to animate Arte Povera – just as it had driven the dismantling of a pictorial aesthetic in the work of the 1950s. The legacy of that moment is not over yet.

Piero Manzoni
Achrome, 1961

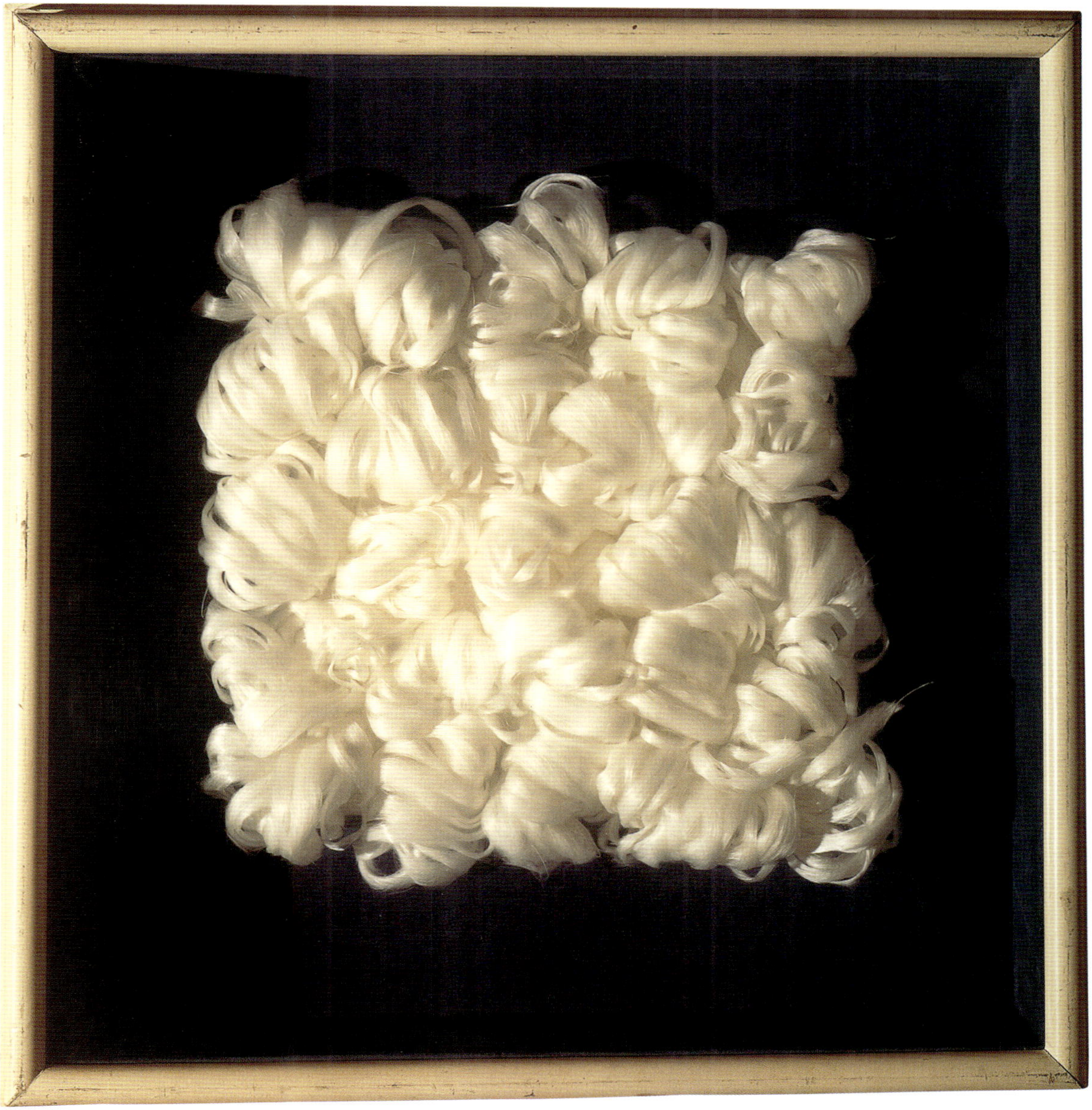

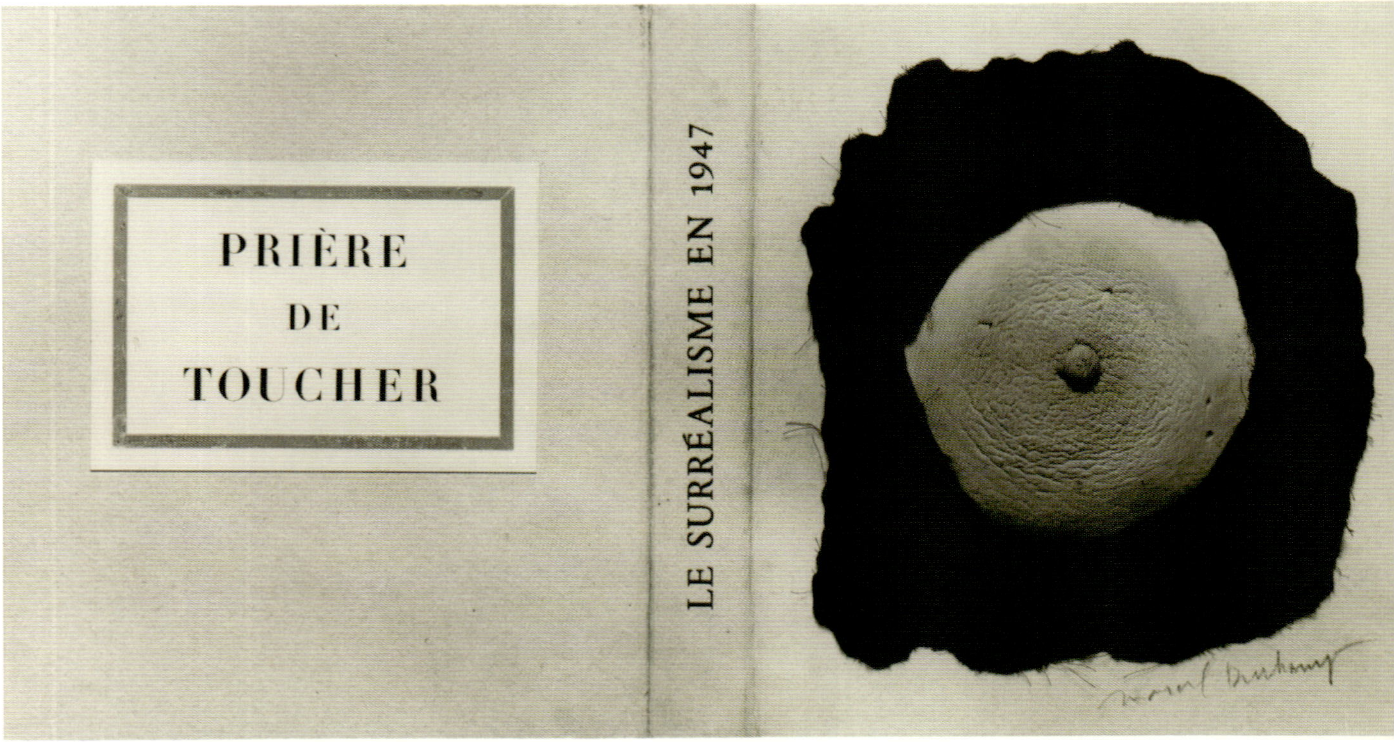
PRIÈRE
DE
TOUCHER
LE SURRÉALISME EN 1947

NOTES

1 Donald Judd, *Complete Writings, 1959–1975* (Halifax: The Press of Nova Scotia College of Art and Design; and New York: New York University Press, 2005), 69.

2 The groundbreaking study of the role of color for the neo-avant-garde was Benjamin Buchloh's essay "The Primary Colors for the Second Time: A Paradigm Repetition of the Neo-Avant-Garde," *October* 37 (Summer 1986). This essay makes important reference to the Italian neo-avant-garde but concentrates on Yves Klein.

3 For a discussion of the excremental and bodily fantasies that attach to Rauschenberg's early work, see Helen Molesworth, "Before Bed," in Brandon Joseph, ed., *Robert Rauschenberg* (Cambridge, Mass.: The MIT Press, 2002), 75–92.

4 "Panoramas terrifiants: Des cendres dans les yeux, du sang dans les yeux," cited by Carolyn Christov-Bakargiev in her interesting essay "Alberto Burri: The Surface at Risk," in *Burri 1915–1995 Retrospektive* (Milan: Electa, 1997), 80.

5 Roland Barthes, "Cy Twombly: Works on Paper," in *The Responsibility of Forms: Critical Essays on Music, Art, and Representation* (Oxford: Oxford University Press, 1986), 166.

6 Sarah Whitfield, "Handling Space," in *Lucio Fontana* (London: Hayward Gallery, 2000), 31.

7 Richard Tuttle, "A Love Letter to Fontana," in *Lucio Fontana* (Amsterdam: Stedelijk Museum Amsterdam; and London: Whitechapel Art Gallery, 1988), 60.

8 Fontana interviewed by Daniele Palazzoli, *Bit,* no. 5, Milan, October–November 1967, in *Lucio Fontana* (London: Hayward Gallery, 2000), 136.

9 See Yve-Alain Bois, "Kitsch," in Yve-Alain Bois and Rosalind Krauss, *L'Informe: Mode d'emploi* (Paris: Centre Georges Pompidou, 1996), 107–12.

10 Robert Smithson quoting Mallarmé from "Hérodiade," in "Entropy and the New Monuments" (1966), in *Robert Smithson, The Collected Writings* (Berkeley and Los Angeles: University of California Press 1996), 20.

11 Samuel Beckett, quoted by Deirdre Bair, *Samuel Beckett: A Biography* (New York: Harcourt Brace Jovanovich, 1978), 523.

12 Mignon Nixon discusses Duchamp's work in relation to Klein's theory of the part-object and relates it to Eva Hesse's *Ringaround Arosie,* in *Fantastic Reality: Louise Bourgeois and a Story of Modern Art* (Cambridge, Mass.: MIT Press, 2005), 213.

13 David Batchelor, *Chromophobia* (London: Reaktion Books, 2000), 71.

Marcel Duchamp
Cover for deluxe edition Le Surréalisme en 1947
"Prière de Toucher" ("Please touch") 1947

CONGO
BINGA

ALBERTO BURRI 1915–1995

Although Alberto Burri's career has languished in the United States, he was an important member of the postwar trans-Continental neo-avant-garde. As a young man, he abandoned his medical studies to pursue a career in art. Ironically, he was to begin painting during World War II, while held as a prisoner of war in a detention camp in Hereford, Texas. Upon his return to Italy after the war, he exhibited at The Art Club, an important gallery in Rome founded by the futurist artist Enrico Prampolini. Burri also was included in important exhibitions in the United States, notably the influential *Art of Assemblage* at the Museum of Modern Art, and exhibited at the most important New York galleries of the 1950s, Betty Parsons and the Stable Gallery. In addition to being included in these influential venues, Burri also exerted a strong influence on contemporary artists on both sides of the Atlantic, setting an important example for fellow Italian Lucio Fontana and American artists Lee Bontecou, Robert Rauschenberg, and Cy Twombly.[1]

Burri himself was influenced by fellow artist Prampolini, whose involvement in Dada and Surrealism shaped Burri's approach to art. What the Italians called "poly materialism," the ability of a single work of art to contain a variety of material effects, led Burri to Paris in 1949. He had already seen the work of Paul Klee, Jean Arp, and Joan Miró in Rome, but in Paris he met the artists and became even more familiar with their practices. Burri rarely made public statements about his work, taking a lesson perhaps from that great master of silence, Marcel Duchamp, but one can surmise that the gentle biomorphism of these artists in Paris appealed to him. So too Arp's lifelong experimentation with relief sculpture and painting must also have influenced Burri and led to his growing awareness of the limits of painting.

After his Paris sojourn Burri began to experiment with large-scale wall reliefs, using materials such as burlap, wood, and plastic, forms and materials that he would deploy throughout his career. Using raw burlap, Burri began patching pieces of the fabric together, sometimes sewing them, as in *Grande Sacco: Congo Binga*, and sometimes painting underneath the holes, tears, and apertures in the burlap, as in *Sacco*. By using the burlap as the active agent in the work rather than simply as the ground, Burri turned away from the traditional norms of painting, moving instead toward the terms of sculpture, so much so that art historian Maria Grazia Tolomeo concluded that "we are no longer dealing with a painting, but with an object, a material object."[2]

The materiality of the burlap not only pushed Burri's painting into the realm of object and sculpture but also into the lived reality of postwar Italian life. Much of the burlap Burri used came from the sacks of grain sent to Italy under the Marshall Plan. For Burri, burlap became a metaphor for skin – punctured, and possibly wounded, as in *Sacco*, or delicately sutured, and holding hope of regeneration, as in *Grande Sacco: Congo Binga*. In one of his few public reflections on his own work, Burri said that whatever he found to work with "must function as surface, material and idea. In burlap I find that perfect measure of tone, material and idea which would be impossible to achieve with paint."[3]

Burri was too inventive, however, for burlap to be perfect forever. Working in large series, he began systematically to explore other rough-hewn materials – wood, Masonite, plastic – working on dozens of pieces, then moving on to a new material after exhausting the possibilities of the previous one. These materials also functioned as building blocks of a sort. Mario Perniola describes Burri's materials as "ordinary household and industrial materials which define the 'origin' of daily life."[4] *Martedi Grasso (Fat Tuesday)* is an extraordinary example of Burri's collaging of rags and various types of flooring materials. The object's gestalt is marvelous in that it can be read, with near simultaneity, as a tiled floor or a mosaic wall. It also provides an intensely haptic field of vision, in which every surface butts up against another that is equally tactile. The shift between the vertical and the horizontal, combined with the work's intense tactility, culminates in a "painting" that appears to masquerade, or misbehave, as a sculpture. This game of mistaken identity continues in *Legno e rosso 3*, in which a red canvas is covered with pieces of wood that have been burned or lacquered, or both. It is Burri's extraordinary economy of means, his ability to produce a work of art from the ordinary materials of daily life, that makes him such an interesting figure well worth considering after decades of the high production values that Pop and Minimalism initiated. Perhaps he has been overlooked in America for so long precisely because he rejected the shiny new commodity form as art's primary interlocutor. For Burri, the object world is precisely *not* the phantasmagoria of the object in spectacle culture. Instead he produces objects whose surfaces retain a high degree of traction, such that they can hold on to – and embrace – the double terrain of art and object.

ALBERTO BURRI 1915–1995

Although Alberto Burri's career has languished in the United States, he was an important member of the postwar trans-Continental neo-avant-garde. As a young man, he abandoned his medical studies to pursue a career in art. Ironically, he was to begin painting during World War II, while held as a prisoner of war in a detention camp in Hereford, Texas. Upon his return to Italy after the war, he exhibited at The Art Club, an important gallery in Rome founded by the futurist artist Enrico Prampolini. Burri also was included in important exhibitions in the United States, notably the influential *Art of Assemblage* at the Museum of Modern Art, and exhibited at the most important New York galleries of the 1950s, Betty Parsons and the Stable Gallery. In addition to being included in these influential venues, Burri also exerted a strong influence on contemporary artists on both sides of the Atlantic, setting an important example for fellow Italian Lucio Fontana and American artists Lee Bontecou, Robert Rauschenberg, and Cy Twombly.[1]

Burri himself was influenced by fellow artist Prampolini, whose involvement in Dada and Surrealism shaped Burri's approach to art. What the Italians called "poly materialism," the ability of a single work of art to contain a variety of material effects, led Burri to Paris in 1948. He had already seen the work of Paul Klee, Jean Arp, and Joan Miró in Rome, but in Paris he met the artists and became ever more familiar with their practices. Burri rarely made public statements about his work, taking a lesson perhaps from that great master of silence, Marcel Duchamp, but one can surmise that the gentle biomorphism of these artists in Paris appealed to him.[2] So too Arp's lifelong experimentation with relief sculpture and painting must also have influenced Burri and led to his growing awareness of the limits of painting.

After his Paris sojourn Burri began to experiment with large-scale wall reliefs, using materials such as burlap, wood, and plastic, forms and materials that he would deploy throughout his career. Using raw burlap, Burri began patching pieces of the fabric together, sometimes sewing them, as in *Grande Sacco: Congo Binga*, and sometimes painting underneath the holes, tears, and apertures in the burlap, as in *Sacco*. By using the burlap as the active agent in the work rather than simply as the ground, Burri turned away from the traditional norms of painting, moving instead toward the terms of sculpture, so much so that art historian Maria Grazia Tolomeo concluded that "we are no longer dealing with a painting but with an object, a material object."[3]

The materiality of the burlap not only pushed Burri's painting into the realm of object and sculpture but also into the lived reality of postwar Italian life. Much of the burlap Burri used came from the sacks of grain sent to Italy under the Marshall Plan. For Burri, burlap became a metaphor for skin – punctured, and possibly wounded, as in *Sacco*, or delicately sutured, and holding hope of regeneration, as in *Grande Sacco: Congo Binga*. In one of his few public reflections on his own work, Burri said that whatever he found to work with "must function as surface, material and idea. In burlap I find that perfect measure of tone, material and idea which would be impossible to achieve with paint."[4]

Burri was too inventive, however, for burlap to be perfect forever. Working in large series, he began systematically to explore other rough-hewn materials – wood, Masonite, plastic – working on dozens of pieces, then moving on to a new material after exhausting the possibilities of the previous one. These materials also functioned as building blocks of a sort. Mario Perniola describes Burri's materials as "ordinary household and industrial materials which define the 'origin' of daily life."[5] *Martedì Grasso* (*Fat Tuesday*) is an extraordinary example of Burri's collaging of rags and various types of flooring materials. The object's gestalt is marvelous in that it can be read, with near simultaneity, as a tiled floor or a mosaic wall. It also provides an intensely haptic field of vision, in which every surface butts up against another that is equally tactile. The shift between the vertical and the horizontal, combined with the work's intense tactility, culminates in a "painting" that appears to masquerade, or misbehave, as a sculpture. This game of mistaken identity continues in *Legno e rosso 3*, in which a red canvas is covered with pieces of wood that have been burned or lacquered, or both. It is Burri's extraordinary economy of means, his ability to produce a work of art from the ordinary materials of daily life, that makes him such an interesting figure well worth considering after decades of the high production values that Pop and Minimalism initiated. Perhaps he has been overlooked in America for so long precisely because he rejected the shiny new commodity form as art's primary interlocutor. For Burri, the object world is precisely not the phantasmagoria of the object in spectacle culture. Instead he produces objects whose surfaces retain a high degree of traction, such that they can hold on to – and embrace – the double terrain of art and object.

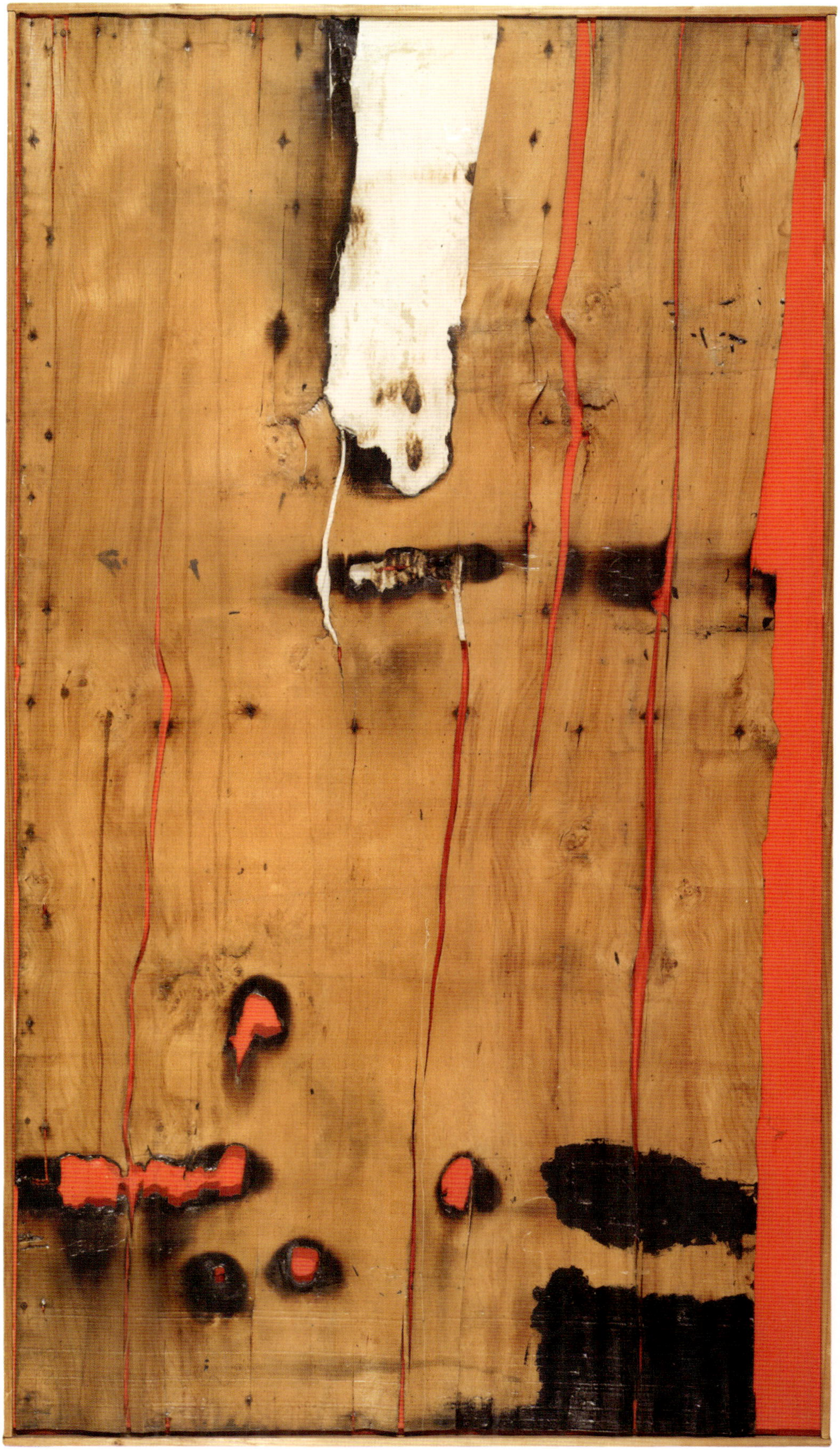

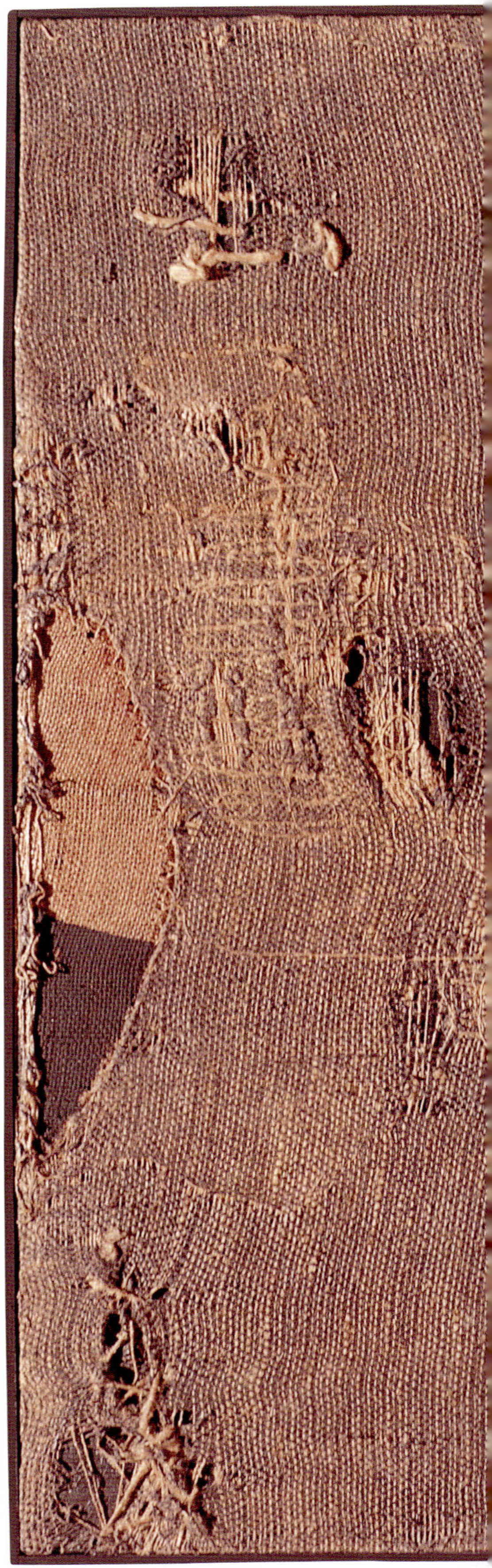

previous spread: left **Grande Sacco: Congo Binga**, 1961

previous spread: right **Legno e rosso 3** (Wood and Red 3), 1956

right **Sacco**, 1952

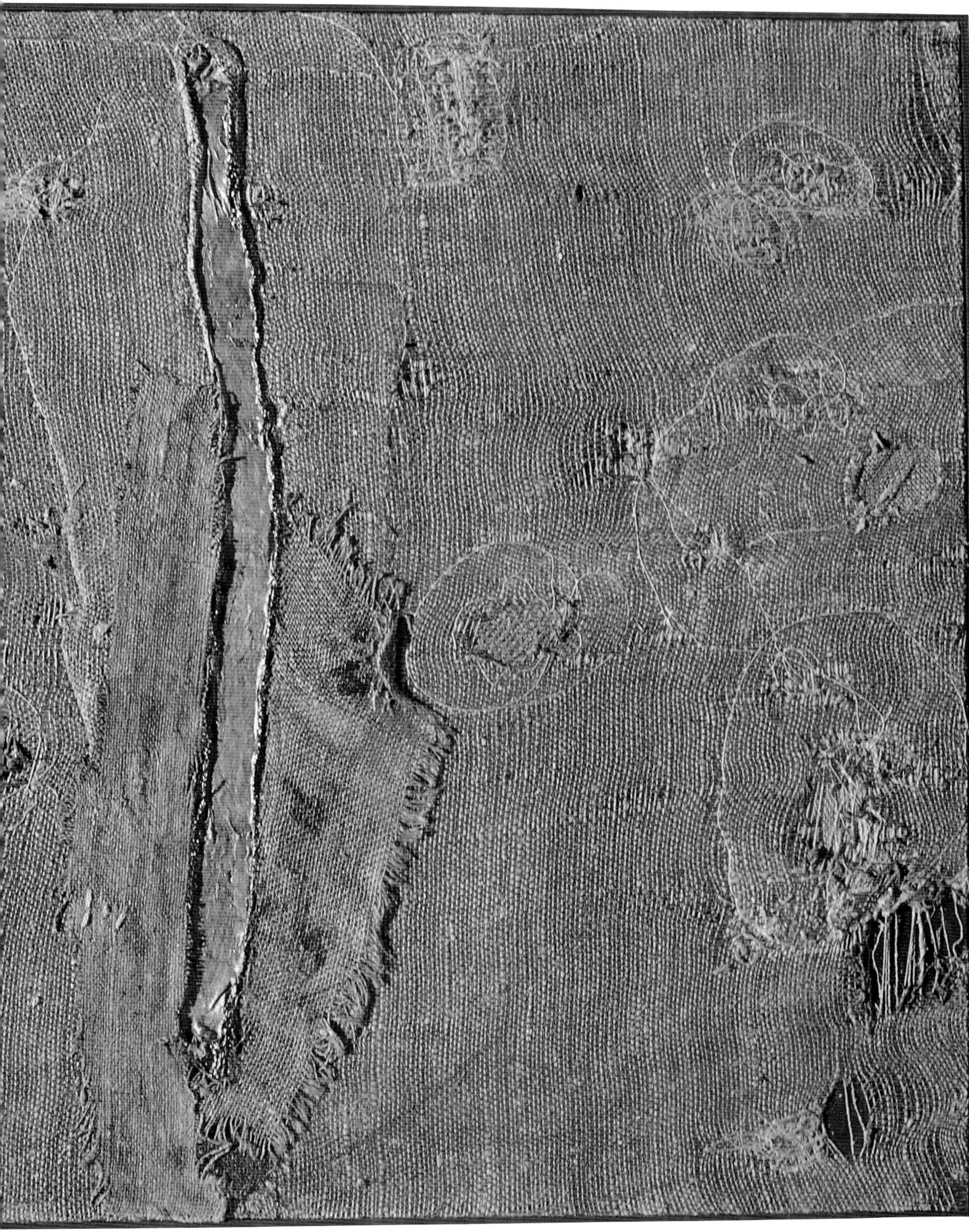

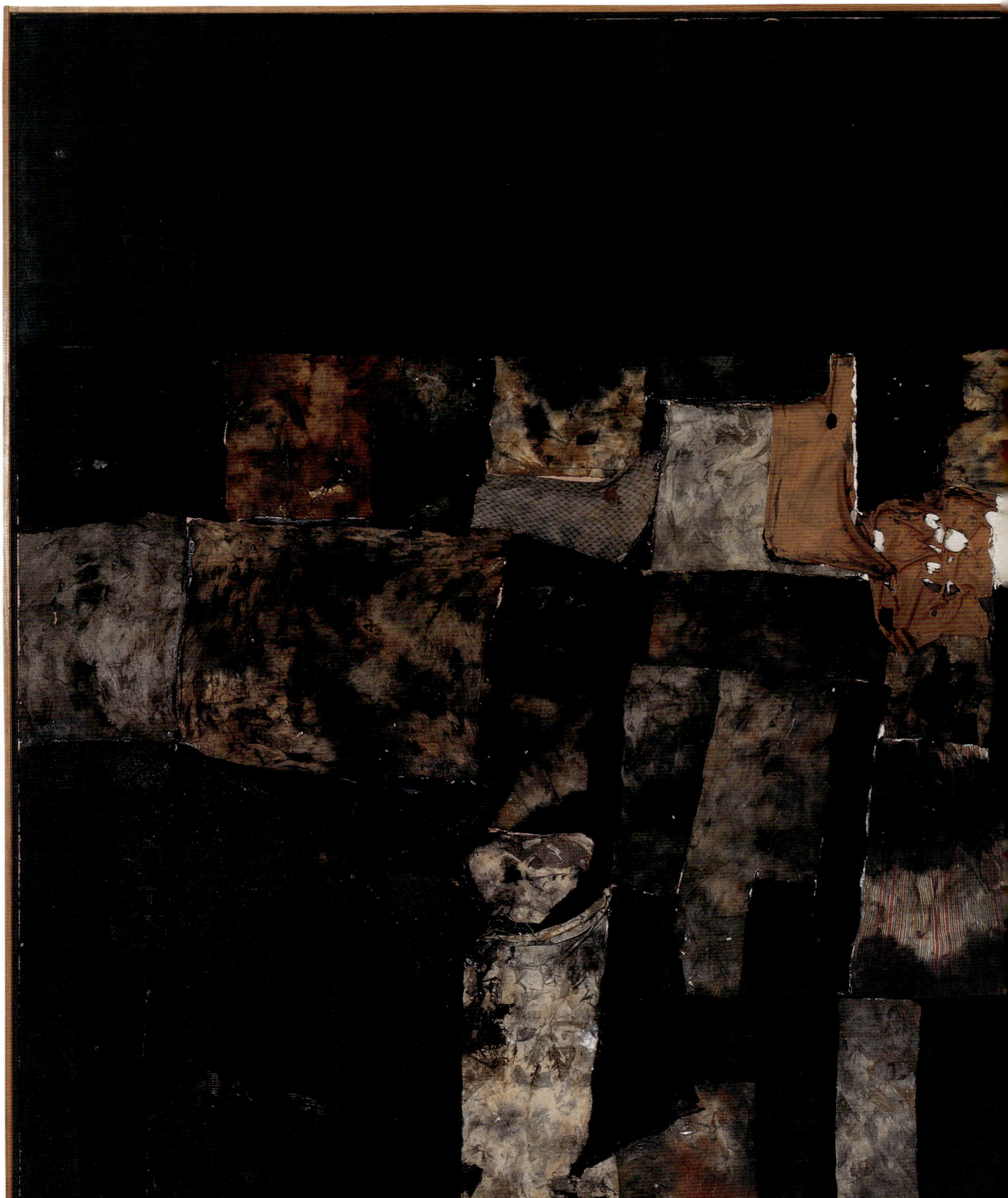

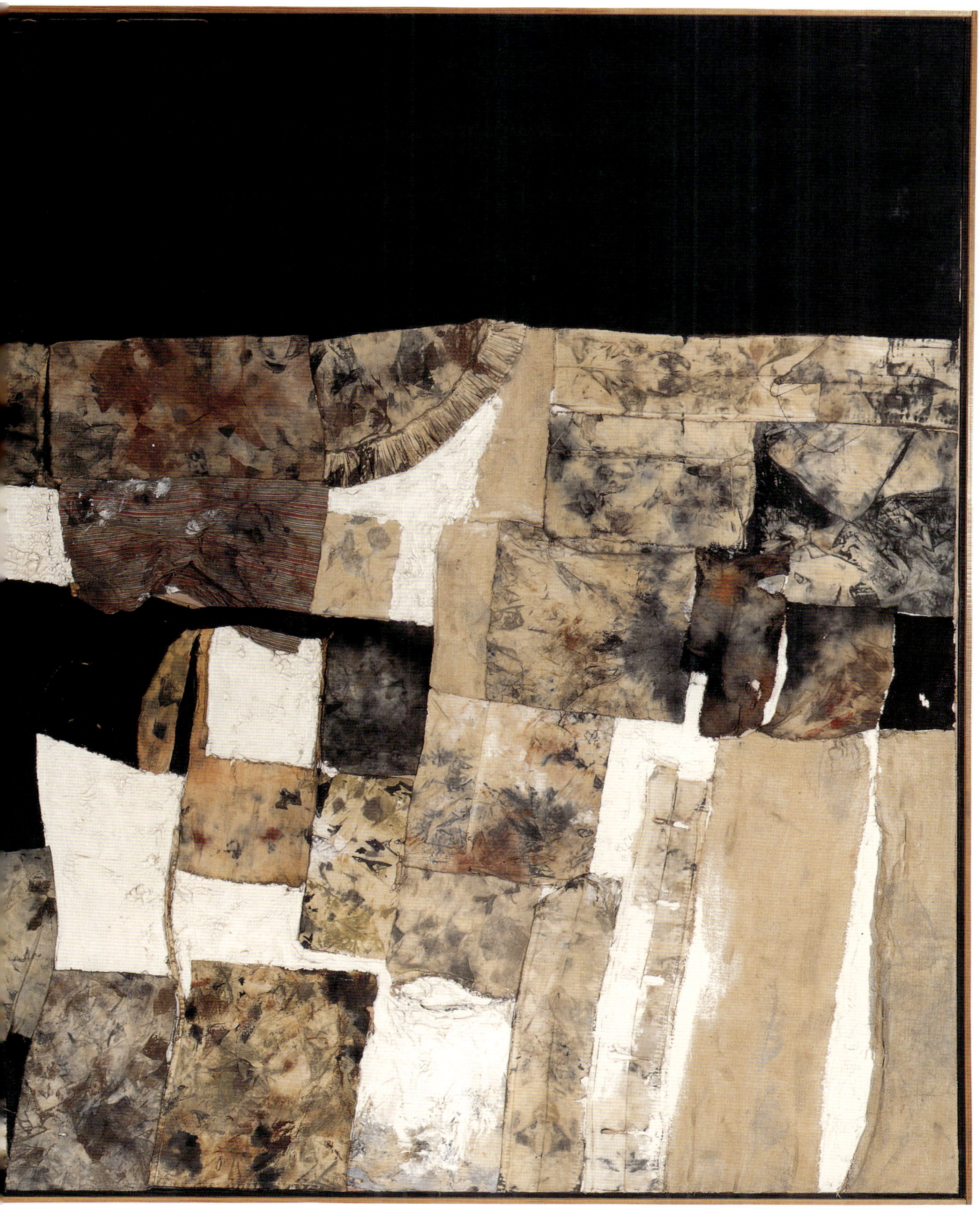

previous spread **Martedi Grasso** (Fat Tuesday), 1956

right **Nero Plastica**, 1961

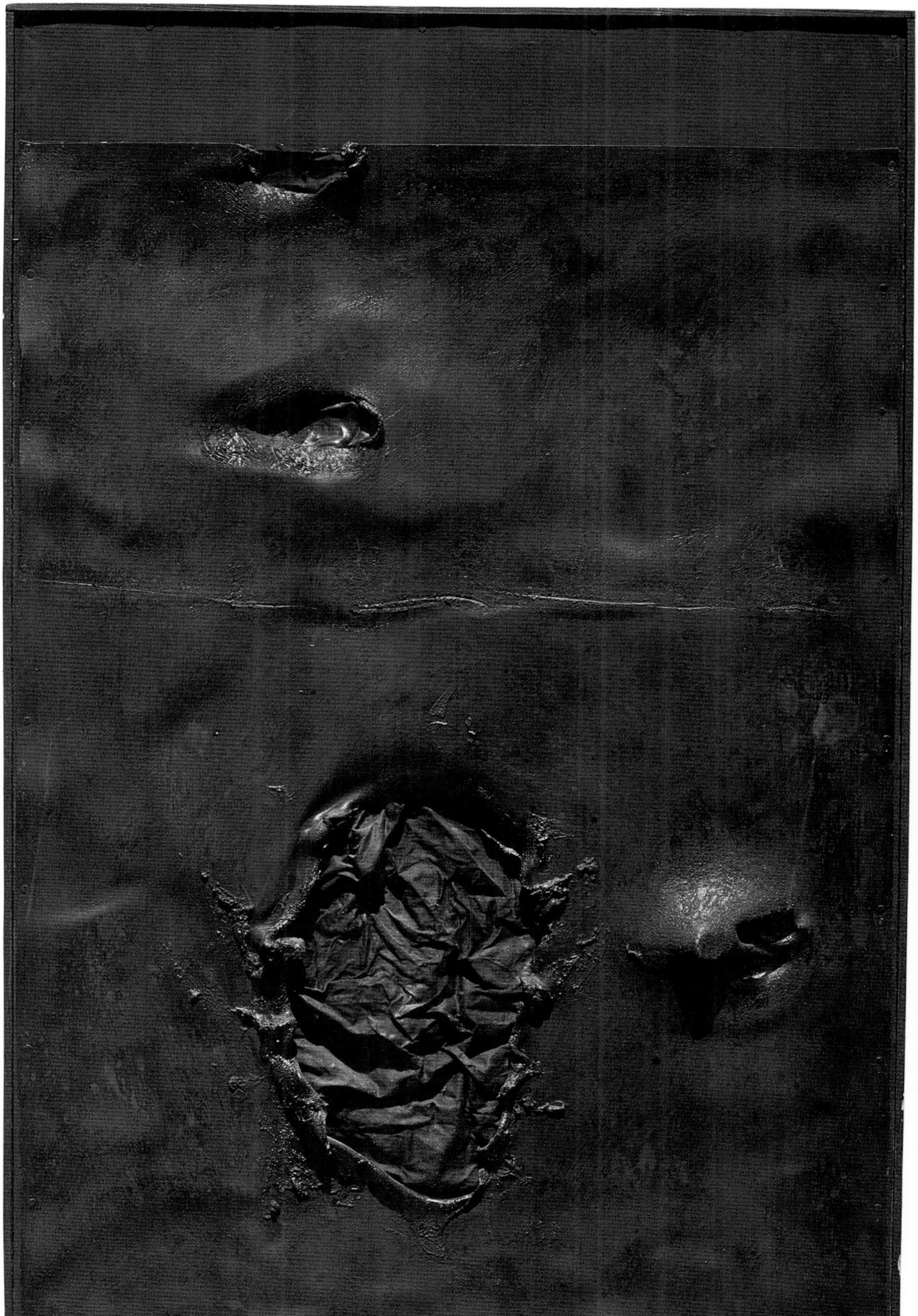

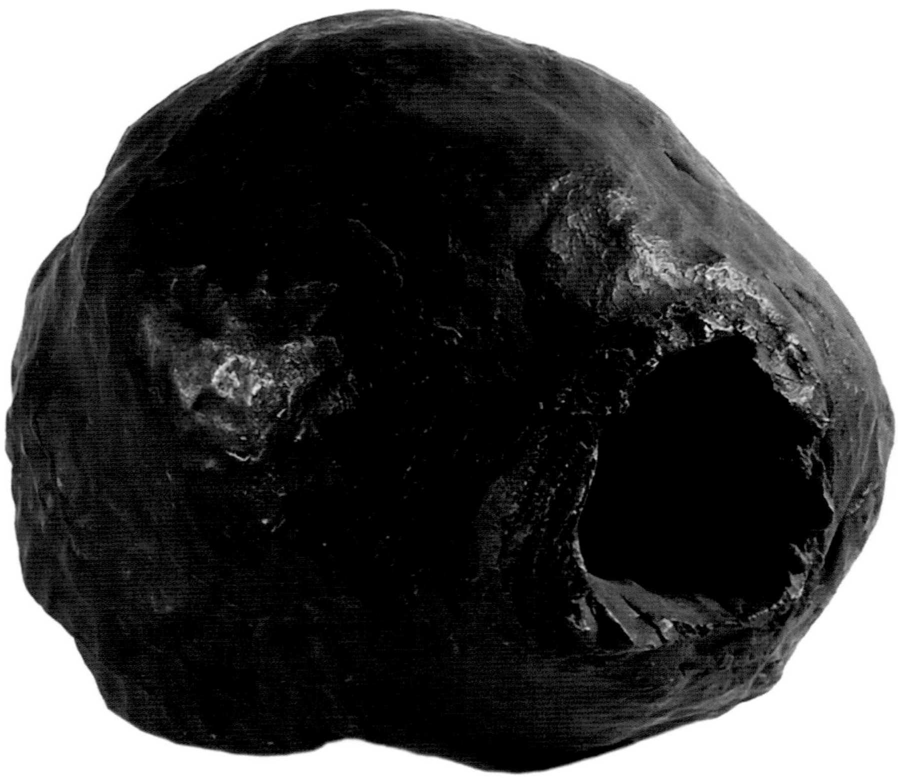

both images **Concetto spaziale, Natura**
(Spatial Concept, Nature), 1959–60

LUCIO FONTANA 1899–1968

Although Lucio Fontana is almost exclusively known for the *Buchi (Holes)* and *Tagli (Cuts)* that he began producing in 1949 and 1958, respectively, those canvases are poorly understood if they are viewed apart from Fontana's whole oeuvre. Specifically, they should be seen in relation to the much larger, more diverse sculptural production, a fact that Fontana himself signaled by giving his canvases the same generic title that he used for several late-period sculptural series: *Concetto spaziale (Spatial Concept)*.

Part painting, part sculpture, the *Buchi* and *Tagli* might even be said to have emerged out of Fontana's 1947 *Concetto spaziale: Scultura nera* (*Black Sculpture*). Cobbled together from bits of lumpish matter that contradict the elevated verticality of its form, the *Black Sculpture* heralds the appearance within Fontana's oeuvre of both a distinctively *base* materialism and a preoccupation with the *informe* (or formless).[1] Previously (and even for a while after the *Black Sculpture* was made) Fontana's output consisted chiefly of small, figurative, polychrome ceramic pieces – pairs of pink and black horses or pearly butterflies – that appear to be the complete antithesis of his later avant-garde production. These kitschy works are all the more difficult to reconcile with the existing image of Fontana in that they cannot be dismissed as ironic appropriations of the lowbrow, à la Pop art. As Yve-Alain Bois has argued, Fontana "did not have to appropriate kitsch (nor could he have done so), for he was mired in it ever since the very beginning of his career: with him, the tight wall separating commercial kitsch from avant-garde art had become utterly porous."[2]

Fontana's infatuation with kitsch is especially important to bear in mind when confronted by his shocking pink *Concetto spaziale* of 1962. Not only does that work's color recall the confectionary glaze of Fontana's earlier ceramic *Horses*, but it also conjures strong associations with bubblegum, so that it seems tacky in every sense of the word. In the context of *Part Object Part Sculpture*, the pink *Concetto* resonates as well with Duchamp's *Wedge of Chastity*, principally via the rosy dental plastic used for that piece's lower, enfolding form.[3] Like the *Wedge*, the holes of Fontana's canvas are clearly anatomically suggestive, their genital or (more precisely) vaginal associations also coupled with an undercurrent of violence.[4] Indeed critics have found the intimated sexual aggression of Fontana's *Buchi* difficult to overlook, even as they draw attention to the occasionally cruciform shape or pattern of their holes.[5] Such works are the very epitome of the *informe*, in that they simultaneously embody any number of seemingly absolute oppositions: the avant-garde *and* the kitsch, the sensual *and* the violent, the sacred *and* the profane.

Fontana's *Concetti* might also be seen as analogous to the Freudian unconscious, to the extent that, like it, they defy the law of noncontradiction basic to reason. Significantly, Freud claimed to have fully grasped the contradictory nature of unconscious thought only after learning that the Latin word *sacer* (from which the English "sacred" derives) originally conveyed entirely antithetical meanings; it connoted both the holy and the damned.[6] Freud believed that contradictory processes also govern dream "logic," so it is perhaps no accident that many of Fontana's *Buchi*, including the 1956 blue *Concetto spaziale* exhibited in *Part Object Part Sculpture*, evoke the Surrealist "dream paintings" of Joan Miró.[7] One thinks especially of the nearly monochromatic *Painting* of 1925 (Paris, Collection Maeght) or *The Catalan*, from that same year (Paris, Centre Pompidou), whose surface is pitted by six small holes. Although most critics have discussed Miró's dream paintings in terms of innocent, childlike reveries, a few have recognized their inherently "base materialism." Writing in 1929, Michel Leiris described the paintings as "so many malicious pebbles that cause circular and vicious ripples, the more one throws them into the marsh of our understanding."[8] The "stones" in Fontana's 1956 *Concetto* resemble Miró's "malicious pebbles" – not simply because they are *pietre* (stones), but because they generate an ever-widening circle of associations, "vicious" in its apparent self-contradiction.[9] Appearing as if they were the product of some ejaculatory spray, the stones, in effect, underscore the fact that childish "innocence" is often accompanied by a powerful anal-sadistic impulse.[10]

Fontana's pair of terracotta *Nature (Natures)* likewise spawn a host of references, many of them antithetical. As with the *Buchi*, the fleshy holes of the *Natures* simultaneously suggest a wound – and so violence – and the intimacy of the erogenous zones, even as the location and gender of those zones remain open. Like the singular spheres within the same series, these two *Natures* are coded feminine, suggesting both breasts and a woman's genitals. (It comes as little surprise to learn that the Italian *natura* is slang for "vagina.") But their testicular shape – and the fact that Fontana often referred to them as *palle* (balls) – equally casts them as male, a possibility also raised by the protuberance of the one ball in the pair. Their generally anthropomorphic suggestiveness is further supplemented by botanical ("seed pods") and geological associations. And they are no less ripe with art-historical allusion. Gesturing toward Miró's *The Kiss* (1924), in which single-celled lovers part mitotically, and Duchamp's ambivalent *Objet-Dard* (as well as his other erotic objects), Fontana's *Natures* suggest the composite figures of dreams, produced through the unconscious process Freud termed "condensation." That process allows two, three, or even a dozen disparate things to occupy a single location. Such, according to Freud, is the space of the unconscious. And such, we might add, is the complex space created and occupied by Fontana's work – or at least that portion of it bearing the title *Concetto spaziale*.

LISA FLORMAN

Although Lucio Fontana is almost exclusively known for the *Buchi* (Holes) and *Tagli* (Cuts) that he began producing in 1949 and 1958, respectively, those canvases are poorly understood if they are viewed apart from Fontana's whole oeuvre. Specifically, they should be seen in relation to the much larger, more diverse sculptural production, a fact that Fontana himself signaled by giving his canvases the same generic title that he used for several late-period sculptural series: *Concetto spaziale* (Spatial Concept).

Part painting, part sculpture, the *Buchi* and *Tagli* might even be said to have emerged out of Fontana's 1947 *Concetto spaziale: Scultura nera* (Black Sculpture). Cobbled together from bits of lumpish matter that contradict the elevated verticality of its form, the *Black Sculpture* heralds the appearance within Fontana's oeuvre of both a distinctively base materialism and a preoccupation with the *informe* (or formless).[1] Previously (and even for a while after the *Black Sculpture* was made) Fontana's output consisted chiefly of small, figurative, polychrome ceramic pieces – pairs of pink and black horses or pearly butterflies – that appear to be the complete antithesis of his later avant-garde production. These kitschy works are all the more difficult to reconcile with the existing image of Fontana in that they cannot be dismissed as ironic appropriations of the lowbrow, à la Pop art. As Yve-Alain Bois has argued, Fontana "did not have to appropriate kitsch (nor could he have done so), for he was mired in it ever since the very beginning of his career: with him, the tight wall separating commercial kitsch from avant-garde art had become utterly porous."[2]

Fontana's infatuation with kitsch is especially important to bear in mind when confronted by his shocking pink *Concetto spaziale* of 1962. Not only does that work's color recall the confectionary glaze of Fontana's earlier ceramic *Horses*, but it also conjures strong associations with bubble-gum, so that it seems tacky in every sense of the word. In the context of *Part Object Part Sculpture*, the pink *Concetto* resonates as well with Duchamp's *Wedge of Chastity*, principally via the rosy dental plastic used for that piece's lower, enfolding form.[3] Like the *Wedge*, the holes of Fontana's canvas are clearly anatomically suggestive, their genital or (more precisely) vaginal associations also coupled with an undercurrent of violence.[4] Indeed critics have found the intimated sexual aggression of Fontana's *Buchi* difficult to overlook, even as they draw attention to the occasionally cruciform shape or pattern of their holes.[5] Such works are the very epitome of the *informe*, in that they simultaneously embody any number of seemingly absolute oppositions: the avant-garde and the kitsch, the sensual and the violent, the sacred and the profane.

Fontana's *Concetti* might also be seen as analogous to the Freudian unconscious, to the extent that, like it, they defy the law of noncontradiction basic to reason. Significantly, Freud claimed to have fully grasped the contradictory nature of unconscious thought only after learning that the Latin word *sacer* (from which the English "sacred" derives) originally conveyed entirely antithetical meanings: it connoted both the holy and the damned.[6] Freud believed that contradictory processes also govern dream "logic," so it is perhaps no accident that many of Fontana's *Buchi*, including the 1956 blue *Concetto spaziale* exhibited in *Part Object Part Sculpture*, evoke the Surrealist "dream paintings" of Joan Miró.[7] One thinks especially of the nearly monochromatic *Painting* of 1925 (Paris, Collection Maeght) or *The Catalan*, from that same year (Paris, Centre Pompidou), whose surface is pitted by six small holes. Although most critics have discussed Miró's dream paintings in terms of innocent, childlike reveries, a few have recognized their inherently "base materialism." Writing in 1929, Michel Leiris described the paintings as "so many malicious pebbles that cause circular and vicious ripples, the more one throws them into the marsh of our understanding."[8] The "stones" in Fontana's 1956 *Concetto* resemble Miró's "malicious pebbles" – not simply because they are *pietre* (stones), but because they generate an ever-widening circle of associations, "vicious" in its apparent self-contradiction.[9] Appearing as if they were the product of some ejaculatory spray, the stones, in effect, underscore the fact that childish "innocence" is often accompanied by a powerful anal-sadistic impulse.[10]

Fontana's pair of terracotta *Nature* (Natures) likewise spawn a host of references, many of them antithetical. As with the *Buchi*, the fleshy holes of the *Natures* simultaneously suggest a wound – and so violence – and the intimacy of the erogenous zones, even as the location and gender of those zones remain open. Like the singular spheres within the same series, these two *Natures* are coded feminine, suggesting both breasts and a woman's genitals. (It comes as little surprise to learn that the Italian *natura* is slang for "vagina.") But their testicular shape – and the fact that Fontana often referred to them as *palle* (balls) – equally casts them as male, a possibility also raised by the protuberance of the one ball in the pair. Their generally anthropomorphic suggestiveness is further supplemented by botanical ("seed pods") and geological associations. And they are no less ripe with art-historical allusion. Gesturing toward Miró's *The Kiss* (1924), in which single-celled lovers part mitotically, and Duchamp's ambivalent *Objet-Dard* (as well as his other erotic objects), Fontana's *Natures* suggest the composite figures of dreams, produced through the unconscious process Freud termed "condensation." That process allows two, three, or even a dozen disparate things to occupy a single location. Such, according to Freud, is the space of the unconscious. And such, we might add, is the complex space created and occupied by Fontana's work – or at least that portion of it bearing the title *Concetto spaziale*.

LISA FLORMAN

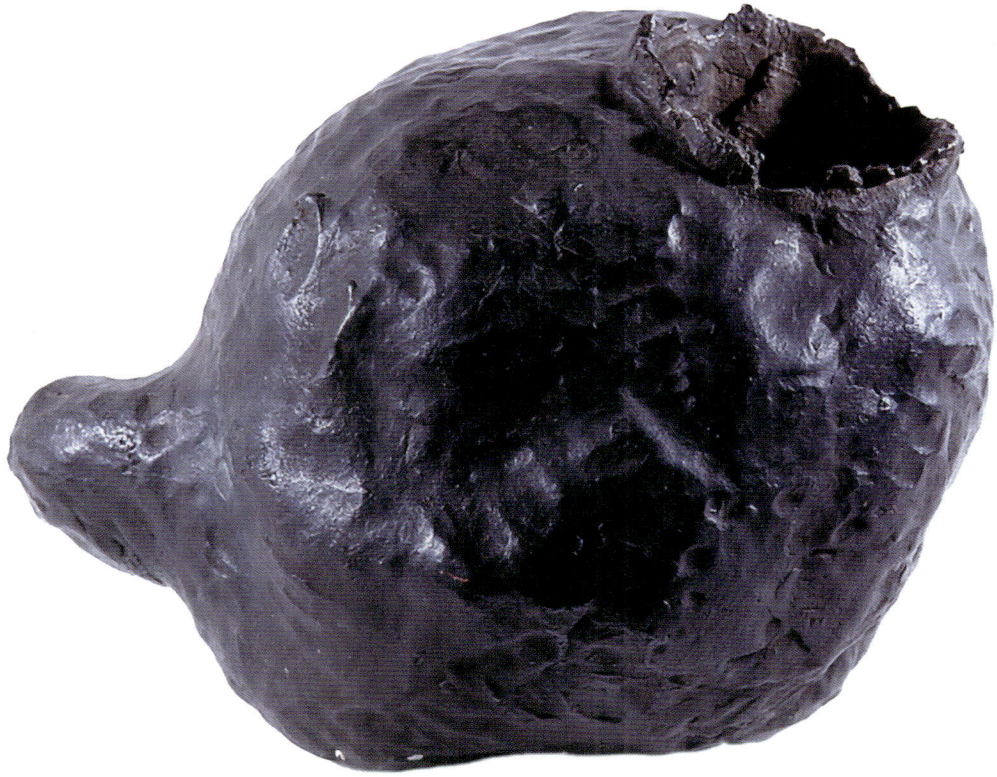

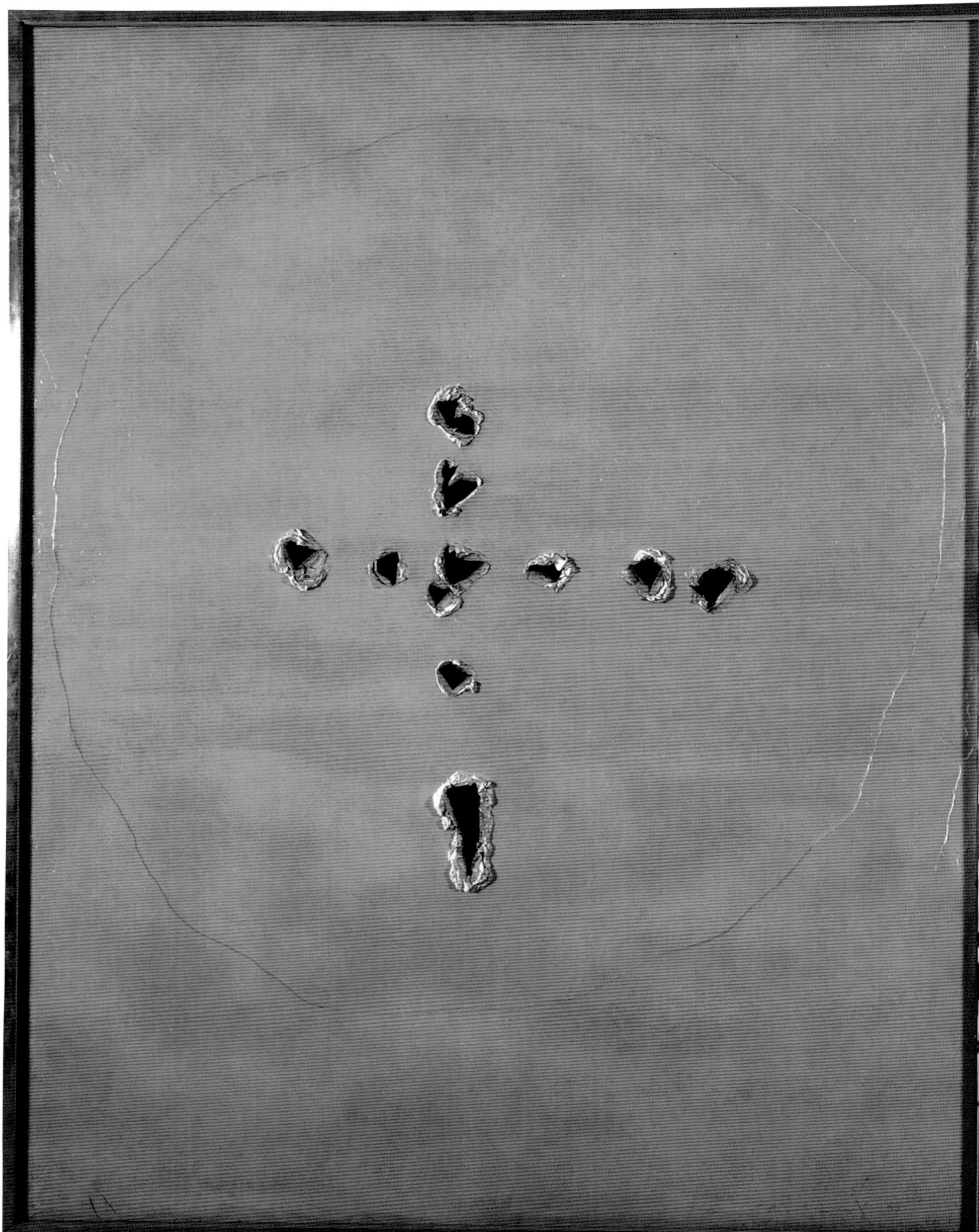

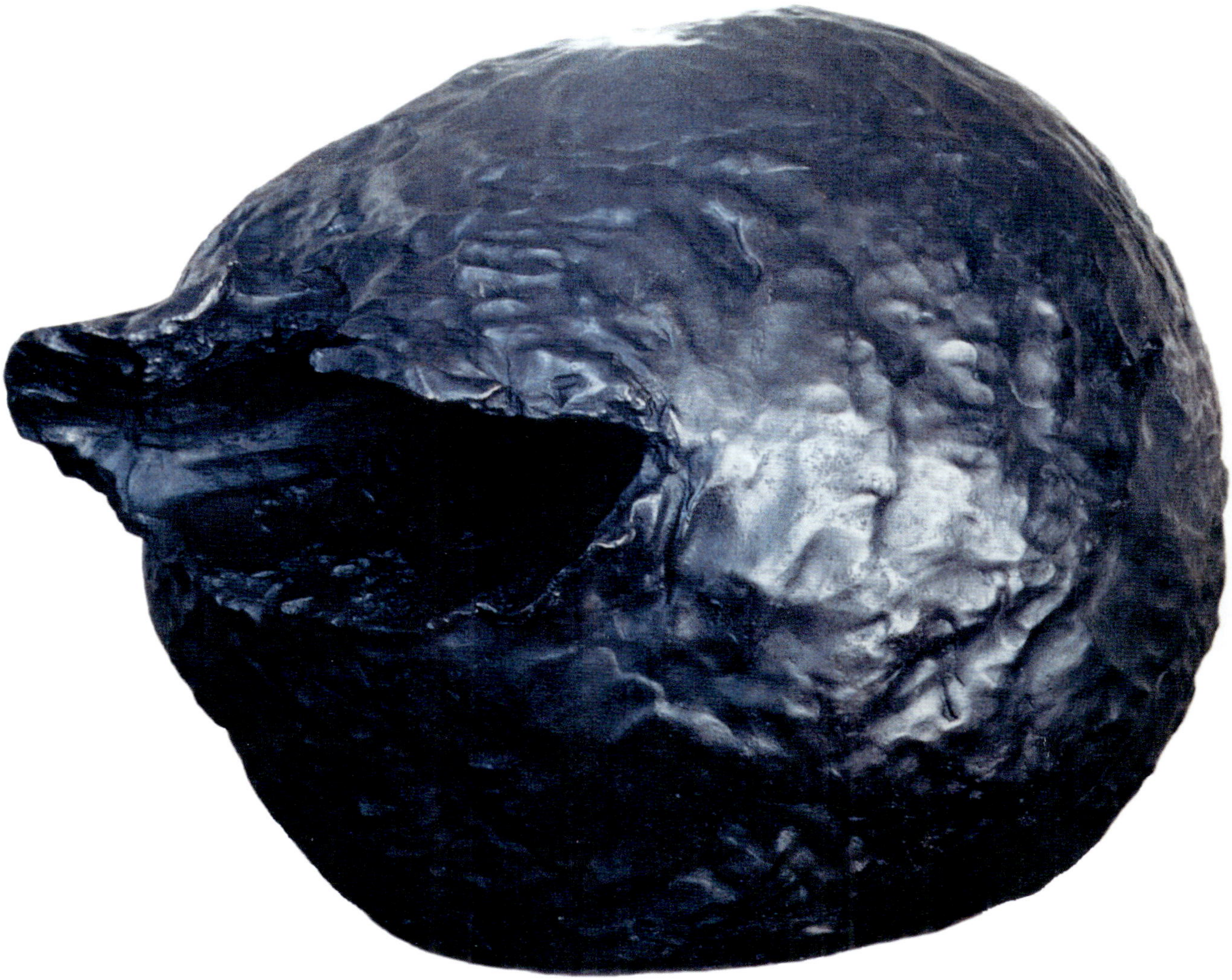

Concetto spaziale, Natura
(Spatial Concept, Nature), 1959–60

left **Concetto spaziale**
(Spatial Concept), 1962

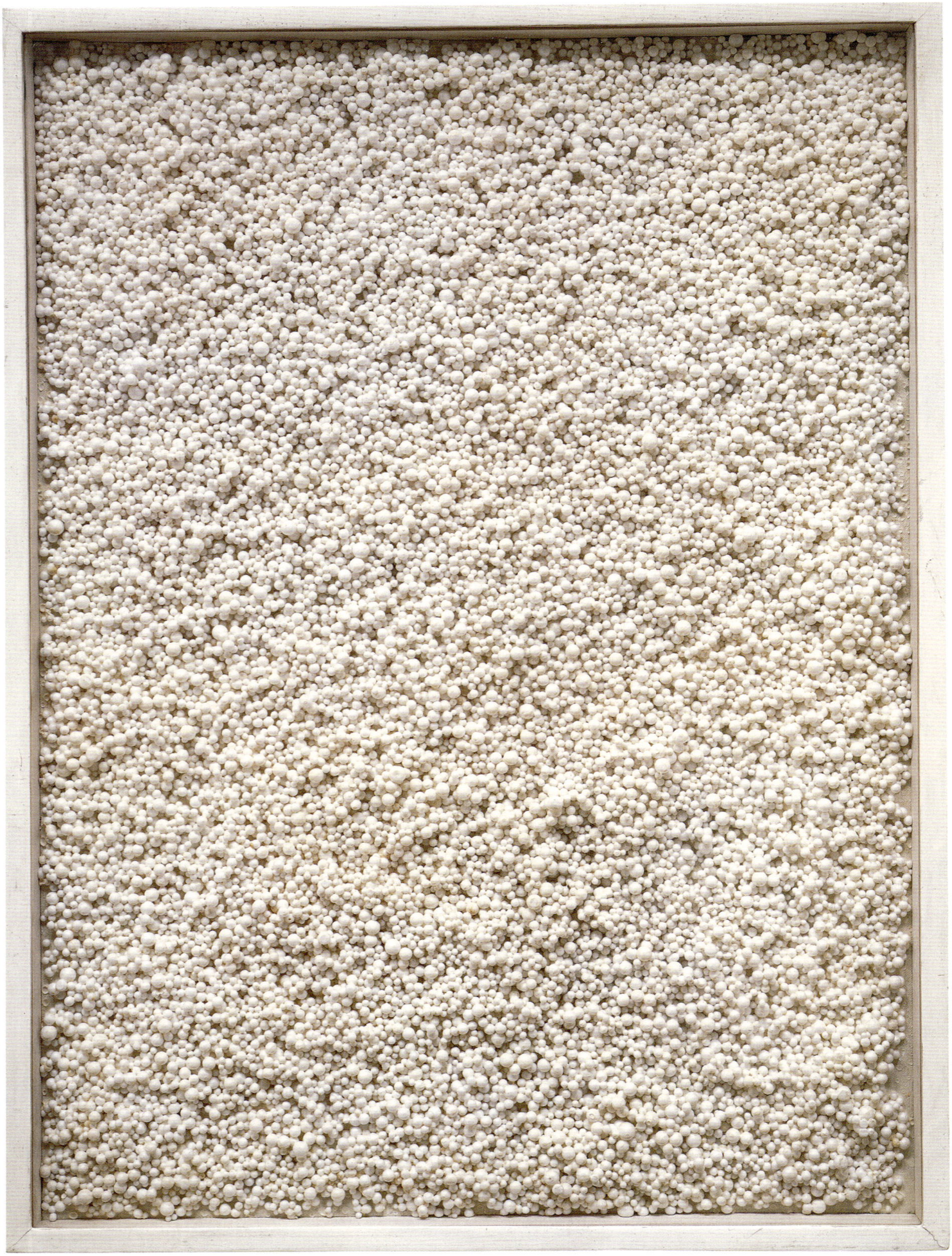

PIERO MANZONI 1933–1963

In a 1963 interview given shortly after Piero Manzoni's stunningly premature death, Lucio Fontana drew attention to the young artist's *Achromes*, focusing on the "obsessional white" of that series. His diagnosis seems remarkably apt; not only the unrelieved colorlessness of the works but also their incessant repetition calls up associations with the Freudian death drive (characterized by just such a compulsion to repeat), and specifically with the symptomatic rituals of obsessional neurosis.

The first of Manzoni's *Achromes*, done in 1957, consisted simply of gesso troweled onto canvas. By the following year the gesso had largely been replaced by kaolin (a superfine clay used for porcelain) and the canvases themselves were now wrinkled or creased. Later the *Achromes* would come to be defined by a subtly gridded surface, produced through the overlapping or stitching together of fabric squares. Then came the canvases filled with one form or another of readymade material: cotton, polystyrene, pebbles, bread rolls, fiberglass.... Driven by no evident logic, the permutations seemed, at least potentially, endless. Or rather, as Briony Fer has suggested, through them, "endlessness played its own sort of endgame: the exhaustion of something going on interminably, the tedium of the repetition."[1]

The immediate trigger for the *Achromes* seems to have been "Propositions monochromes," an exhibition of Yves Klein's work held at the Galleria Apollinaire in Milan in January 1957. There Klein unveiled his recent "blue period" paintings, ultramarine monochromes that, the artist said, took their cue from Giotto's frescoes at Assisi, specifically the deep, uniform blues of his skies and heavens. Like them, Klein's blue monochromes were to be seen as wholly immaterial, even spiritual – not pigment on canvas, then, but cosmic forces miraculously rendered visible.[2]

Manzoni, in describing his own works as "Achromes," clearly hoped to underscore their fundamental difference from Klein's monochromatic paintings. In a 1960 essay, "Libere dimensione" (*Free Dimension*), he attempted to articulate the particular terms of that difference:

> It is not a question of "painting" blue on blue or white on white (either in the sense of composition or of self-expression). It's exactly the opposite: the question as far as I'm concerned is that of rendering a surface completely white (integrally colorless and neutral) far beyond any pictorial phenomenon or any intervention extraneous to the value of the surface. A white that is not a polar landscape, not a material in evolution or a beautiful material, not a sensation or a symbol or anything else: just a white surface and nothing more (a colorless surface that is just a colorless surface).[3]

Manzoni's statement was clearly intended to mark a distinction between the brute, untransmuted materiality of the *Achromes* and the purported transcendence of Klein's paintings (or, for that matter, Malevich's – one thinks especially of his *White on White* – or any number of other Modernist monochromes). The insistence on the closure of the surface of the *Achromes* to all forms of self-expression was evidently intended to set them apart as well from the work of the Abstract Expressionists, who were beginning to make their presence felt on the Italian scene.

Yet, despite that insistence on the impersonal, nonexpressive nature of his work, Manzoni repeatedly spoke of its "unconscious" underpinnings. Fontana's remark about the obsessive-compulsive quality of the *Achromes* likewise suggests a psychoanalytic (if not exactly self-expressive) frame of reference. Perhaps there is no real contradiction here – only a need for clarification. If we speak of the "obsessive" nature of the *Achromes*, it must be understood that the obsession belongs less to Manzoni's personal psyche than it does to the unconscious of modernist painting itself.[4]

According to psychoanalytic theory, obsessional neurosis marks a regression to an earlier (anal) stage of development. Arising from an acute need to control base impulses, its symptoms signal precisely the subject's failure to achieve that measure of control. Those symptoms in effect constitute a return of the repressed. In the case of modernist painting, we might say that the repeated denial of the materiality of the surface – a denial born presumably out of a deep-seated anxiety over the potential meaninglessness of a work reduced *simply* to surface – necessarily led to something like Manzoni's *Achromes*. Significantly, in many of the *Achromes*, the readymade materials are rectangular and repetitively arranged, thereby explicitly evoking those two hallmarks of modernism, the monochrome and the grid. This structural similarity or overlap appears to insinuate the *Achromes* within the very field of modernist painting, as if they had been there all along, resurfacing only in the present.[5] If it seems wrong to say that they represent the return of modernism's repressed materiality, it's only because the materiality of the *Achromes* presents itself as thoroughly nonrepresentational–"not a sensation or a symbol or anything else: just a white surface and nothing more (a colorless surface that is just a colorless surface)."

The untransmuted materialty of the *Achromes* has a counterpart of sorts in those "works" for which Manzoni is, rightly or wrongly, best known: the *Merda d'artista,* those cans of the artist's own shit, which were sold for (quite literally) their weight in gold. No doubt those critics are right who have seen the *Merda* as part of "an effective critique of institutional modernism, which was consecrated in an unholy alliance between artistic production and the demands of an increasingly active and dominant art market."[6] But those cans of shit also stand to remind us, should we have missed the more subtle indications of the *Achromes,* that Manzoni's work is to be understood as symptomatic of a regression to the anal stage, its obsessiveness born of modernism's need to repress or sublimate a materiality that always managed to exceed its control.

LISA FLORMAN

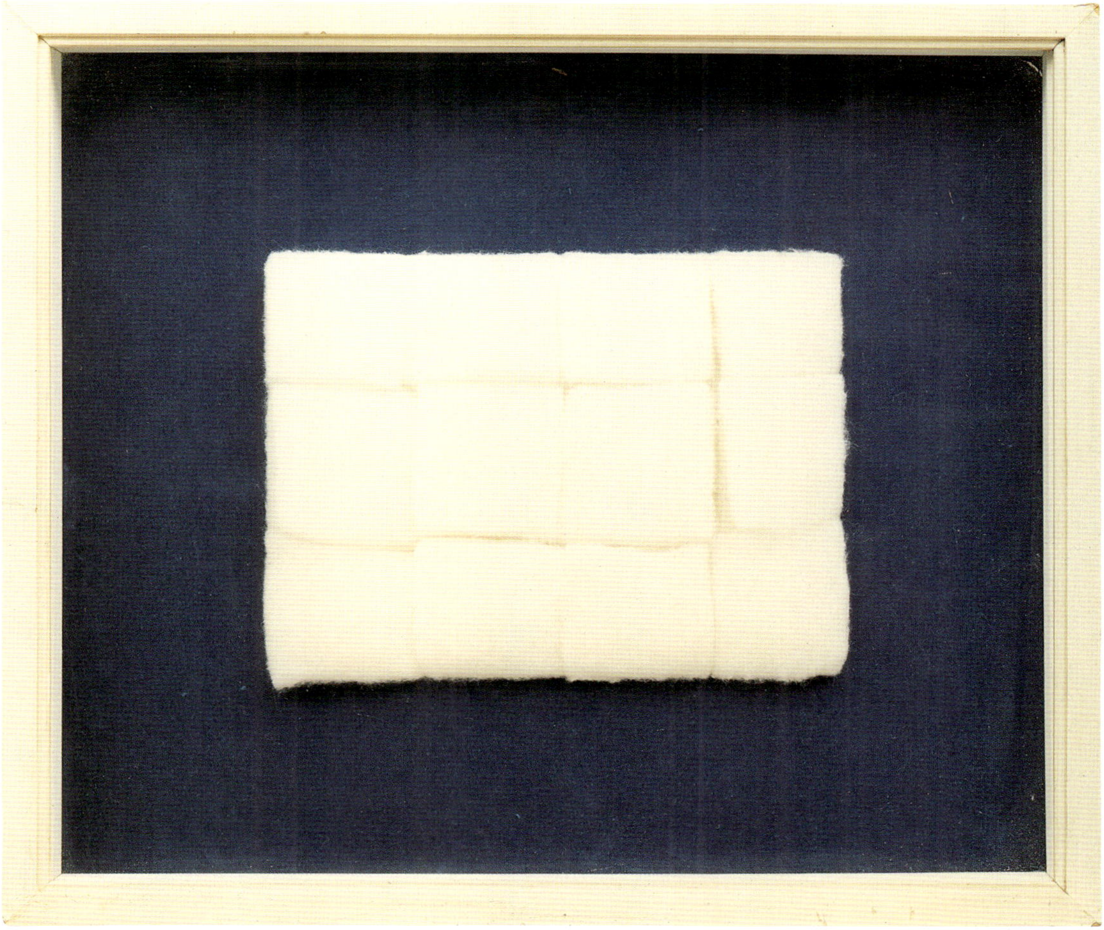

previous left **Achrome**, 1960–61

previous right **Achrome**, 1962

right **Achrome**, 1962

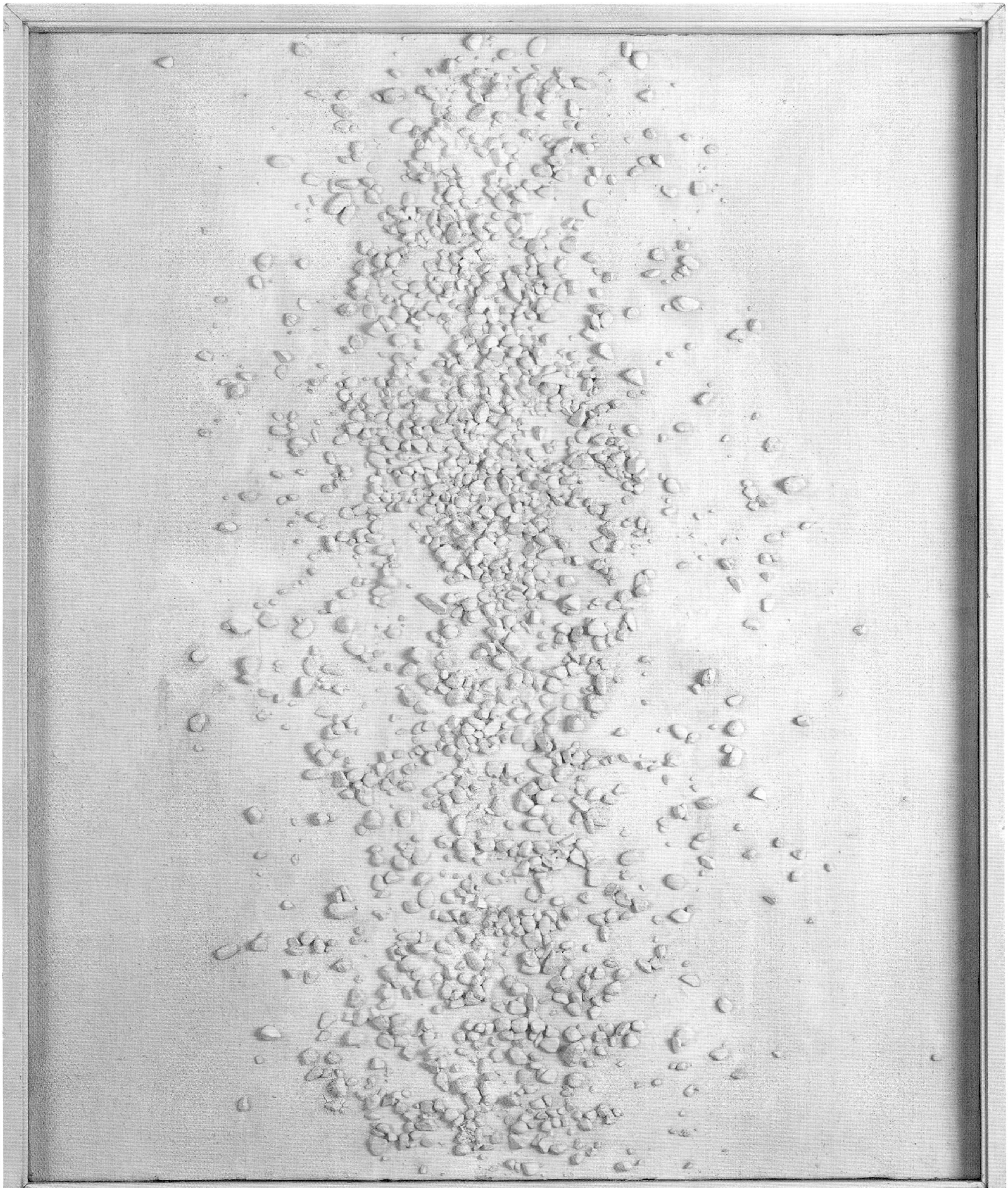

ROSALIND E. KRAUSS

OBJET (PETIT) a

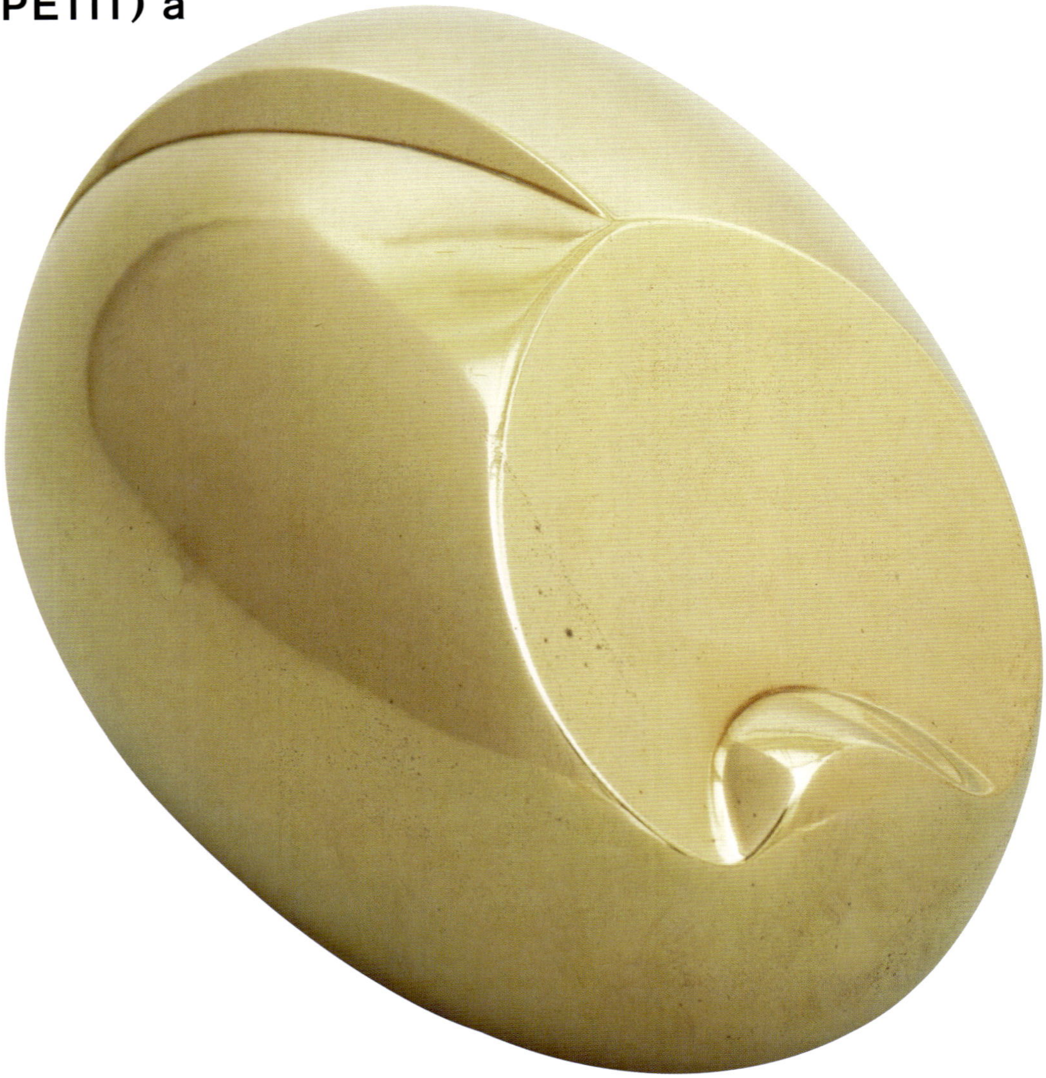

Without doubt, modern sculpture was born from classical archaeology. The unearthing of sculptural fragments of previously whole bodies, resulting in the caches of armless and legless torsos or detached body parts, such as elegant hands or feet, produced the experience of aesthetic pleasure in front of the muscular fragment's instruction in the lessons of metonymy: the entirety of the polygonal stone block as a proxy for the entirety of the whole body. Auguste Rodin's pitted bronze torsos or other partial figures are unimaginable without these earlier examples. Brancusi, in his apprenticeship in Rodin's studio, undoubtedly focused his own imagination on the beauty and aesthetic "completeness" of the fragmented body, leading to the daring conception of detached heads as nothing but gleaming ovoids (*The Newborn*, 1923; *Sculpture for the Blind*, 1916; *Sleeping Muse*, 1912) or the daringly suggestive body parts: *Torso* (1909) and *Princesse X* (1918). Brancusi's surprising relationship with Marcel Duchamp (they met at an exhibition of industrial products while looking at an airplane propeller, with Duchamp asking whether any sculptor could do better than that and Brancusi deciding – with his *Bird in Space,* 1924 – to match its sleek elegance) might provide the background for Duchamp's own experimentation with sculpture as partial object, as in the foam-rubber breast, *Prière de toucher* (1947), or the suggestive cast of the pudendum, *Feuille de Vigne Femelle*, not to speak of the torsolike *Mallic Moulds* of *The Large Glass*'s *Bachelor Machine.*

To speak of the partial object is to invoke the theories of Melanie Klein and Jacques Lacan, both of whom saw an infant's subjectivity as shaped by a strong identification with the parts of the body to which the infant is directly exposed – whether to the mother's breast during nursing or to her gaze as she admires her newborn. Klein took identification all the way to incorporation, as when the suckling baby fantasizes the consumption of the breast, which then enters its body, and, moving from "good object" to "bad" and threatening object, induces a depressive position in the frightened infant. Calling these part objects the *"objet (petit) a,"* Lacan constructed a period during infancy that he called the "mirror stage," reasoning that, when babies are held in their mothers' arms in front of a mirror, where they suddenly see their inchoate and uncontrollable bodies as vertical and well formed, they identify with this mirror reflection as offering a good gestalt, and it is this whole, organized form that shapes their ego in its own structured image. Calling this system of visual identification the "imaginary," Lacan followed Klein in formulating his own version of the part object in his *objet (petit) a.*

Insofar as the part object takes the form of an alphabetical letter in this formulation, and such a letter is a "signifier" in the structural linguistic theory of the sign, the part object supported Lacan's position that the subject is always a function of the signifier, which has preeminence over the subject. "The subjects take up their roles in relation to the letter [the signifier]," he wrote. "Should they pass beneath its shadow, they become its reflection." A banal example of this would be the letters M or W on the doors of lavatories, producing the channels through which any individual subject must pass.

Constantin Brancusi
The Newborn (version I, 1920, close to the marble of 1915)

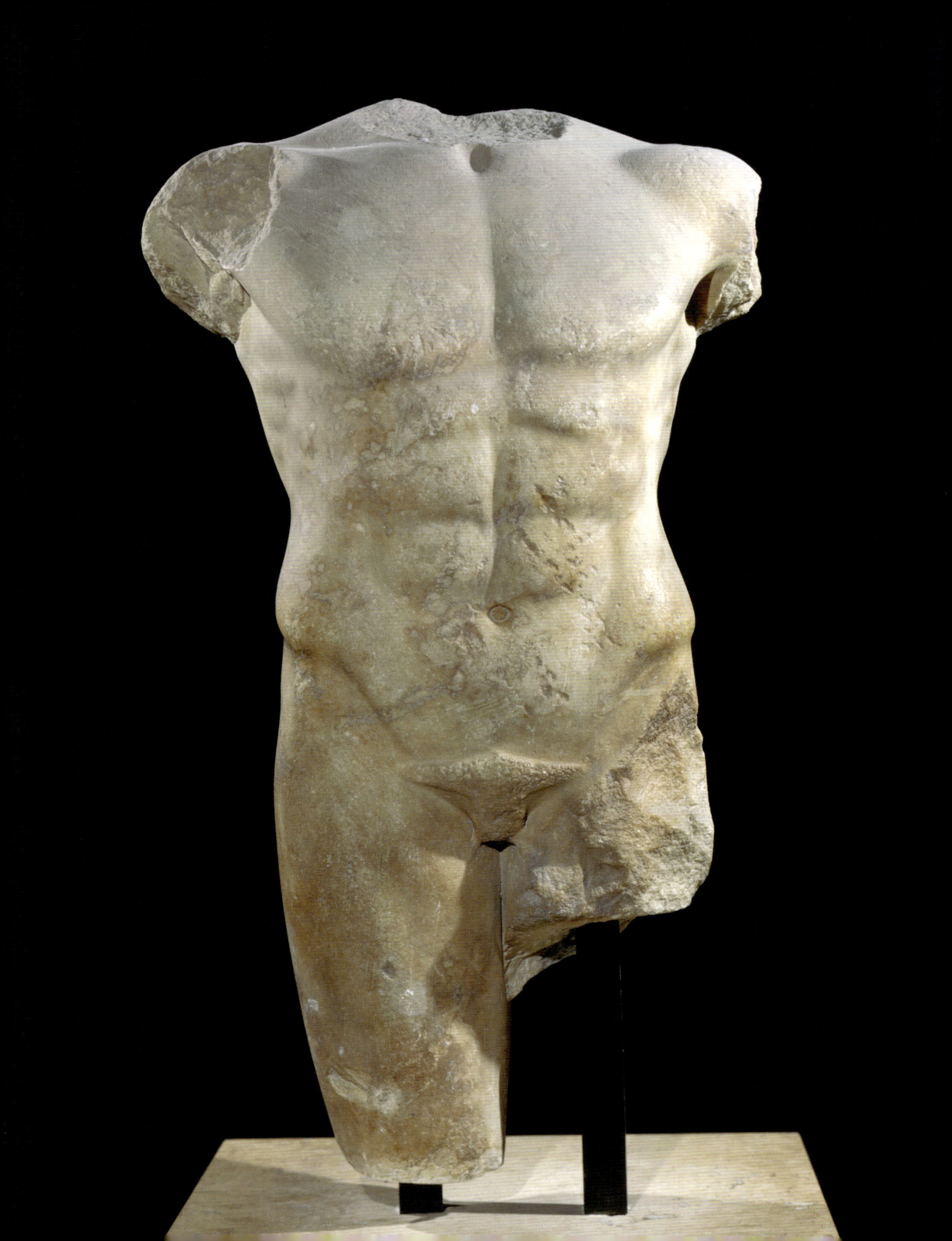

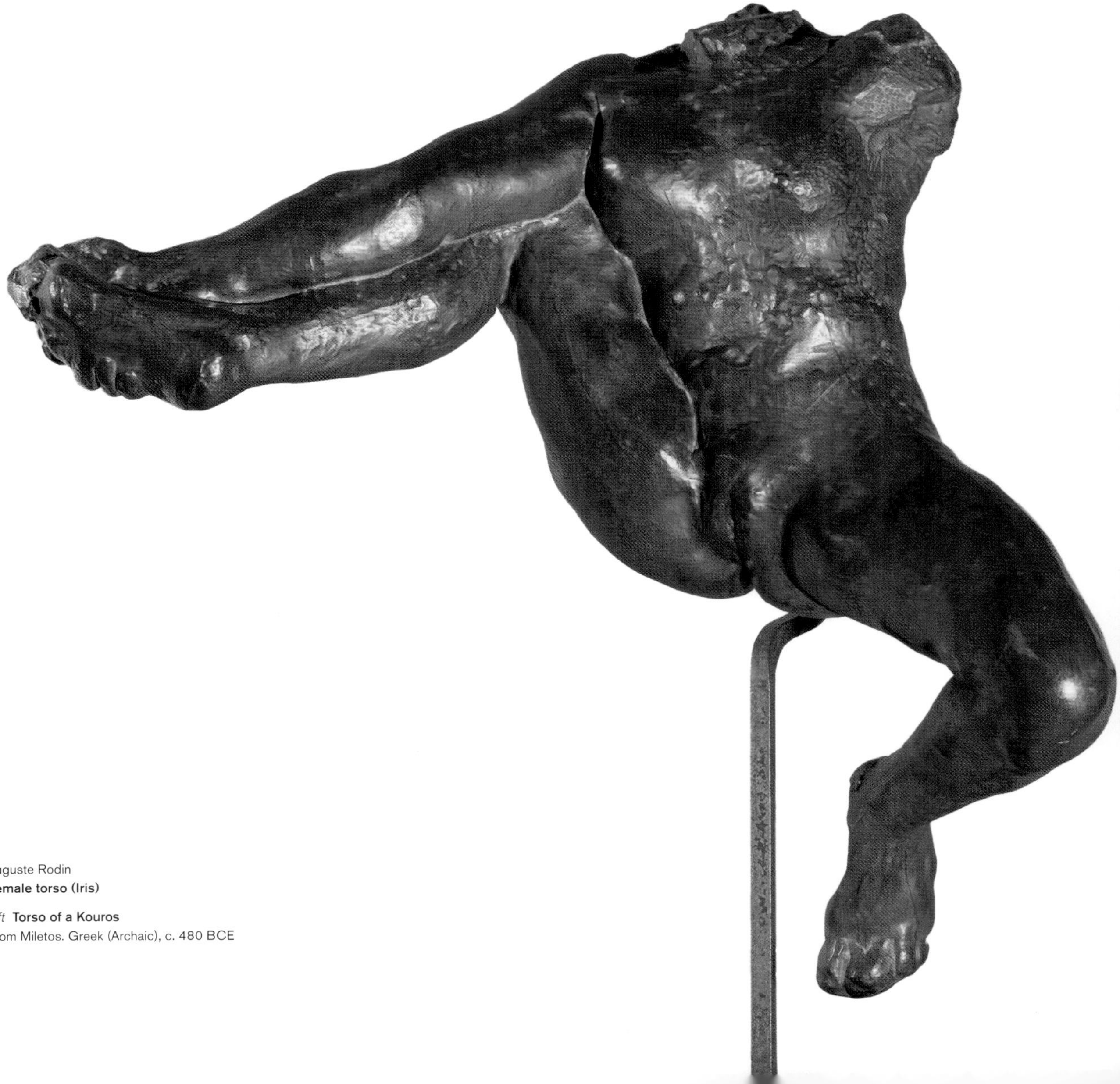

Auguste Rodin
Female torso (Iris)

left **Torso of a Kouros**
From Miletos. Greek (Archaic), c. 480 BCE

With his own cast objects, Duchamp achieved a position apart from his confreres, in this as in so many other instances. The cast body parts obviously functioning as the Lacanian *objet (petit) a* are an extension of the infant's image bank – on an axis that Lacan names the "imaginary." In shaping the infant's self-image, the *objet a* seems to point to the developing subject, in a relation that semiology terms "deictic." Duchamp projected his readymades as existing on the deictic axis as well, as when in the note he wrote on the matter he specified: "In projecting at a future moment (such a day, such a date, such a minute), 'to inscribe a readymade.' – the readymade can subsequently be sought (with all kinds of delays). The important thing is thus this clocktime, this snapshot, like a discourse pronounced on no matter what occasion but at such and such an hour. It is a kind of appointment." The deictic function of capturing the subject thus marries the corporeal part object to the sculptural fragment with all its associations to casting. Jasper Johns carries this possibility forward with the phallic implication of his *Flashlights*, and Lucio Fontana joins forces with this through the uterine connotations of his split pods.

Because of the deictic's capture of the subject in the mold of its image, it is a use of casting that seems to escape the fate of kitsch, despite the dire predictions of a writer like Walter Benjamin. Duchamp's eccentric posture never committed him to carrying forth any of his ideas consistently. With the readymades, as with so many other of his practices, he broke the strict condition of the readymade to fashion some of these objects (including *Fountain*) by hand. When he turned to making a kind of retrospective of his entire oeuvre with the reproductions of *Boîte-en-Valise*, he behaved no differently. Here was the perfect instance of Benjamin's mechanical reproductions, with their withered aura. But Duchamp took the black-and-white prints and laboriously added color to them individually. Never hesitant about labeling any part of his fastidious practice, he named this action "coloriage."

Still another reflection on the predominance of part object over the viewer's subjectivity is to be found in Benjamin's important essay "The Work of Art in the Age of Mechanical Reproduction." To feel its relevance, we need to return to the example of Brancusi and the variety of materials he used for the expression of his heads and torsos, moving from marble, to oak, to polished bronze. In one curious instance, he worked with the architect Jean Prouvé to cast *The Newborn* in stainless steel for a commission from the duc de Noailles. This little object, part sculpture/part ball bearing, enters the aesthetic domain as an industrial form: as serialized and multiply produced as a tin can or a screwdriver. Benjamin's theory of the effect of mechanical reproduction on the traditional art object turns on the issue of authenticity, since, he argues, only the authentic object (and not a secondary copy) can work the magical, healing effect of the original, cult object. This unique power Benjamin calls "aura," arguing that "what withers in the age of mechanical reproduction is the aura of the work of art." Returning to Lacan's and Klein's issues of identification in the formation of subjectivity, we hear Benjamin's caution: "To pry an object from its shell, to destroy its aura, is the mark of a perception whose 'sense of the universal equality of things' has increased to such a degree that it extracts it even from a unique object by means of reproduction."

Reproduction plays a role in yet another phase of modernism. At the Bauhaus in the 1920s, the introductory design course waged war on mechanical reproduction by forcing students to analyze the specific character of individual materials – glass, steel, paper – in different conditions of light, orientation, and physical stress. The course was meant to wean these future designers from the fake effects of die casting or industrial reproduction, which turns the artisan's work with the properties of a particular material – the ductility of silver, for example – into a lifeless imitation of the authenticity of specific design. The word used for these fake effects was "kitsch," the very enemy of art Clement Greenberg singled out in his essay "Avant-Garde and Kitsch" (1939). For his analysis, it was the corruption of taste wrought by kitsch's "simulacrum of genuine culture" that the avant-garde was pledged to fight by following the Bauhaus's exhortation to honor the properties specific to a particular material.

In his novel *The Unbearable Lightness of Being* (1984), Milan Kundera ratchets the attack on kitsch up a notch when he speaks of man's need to deny the most basic facts of his own existence, such as defecation, or, as Kundera writes, "shit." This dissimulation, which he names kitsch, is the witless embrace of cliché as a defense against the weight of human reality. Because of this defense, he says, "human existence loses its dimensions and becomes unbearably light." The types of kitsch multiply: Soviet kitsch, totalitarian kitsch, and communist kitsch. Common to them all, however, is abject inauthenticity. Brancusi's stainless-steel *Newborn*, gleaming in the fake silver shine of its metallic surface, is the perfect example of kitsch, abandoning the sculptor's meticulous explorations of the massive resistance of oak to the action of his chisel, or of the ponderous resistance of bronze to weightless verticality.

As the century unfolded, Pop art celebrated the disappearance of "aura" by fashioning sculptural objects as though they were assembly-line products: so many Brillo boxes, or Campbell's soup cans, or helium-filled balloons. In assuming the readymade in this manner, they also adopted the penchant of the readymade's father – Marcel Duchamp – for the cast body part: the fig leaf, the breast, the "chastity belt." The cast readymade welcomed, of course, the resulting confusion about which object in the series was the aesthetic original, as it courted the loss of material specificity. In this sense, Allan McCollum's multicolored plaster casts of Grecian urns or archaeological specimens radiate the feeling of that "simulacrum of genuine culture" that Greenberg had baptized "kitsch."

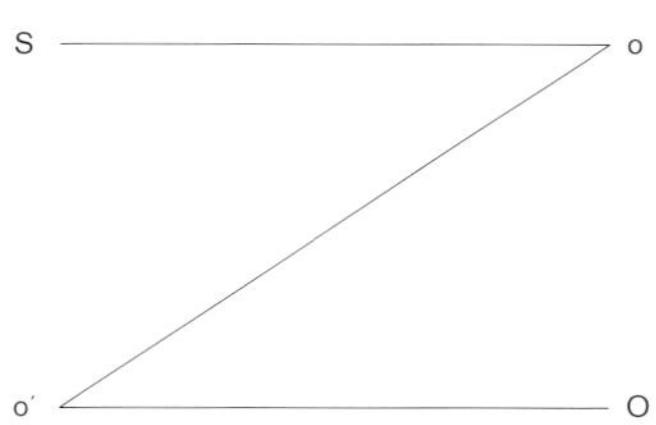

Jacques Lacan,
Schema L

Sculptors can exploit ready-made materials in many ways without descending into the mechanical language of casting. According to Robert Smithson, Eva Hesse was the specialist of Canal Street plumbing supply stores, where she found the rubber tubing and Styrofoam that she melted and wove into the steel mesh fashioned boxes and other polygonal supports. *Accession II* (1967–69), with its tufted interior, fashions a sexual part object without any of the kitsch associations of casting it. Such a piece, in addition to so much else of her work (like the arterial *Repetition Nineteen*), makes it clear that late modernist sculpture is unthinkable without the idea of the part object.

Eva Hesse
Accession II, 1967

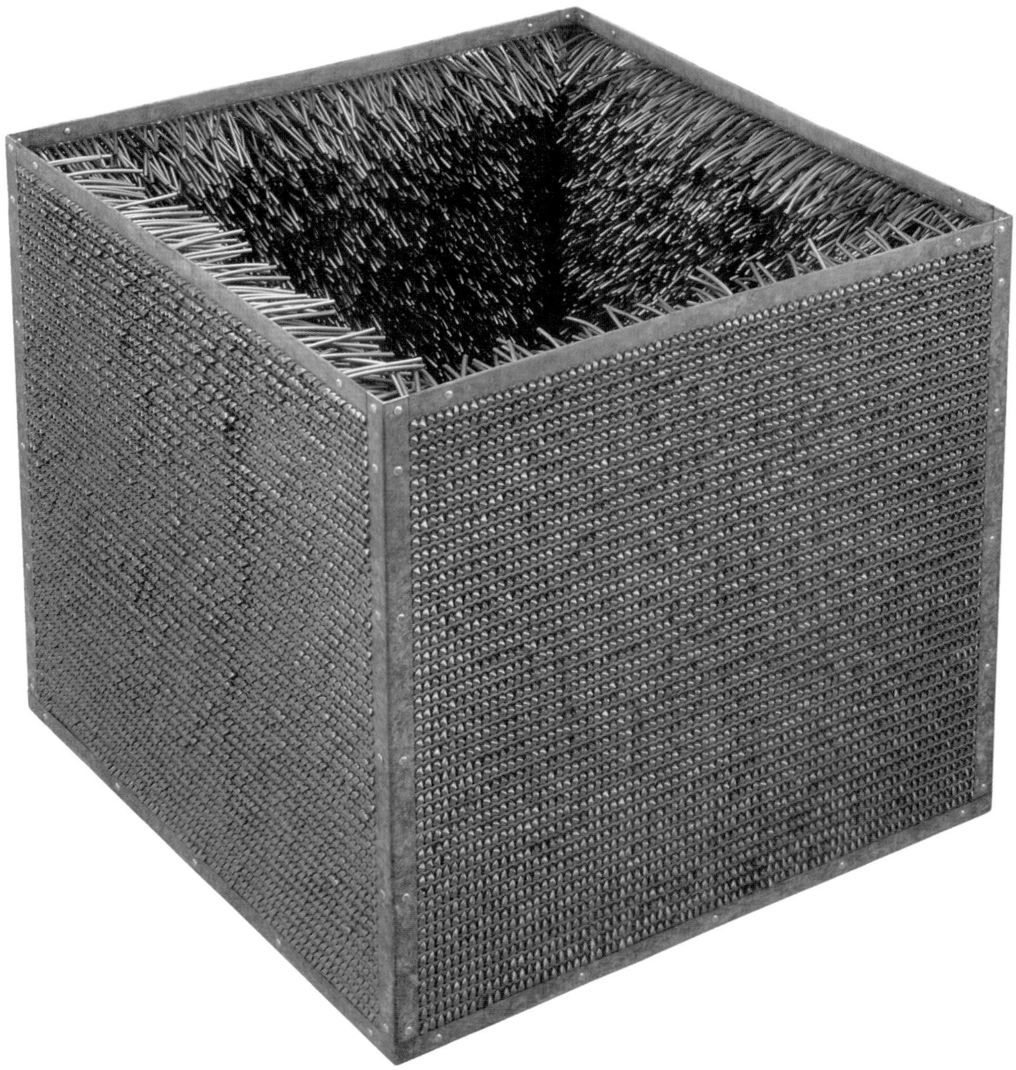

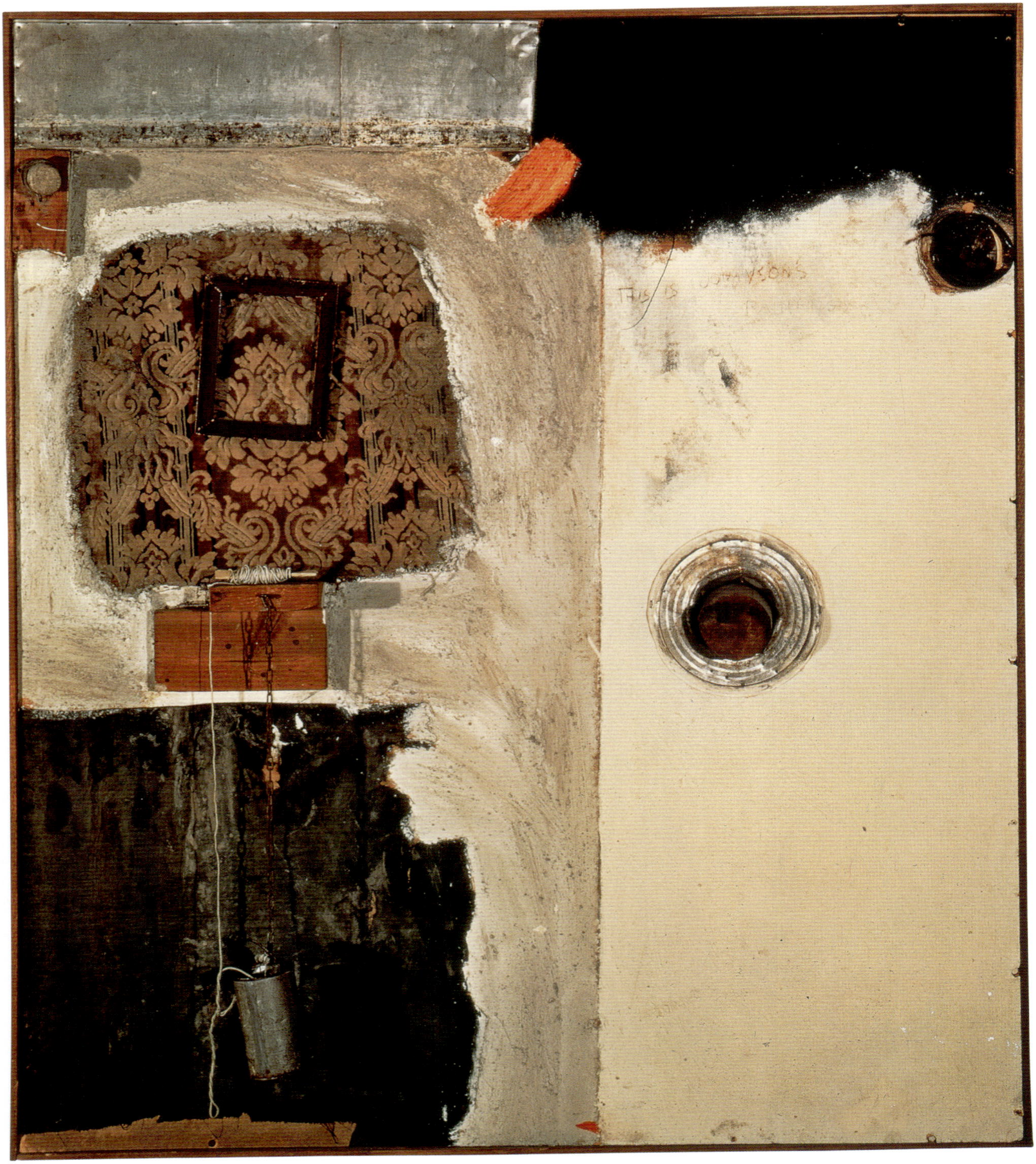

ROBERT RAUSCHENBERG 1925–

In many ways Robert Rauschenberg did more to elasticize the boundaries of sculpture than any other artist of the postwar period. His now canonical Combines of the mid- to late 1950s were a self-articulated mixture of painting and sculpture, producing a third term that remains emblematic of the slippages between media that define contemporary art in the twentieth century. The Combines, however, did not spring Athena-like from the head of Zeus. The work Rauschenberg made in the early 1950s already put into motion a complicated relationship to any preconceived notions about sculpture's relation to the monument.

In 1951 Rauschenberg attended both the Art Students League and the experimental art school Black Mountain College along with fellow artist and friend Cy Twombly. While at Black Mountain, Rauschenberg began to make paintings with a highly tactile surface covered in stones, dirt, and old newspapers. In 1952, Twombly and Rauschenberg set off for Europe together, where they settled in Rome. While in Italy, Rauschenberg continued his avid interest in the work of other contemporary artists and visited the studio of Alberto Burri, where he most likely saw Burri's large wall works that incorporated burlap sacks, as well as a wide range of detritus such as all sorts of flooring material, wood, and plastics.[1]

When Rauschenberg ran out of money, he went to Morocco to search for work, and during a nine-month sojourn there he made a group of hanging assemblages and small boxed fetishes. These works were subsequently exhibited in 1953 at the Galleria dell'Obelisco in Rome and at the Galleria d'Arte Contemporanea in Florence, where after receiving a review in which the critic suggested the works deserved to be thrown in the river, Rauschenberg complied and tossed the works into the Arno. Before discarding these pieces, however, Rauschenberg photographed them installed suspended from trees and draped over statuary.

Entitled *Scatole Personali* or *Feticci Personali* (Personal Boxes and Fetishes), these small, intensely handmade objects offer a very particular version of sculpture. Fabricated from string, wooden boxes, shells, dirt, bird feathers, and bits of mirror, they express an extremely modest economy of means, a desire to make art with the objects found in both the natural world and the space of daily life. These are constructions, as if made by ravens; they seem to be continuous with the world around them. These are not objects destined for pedestals and vitrines. Rather, their very placement seems to present a quandary of sorts for Rauschenberg, as the photographs attest. So too the titles intimate that these are objects with quasi-magical powers. In a typewritten statement about the works, Rauschenberg wrote: "The materials used for these constructions were chosen for either of two reasons: the richness of their past... or for their vivid abstract reality."[2]

Even though Rauschenberg threw the assemblages into the river Arno, many of the small box constructions are extant. While they easily bring to mind the wondrous dioramas of Joseph Cornell, they are much more rough-hewn, filled with dirt, stones, and dead bugs, disallowing the kind of preciousness that overcomes Cornell's work. Rauschenberg sometimes gave these boxes as gifts to friends, and now they reside in the collections of such friends as Twombly and Jasper Johns. Alberto Burri also recalls receiving a *Scatole Personali* from Rauschenberg, "a little box filled with sand and a dead fly."[3] This gift economy, borne of intimacy, respect, and generosity, suggests that these boxes existed in a particularly liminal state between sculpture and object, a threshold Rauschenberg would enact in a more public dimension with the Combines. Rauschenberg said of the objects: "You may develop your own ritual about the objects. The order and logic of the arrangements are the direct creation of the viewer assisted by the costumed provocativeness and the literal sensuality of the objects."[4]

When Rauschenberg returned to New York in 1953, he moved away from the small box constructions toward slightly larger and more open objects called the Elemental Sculptures. In these works, rocks predominated, and they were often attached in some way to another object, often with rope, or held on a wooden plank or within a wooden box with nails. Rauschenberg continued his interest in three-dimensional objects created through an additive process. It is as if, for Rauschenberg, one plus one never only equals two, as if the repeated act of accumulation leads to an accretion of both meaning and emotional intensity. This is perhaps best seen in *Soles* (1953), a narrow box that, when opened, reveals several cloth-wrapped objects, which range from a lump of dirt, to rocks, to a piece of broken glass and a fragment from a Roman fresco. At first, the repetition of the cloth-bound objects in the box seems to suggest sameness, yet upon opening them (following again the logic of the gift), the homogeneous cloth gives way to a heterogeneous array of objects. But the play of sameness and difference does not end there, for as Walter Hopps has noted: "With the objects unwrapped, revealed as a charm or a talisman, one finds that Rauschenberg's intent is to establish the coequal value of objects, ranging from the most primordial to the most civilized and most sophisticated."[5]

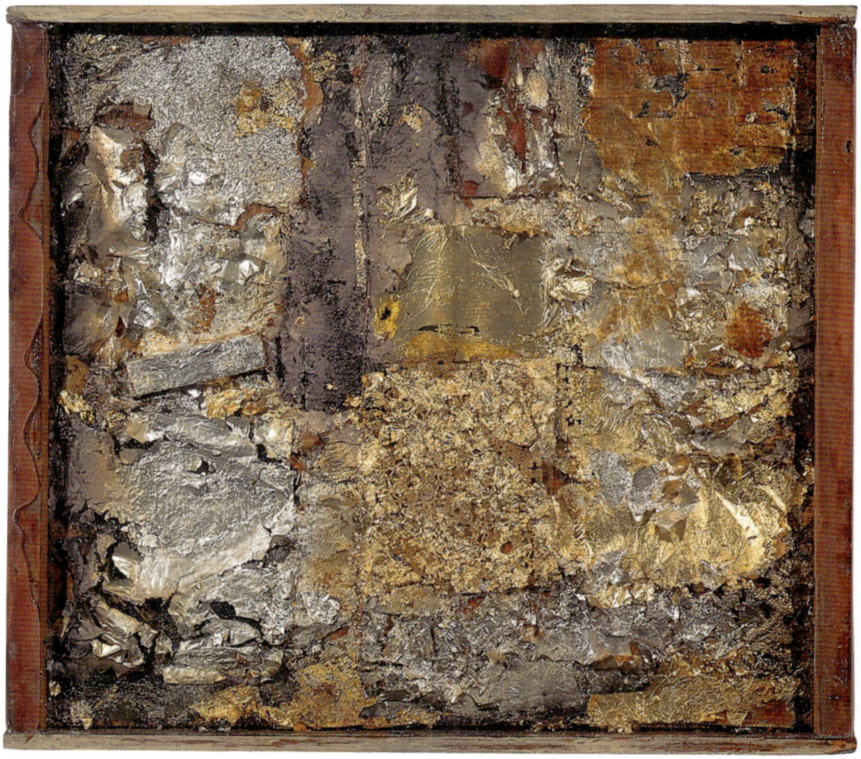

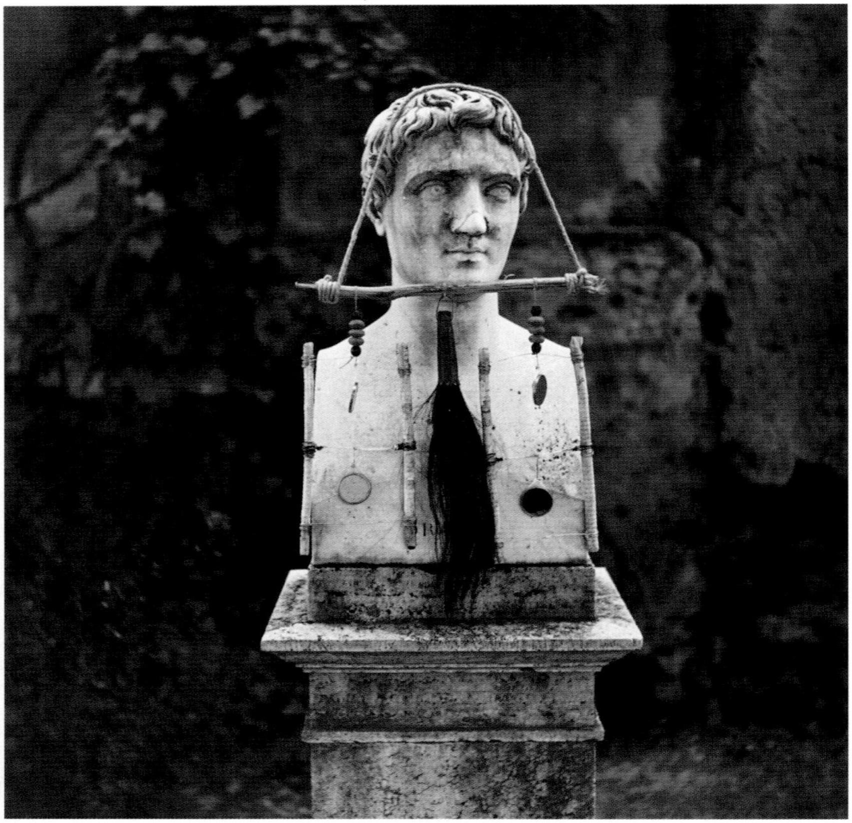

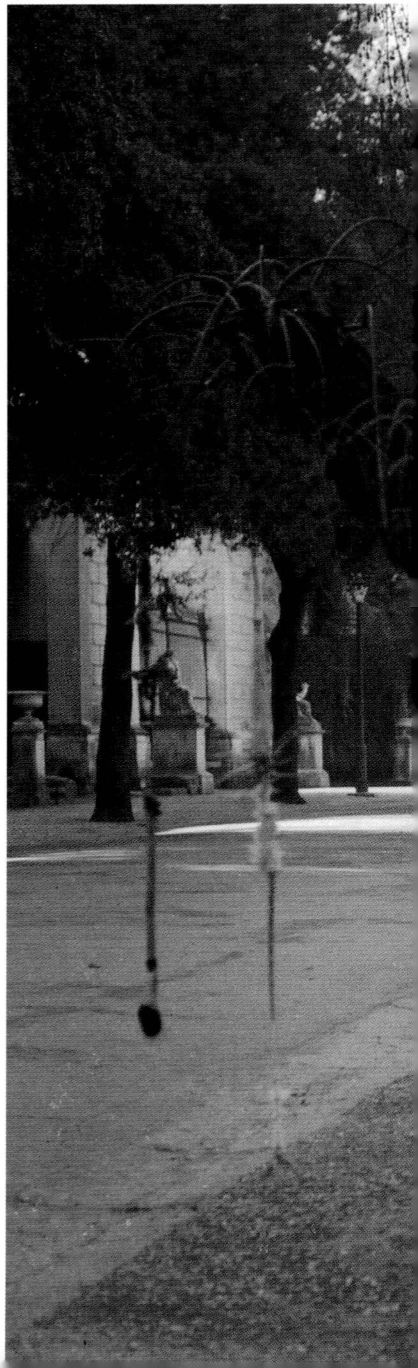

previous spread: left **Johanson's Painting**, 1962

previous spread: right **Untitled (Gold Painting)**, circa 1953

above **Untitled Hanging Assemblage**, 1952

right **Nine Untitled Hanging Assemblages**, 1952

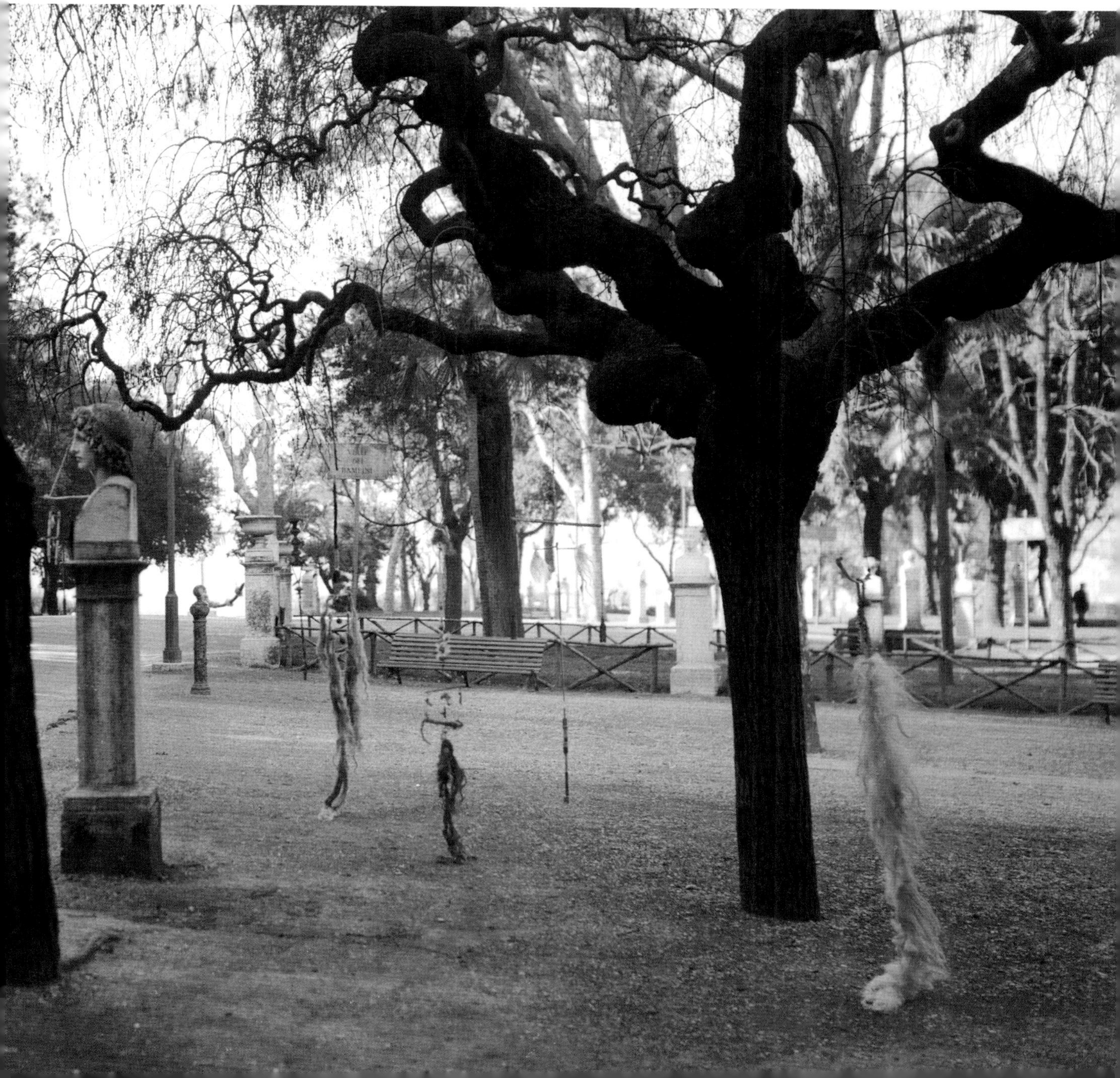

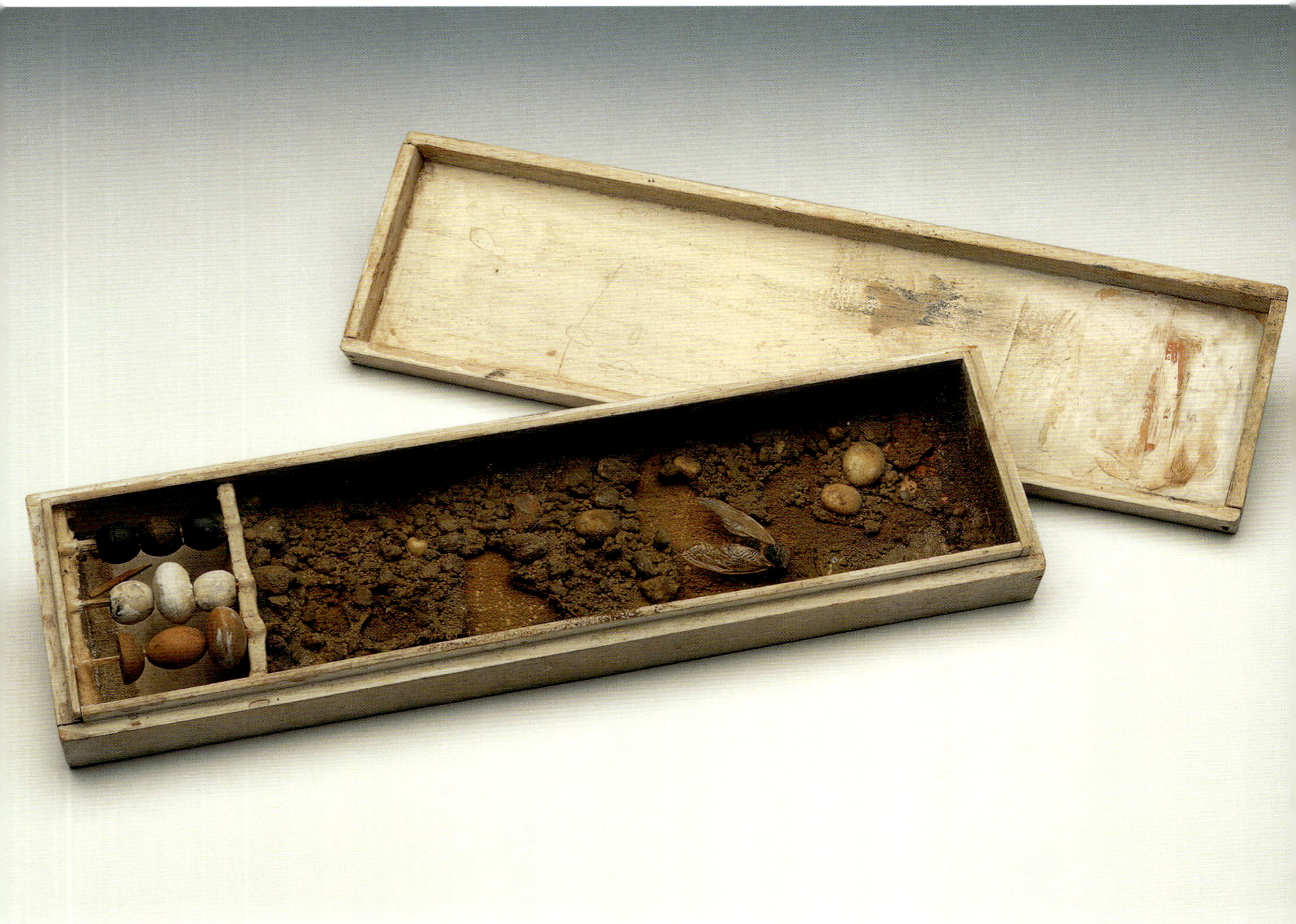

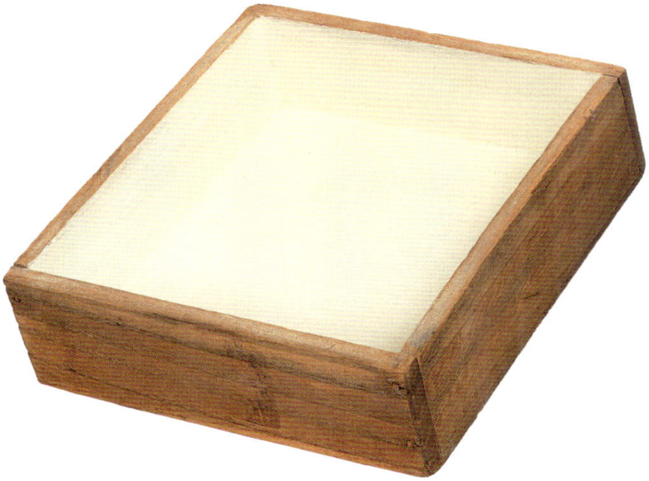

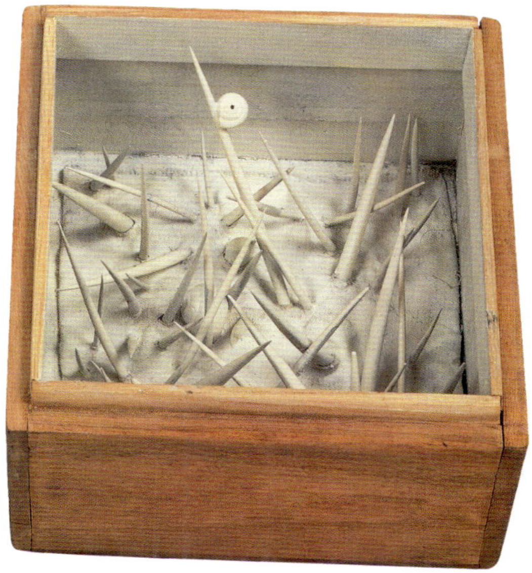

Untitled (Scatole Personali), 1952

left **Untitled (Scatole Personali)**, 1951

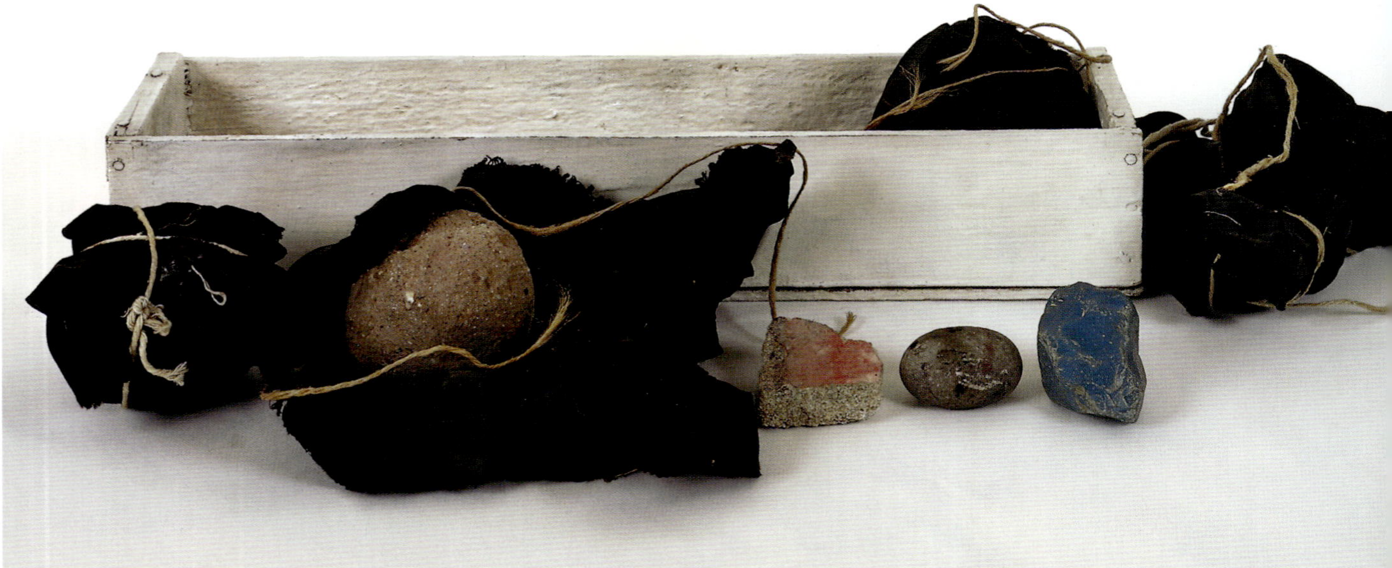

Soles, 1953

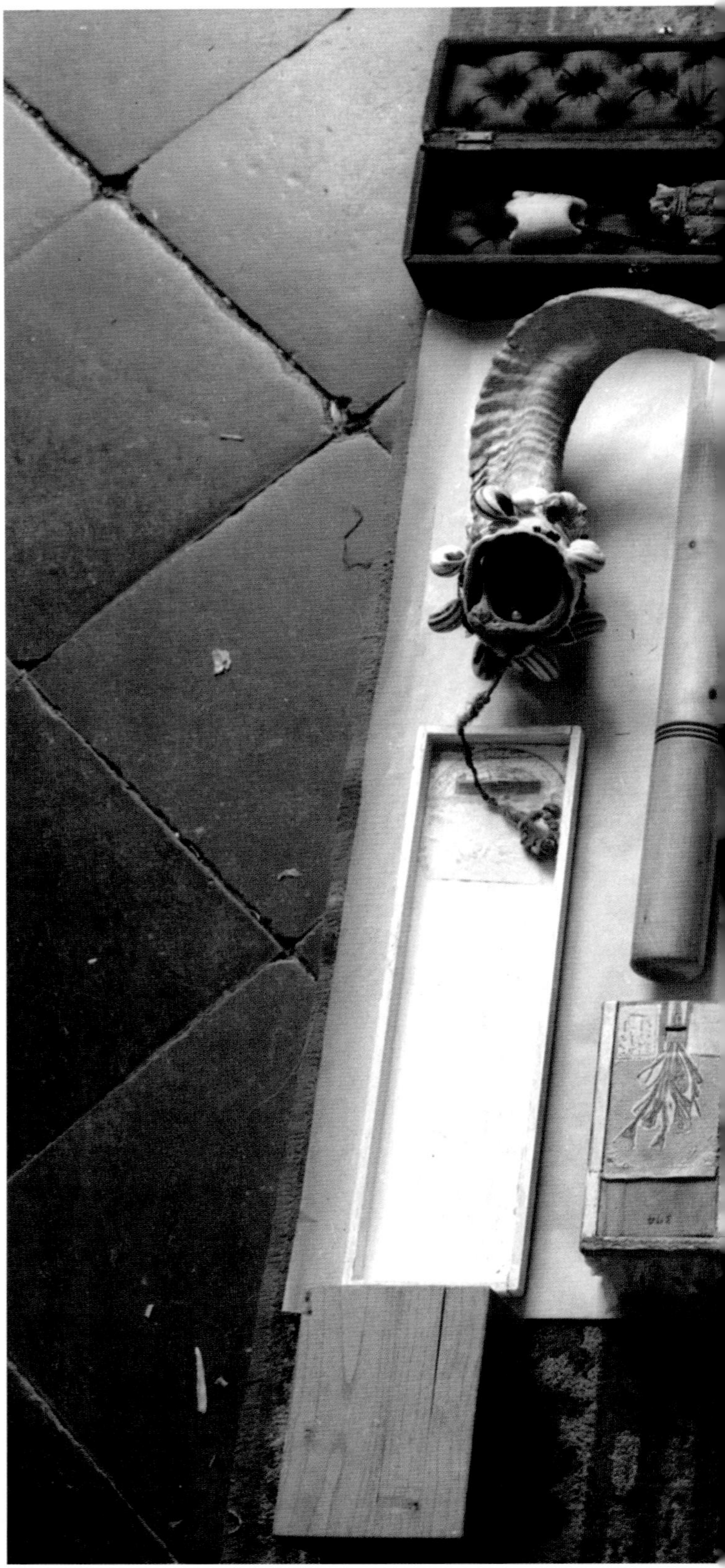

Thirty Scatole Personali, 1952

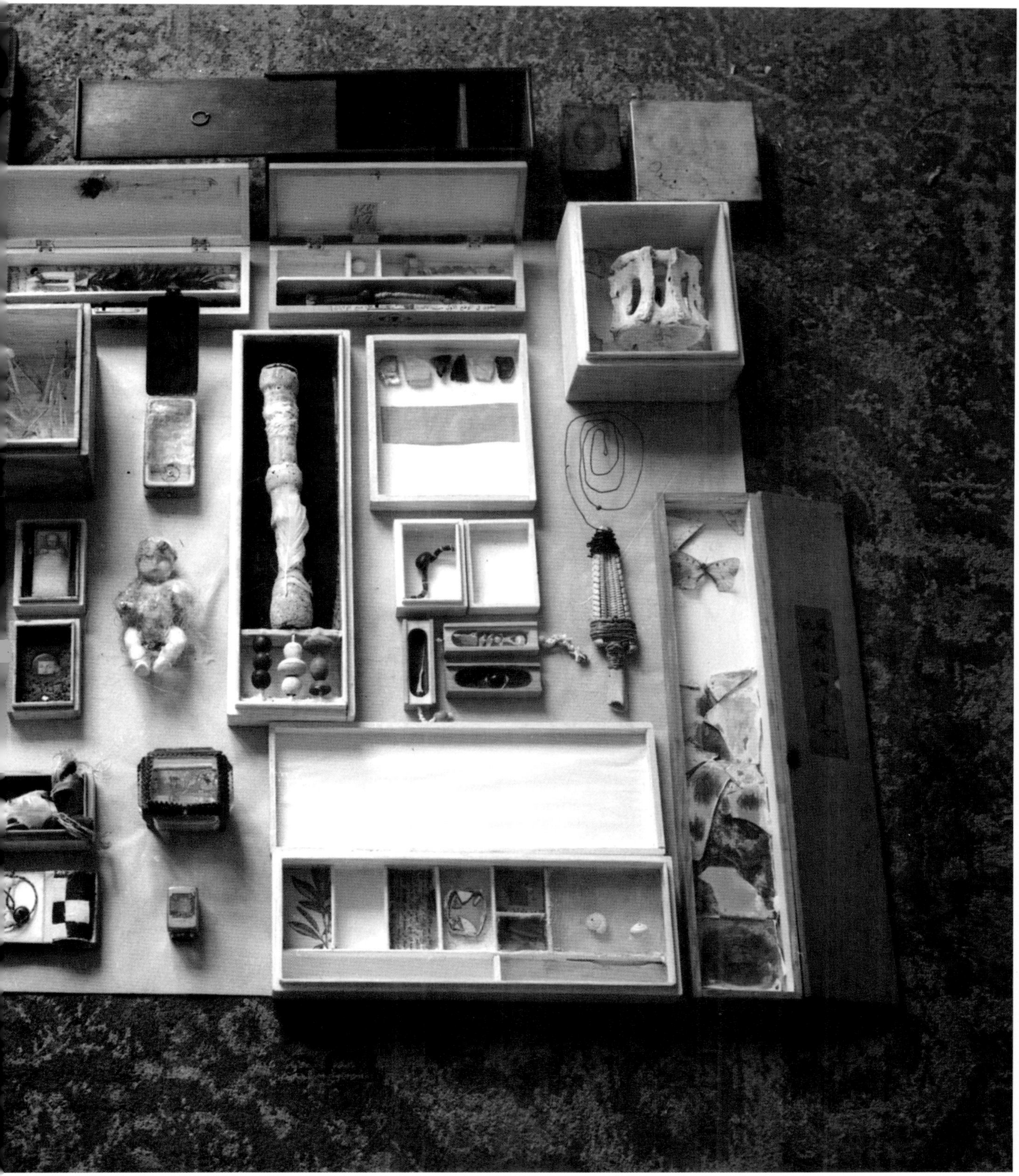

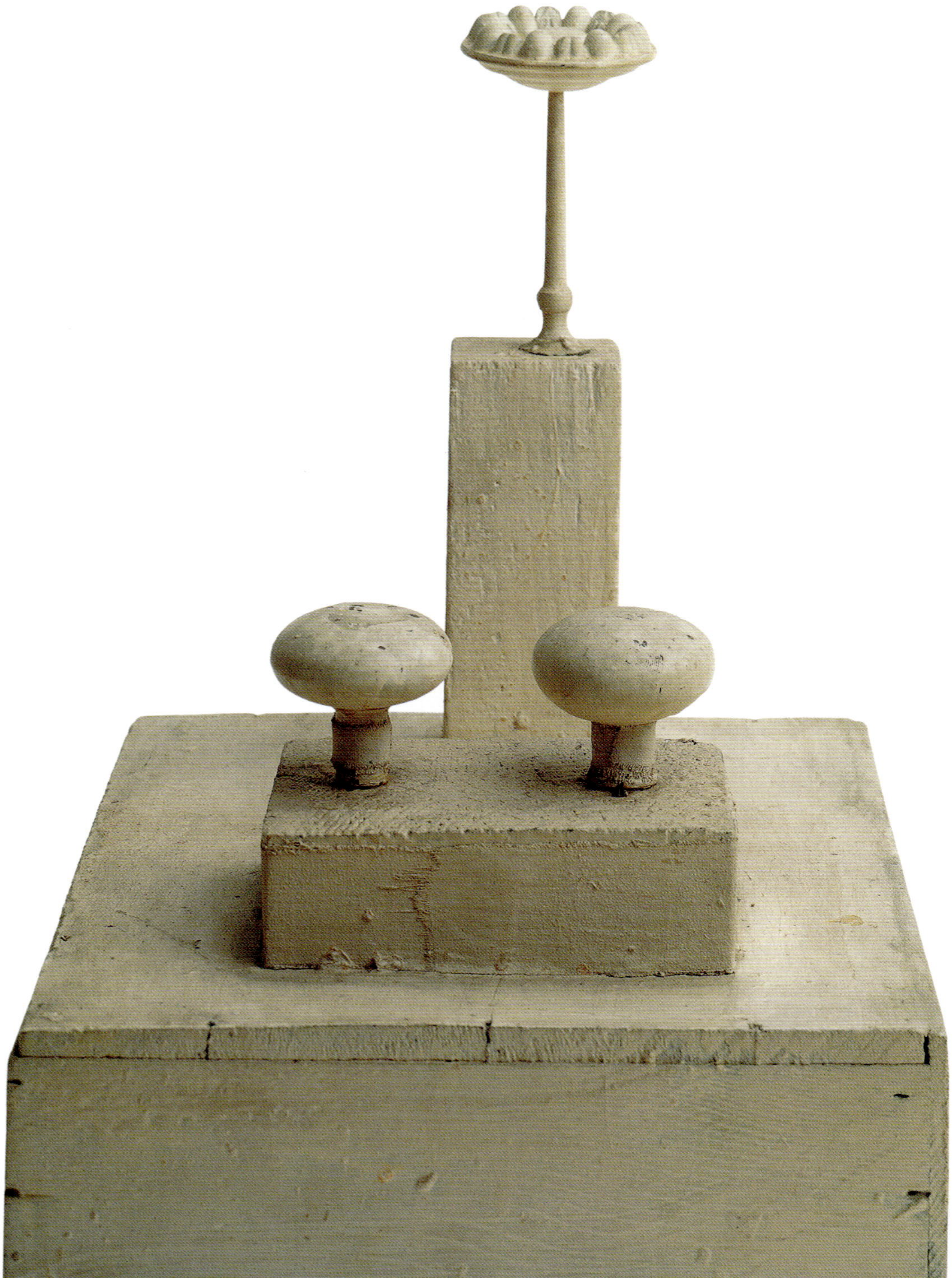

CY TWOMBLY 1928–

Although best known as a painter and draftsman, Cy Twombly has made sculpture throughout his entire career. From the late 1940s through the early 1950s, Twombly was enrolled in several art schools, most notably the Arts Students League, where he met Robert Rauschenberg, and Black Mountain College. Rauschenberg and Twombly were to become fast companions. They traveled extensively together throughout the United States and then to Italy, where Twombly would eventually take up permanent residence. Perhaps there was something about sculpture that made sense with this peripatetic life, as many of Twombly's works from these years are diminutive in scale, fabricated from crude materials – wood scraps, fabric, rope, discarded boxes or crates – and were assembled through the "simple" activities of binding, wrapping, nailing, and tying. Similar in conception to Rauschenberg's early sculptures, Twombly's work has an intensely handmade, rough-hewn nature. His sculptures, formed through accumulation and accretion, seem to possess an unexpected aura that is surprising in its intensity given the ordinary nature of its components.

Despite the similarities in Rauschenberg's and Twombly's early work, there is much to distinguish these two bodies of sculpture. Twombly's work is usually monochromatic; if the sculptures are painted, white predominates. Even when the works are not painted, as in *Untitled* (New York) (1953) and *Untitled* (New York) (1955), white or ecru prevailed because of his use of relatively undyed fabrics. This monochromism has numerous effects. It acts as a kind of cohesive element, as the white paint papers over the disparate nature of the object's internal parts. But it also heightens dramatically the textural qualities of the works. In *Untitled* (Lexington) (1948), for instance, white paint is unevenly applied over the entire surface of the sculpture, from the upended box, which serves as a base, to the two small rectangular pieces of wood, which act as perches for two small knobs in the front, and an assemblage of small objects in the back resembles a footed vase with fruit or perhaps a flower in full bloom. Even as the white paint binds the disparate objects together into a unified visual field, so too it accentuates the differences among and between the sculpture's disparate parts. It highlights the wood grain of the two "plinths"; it drips down over the "base"; it both coats and chips off the knobs. And yet even though the white paint promotes the heterogeneousness of the individual objects, the uniformity with which Twombly uses it helps to accentuate the highly repetitive nature of these works. But even as their whiteness makes us aware of Twombly's ongoing return to a set of aesthetic problems, the paint also furthers the distinction between the "used up" quality of the materials and their detritus-like feel in a manner that seems exponential in relation to the putative purity of the whiteness that encases them.

The repetitiveness is carried through in the objects themselves. In *Untitled* (New York) (1953), eleven small pieces of thin wood are bound together with a gauzy material and additionally are secured with nails. Ganged up, as if for a line up, or squeezed together, as if for a family photo, the work at once seems like an arbitrary slice of a potentially limitless arrangement and evokes the flute of Pan. This play between formal and more "narrative" concerns is typical of Twombly's sculptures. In *Untitled* (New York) (1955), five pieces of wood are held together like a fan and are bound to a base that looks either like a handle (if the work is a fan) or like a trunk or branch (if the work is an opening plant). Again our articulation of the object moves between inanimate and animate metaphors. This vacillation is heightened by the bound quality of the wood lathes, all but the middle one, which is painted white. The binding of each piece is different, as sometimes the string crosses over itself and other times runs parallel around the object. In each instance, however, Twombly appears to be playing a game of "transparency and concealment,"[1] one not entirely dissimilar from his use of the white paint.

The skinlike nature of both the white paint and the bound fabric is part and parcel of the hide-and-seek at play in Twombly's work. Another mode of display or presentation that Twombly explored is in the many photographs of the works, many of them taken by Rauschenberg. The photos are reminiscent of Brancusi's studio shots, in which sculptures and furniture stand in mute dialogue with one another. For Brancusi, these images were a way of registering the contiguity of his objects with other objects, to show that they existed in the space of the world. In the photographs of Twombly's work, something else happens: Twombly often appears in the images, and he uses the sculptures to obscure himself. In an image in Rauschenberg's Fulton Street studio, we see Twombly, hidden, except for his face and hands, by both his sculpture and an early painting. In another photograph, he appears in profile, arm extended over a sculpture so that he seems to be part of a wall relief, made sculpture-like by his encounter with his own work.

Poet Charles Olson described Twombly's sculptures in a way that can help to untangle the repetitions within the pieces and these photographs of it. However secretly they may operate, the repetitions are constitutive of the self. In Olson's words, "These sculptures of his also show how accurate his penetration of the reality bearing on us is: these are the artifacts he finds surrounding himself in the same diggings out of which he is digging himself."[2]

CY TWOMBLY 1928–

Although best known as a painter and draftsman, Cy Twombly has made sculpture throughout his entire career. From the late 1940s through the early 1950s, Twombly was enrolled in several art schools, most notably the Arts Students League, where he met Robert Rauschenberg, and Black Mountain College. Rauschenberg and Twombly were to become fast companions. They traveled extensively together throughout the United States and then to Italy, where Twombly would eventually take up permanent residence. Perhaps there was something about sculpture that made sense with this peripatetic life, as many of Twombly's works from these years are diminutive in scale, fabricated from crude materials — wood scraps, fabric, rope, discarded boxes or crates — and were assembled through the "simple" activities of binding, wrapping, nailing, and tying. Similar in conception to Rauschenberg's early sculptures, Twombly's work has an intensely handmade, rough-hewn nature. His sculptures, formed through accumulation and accretion, seem to possess an unexpected aura that is surprising in its intensity given the ordinary nature of its components.

Despite the similarities in Rauschenberg's and Twombly's early work, there is much to distinguish these two bodies of sculpture. Twombly's work is usually monochromatic; if the sculptures are painted, white predominates. Even when the works are not painted, as in *Untitled (New York)* (1953) and *Untitled (New York)* (1955), white or ecru prevailed because of his use of relatively undyed fabrics. This monochromism has numerous effects. It acts as a kind of cohesive element, as the white paint papers over the disparate nature of the object's internal parts. But it also heightens dramatically the textural qualities of the works. In *Untitled (Lexington)* (1948), for instance, white paint is unevenly applied over the entire surface of the sculpture, from the upended box, which serves as a base, to the two small rectangular pieces of wood, which act as perches for two small knobs in the front, and an assemblage of small objects in the back resembles a footed vase with fruit or perhaps a flower in full bloom. Even as the white paint binds the disparate objects together into a unified visual field, so too it accentuates the differences among and between the sculpture's disparate parts. It highlights the wood grain of the two "plinths"; it drips down over the "base"; it both coats and chips off the knobs. And yet even though the white paint promotes the heterogeneousness of the individual objects, the uniformity with which Twombly uses it helps to accentuate the highly repetitive nature of these works. But even as their whiteness makes us aware of Twombly's ongoing return to a set of aesthetic problems, the paint also furthers the distinction between the "used up" quality of the materials and their detritus-like feel in a manner that seems exponential in relation to the putative purity of the whiteness that encases them.

The repetitiveness is carried through in the objects themselves. In *Untitled (New York)* (1953), eleven small pieces of thin wood are bound together with a gauzy material and additionally are secured with nails. Ganged up, as if for a line-up, or squeezed together, as if for a family photo, the work at once seems like an arbitrary slice of a potentially limitless arrangement and evokes the flute of Pan. This play between formal and more "narrative" concerns is typical of Twombly's sculptures. In *Untitled (New York)* (1955), five pieces of wood are held together like a fan and are bound to a base that looks either like a handle (if the work is a fan) or like a trunk or branch (if the work is an opening plant). Again our articulation of the object moves between inanimate and animate metaphors. This vacillation is heightened by the bound quality of the wood lathes, all but the middle one, which is painted white. The binding of each piece is different, as sometimes the string crosses over itself and other times runs parallel around the object. In each instance, however, Twombly appears to be playing a game of "transparency and concealment," one not entirely dissimilar from his use of the white paint.

The skinlike nature of both the white paint and the bound fabric is part and parcel of the hide-and-seek at play in Twombly's work. Another mode of display or presentation that Twombly explored is in the many photographs of the works, many of them taken by Rauschenberg. The photos are reminiscent of Brancusi's studio shots, in which sculptures and furniture stand in mute dialogue with one another. For Brancusi these images were a way of registering the contiguity of his objects with other objects, to show that they existed in the space of the world. In the photographs of Twombly's work, something else happens. Twombly often appears in the images, and he uses the sculptures to obscure himself. In an image in Rauschenberg's Fulton Street studio we see Twombly, hidden, except for his face and hands, by both his sculpture and an easel painting. In another photograph, he appears in profile, arm extended over a sculpture so that he seems to be part of a wall relief, made sculpture-like by his encounter with his own work.

Poet Charles Olson described Twombly's sculptures in a way that can help to untangle the repetitions within the pieces and these photographs of it. However secretly they may operate, the repetitions are constitutive of the self. In Olson's words, "These sculptures of his also show how accurate his penetration of the reality bearing on us is: these are the artifacts he finds surrounding himself in the same diggings out of which he is digging himself."

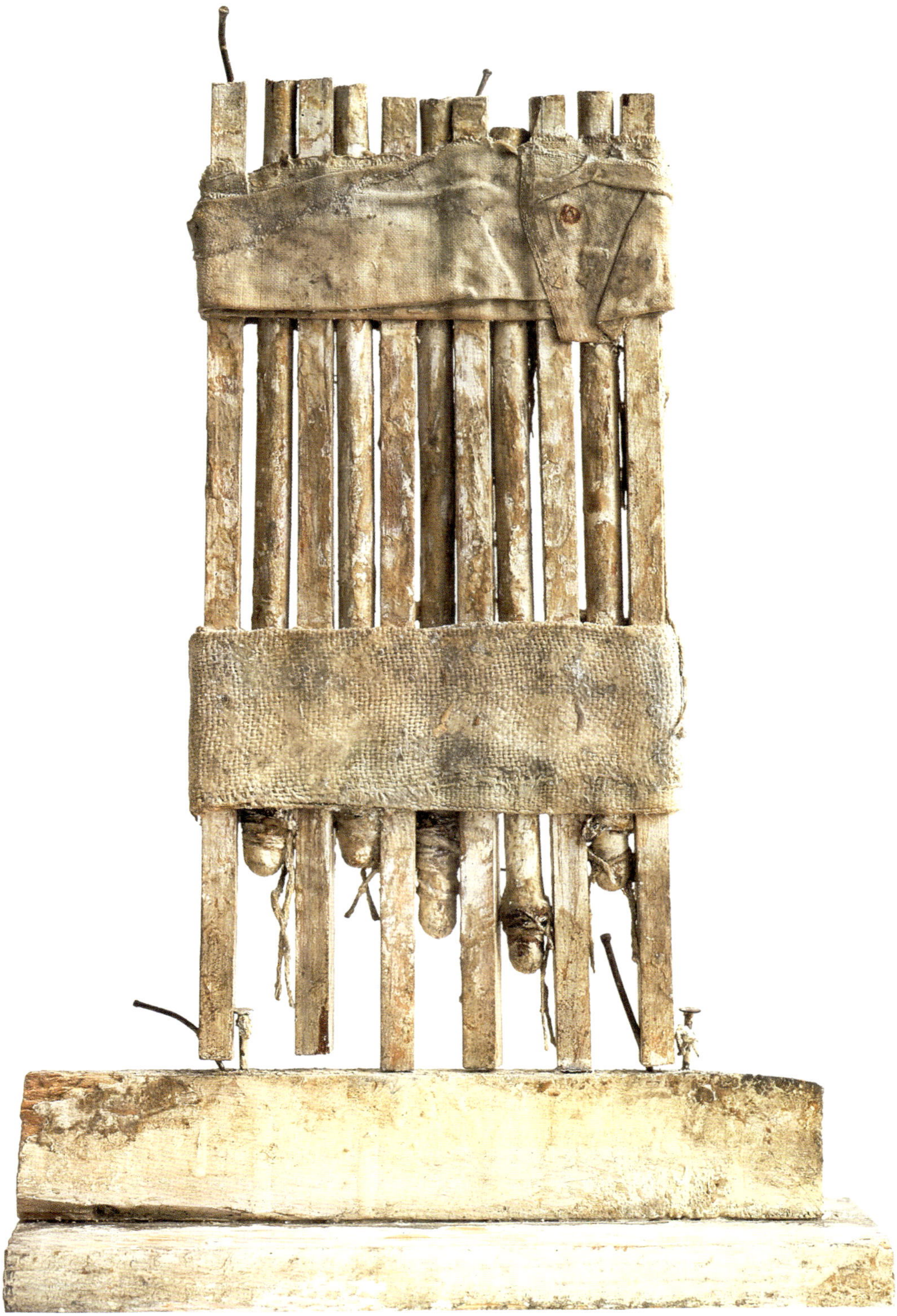

previous spread: left **Untitled, Lexington**, 1948

previous spread: right **Untitled, New York**, 1953

right **Untitled, New York**, 1955

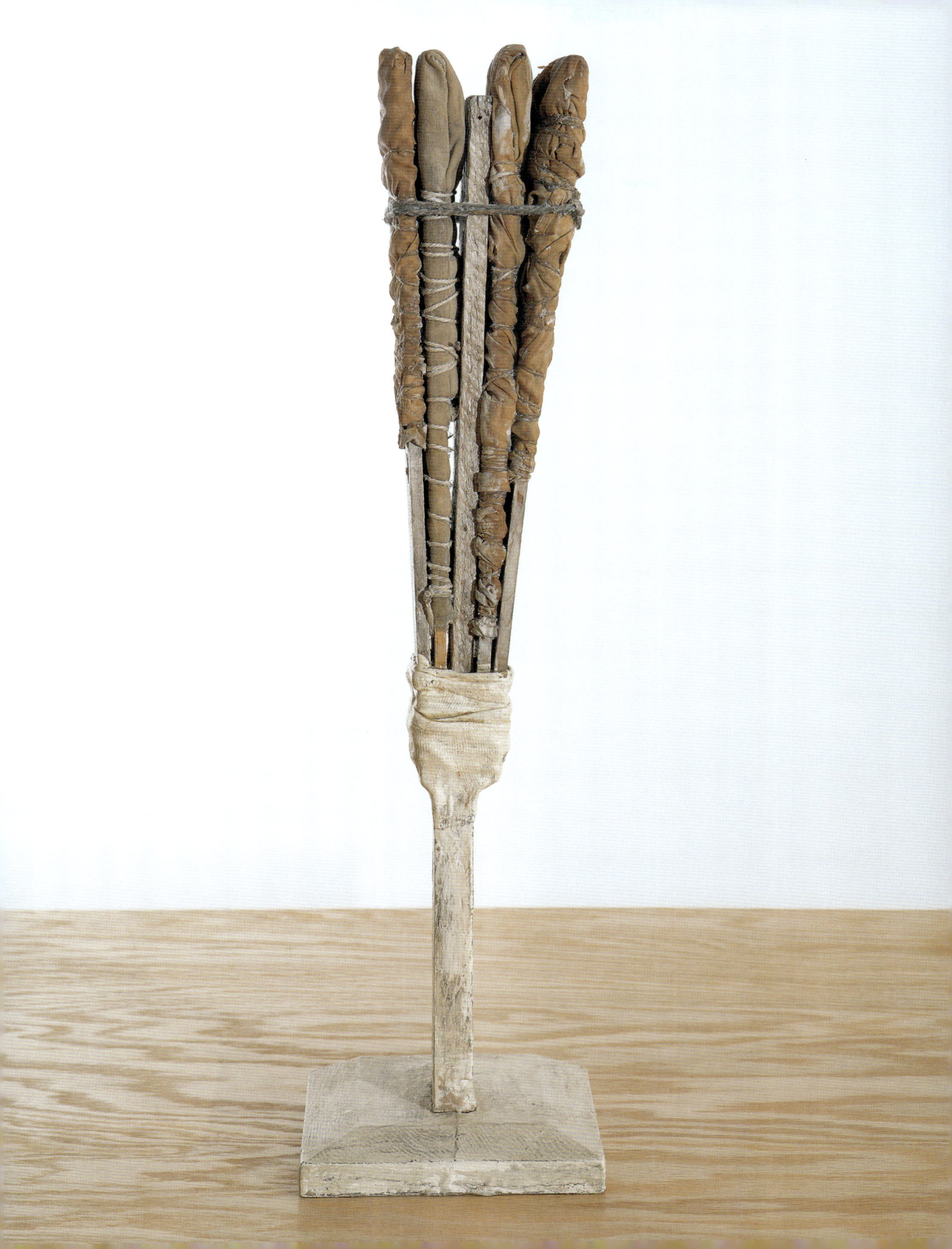

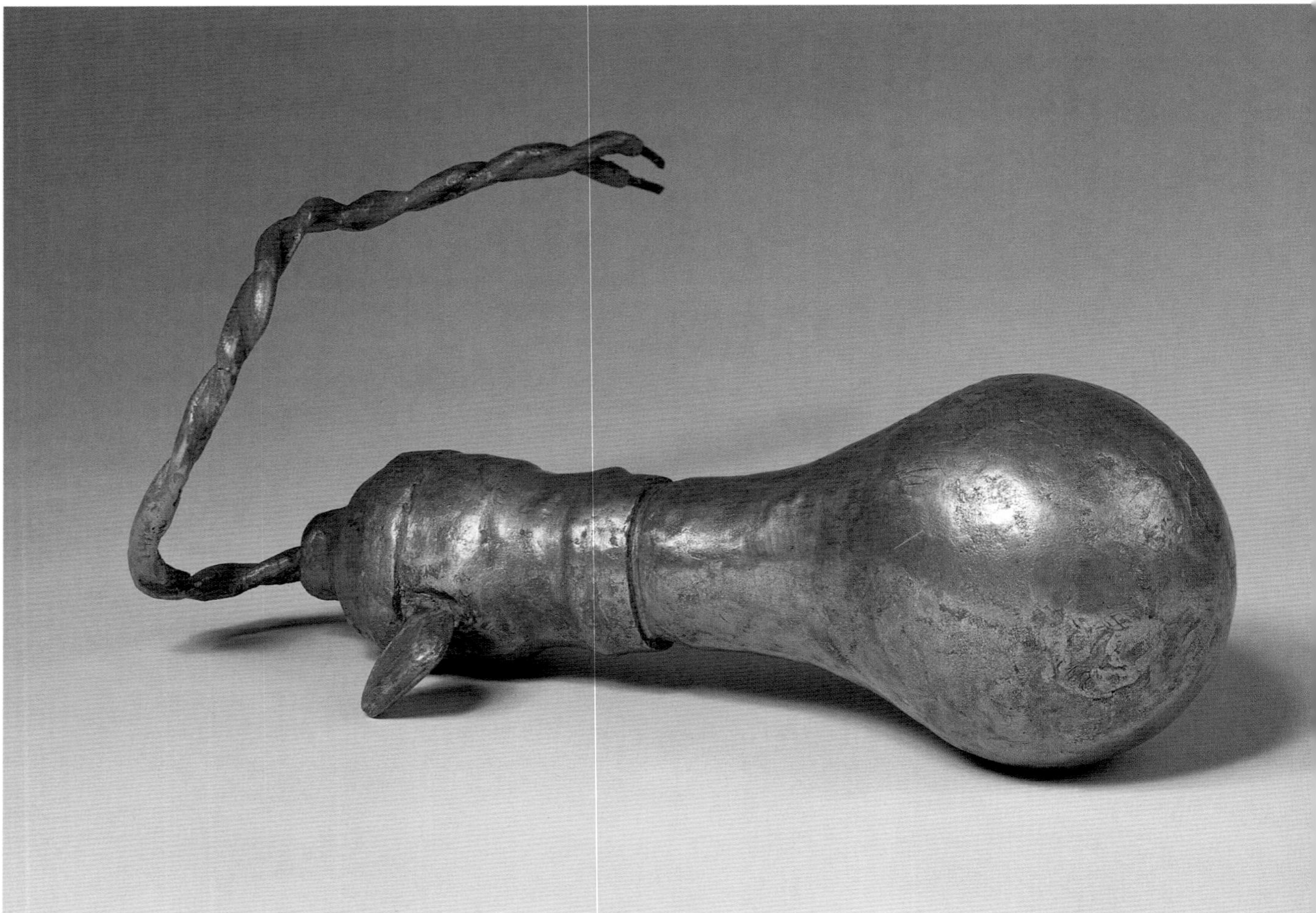

Light Bulb II, 1958

right **Flashlight II**, 1958

JASPER JOHNS 1930–

Although Jasper Johns is primarily known as a painter (with a high degree of interest in drawing and printmaking), his early work in sculpture, while modest in both scale and number, has left a lasting legacy in the history of postwar art; we need only think of Robert Gober's and Josiah McElheny's work to see its enduring resonance. Begun in the late 1950s, Johns's sculptures share two features: they are all of relatively banal objects, and they explore a variety of materials through the process of casting. As a sculptural technique, casting has traditionally been seen as a degraded form, one inherently devoid of skill, bent upon the reproduction of an existing form as opposed to the creation of a new one. By the late 1950s, casting probably had stronger associations with the marvels of plastic and the endless production of everyday commodity goods than it did with high art. Part of Johns's overall project was the problematizing of such boundaries between high and low art and skill versus technique, as his alphabet, number, and flag paintings attest. And yet the sculptures seem to work on other fronts as well; they are not merely an extension of Johns's exclusively painterly concerns.

It is unclear when Johns first saw the three erotic objects of Marcel Duchamp, although by the mid-1960s he owned a copy of each of them. This is not to say that these objects were a direct influence on Johns; the relations between Johns and Duchamp at this point were likely to have been reciprocal. As most of Johns's sculptures were made *before* Duchamp authorized the 1964 set of readymades to be made by hand, it might, in this regard, have been Johns who influenced Duchamp. But he has stated that he was interested in work of such a diminutive scale, especially in sculpture: "The impact of his three small works perhaps was to confirm that works of modest size could be full, complete, accurate, impressive sculptures. The 'obscurity' of the Duchamp forms was, of course, very different from the 'obviousness' of my own."[1]

The early sculptures were of flashlights and light bulbs, seemingly innocuous objects, and are definitively less charged than the highly fragmented cast body parts of friends that appear in *Target with Plaster Casts* (1955) and *Target with Four Faces* (1955). However mundane the light bulbs and flashlights may be, Johns recalled having difficulty in picking the correct object:

> I had a particular idea in my mind what a flashlight looked like – I hadn't really handled a flashlight, since, I guess, I was a child – and I had this image of a flashlight in my head and I wanted to go and buy one as a model. I looked for a week for what I thought looked like an ordinary flashlight, and I found all kinds of flashlights with red plastic shields, wings on the sides, all kinds of things, and I finally found one that I wanted. And it made me very suspicious of my idea, because it was so difficult to find this thing I had thought was so common.[2]

It is certainly easy to hear echoes of Duchamp's claim that the readymades were chosen with complete aesthetic indifference. But it's hard not to attach at least some symbolic attributes to these apparatuses of light and illumination, with all their humanistic implications about the nature of art. And yet, the very thingness, and the life-size scale of these objects, belies, almost immediately, such old-fashioned iconographical readings. What we encounter instead in the mute physicality of these objects is that they seem to be about touch, about the residue of the hand, about a registration of the very carefulness with which they were made to resemble a mass-produced object without ever being able to be mistaken for one.

Light Bulb II (1958) is a study in a kind of dull blankness. Made of sculp-metal, the surface of the light bulb resembles the wear and tear on an old coin – burnished, nicked, worn. As the title implies, this work is one in a series. The first light bulb sits atop, or amid, or emerges from, a somewhat expressionistic papier mâché base. So too all the *Light Bulbs* of 1960 (there is one in plaster, one in bronze, and one in painted bronze) sit on a small base made out of the same substance as the light bulb itself – a Brancusian joke of sorts. But *Light Bulb II* is truly nomadic, unattached, the only thing that stops it from rolling off its surface is the switch at its base. The series offers the repetition of the same object in different materials, each with slightly different distinguishing characteristics. For instance, the painted bronze *Light Bulb* from 1960 is the only one with the denotation of the wattage carefully replicated. Such incremental adjustments put into play the very differences of the operations at work in the sculptures. The replication of a mass-produced, store-bought object is compounded by its repetition as an artistic performance or activity. In this regard it's sometimes hard to know exactly what we are looking at; much like looking at a *Flag* painting provokes a rhetorical question, "Is it a flag or is it a painting?"[3] Although we know the light bulbs are not functional (we can never use them in a pinch in the way we might be able to "use" *Flag*), we don't know if what we are apprehending is a sculpture, an object, or an instantiation of repetition and reproduction as such. Alan Solomon, who curated Johns's first retrospective in 1964 at the Jewish Museum, understood this problem when he wrote, almost plaintively, in the exhibition catalogue: "We encounter a perplexing uncertainty over whether or not he simply cast the real objects in Sculpmetal or bronze, or even just coated them with Sculpmetal, since they appear so true to life.... The result is that these pieces give the effect of objects trying to be sculpture, and we are plunged right back into that now familiar realm of ambiguity."[4] The struggle of an object to be a sculpture was not for Johns alone, although no other works of the postwar period elicited such a direct assessment of this particularly vexed problem, and no other works play out the coordinates of everyday object, handmade object, repetition, and sculpture so matter-of-factly.

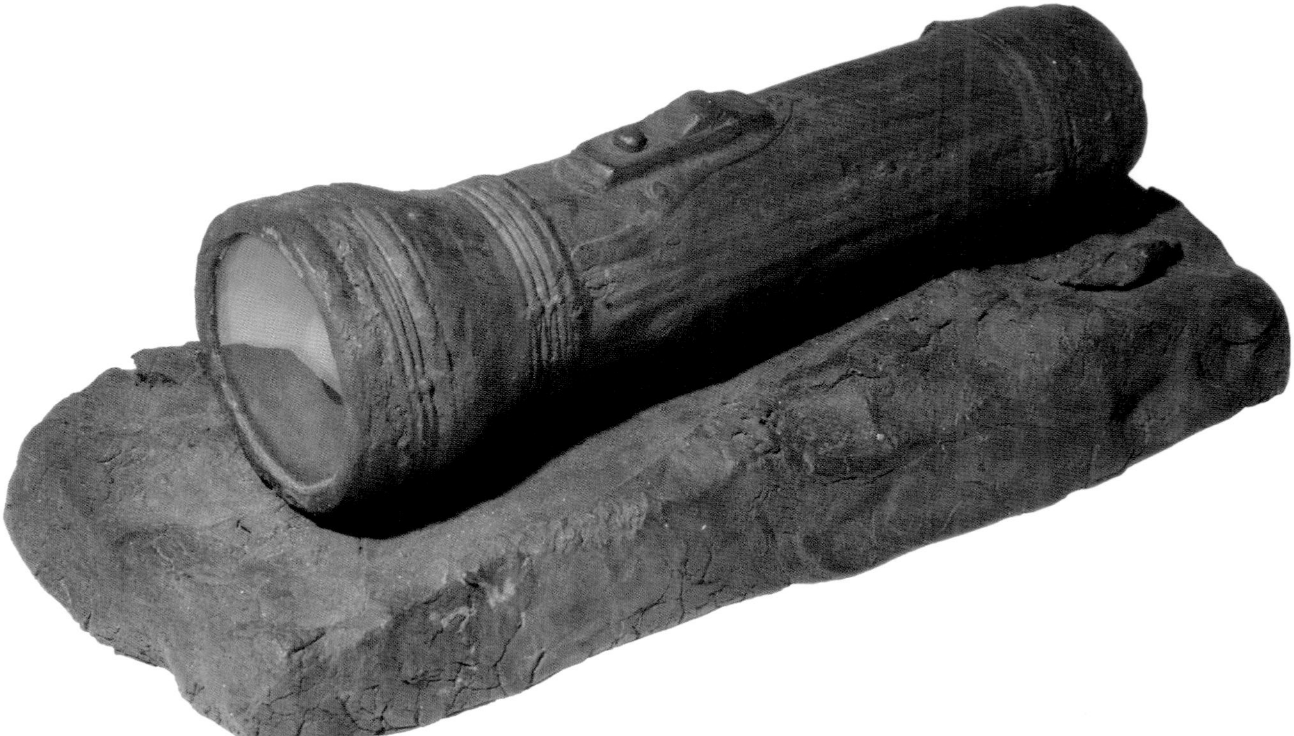

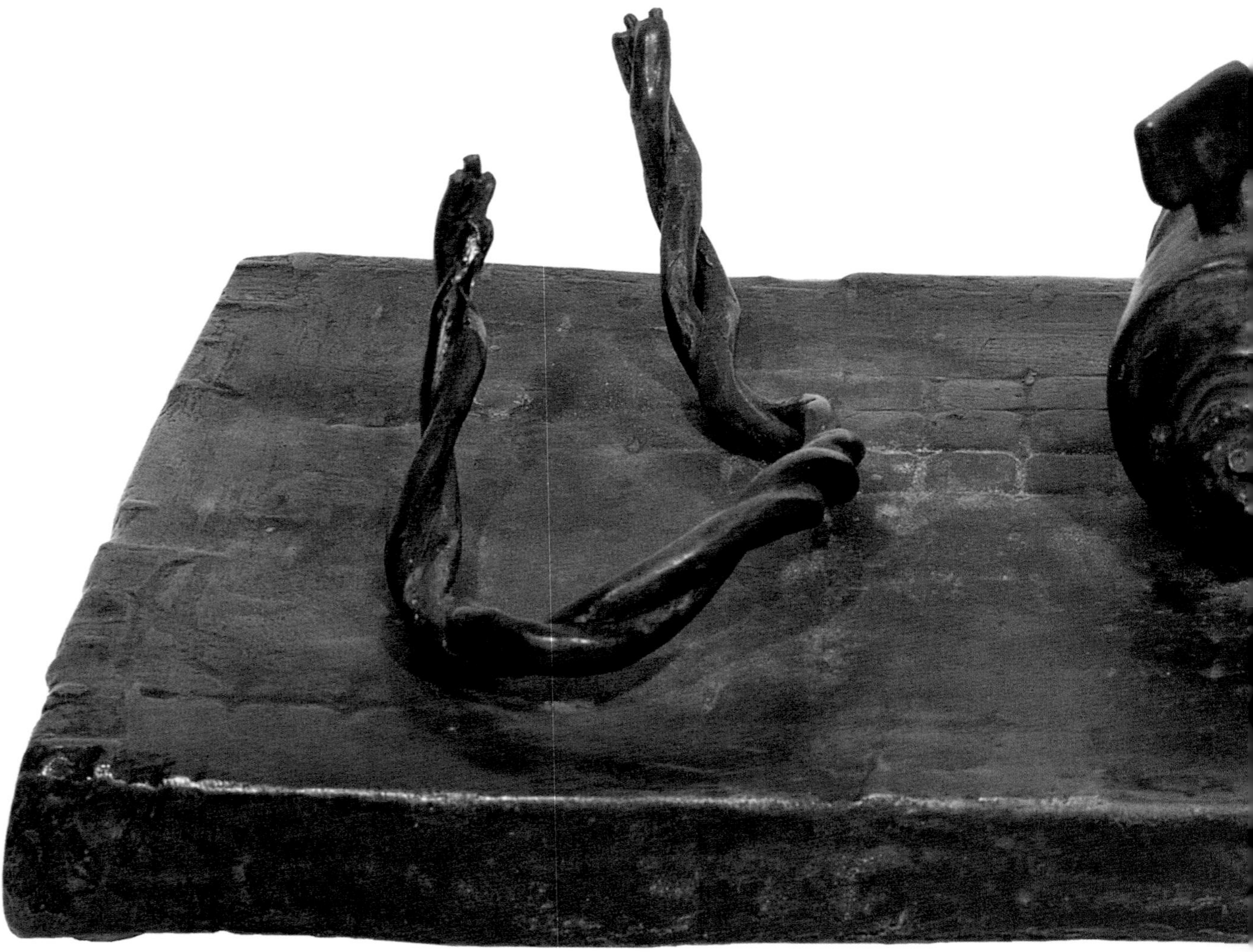

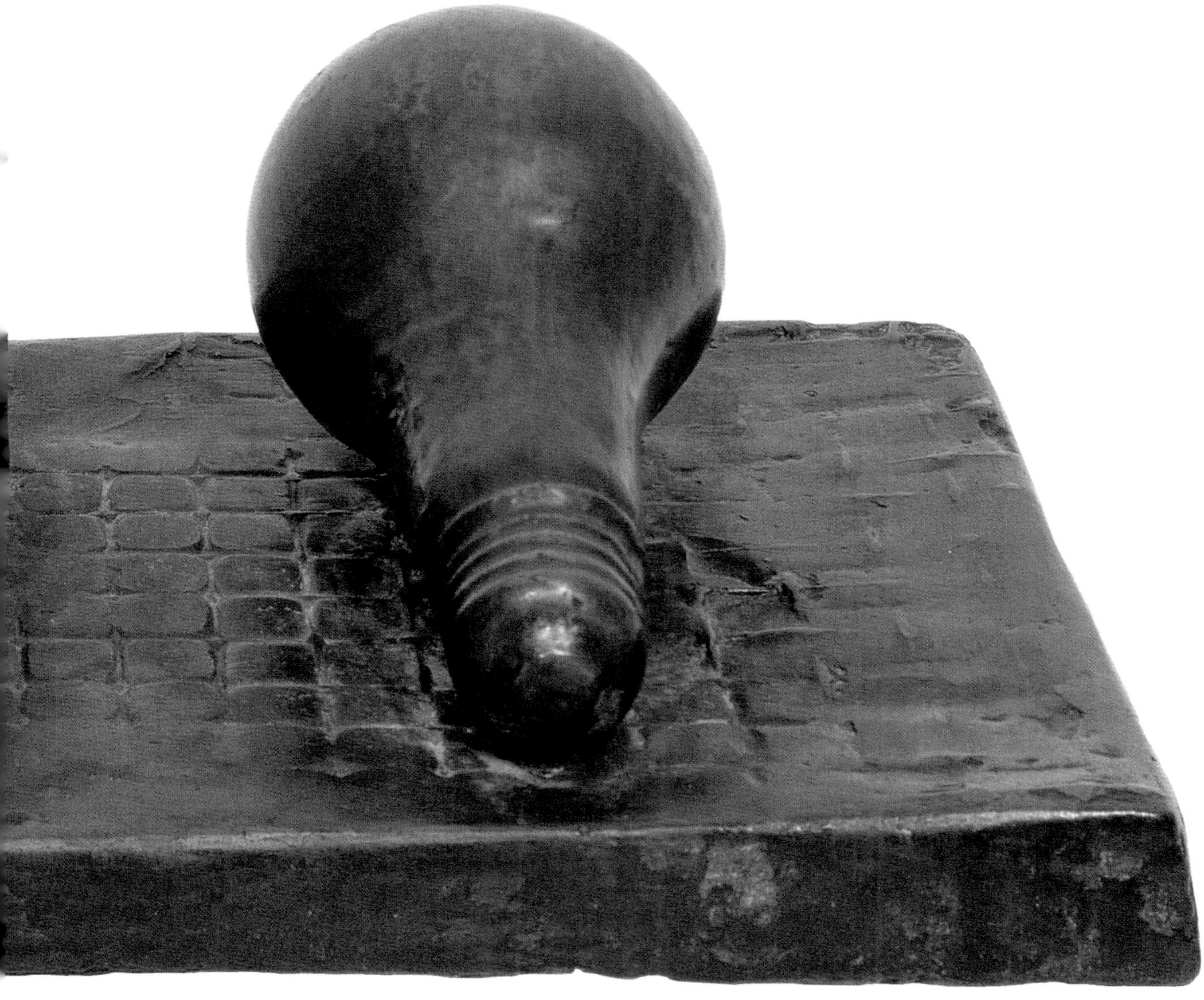

previous spread **Bronze**, 1960–61

right **Do It Yourself (Target)**, 1960

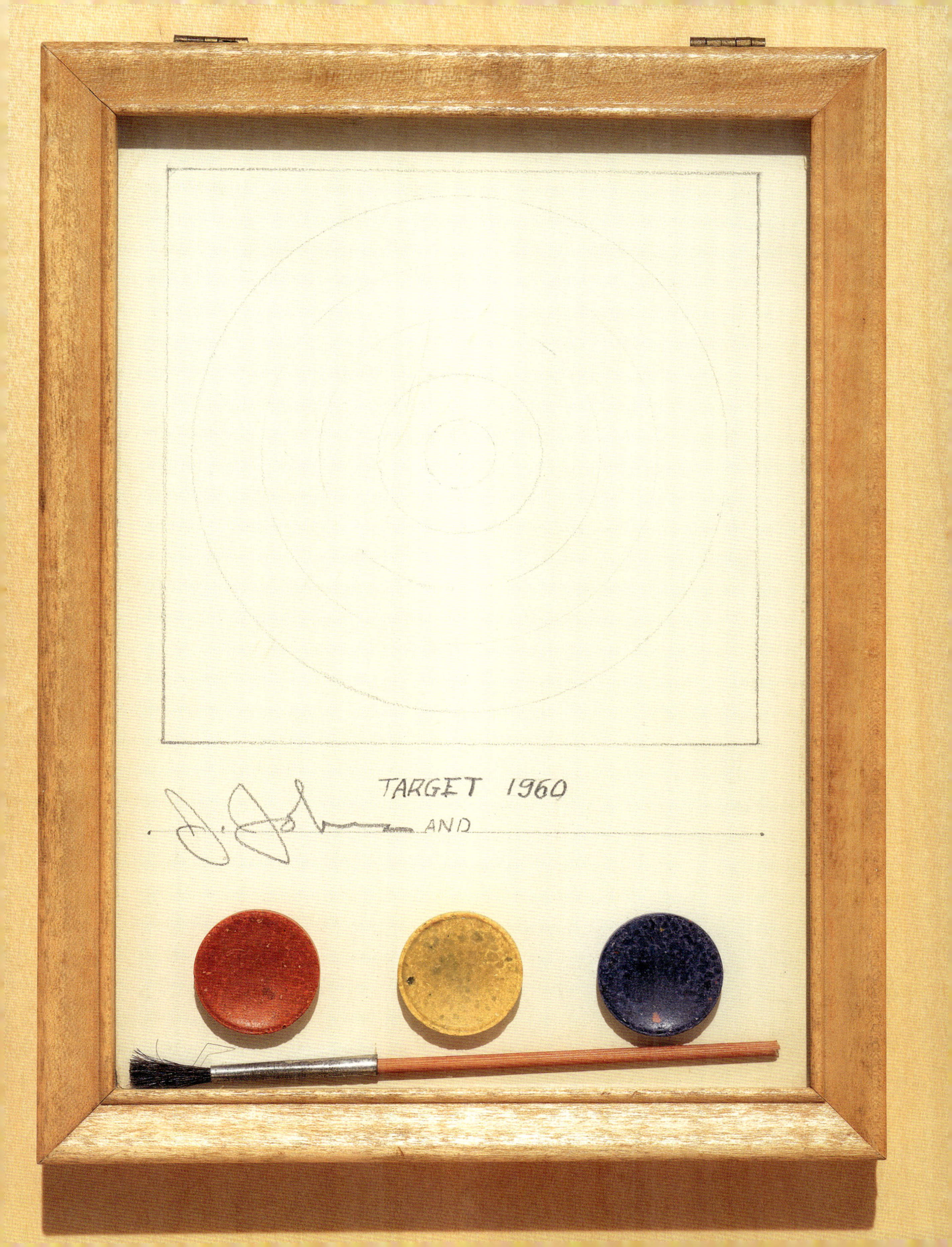
TARGET 1960
AND

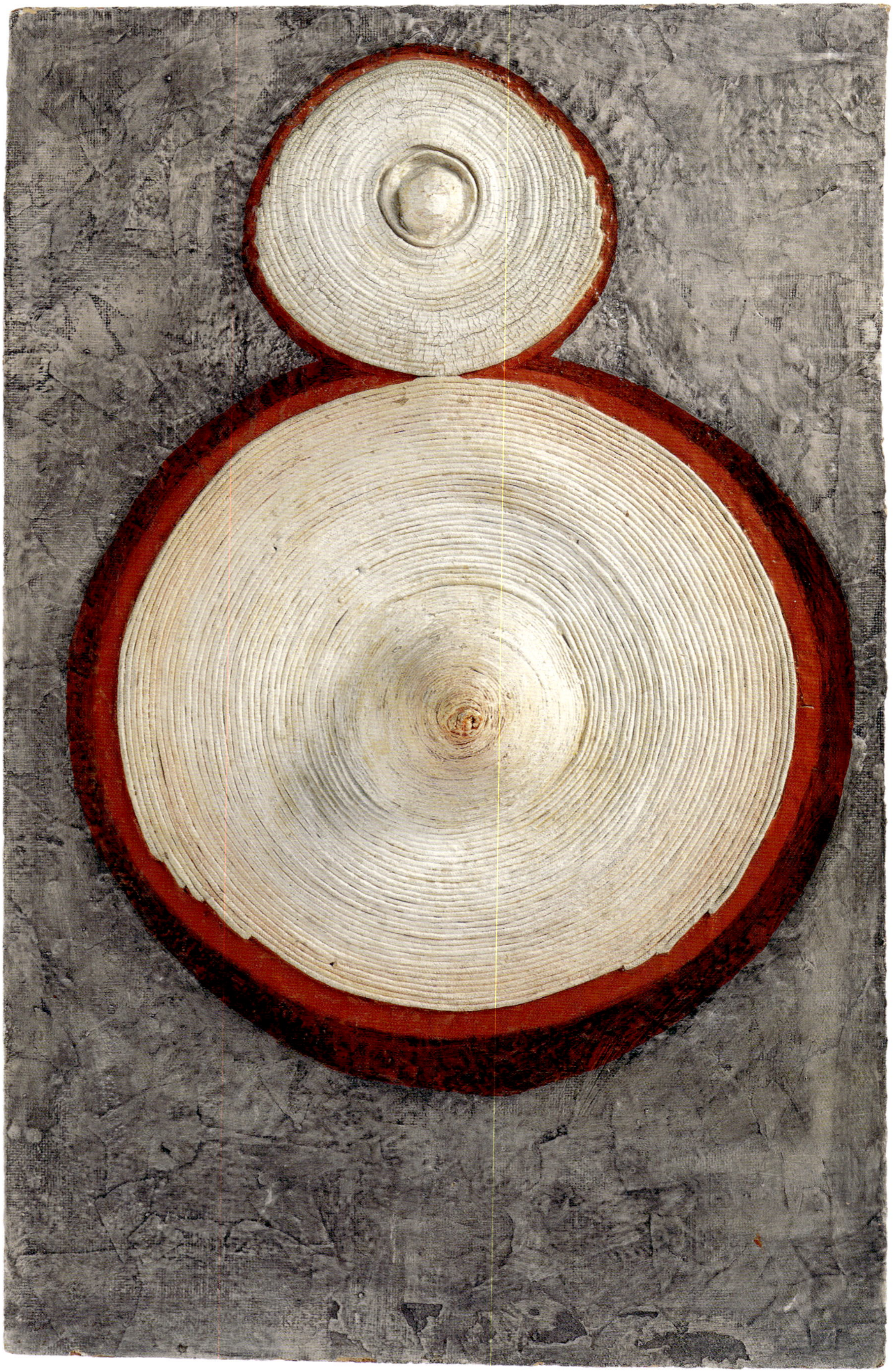

EVA HESSE 1936–1970

In June 1964, Eva Hesse left the United States for a fifteen-month sojourn in Germany. The invitation of a wealthy industrialist to her then-husband, artist Tom Doyle, prompted the trip, and both were offered studios in an abandoned textile factory in Kettwig. This trip would prove to be transformative for Hesse, for it marks the occasion of her first experiments with relief sculpture, her first radical break from the two-dimensionality of the picture plane into a space where object, sculpture, and drawing were to mix ineluctably. During this period, Hesse produced fourteen reliefs, all brightly colored, all deploying both readymade and found objects that protrude from the picture plane, and all related to a group of approximately sixty mechano-morphic drawings. For many years these works were relatively unknown, most likely because Hesse left many of the reliefs in Germany when she returned to the States, and because their wild palette was not in keeping with the vogue for grays and whites that were to dominate Minimalism. However, recent scholarship has paid renewed attention to these works, seeing them not as juvenilia but as a full-fledged passage within Hesse's overall career.[1]

The first relief was the extraordinary and iconic *Ringaround Arosie*. From the rough collaged and scuffed gray surface, a buildup of papier-mâché on Masonite, rise two circles, one smaller circle above a larger one. The circles are comprised of tightly wound electrical wire that has been covered with cloth. Rimmed in red that blushes to pink, the two circles appear as breasts, a snowman, a stoplight, an on/off switch, all out of whack. The larger, lower circle culminates in a nipple that sticks out from the surface by nearly three inches. Between the gradation of color from red to pink, the industrial feel of the wire leading up to the tip, and then the remarkably lifelike nature of the nipple itself, *Ringaround Arosie* has a tendency to be oddly disconcerting and embarrassing. The intense viscerality of the piece is far from self-evident, however, as the work is neither exclusively a breast nor a circle. Rather, the image/object seems to vacillate wildly between a variety of identities – haptic/optic, menacing/hilarious, sexual/geometric, intensely colorful/monochromatic.

What gets started in *Ringaround Arosie* is much elaborated in *Oomamaboomba*. The incipient abstraction is full blown as the yellow boomerang shape implies motion and contains orifices. Its circles are eyes, its black-and-white strips teeth and hair, as well as being absolutely none of these things. Hesse again deploys the tight wrapping of cord, this time around a metal armature that swings up and away from the canvas, only to re-secure itself, as if its job is to attach the canvas to itself. (Hesse expands this gesture in *Hang Up*, 1966.) Both the palette, with its gaudy Floridaesque play of hot pink and lemon yellow, and the vowel-filled openness of the title suggest a kind of slap-happy playfulness.

This slightly slapstick quality comes from the confluence between the clearly inanimate and industrial nature of the materials and the intensely biomorphic nature of the shapes and organic quality of movement and color in the works. The porosity of body and machine in these reliefs demonstrates a wonderfully humorous elaboration of Duchamp's interest in the mechanics of desire and the relays established by the readymades between bodies and objects. Hesse had been exposed to Duchamp's work early in her career, notably while a student at Yale, where the important relief *Tu M'* was on view. Certainly, the use of readymade materials was intellectually available to Hesse at any juncture of her career. Yet it remains interesting that she first began to do so in a factory environment, in which industrial detritus littered the studio. During this period, she saw (among many exhibitions) an important exhibition of works by Duchamp held in Bern in October 1964. Although it is circumstantial, it seems likely that this exhibition helped to jog Hesse's fertile creativity.

However indebted Hesse's reliefs may be to Duchamp, they possess an ineffable uniqueness of their own, particularly in their mode of psychic address. On the one hand, they play out a Kleinian notion of the part object, as they toy with the boundaries between inside and outside (the push-pull of *Oomamaboomba*), and, on the other, they stage the dispersal of emotional effects across body parts that are neither fully real nor entirely fantasy (*Ringaround Arosie*). Repetition functions as a source of pleasure in these works as well. In *Eighter from Decatur*, thick sunflower-yellow cord is nailed to the Masonite ground in a radiating pattern. The radial is doubled by the pinkish claw-arms that emanate from yet another breast/nonbreast. As if the title weren't funny enough, the contraption moves, a merry-go-round of sex, a clock that can't tell time, a sundial of the body, a hubcap, a steering wheel, a pinwheel. All forms of movement activated by the body, they subsequently produce yet another bodily effect through vision – dizziness, hilarity, vague nausea, laughter, desire. From the breast to the eye and back again, Hesse's reliefs offer us the adult version of Freud's famous fort – da game, in which a little boy throws and retrieves a toy endlessly in order to overcome the loss of his father. Here, instead of mastery, we have its promise and its ever-present retreat. As Hesse once wrote in her diary, "Endless repetition can be considered erotic."[2]

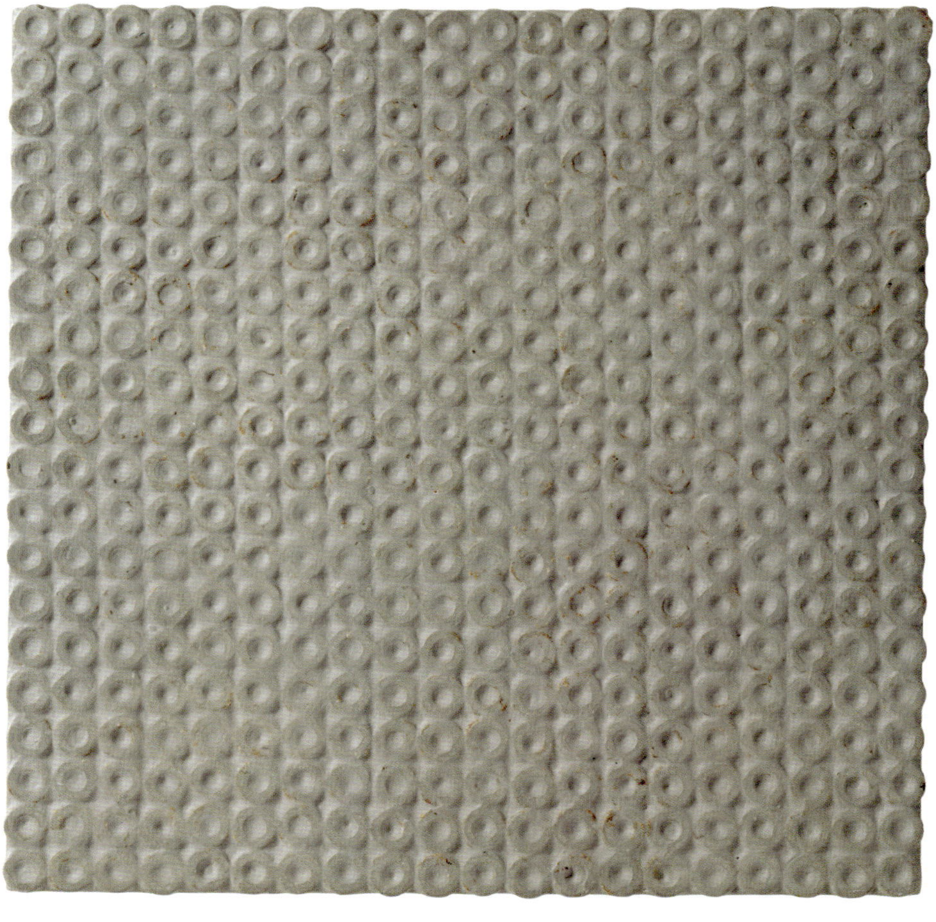

previous spread: left
Ringaround Arosie, 1965

previous spread: right **Compass**, 1967

right **Eighter from Decatur**, 1965

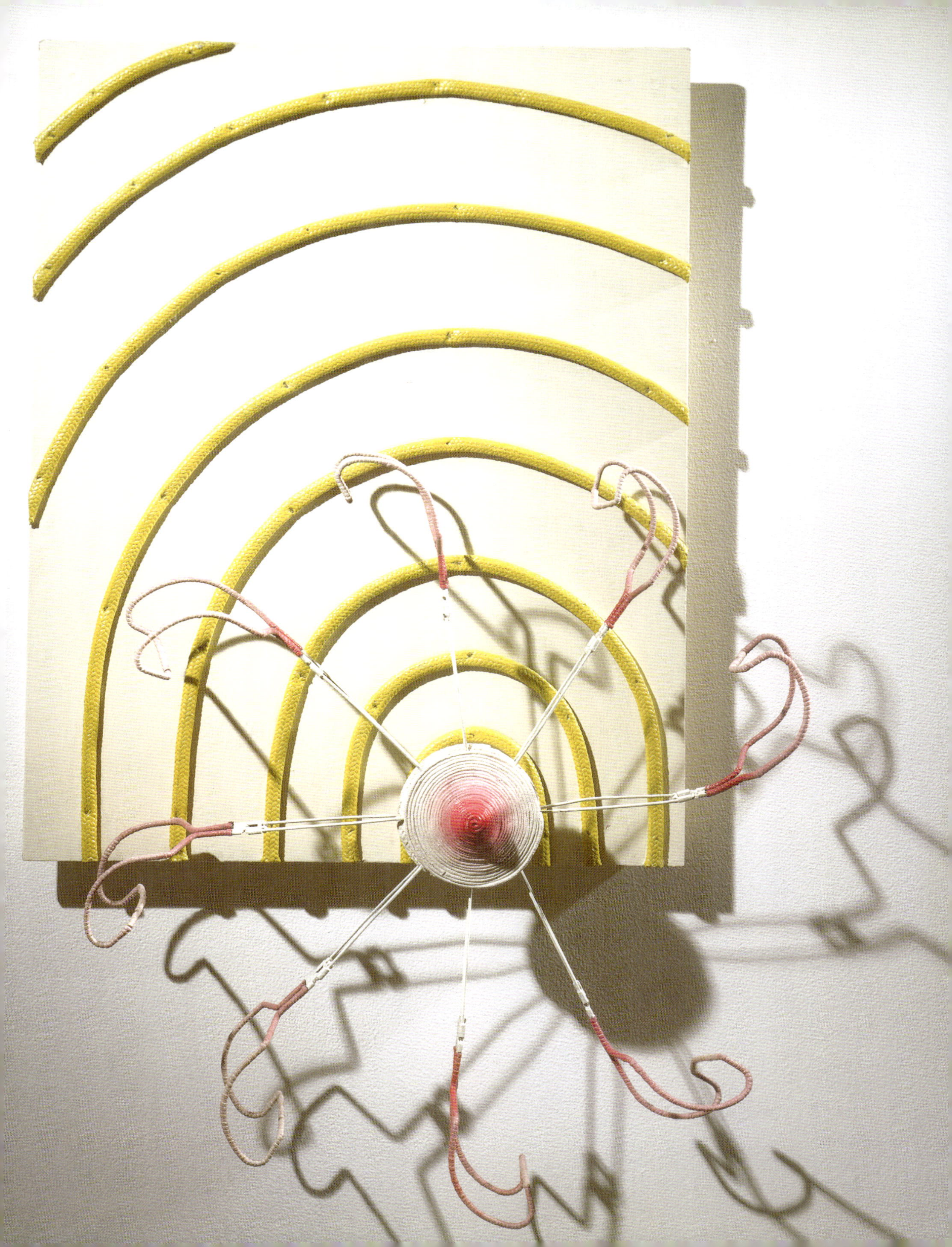

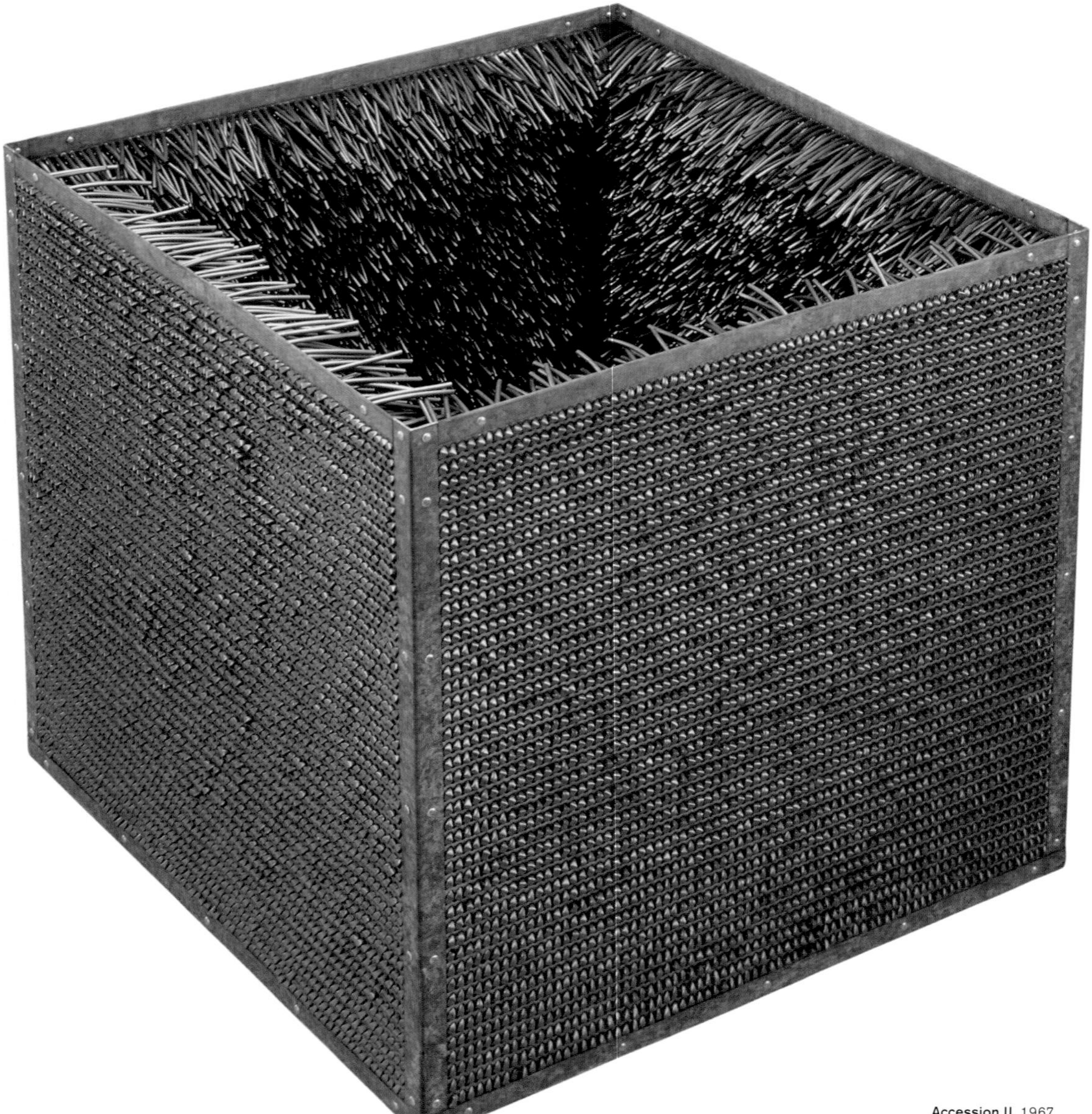

Accession II, 1967

right **Accession II** (detail), 1967

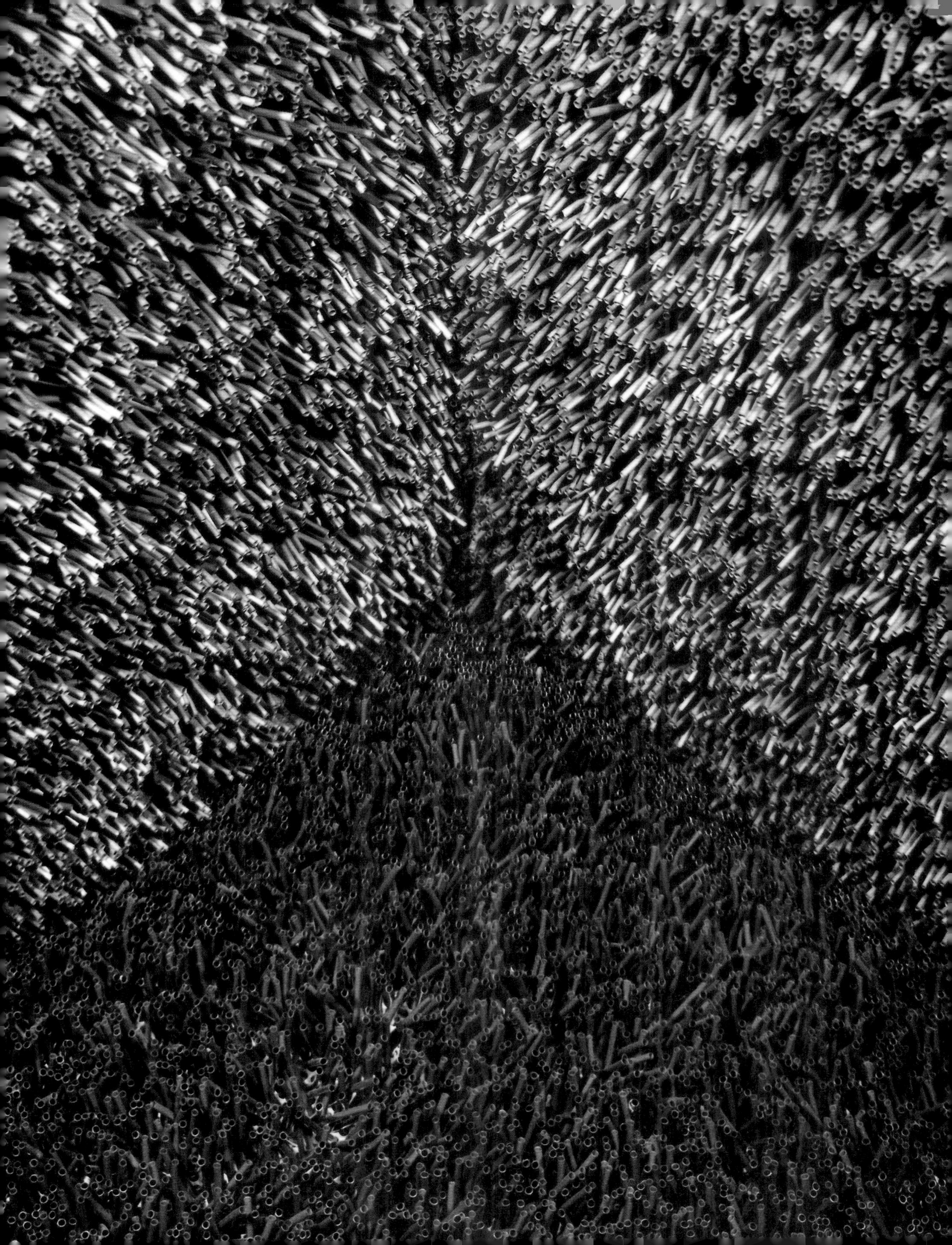

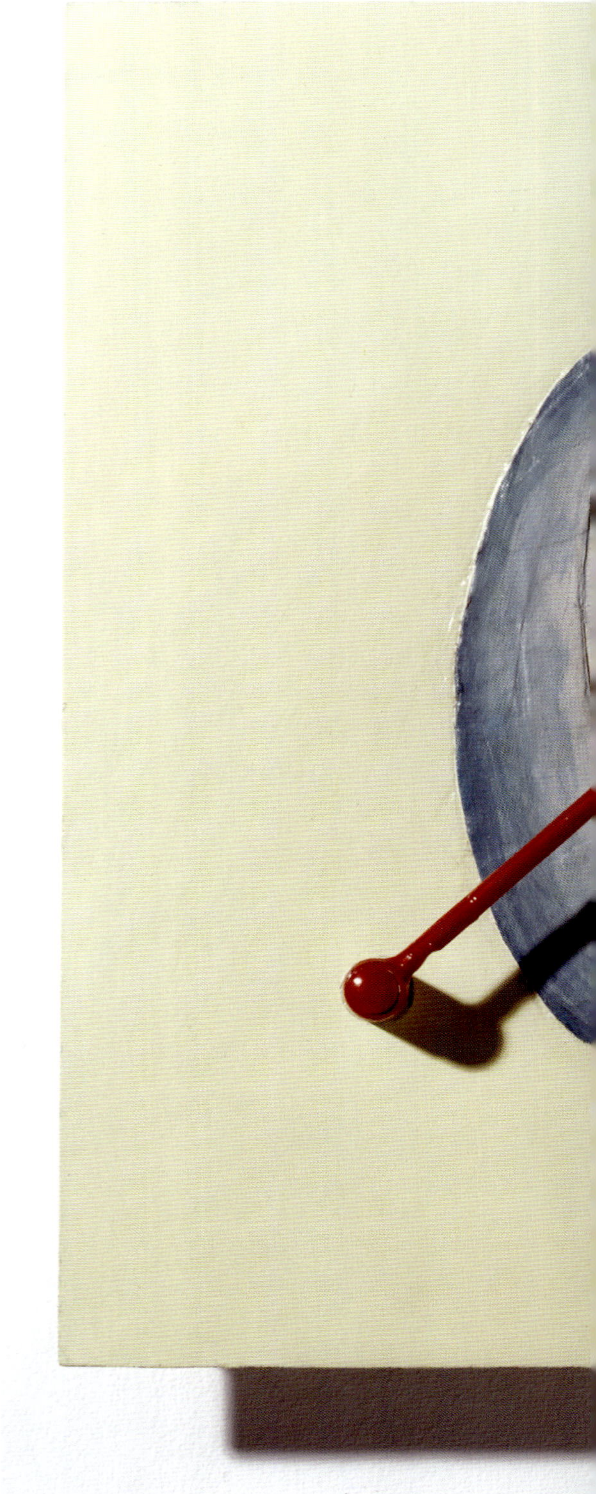

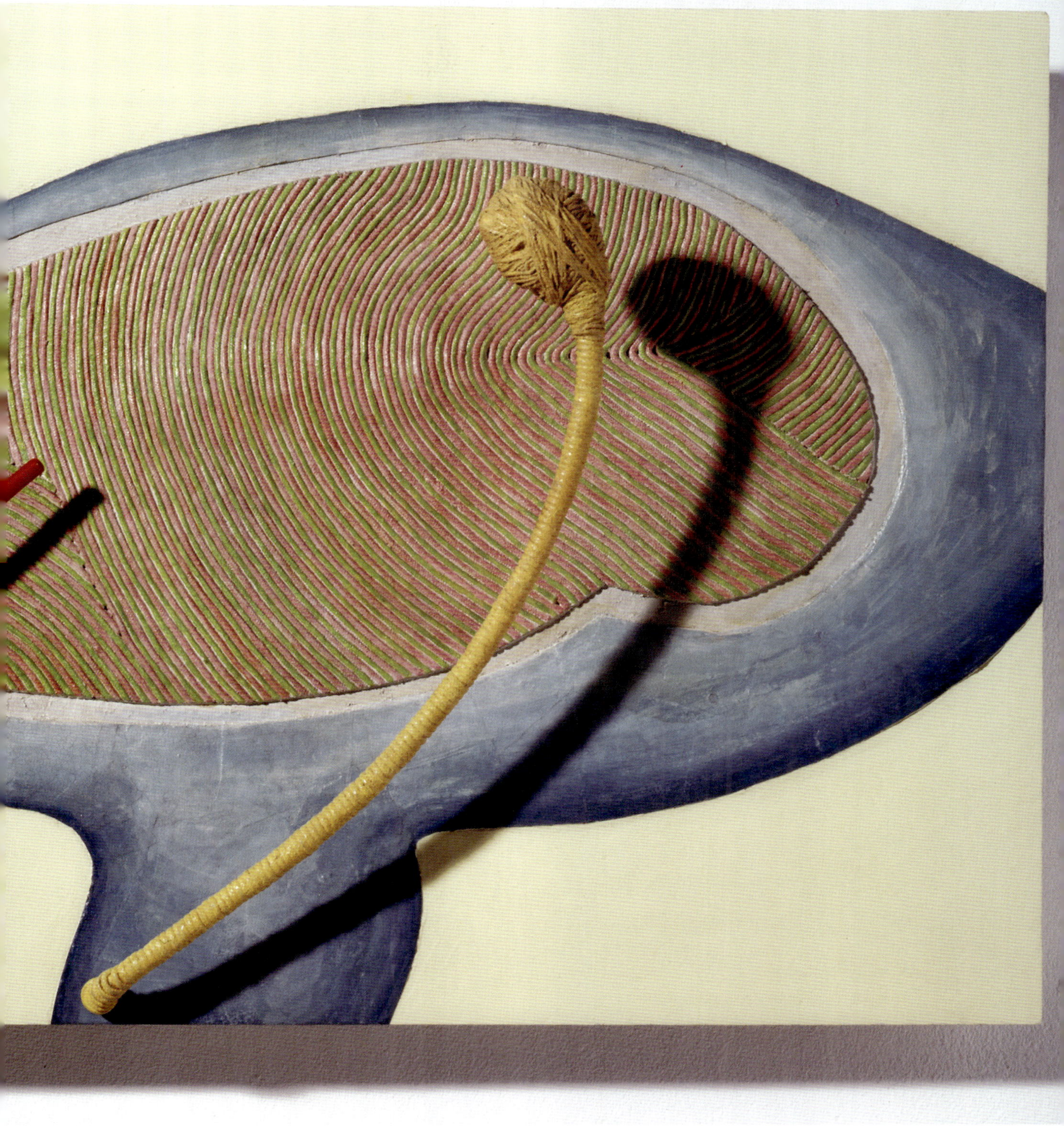

Legs of a Walking Ball, 1965

Oomamaboomba, 1965

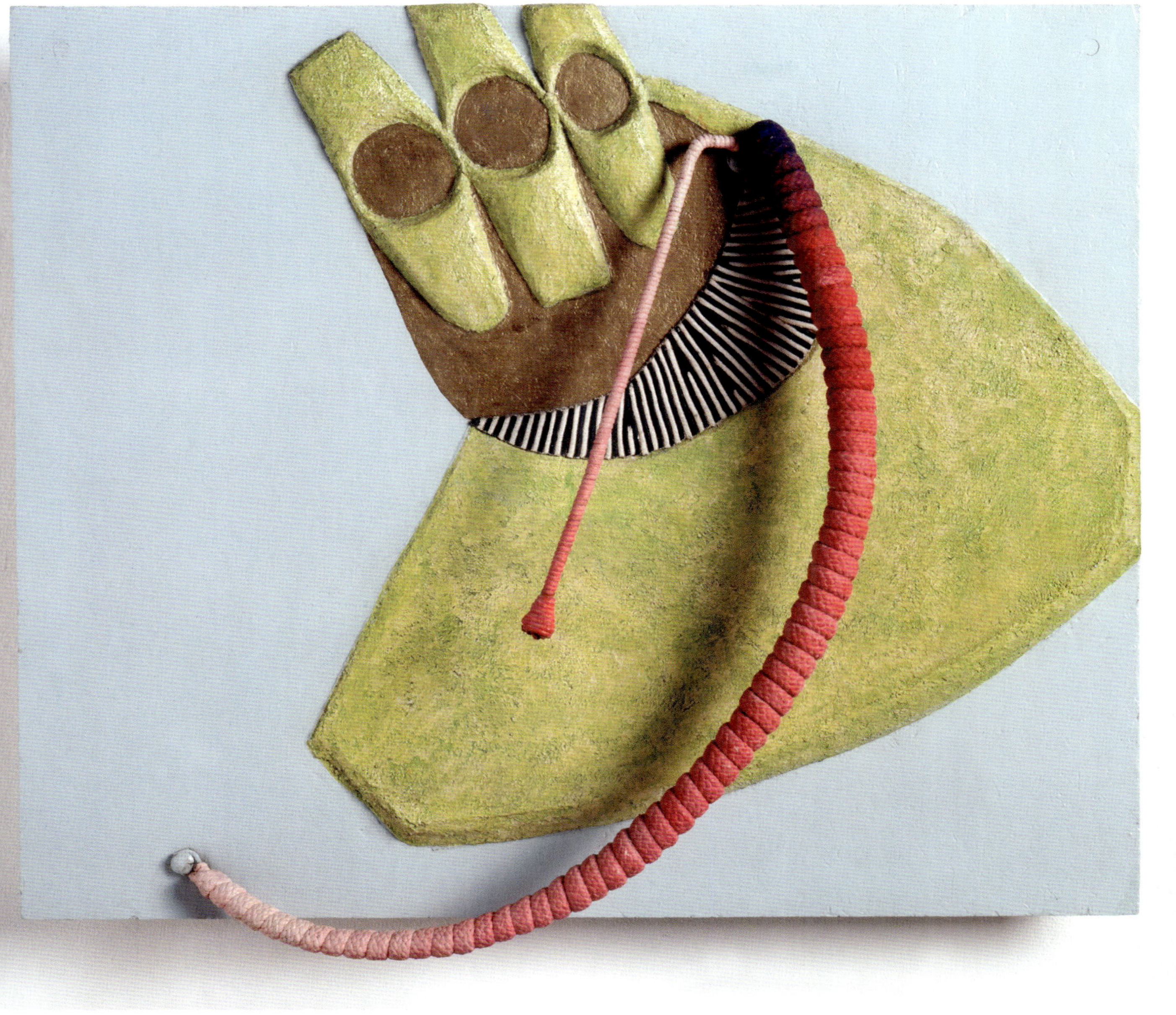

RACHEL HAIDU

LAUGHTER

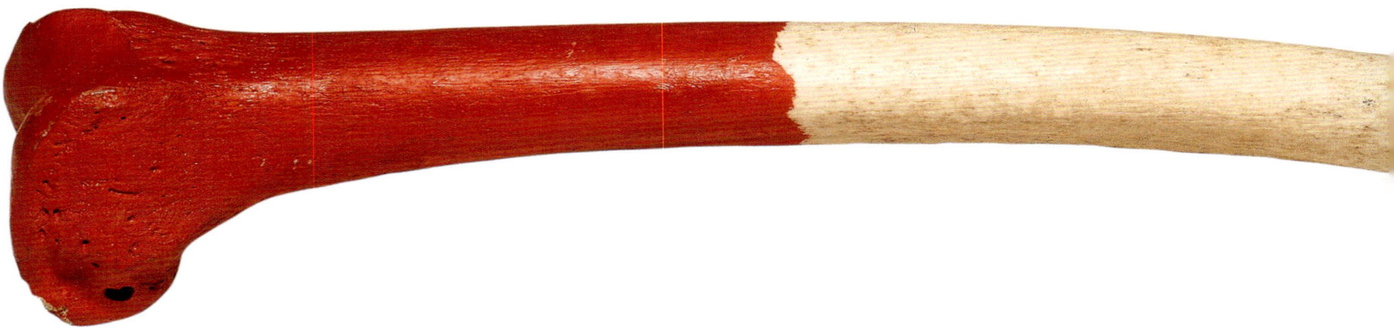

In 1965 Marcel Broodthaers acquired a femur, painted it with the colors of the Belgian flag, and entitled it *Fémur d'homme belge* for the purpose of artistic exhibition. In all its colorful ghoulishness, the object seems to set up Belgian identity as the target of a visual joke: the nation-state as skeleton, or perhaps a Belgian-style bone to be given to a dog. Or perhaps the target of the joke is not Belgium itself but something like *belgitude,* the recently-coined term designating "a sense of belonging to a no man's land, a country in the void that can only get out by privileging the imaginary."[1] Even if the term is new, it reflects an old understanding of the vacuum known as Belgian identity: as Charles Baudelaire wrote in the mid-1860s (thirty years after the state's founding): "There is no Belgian people, properly speaking" – but also, "A Belgian is his own hell."[2] It follows from such characterizations that the symbolic manifestation of a hollowed-out national identity – an identity in search of an entity – would be only as "real" as it is "over," and only as iconic as it is pathetic.

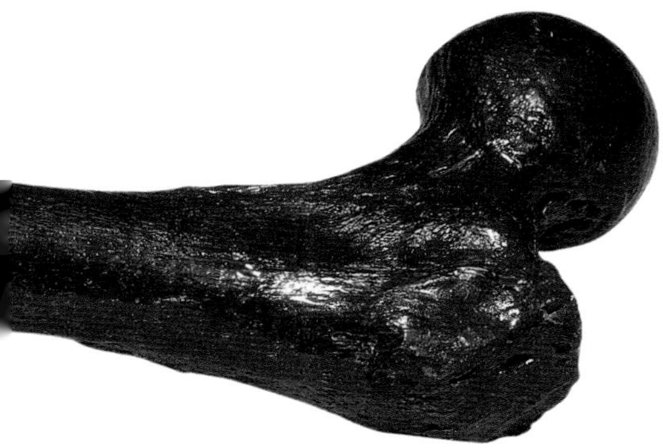

Broodthaers's *Fémur* is deeply engaged with the legacy of Magritte. It transforms a unique "relic" with an infinitely transferable and recognizable sign – a flag. What is more, the marriage of the somatic and the readymade happens instantaneously: the object is just paint on bone; it is quick, resisting deep contemplation or extended viewing. There are fertile painterly enterprises like Jasper Johns's *Flag* paintings, which convert the iconic flatness of the Stars and Stripes into depth and complexity; and then there is the *Fémur.* Taking the strongest bone in the human skeleton and draping it in unmixed, straight-from-the-can colors, Broodthaers arrests any sense of the potential infinity of artistic signification with a kind of flat "that's all, folks."

But why? Doesn't Belgium merit the kind of rich painterly endeavor that Johns's United States did ten years before? Is that the question here? In 1965 Broodthaers's tricolor signified a state that had just lost its claims to empire. But Belgium's claims to nationhood have always been peculiarly contingent, having been first drawn up by international treaty, then legitimated only as a seat of political "neutrality" in an eternally divided Europe. Always rooted in an administrative definition of statehood, always outside anything like even a fantasy of linguistic or cultural unity or coherence, Belgium's claims to nation-state identity can appear as a kind of joke. But the operation of the one-liner that Broodthaers exploits with the *Fémur* does more than merely tease or mock: it suggests, rather, that his national identity is one that cannot be said "straight." For what the joke-form articulates is that what it wants to say is actually unsayable – that for which jokes provide the necessary cover.

What remains unclear is whether the problematic nature of national identity as it is revealed in Broodthaers's work is peculiar to *certain* European states in the 1960s or whether it describes a more general condition for the expressibility of national identity in the postwar period. Since the publication of Benedict Anderson's *Imagined Communities* in 1983, it has become almost a truism to refer to nationality as a site of "imagined community." Anderson defines such a community as one that is not so much phantasmagorical or nonexistent

Marcel Broodthaers
Fémur de la femme francaise, 1965

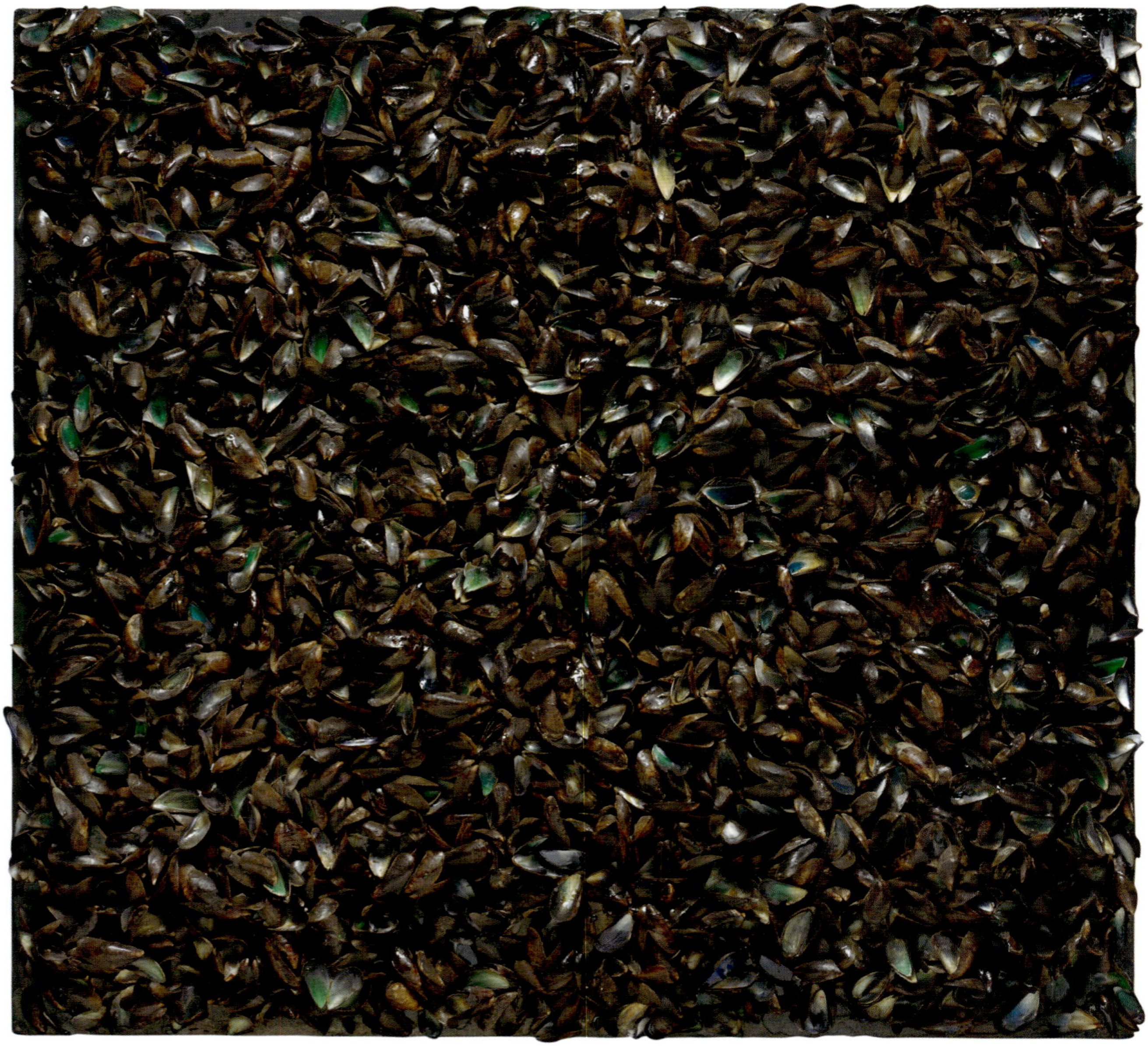

Marcel Broodthaers
Panneau de Moules (Panel of Mussels), 1966

as one that is consolidated through the disseminating, civilizing factors of print culture, vernacular languages-of-state, and correlative shifts in conceptions of time.[3] And, as the writing of James Joyce or John Dos Passos suggests, modernist literary form eventually constructs an audience that admits to the boundaries, dialects, and conventions of "imagined communities" as one of its founding conditions. In other words, the book-site through which such "imagined communities" come together eventually becomes reflexive, making the conditions of community-formation into the forms it identifies as its own. What I would like to investigate are the ways that the joke-form can retread and perhaps constructively *mess up* these footsteps. The project of discerning the reflexive forms of (prewar) literary modernism from those that I detect in jokelike (postwar) visual experiments demands a kind of cautious history that I can only suggest here, with Broodthaers as a natural point of departure, his investment in literary modernism one of the most striking and singular features of his work.

In the following pages I address the reflexive, joking forms that national identity takes in the work of Broodthaers and his younger, Italian colleague, Piero Manzoni. The two met in 1962, just before Manzoni's death and just before Broodthaers – poet, rare-books dealer, and museum docent – turned to artistic object-production in 1963. Most of Broodthaers's early works, produced from 1963 to 1966, exploit the "materials" that he named in the title of his 1966 exhibition at the Wide White Space Gallery: *Moules Œufs Frites Pots Charbon.* All share an *echt*-Belgianness that his audience – an audience still extremely local in the mid-1960s – would have instantly recognized. The most iconic of these are the mussel shells, whose qualities he venerated in "La Moule," a poem included in the 1964 volume, *Pense-Bête*: "This trickster has avoided the mold of society / She's cast herself in her very own / Others, look-alikes, share with her the anti-sea. / She is perfect."[4] In 1965, Broodthaers began placing emptied, glued mussel shells onto painted canvases, suggesting a kind of ultra "Belgian" response to the proclaimed universality of the monochrome.

Rosalind Krauss has pointed to the sea as "a special kind of medium for modernism, because of its perfect isolation, its detachment from the social, its sense of self-enclosure, and above all, its opening onto a visual plenitude that is somehow heightened and pure, both a limitless expanse and a sameness, flattening it into nothing, into the no-space of sensory deprivation."[5] In her description of the "visual plenitude" associated with the modernist canvas, Krauss gives us one sea: pure, limitless, and almost monotonously uniform ("the no-space of sensory deprivation"). Upturned and amassed on the *Panneaux* are messengers from another sea: the hidden world of mollusks and bottom feeders, those creatures that live on drifting debris and reproduce while attached to other objects. In the *Panneaux,* the shells of these creatures invade and encrust a particular kind of painting, whose uniformity and blankness ("limitless expanse and sameness") epitomize the alleged autonomy ("perfect isolation") of the art-object.[6] If mussels are self-regenerative yet utterly dependent, parasitical *in* their sovereignty, then they signify a special twist on "autonomy" that they transmit to the painted canvas, overturning the analogy between "sea" and "pure seeing."[7]

But the *Fémur*, that "joke," is not a painting, it is an object, as are most of Broodthaers's early works containing mussels, eggshells, coal, or *frites*. In some, mussel shells hold up the lids of casseroles, while in others eggshells appear like blank eyes staring out of old-fashioned cabinets and mirrors. When, in the early- to mid-1960s, Arman and Warhol were collecting metro tickets and soup cans, Broodthaers chose traditional *objets ménagers* – spindly chairs and enameled casseroles. These objects of the domestic everyday flaunt their histories as salable and resalable commodities, alluding to the obsessive, specular dimensions of the shop-window, and to Belgium's particular proclivity for the recycled and recyclable. Once Broodthaers's objects enter a gallery, the framework of reclaimed, repainted, and resold discards enlarges to include historical tropes, such as the surrealist *objet trouvé* and the Duchampian readymade. There, the possessive power of these historical tropes is (or appears to be) reduced to a simple pecuniary matter, initiating one aspect of Broodthaers's frequent satire of the art market.

Broodthaers was often called a "Belgian Pop artist" in the 1960s.[8] Given that Pop art gained its notoriety by "recycling" postwar popular culture, it faces a perverse obstacle in a culture that is itself built out of a recycled (prewar) material culture. Anticipating such absurd handles, his early works seem to ask what "Pop," an utterly American idiom, would look like in a country devotedly shopping at flea markets. More fundamentally, they ask what it would mean for an artist to translate an artistic idiom from one national context into another. Such a "translation" would have to admit to a kind of reflexivity of the sort I mention above, which builds its audience through recognition of the conventions of its "imagined community." After all, the artworks that precede the *Panneaux*, that break up lines of direct historical filiation through the framework of the discard, demonstrate the impossibility of a "Belgian Pop art." But as the *Panneaux* fit Broodthaers's use of mussel- and eggshells into the framework of the pristine modernist canvas, they infect its utterly "reflexive," pure space, making it only as self-determined as it is parasitical. The critique of modernism that they perform is both insistently local and perpetually laughing, for Broodthaers's audience would have to admit not only to its "Belgian" collective identity, but to the aesthetic handicap that identity imposes.

At the moment of their encounter in 1962, Piero Manzoni presented Broodthaers as a signed and certified work of art – a "joke"-like artwork if ever there was one.[9] But the more complex reading of Manzoni's work performs a strong critique of historical agency, and along with it a reconceptualization of authorship. Manzoni's work breaks with the kind of uninterruptible, uncorruptible physical immediacy, resolutely outside commodification, that served as the basis of a (largely American) model of authorship, as described in Robert Rauschenberg's retrospective discussion of his time at Black Mountain College in the early 1950s: "I could have gone on painting with my hands, I think, and making messes forever because I really loved painting. I guess the physicality of my personality was emerging, and so I had to paint with my hands. I couldn't stand a brush coming between me and the canvas. Naturally I cleaned my 'brushes,' which were my hands, on my clothes."[10] As radical as Rauschenberg's practice was – and as influential for emerging European artists – his model for authorship in the 1950s could not have been more neo-Pollockian or, by 1960, more obsolete, as Manzoni's practice would demonstrate.

In 1961, Manzoni began covering his canvas with unbaked bread rolls. The use of bakery goods radically modified Manzoni's two-year series of *Achromes*, "colorless," unpainted canvases. Instead of preparing his canvas with gesso or kaolin and then creasing, pleating, pockmarking, scraping, or pebbling it, he piled on tight, constipated rows of small, doughy buns, coated them in kaolin, and let them signify the "*achrome*" – the absence of color, but also the artist's own signature series. In place of the restraint inherent in working the canvas itself, Manzoni offers bread rolls, an outlandish accumulation and accretion that both hides and ornaments the canvas. The shift, more surprising than it at first appears, was wildly productive. Manzoni's earlier *Achromes* seem to demonstrate only the canvas's resilience to the artist's rude tests. When he pleated and bunched the canvas, he emphasized its suppleness; when he combined it with cotton wadding stitched together in quilt fashion, he reiterated the grid structure fundamental to modernist painting. But when he introduces *pane* onto the surface of his canvas, this testing abruptly ends. From the moment of that initial Freudian joke, the *Achromes* become noticeably looser, weirder, perverse, and even, at times, explicitly flamboyant: the cotton wadding of 1960 is treated in lurid cobalt chloride in 1961, while backgrounds are suddenly painted scarlet, vivid blue, and chartreuse, enhancing the snowy, whiskery fiberglass fur or poodle-like pelts attached to the canvas. The qualitative shift that took place in 1961 with the introduction of little bread rolls consists precisely in covering up the canvas's materiality. At last, the *Achrome* provides a means of perverting – rather than proving – the canvas's resilience. In this way Manzoni sets up a kind of antiheroics of painting that is uniquely capable of unraveling the painting's authority. By performing his antiheroics with a banal stuff of daily life – dough – he drags his canvas down into something even below the quotidian.

Bread rolls are by no means merely or even primarily "Italian"; they do not signify nationality in a manner comparable to Broodthaers's *Moules Œufs Frites Pots Charbon* series. Manzoni's obsession with the commodification of the somatic has to be read against Italy's postwar struggle for solvency and economic independence. It is an obsession that extends well beyond the *Achrome.* In works such as *Fiato d'artista* (*Artist's Breath*: deflated balloons pinned to wood panels bearing on a lead seal the title of the work and the artist's name), *Merda d'artista* (carefully labeled tins of "artist's shit"), and *Uova con impronta* (signed and dated boxes for eggs that bear the artist's thumbprint), Manzoni continually fabricates art out of packaging emptiness and relates that commodified emptiness to the body. Objects of no value – empty eggshells, deflated balloons, shit – signify worthlessness but also extend the body into the art object and its packaging. Yet it is the artist's "extended" body as a packaging and labeling

system that creates the self-sustaining, value-generating system of distribution. In this, Manzoni does more than point to art as something whose value rests in its immateriality; he parodies the notion of the commodity system as an "unnatural" evil. Even the infinitely generative capacity of the commodity merely augments the human, the corporeal, the organic.

The parodic element in Manzoni's work becomes even sharper when read against "national" goals. In the late 1950s, Italy attempted to shift from an agrarian economy to the competitive late-industrial global arena. Manzoni's work, pointing out the "emptiness" of packaging, appears almost obscenely antinationalist. Arguably, the bread roll *Achromes* are the most forceful of these parodies inasmuch as they evoke a system of manual production that has been subjected to industrial standards of uniformity and efficiency. On the painter's canvas, where manual skill is normally displayed, Manzoni gives us manual production that simulates industrial production. What is more, the gridded uniformity and "perfection" of his bread rolls knot together the anality of obsessive kneading and the orality of consumption.

Manzoni, much like Broodthaers, was not making antinationalist work: he made work that jokes. A joke's success, as Freud explains, lies in its ability to protect itself from being taken "seriously," as if being said "straight." This is why jokes cannot be explained without losing their funniness. But while Freud defines a joke's meaning as lying in its *form,* he acknowledges the way in which the nature of the joke handicaps the jokester: "It seems as though...the *other* person has the decision passed over to him on whether the joke-work has succeeded in its task – as though the self did not feel certain on its judgment on the point" (italics added).[11] There is, in joke-telling, an excess of the dialogic. But it is humor that works to undermine the traditional vectors of sense-making: "I mean x" is emptied from language itself, so that another meaning, "y," can operate, *without* having been authorized by "I." "I" gets off scot-free (his reputation as a joke-teller enhanced), while the audience is exactly what is named by the phrase "in on the joke." The decision that is passed over to a second person as to whether a joke is "funny" robs the joker of his sovereignty.

But besides being "in on it," the audience is formed by the joke: the audience is comprised of whatever individual or collective gets the joke's meaning. When Henri Bergson set out to define laughter (just six years after Freud's *Jokes and Their Relation to the Unconscious*), he too argued that it "appears to stand in need of an echo.... Our laughter is always the laughter of a group." But he soon qualified the makeup of that group: laughter's "secret freemasonry, or even complicity" turns out to mean that we laugh only "with other laughers, real *or imaginary*" (italics added).[12] There is nothing sacred or necessary about the *reality* of laughter's community. According to Bergson, it can just as well be *imaginary.* What counts is that the community exists as a set of boundaries in the mind of the subject; that it creates its own rules of exclusion and inclusion. To make his point, Bergson resorted to this anecdote: "A man who was once asked why he did not weep at a sermon, when everybody else was shedding tears,

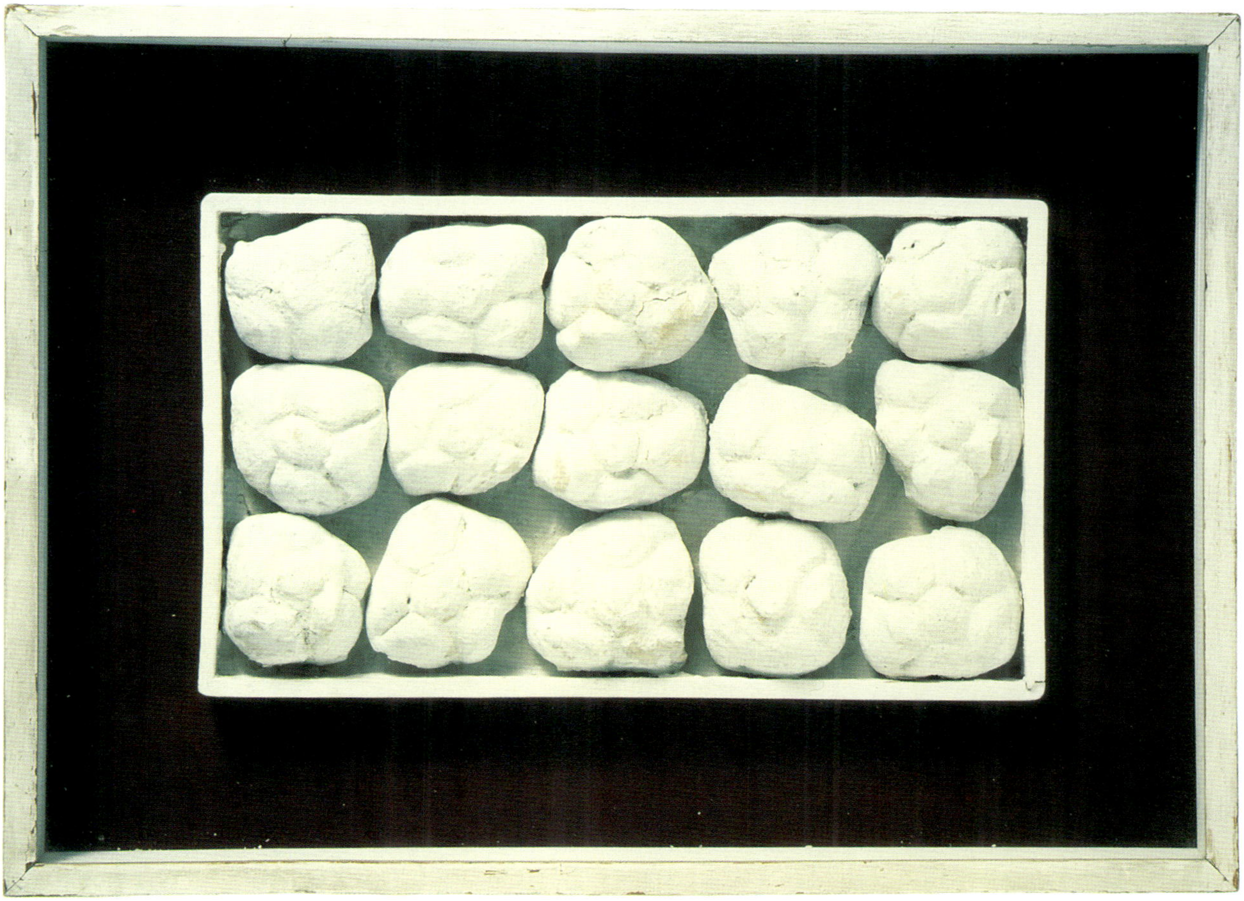

Piero Manzoni
Achrome, 1962

replied 'I don't belong to the parish!' What that man thought of tears would be still more true of laughter."[13] What counts in Bergson's anecdote is that he does not describe merely ephemeral groups: laughter can suggest even a community as formal as that of a parish.

The resurgence of comic structures in artworks of the 1960s need not be regarded as innocently playful or defensive, though they might be that as well. They represent Belgianness and Italianness rather straightforwardly, and yet also jokingly. The paradox leads to several hypotheses. One is that the construction of national identity in postwar Europe, especially in the 1950s and 1960s, was a nervous process. As even the notion of a local material culture was being voided by the increasingly global face of postwar consumption, Broodthaers's and Manzoni's work reacts almost like mimetic echoes. They riff on "emptiness" in a way that parodies the celebration of the supposedly "heroic and original" – universal and internationalist, in modernist art. Yet even as they maintain the blankness of the canvas or the regularity of its grid, they also insist on a notion of the national become fatuous, corny, all-but-obsolete. The send-up of emptiness and the send-up of the national turn out to be mutually dependent, even entwined. The "snapshots" of material culture in Broodthaers's and Manzoni's works – the artisanal backwardness of Broodthaers's *objets ménagers* or the clichés invoked by his *moules-frites*; Manzoni's obsessively kneaded and gridded *pane* – show off the hackneyed quality of their signifiers and the obsolescence of what they signify. The "national" becomes empty, and "emptiness" becomes packaging. It falls to Manzoni to underscore the unbearable truth of packaging – the manner in which it is merely an extension of our most bodily selves.

And it falls to Broodthaers to refine the form peculiar to jokes. Joking relieves the artist of sovereign responsibility for a work's meaning by extending that responsibility to an "imagined community." To laugh, as Bergson writes, the group has to be "real or imaginary": even if the entity is unreal, it must exist in the imaginary of the laughers. A deadpan work like the *Fémur* calls this contingent, utterly unreal group into being, "as though the self did not feel certain on its judgment." It *waits* for this group to assemble in order to come into being; as with a joke, the audience's recognition is necessary for the *Fémur* to function as a work of art. Yet there is little, if anything, that is anticipatory about Broodthaers's wooden chairs and iron casseroles. These objects are antiquated, bygone. They represent a pastness to the identities they configure, and they transmit that pastness to the "group" they name. They anticipate collectivity, *imagine* it, but they also undermine it by suggesting that the "unity" to which one might now belong has already passed by.

The author would like to thank Maria Gilissen and Marie-Puck Broodthaers for their assistance with this text.

NOTES

1 Jean-Pierre Stroobants, "La Belgique, genie du rêve et de la derision," *Le Monde*, March 7, 2005.

2 Charles Baudelaire, "Divertissements Belges," in *Fusées. Mon cœur mis à nu. La Belgique déshabillée*, ed. André Guyaux (Paris: Gallimard, 1975–86), 234, 278.

3 "Nothing perhaps more precipitated this search [for 'a new way of linking fraternity, power and time meaningfully together'], nor made it more fruitful, than print-capitalism, which made it possible for rapidly growing numbers of people to think about themselves, and to relate themselves to others, in profoundly new ways." Benedict Anderson, *Imagined Communities: Reflections on the Origin and Spread of Nationalism*, rev. ed. (London and New York: Verso, 1991), 36.

4 This poem, "La Moule," forms the basis of Jaleh Mansoor's masterly essay, "Piero Manzoni: 'We Want to Organicize Disintegration,'" *October* 95 (Winter 2001): 29–54. My own reflections here owe everything to years of friendship, collaboration, and art-viewing with Jaleh.

5 Rosalind E. Krauss, *The Optical Unconscious* (Cambridge: The MIT Press, 1993), 2.

6 The *egg*shells that Broodthaers spreads on canvases during this period fare no better. Thanks to their smoothly monochromatic, neutral coverings, eggs are perhaps nature's other "special kind of medium for modernism." But once cracked, drained, and glued to canvas, Broodthaers's eggs are dispossessed of precisely those qualities that Krauss associates with the sea and with modernism—"perfect isolation…sense of self-enclosure…plenitude that is somehow heightened and pure." If all those qualities can be imputed to *whole* eggs—as I believe that they are in *Uovo con impronta*, the carefully packaged eggs with thumbprints that Manzoni made in 1960, and in the related 1960s performances in which Manzoni's art audiences ingested the signed, and boiled, eggs that the artist offered to them (see Anna Costantini, "Piero Manzoni in Context, 1933–63," in *Piero Manzoni*, ed. Germano Celant [London: Serpentine Gallery; and Milan: Edizioni Charta, 1998], 270–71)—then their cracked and useless shells in Broodthaers's works of the mid-1960s deduct those very qualities from the canvases they decorate.

7 I am particularly grateful to Maria Gilissen for her suggestions on this point.

8 See the first few sentences of the interview by Jean-Michel Vlaeminckx, "Entretien avec Marcel Broodthaers," in *Degré Zero* 1 (Brussels, 1965): "Marcel Broodthaers, vous êtes Belge. Vous faites du Pop….Quelles sont, d'après vous, les origines du pop'art?"

9 On February 25, 1962, Manzoni signed Broodthaers, making him a *Sculture viventi (Living Sculpture)*, a transformation authenticated by Manzoni's "Certificate of Authenticity No. 71." See Michael Compton, "In Praise of the Subject," in *Marcel Broodthaers*, ed. Marge Goldwater (Minneapolis: Walker Art Center, 1991), 21.

10 Barbara Rose, *Robert Rauschenberg* (New York: Vintage Books, 1987), 23, cited in Helen Molesworth, "Before Bed," in *October* 63 (1993). Jacques Charlier has mentioned in an interview (2001) that Rauschenberg was one of the most influential artists among those whose works Broodthaers encountered in the mid-1960s.

11 Sigmund Freud, "Jokes and Their Relation to the Unconscious" (1905). In *Sigmund Freud*, Standard Edition, ed. and trans. James Strachey (New York: W. W. Norton, 1960), 176.

12 Henri Bergson, *Laughter: An Essay on the Meaning of the Comic*, trans. Cloudesley Brereton and Fred Rothwell (Copenhagen and Los Angeles: Green Integer Books, 1999), 12 (first published by Macmillan and Co. [London], 1911).

13 Ibid., 11–12.

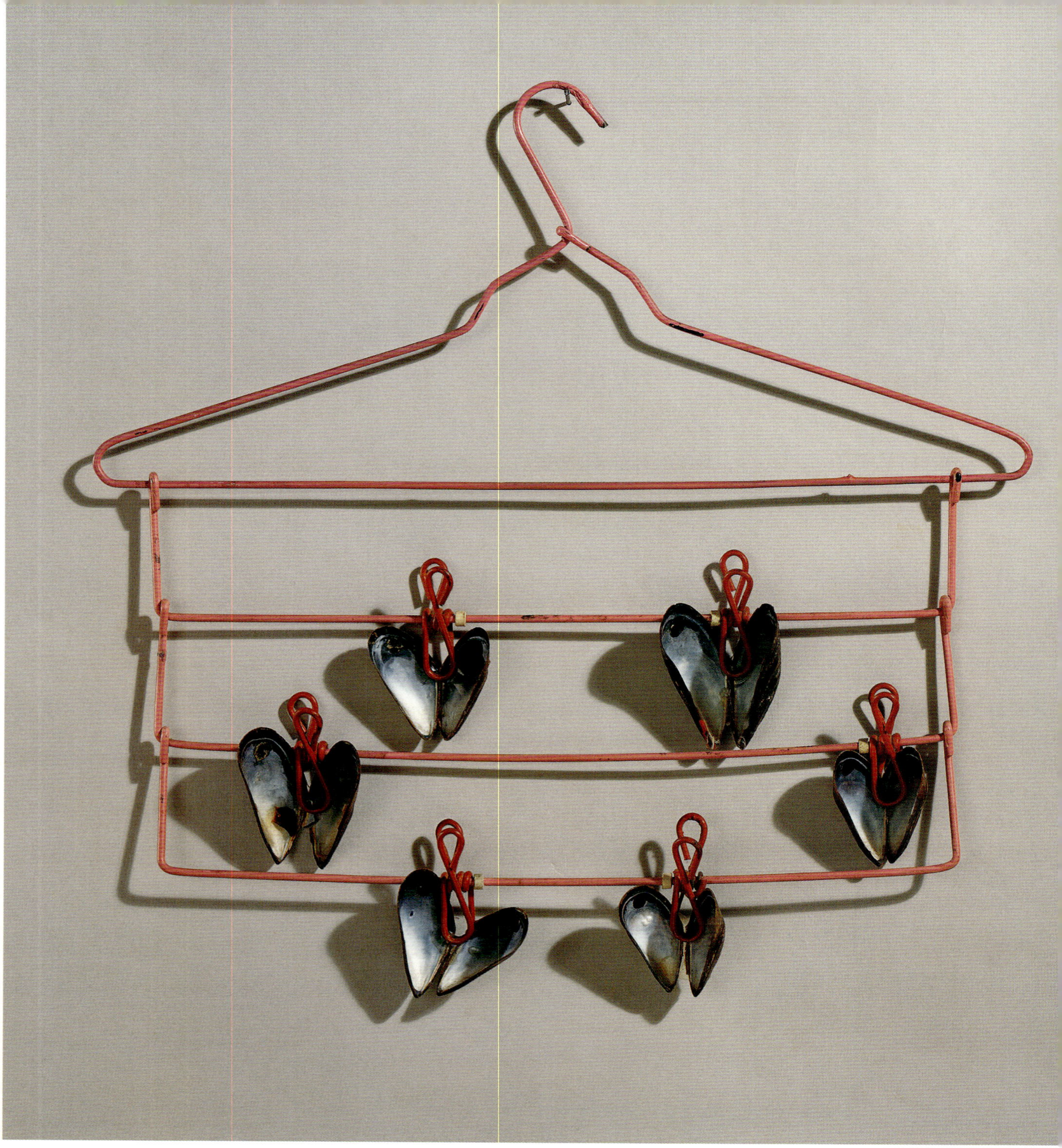

MARCEL BROODTHAERS 1924–1976

Marcel Broodthaers was first, if perhaps not foremost, a poet. Until the last twelve years of his life, poetry was his principal avocation, though one that had earned him very little critical attention and even less money. His career as a visual artist began only in 1964, when he received his first solo exhibition, at the Galerie Saint-Laurent in Brussels. A fourth book of his poetry, *Pense-Bête*,[1] had appeared earlier that year, like its predecessors finding little audience beyond a small circle of friends and acquaintances. Shortly thereafter, as Broodthaers stated in the announcement for the Galerie Saint-Laurent exhibition, the "idea of inventing something insincere finally crossed my mind, and I set to work at once."[2]

The first of these "insincere" visual objects, itself called *Pense-Bête*, consisted of fifty unsold copies of Broodthaers's book, still partially wrapped in paper and embedded in a mound of plaster. Although the plaster rendered the poems inside almost unreadable, one of them in particular – "La Moule" – seems crucial to an understanding of Broodthaers's visual work:

La Moule
Cette roublarde a évité le moule
de la société.
Elle s'est coulée dans le sien propre.
D'autres, ressemblantes, partagent avec
elle l'anti-mer.
Elle est parfaite.

The Mussel
This clever thing avoided society's mold.
She has cast herself in her very own.
Others, look-alikes, share with her the
anti-sea.
She's perfect.

The poem turns on the double sense of *"moule,"* the feminine form of which designates a mussel, while the masculine refers to a cast or mold – in this case, society's, which imposes on the individual a strict conformity. The mussel, then, is that rare creature that secretes her own mold. She is autonomous, the poem suggests, at once self-determining and self-framing. In that sense she represents the ideal not only of bourgeois subjectivity but also of the modernist work of art. Of course, "La Moule" itself was cast in plaster for that first exhibition; and Broodthaers, recalling the event later, confessed his surprise that no one who saw the work seemed inquisitive about the text inside.[3] It was as if "La Moule" and the other poems in *Pense-Bête* had become pure exteriority – all cover (or shell) and nothing more.

Broodthaers's professed surprise at the object's reception resonates with comments he made following the opening, two years earlier, of an exhibition of Piero Manzoni's work at the Palais des Beaux-Arts in Brussels. There Broodthaers had encountered not only Manzoni's *Achromes* and the tins of *Merda d'artista* (*Artist's Shit*), but also Manzoni himself. Evidently drawn to Broodthaers, Manzoni had penned his signature directly on the Belgian poet, then issued a certificate of authenticity declaring him a work of art. In many ways the moment reads as a concrete example of the process that Marx described as reification, for Manzoni's gesture literally reconfigured social relations as relations between and among commodities. Having been declared a work of art on a par with, say, the *Merda d'artista* (whose price was pegged to its weight in gold), Broodthaers realized for the first time, he said, the distance that separates the poem from a material work of "fine art." That distance, he added, was roughly the one separating the "value of the message" from the "notion of the message as merchandise alone."[4]

Clearly it was in relation to the world of merchandise that many of Broodthaers's early objects were situated: the empty mussel shells hung by clothespins from a hanger, like so many off-the-rack garments; the hollowed-out eggshells arranged in neat rows against a red cloth ground; or the open valise, displaying its wares, a seemingly picked-over selection of stenciled black letters. If this last object is perhaps most reminiscent of Duchamp, the other two are especially characteristic of Broodthaers, for whom shells (whether mussel or egg) became almost a medium of their own. The interest of those shells plainly lies in the fact that they suggest simultaneously self-determination and reification – both *la* and *le moule*.

In that sense, Broodthaers's early "shell" pieces might be seen as continuous with his so-called Musée d'Art Moderne installations, which he "administered" from 1968 until his death in 1976. As Benjamin Buchloh has argued, Broodthaers's interventions presented the museum as a normalizing, disciplinary institution even as they valorized it as one of the few parts of the bourgeois public sphere that, historically, had been relatively autonomous, operating outside the forces of commercialization.[5] During a period when the ambition of much of the avant-garde was to dismantle the institution of the museum, and thereby to expose the notion of the autonomous work of art as delusional fantasy, Broodthaers seemed more concerned to show that such a dismantling was part and parcel of the rise to domination of the culture industry.

In the same way, the commercial cooking pots overflowing with empty mussel shells, such as the paint-splattered *Moules Sauce Blanche* in *Part Object Part Sculpture,* seem both caught up in and resistant to the tide of commodity culture. The mussels are so many look-alikes (*ressemblantes*), their claims to individuality resting solely on their shared opposition to that potentially engulfing "sea" (*l'anti-mer*). The catalogue *Moules Œufs Frites Pots Charbon, 1966*, that accompanied an exhibition in Antwerp in which some of these works were shown included a poem by Broodthaers that gave voice to just these concerns. Entitled "Rhetoric," it sputters out its opening lines, the repetition of pronouns suggesting a subjectivity hardening into mere object:

Me I say I Me I say I
The King of the Mussels...

LISA FLORMAN

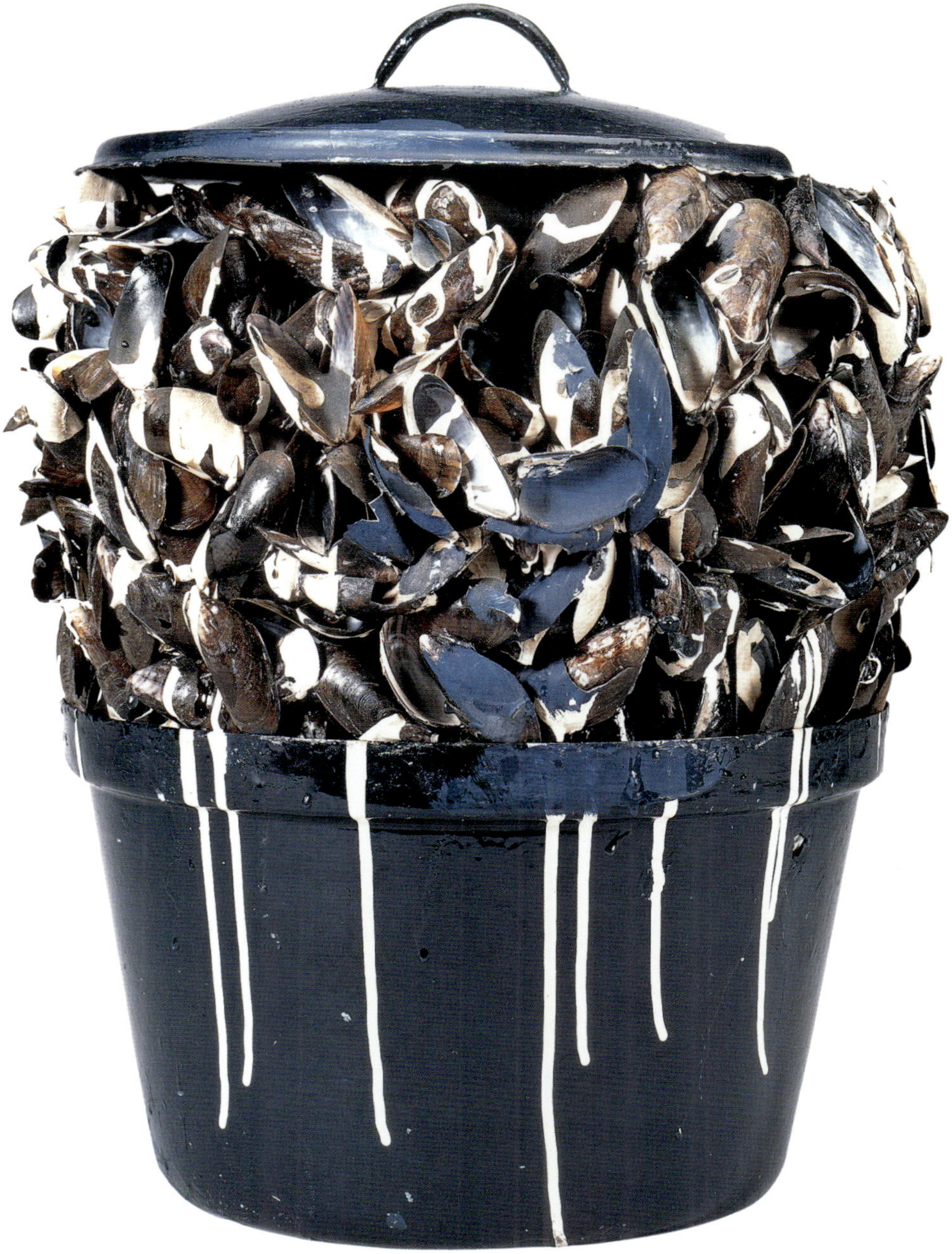

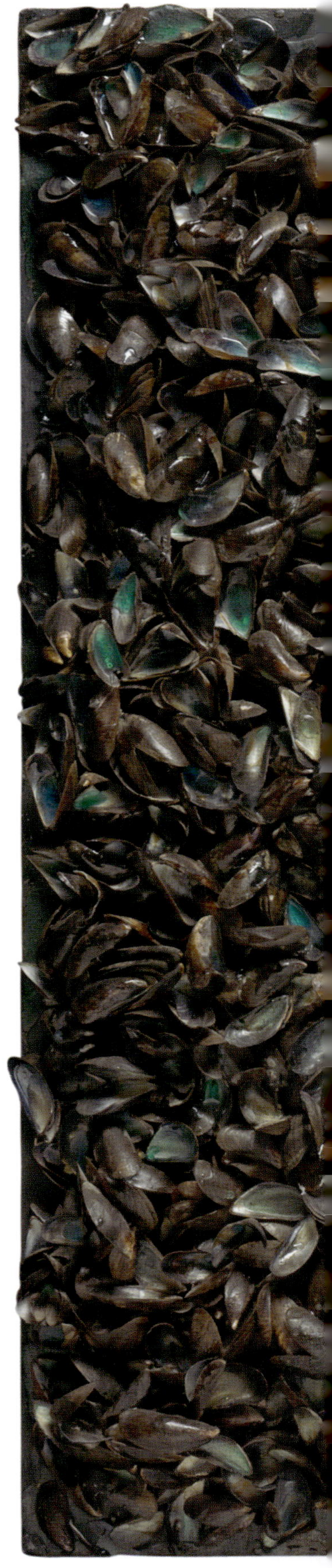

previous spread: left **Portemanteau aux Moules** (Coat Hanger with Mussels), 1965

previous spread: right **Moules Sauce Blanche** (Mussels with White Sauce), 1967

right **Panneau de Moules** (Panel of Mussels), 1966

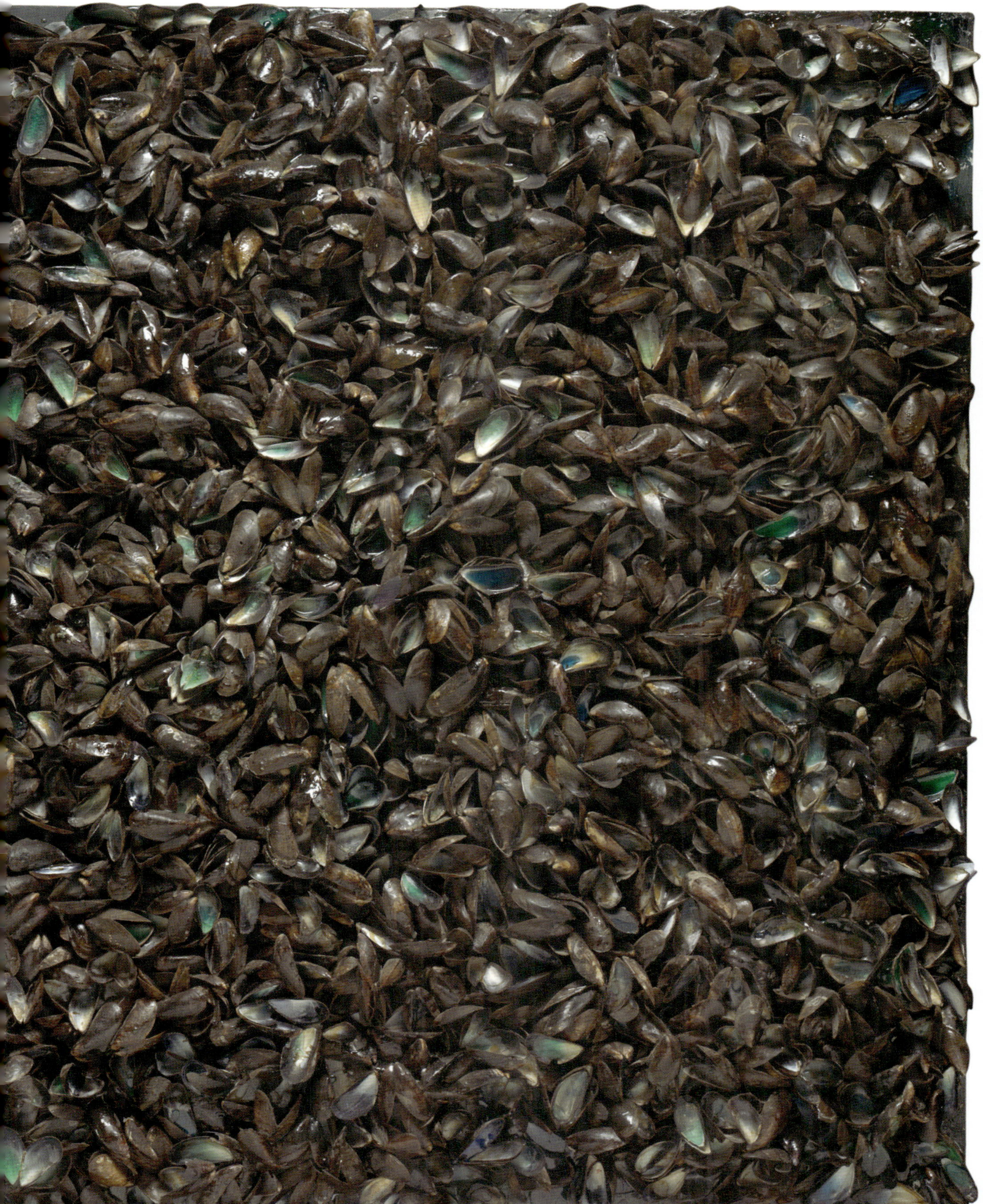

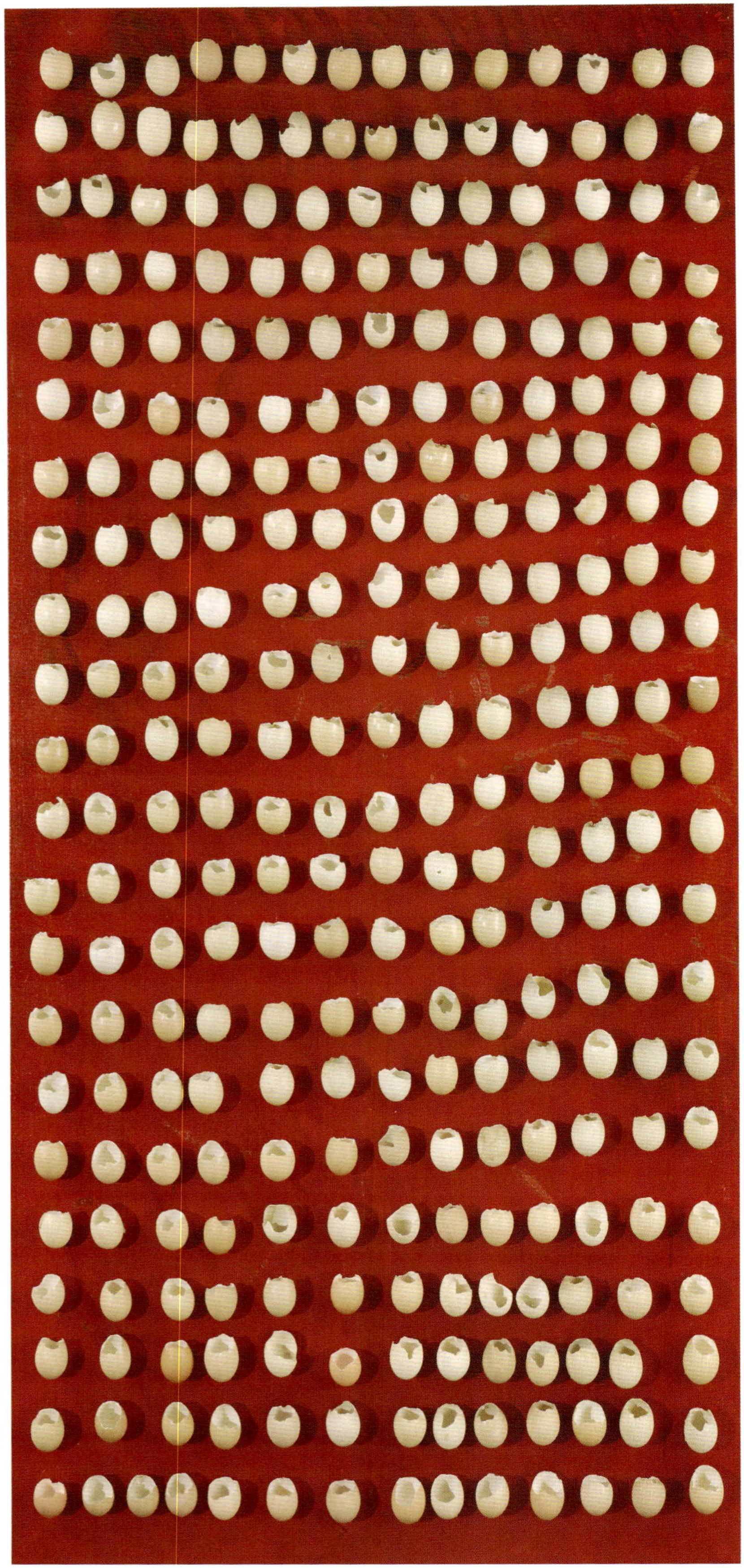

289 Coquilles d'oeufs, 1966

right **Grande Casserole de Moules** (Large Casserole of Mussels), 1966

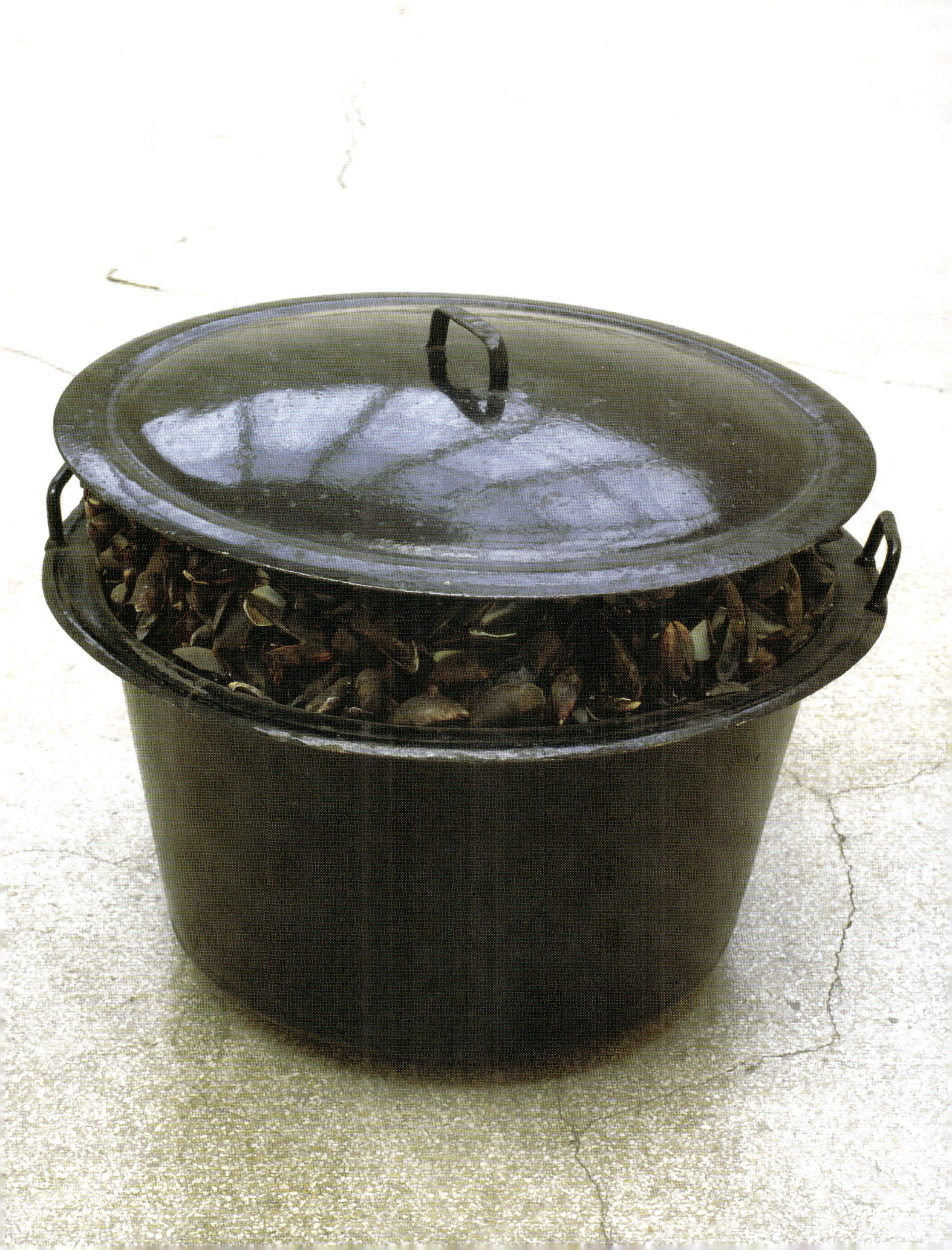

Valise avec Alphabet
(Suitcase with Alphabet), 1973

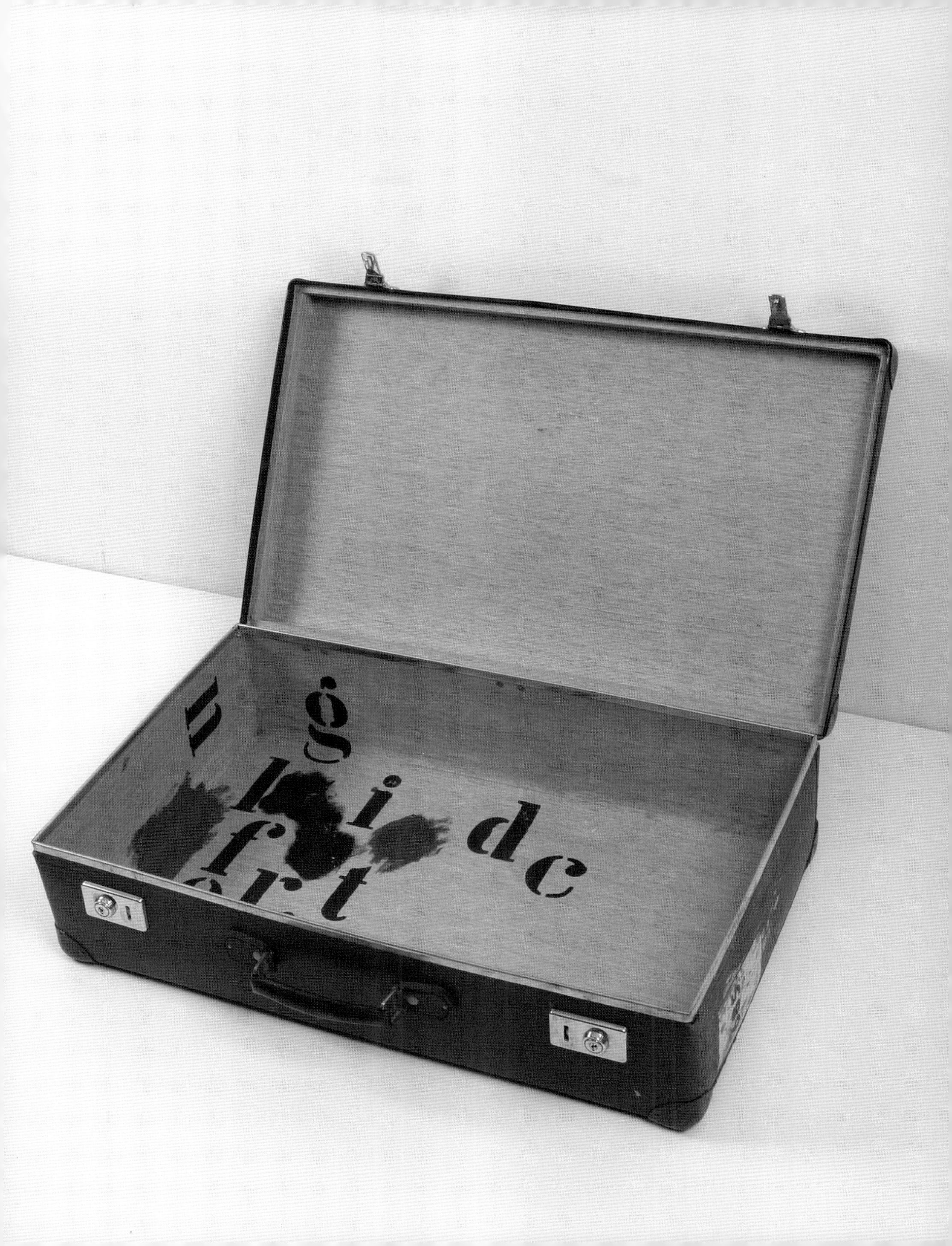

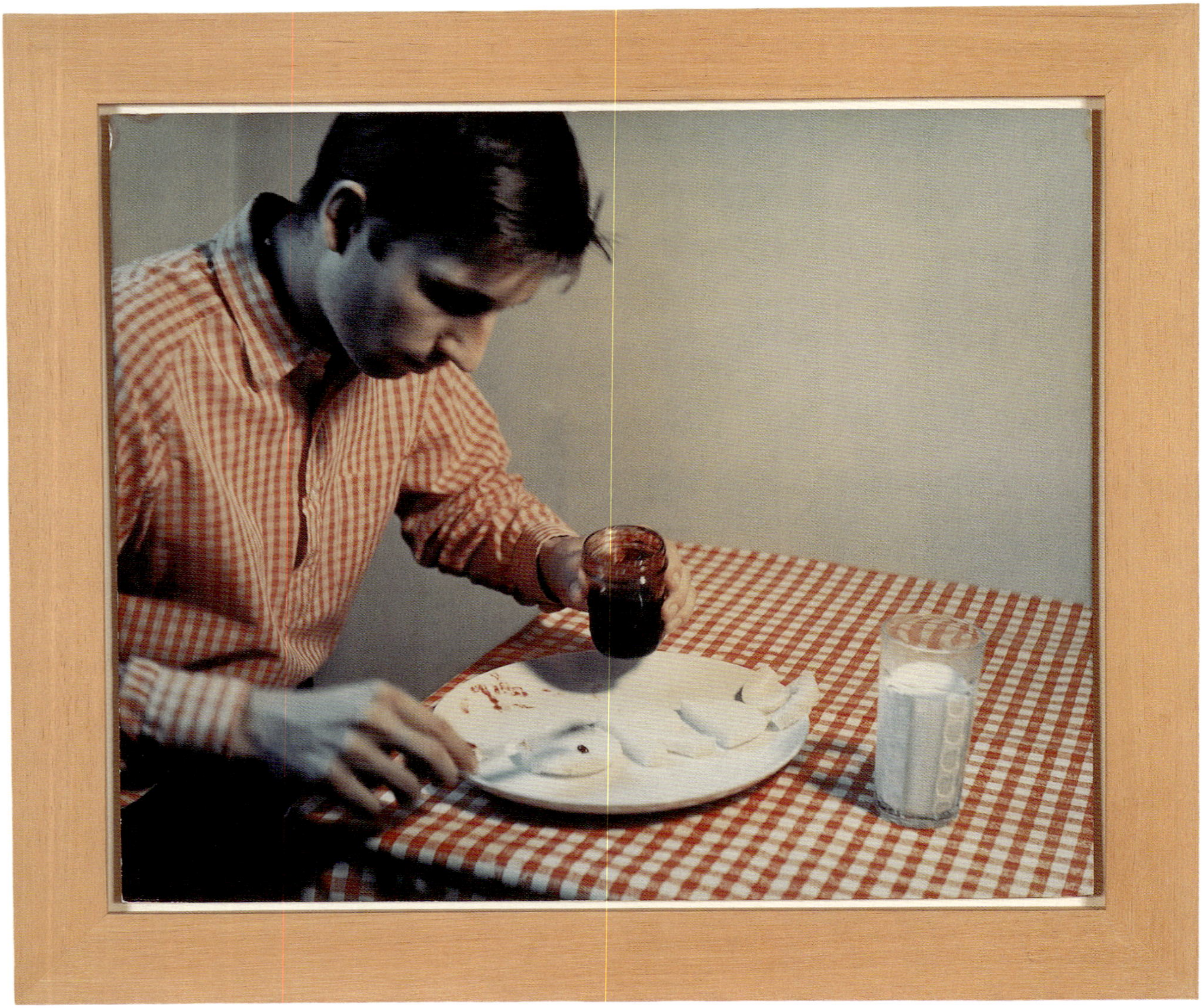

BRUCE NAUMAN 1941–

Bruce Nauman may have done more to stretch the boundaries of sculpture than any other artist of his generation. He has used the human body, particularly his own, as the medium of sculpture, and indeed of art in general. Speaking about this phenomenon, he said: "If you can manipulate clay and end up with art, you can manipulate yourself as well. It has to do with using the body as a tool, an object to manipulate."[1] Nauman's conflation of the body with an object is telling because it speaks directly to the porosity between bodies and things that is predominant in the work presented in *Part Object Part Sculpture*.

Nauman's manipulation of the body can also be said to produce a kind of readymade – a thing that exists in the world, both made by others and similar to others. The experience of the "body as readymade" in Nauman's work is marked by a strong sense that one inherits and inhabits one's body as a kind of alien apparatus. Such is the effect of one of Nauman's early works, *Wall-Floor Positions* (1968), in which he methodically used his body to delineate the difference between it and the floor and the wall. His physical contortions suggest nothing less than a profound lack of ease with "his" body: his body is both his and not his simultaneously. Treating all three elements as equal – wall, floor, and body – Nauman established one of his oeuvre's central terms, the co-equivalence of bodies and objects and bodies and space.

Nauman's examination of his body continued in other ways, notably through the act of casting. In *From Hand to Mouth* (1967) and *Henry Moore Bound to Fail (back view)* (1967), he imagines the human body as a site of repetition and reproduction by offering it, somewhat ironically, as the "original" artistic mold. And yet Nauman's molds are not simple machines for generating copies. They are either a fragment, as in *From Hand to Mouth*, or are bound to a kind of aesthetic failure, as in *Henry Moore Bound to Fail*. Neal Benezra has observed that Nauman's early casts were informed by Jasper Johns, whose *Target with Plaster Casts* (1955) explored the tension and reciprocity between the fragmented body and the readymade sign of a target.[2] To see Nauman within Johns's lineage is to reveal his primary concern with the workings of relief sculpture, in which the wall and the floor are equally available for sculptural activity. Indeed what binds them as sculptural properties is the body of the viewer/participant–an equivalence Nauman makes between the three in his early work – who is potentially made aware of his or her own "readymade" nature.

Just as our bodies are given to us as so many readymades, so too language precedes and molds us as well. Nauman's titles often play with puns or colloquialisms in ways that dramatize the relationships between the visual, the linguistic, and the bodily. Nauman understands, perhaps more acutely than many of his Conceptual contemporaries, that language and the body are not separate but are radically intertwined. In this regard, his work extends this underwritten aspect of Duchamp's oeuvre.[3]

Eleven Color Photographs (1966–1967/1970) is Nauman's most concise rendering of Duchamp's impact on his work. Each photograph shows Nauman working through a sculptural, linguistic, and bodily dilemma that often directly addresses the legacy of Duchamp. In this most explicit image, "Self Portrait as a Fountain," Nauman uses his body to mimic the upended urinal that had become the most famous of Duchamp's readymades. Here Nauman understands the implicit bodily humor that Duchamp's *Fountain* offered, with all its various inversions, not least of which is the substitution of water for urine and the performing body for the industrially produced object. This logic pervades "Drill Team," a photograph of five drill bits in a piece of wood. The visual and linguistic pun is amusing, but there is also a sense of unease at how easily one can substitute people for tools. If Duchamp used everyday objects as a playful means to trip up visitors to his studio (the effect of the readymades in the teens), then Nauman shows us the frustration and limits of the body in its triangulated relationship to language, objects, and space. Importantly, *Eleven Color Photographs* also articulates the crucial role of photography for Duchamp's readymades. Because almost all the original readymades were lost or misplaced, the photographs now stand in for the objects themselves. Intentional or not, Nauman initiated a complex relationship between photography and sculpture that would grow more dynamic and complex in later decades.

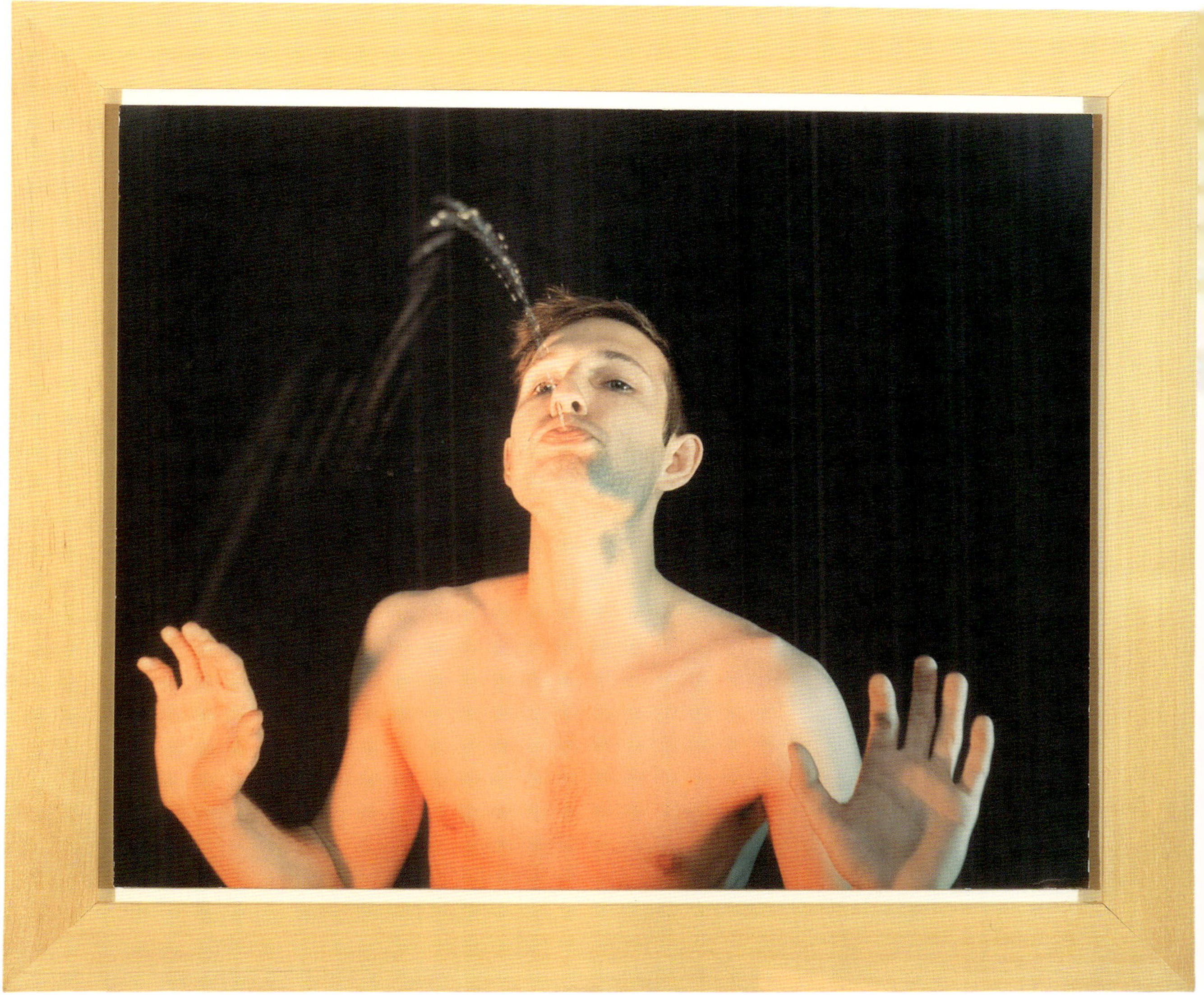

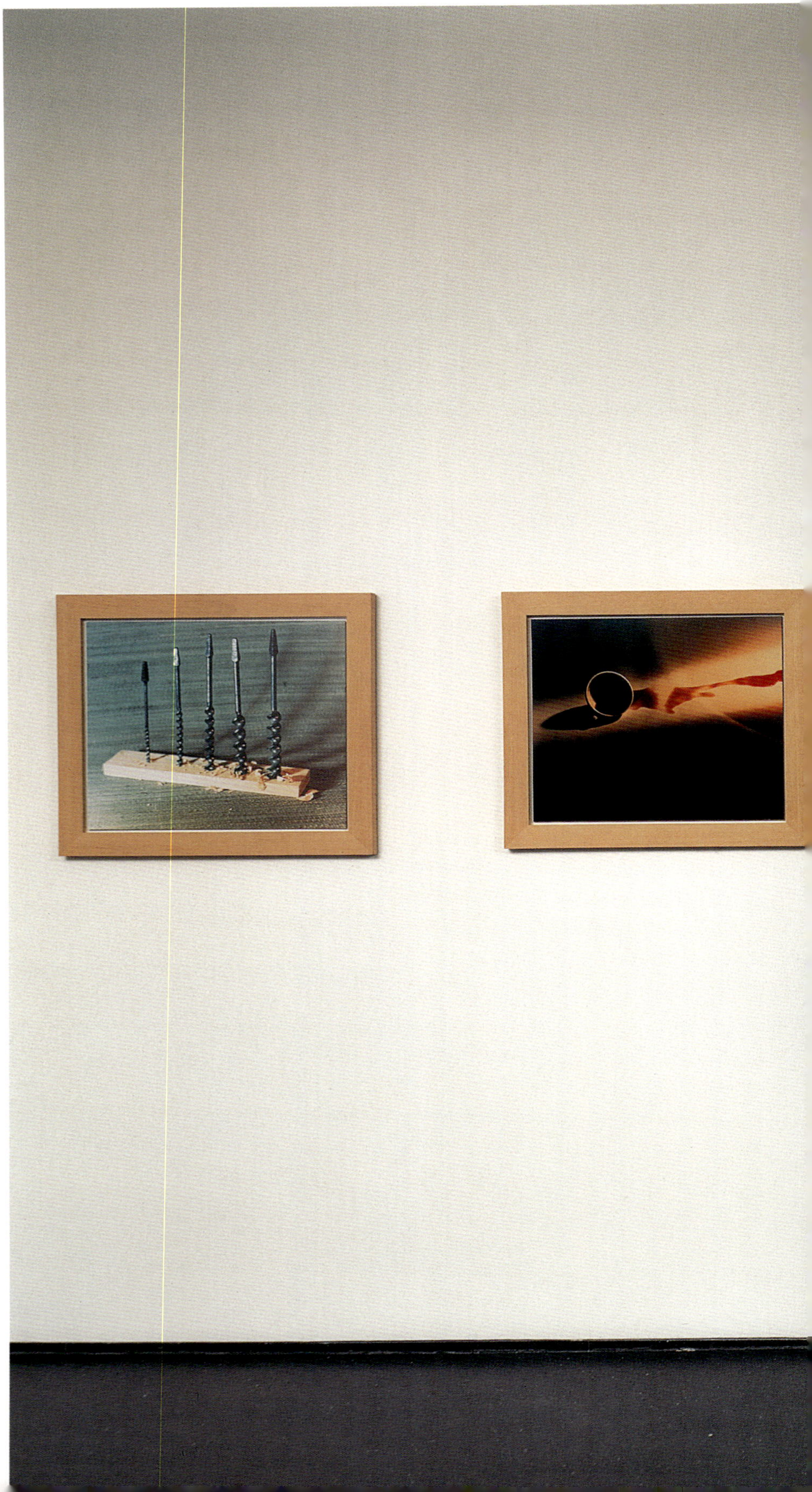

previous spread: left **Eating My Words** (from the portfolio **Eleven Color Photographs**), 1966–1967/1970

previous spread: right **Self-Portrait as a Fountain** (from the portfolio **Eleven Color Photographs**), 1966–1967/1970

right **Eleven Color Photographs**, 1966–1967/1970

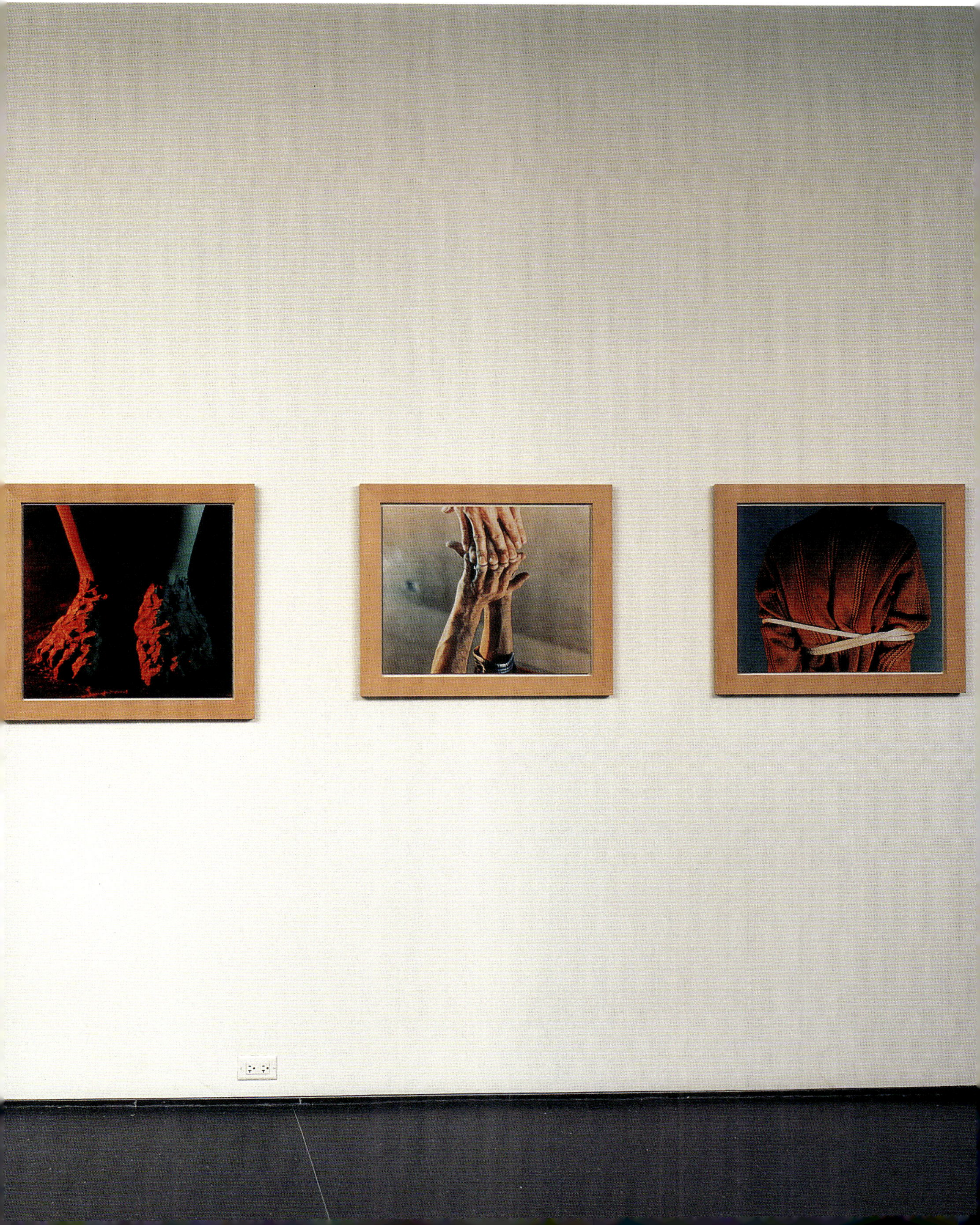

DAVID JOSELIT

MOLDS AND SWARMS

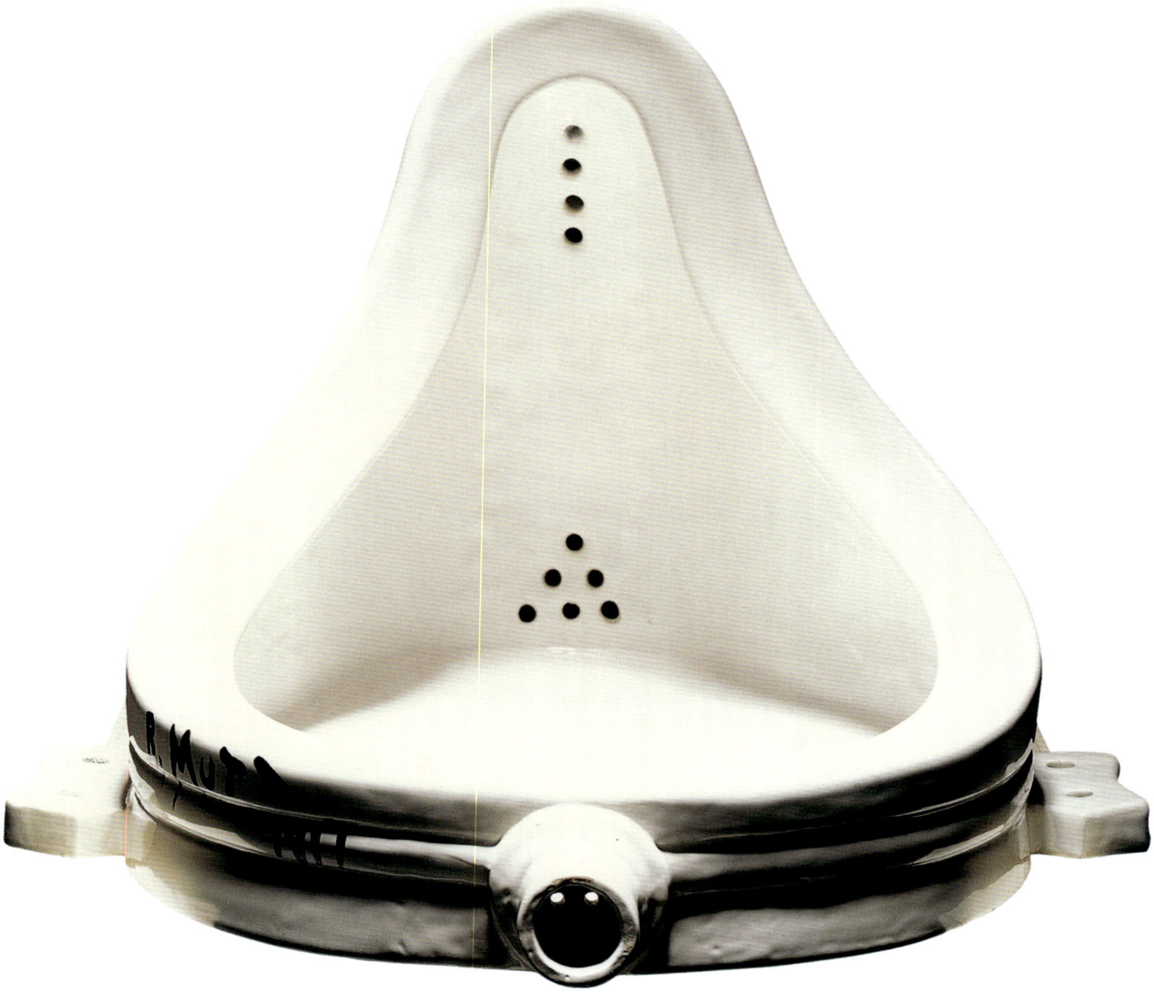

Duchamp's career describes a pathway from **A** to **B,** where, for example:

A = *Fountain* (1917)
and
B = *Female Fig Leaf* (1950)

This trajectory culminates in one of the great aesthetic variables of the twentieth century:

C = *Etant donnés* (1946–66)

Accounting for this transit from commodity to body, or from the readymade to the "bio-readymade," could reshuffle the history of postwar sculpture.[1]

OBJECTION

This terminology is imprecise. How can *Fountain* – a urinal – not be considered a "bio-readymade"?[2] As a receptacle for the penis, a urinary codpiece, it functions as a kind of masculine fig leaf: a twin of its feminine sister thirty-three years in advance.

Moreover, what *is* a readymade?

INSCRIPTION

Following Duchamp's specifications, I propose we provisionally define the readymade as an inscribed object:

> Specifications for "Readymades"
>
> by planning for a moment to come (on such a day, such a date, such a minute), "*to inscribe* a readymade" – The readymade can later be looked for. – (with all kinds of delays)
>
> *The important thing, then, is just* this matter of timing, this snapshot effect, like a speech delivered on no matter what occasion but at *such and such an hour*. It is a kind of rendezvous.
>
> Naturally inscribe the date, hour, minute, on the readymade as information.[3]

This definition encompasses both *Fountain* and *Female Fig Leaf*, which is inscribed, *feuille de vigne femelle*. But it nevertheless leaves hanging (a *pendu femelle?*)[4] the question of commodities versus bodies – the question of a *bio*-readymade.

OBSERVATIONS

It is seductive to argue that between 1917 and 1950 Duchamp moved from things (*Fountain*) to organs (*Female Fig Leaf*) as the ground for his inscription of readymades – not least because such an account offers an interpretive frame for the *Etant donnés*. Unfortunately, everything in Duchamp's oeuvre conspires to undermine such a claim: after all, *The Large Glass* (1915–23) is already both a manifesto and a catalogue of the bio-readymade in which a swarm of organic desiring-machines pinwheel through various procedures. Duchamp understood the instability of his invention as well as its tendency to swing from objects to persons:

Marcel Duchamp
Fontaine (Fountain), 1917, 5th version 1964

> The curious thing about the Ready-Made is that I've never been able to arrive at a definition or explanation that fully satisfies me.... There's still magic in the idea, so I'd rather keep it that way than try to be exoteric about it. But there are small explanations and even general traits we can discuss. Let's say you use a tube of paint; you didn't make it. You bought it and used it as a ready-made. Even if you mix two vermilions together, it's still a mixing of two ready-mades. So man can never expect to start from scratch; he must start from ready-made things like even his mother and father.[5]

This passage makes two provocative insinuations: first, that the readymade occupies the position of origin ("mother and father") that poststructuralism has identified as impossibly mythic, and second, that in the readymade origins are imagined in terms of the formal (and not just commercial) delimitation of matter (such as the flows of vermilion channeled into tubes of paint).[6]

We have been misled by Duchamp's early adoption of things like snow shovels and urinals as his readymades. The point isn't that the readymade is a commodity, or that its election by Duchamp indicates a thoroughgoing condemnation of the (art) market.[7] The radical accomplishment of the readymade is to initiate, as art, those procedures by which any matter is distinguished from other matter and hence delineated as things or organism – a thing or an organism defined through the extreme reduction of the functions and meanings officially assigned or "warranted to it."[8] At the end of his "Specifications for 'Readymades,'" Duchamp pushed through the porous limits of objectivity with a good idea: "Reciprocal Readymade = Use a Rembrandt as an ironing-board." A painting by Rembrandt could function as a tabletop, the canvas patching for a torn sail, or it could be fashioned into a crown for an emperor or exhibited in the Metropolitan Museum of Art. In other words, rather than transparently opening onto a meaning, the readymade possesses "general traits." Readymades are known through their qualities, or actions, and not by a stable meaning. The counter-functionality of an inscription (such as the title *Fountain* and the signature "R. Mutt") returns the urinal to its wildly polymorphous state as matter, just as calling a Rembrandt an ironing board, or using it as an ironing board, makes it that thing. Duchamp knew that language makes a urinal as much as the factory does.

No one describes the problem of matter and signification better than Gilles Deleuze and Félix Guattari. Take, for example, their definition of the double articulation of form:

> The first articulation chooses or deducts, from unstable particle-flows, metastable molecular or quasi-molecular units (*substances*) upon which it imposes a statistical order of connections and successions (*forms*). The second articulation establishes functional, compact, stable structures (*forms*), and constructs the molar compounds in which these structures are simultaneously actualized (*substances*). In a geological stratum, for example, the first articulation is the process of "sedimentation," which deposits units of cyclic sediment according to a statistical order: flysch, with its succession of sandstone and schist. The second articulation is the "folding" that sets up a stable functional structure and effects the passage from sediment to sedimentary rock.[9]

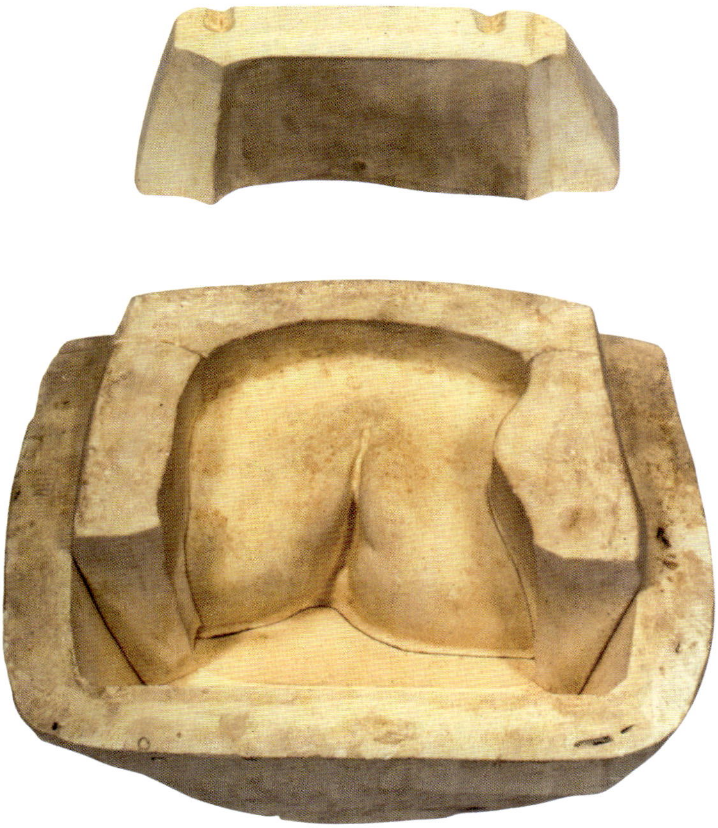

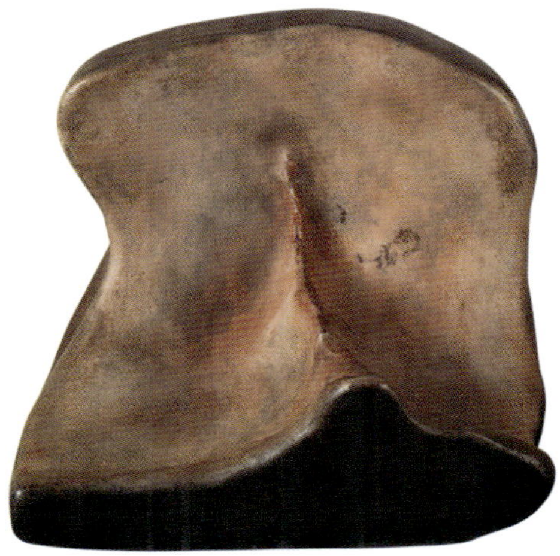

above left Marcel Duchamp
Moule à pièces pour Feuille de Vigne Femelle (Mold for Female Fig Leaf), 1950/1951

above right Marcel Duchamp
Feuille de Vigne Femelle (Female Fig Leaf), 1950

In the double articulation Deleuze and Guattari describe, matter emerges into form (statistically) out of immanent flows as, conversely, form structures matter: there is sedimentation as well as sedimentary rock. In other words, substance aspires to form (sedimentation) as form generates substance (sedimentary rock).

PRELUDE TO A HYPOTHESIS

Given that:

A. The distinction between readymade and bio-readymade is invalid inasmuch as the commodity and the organ were always imagined as equivalents by Duchamp (not to mention in the capitalist regime in which he operated), and:

B. Inscription is not sufficient to define the difference that nonetheless persists in one's understanding of *Fountain* and *Female Fig Leaf*, or *The Large Glass* and *Etant donnés*, then:

C. It appears that we require an additional critical tool.

If, as Deleuze and Guattari suggest, organic and inorganic matter surges through and around us in deterritorialized flows, it is not matter itself (the commodity or the organ) that will allow us to define Duchamp's readymade practice, but rather procedures for organizing matter into form. In this regard, the difference between *Fountain* and *Female Fig Leaf* is plain: the former is recoded through inscription alone, while the latter is imprinted. The *Fig Leaf*, like the related objects, *Not a Shoe* (1950), *Objet-Dard* (1951), and *Wedge of Chastity* (1954), is produced through the logic of the mold.

MOLDS

Duchamp thought about molds a lot, often in conjunction with his theorization of the "infra thin." Here is a long note on the subject, written on two sides of a piece of paper (recto and verso):

> (recto) Infra-thin separation
>
> 2 forms cast in/the same mold (?) differ/from each other/by an infra thin separative/amount –
>
> All "identicals" as/identical as they may be, (and/the more identical they are)/move toward this/infra thin separative/difference.
>
> Two men are not/an example of identicality/and to the contrary move away/from a determinable/infra thin difference – but (verso) there exists the crude conception/of the déjà vu which leads from/generic grouping/(2 trees, 2 boats)/to the most identical "castings"/It would be better/to try/to go/into the/infra thin/interval which separates/2 "identicals" than/to conveniently accept/the verbal generalization/which makes/2 twins look like 2/drops of water. Copenhagen/July 29, [19]37[10]

At the core of the infra thin is the acute awareness of a difference among objects that is erased by language: "It would be better/to try/to go/into the/infra thin/interval which separates/2 'identicals' than/to conveniently accept/the verbal generalization/which makes/2 twins look like 2/drops of water." Language necessarily erases difference: *urinal* refers to all machines for catching the urine of men despite the fact that *every one of them is different.* Even those that came off the same assembly line, or those that stand side by side in the same lavatory, are minutely different, either through the vagaries of manufacture or through the different veils of liquid staining their surfaces. *Inscribing* things was Duchamp's first strategy for allowing the variable materiality underlying any object to surge forth. Calling a urinal *Fountain* and signing it "R. Mutt" introduces difference into the thing. But language can be a blunt instrument. It cannot specify "2 forms cast in/the same mold (?) differ/from each other." The infra thin denotes the intimate touch of the mold and the molded. An impression (of a vaginal cleft) is both empty and full, both itself and other. *Female Fig Leaf* is both mold and molded – or more accurately, it is the infra-thin bond between them.

The inscribed readymades are generally associated with Duchamp's notorious "cerebral" disposition. Not surprisingly, eroticism, the counterintuitive partner to this conceptual bent, is less widely credited despite its status as the engine of *The Large Glass* and the corollary of the mold's intimate encounter between things. Duchamp imagined a mode of reception corresponding to the erotic in which the gray matter of the spectator is bypassed in favor of a direct appeal to his or her guts. There is a hint of this in the note I have quoted: "there exists the crude conception/of the déjà vu which leads from/generic grouping/(2 trees, 2 boats)/to the most identical 'castings.'" Déjà vu is a mental echo, a kind of fissure in reality that Duchamp aligns with the mold or "castings." In a later text he developed a related concept, "esthetic echo," more fully:

> [E]verybody is welcome to look freely at all works of art and try to hear what I call an esthetic echo. We also imply that art cannot be understood through the intellect, but is felt through an emotion presenting some analogy with a religious faith or a sexual attraction – an esthetic echo.... The important point here is to differentiate taste from the esthetic echo....
>
> Quite differently, the "victim" of an esthetic echo is in a position comparable to that of a man in love, or of a believer, who dismisses automatically his demanding ego and, helpless, submits to a pleasurable and mysterious constraint. While exercising his taste, he adopts a commanding attitude. When touched by the esthetic revelation, the same man, in an almost ecstatic mood, becomes receptive and humble.[11]

The esthetic echo is a psychic mold in which the viewer's consciousness conforms to an image, a feeling: it submits the viewer to a *pleasurable and* mysterious *constraint,* a becoming-receptive (like a mold).

Inscription corresponds to the gray matter.
Molds operate through an erotics of things.

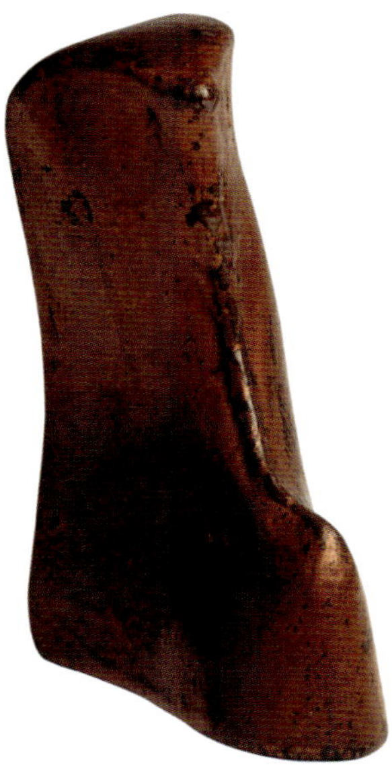

Marcel Duchamp
Not a Shoe, 1950

HYPOTHESIS

In place of the terms "readymade" and "bio-readymade," I have identified two strategies by which Duchamp articulates organic and inorganic matter: inscription and molding. But how do they interact?

The trajectory from **A** to **B,** when

A = *Fountain*
and
B = *Female Fig Leaf*

constitutes an effort to circumnavigate language as the means of specifying things. (Why this was a compelling artistic project at mid-century is worth investigating further.)[12]

The flight from language induces a surge of the body: the waning of inscription corresponds to the waxing of the mold.

A SIDEWAYS PROOF

William S. Burroughs brings together the two sides of the readymade – the word and the mold – on the terrain of his cut-up novels, such as *The Ticket That Exploded* (1962):

> The body is two halves stuck together like a mold – That is, it consists of two organisms – See "the Other Half"
> And:
> The "Other Half" is the word. The "Other Half" is an organism. Word is an organism. The presence of the "Other Half" a separate organism attached to your nervous system on an air line of words can now be demonstrated experimentally. . . . From symbiosis to parasitism is a short step. The word is now a virus. . . . It is now a parasitic organism that invades and damages the central nervous system. Modern man has lost the option of silence. Try halting your sub-vocal speech. Try to achieve even ten seconds of inner silence. You will encounter a resisting organism that *forces you to talk*. That organism is the word.[13]

For Burroughs (as for any ordinary citizen of a media world), the word is an instrument of control, an "other half" that has entered the body in order to colonize it like a virus. For him, the horizon of liberation consists of breaking this stranglehold, this mold. When the word is "rubbed out" (as he exhorted), the body will surge forth:

> The human organism is literally consisting of two halves from the beginning word and all human sex is this unsanitary arrangement whereby two entities attempt to occupy the same three-dimensional coordinate points giving rise to the sordid latrine brawls which have characterized a planet based on "the Word," that is, on separate flesh engaged in endless sexual conflict – [14]

The trajectory from *Fountain* to *Female Fig Leaf* redresses the alienation of Burroughs's "separate flesh" compelled to throw itself upon other bodies in order to compensate for its individuation through the word-virus. When the word is rubbed out, the polymorphous body, no longer tied to any particular individual, may surge forth: the mold is no longer double, but serves, like *Female Fig Leaf*, as the perpetual becoming of the infra thin.

right Lucio Fontana
Concetto spaziale, Scultura nera
(Spatial Concept, Black Sculpture), 1947

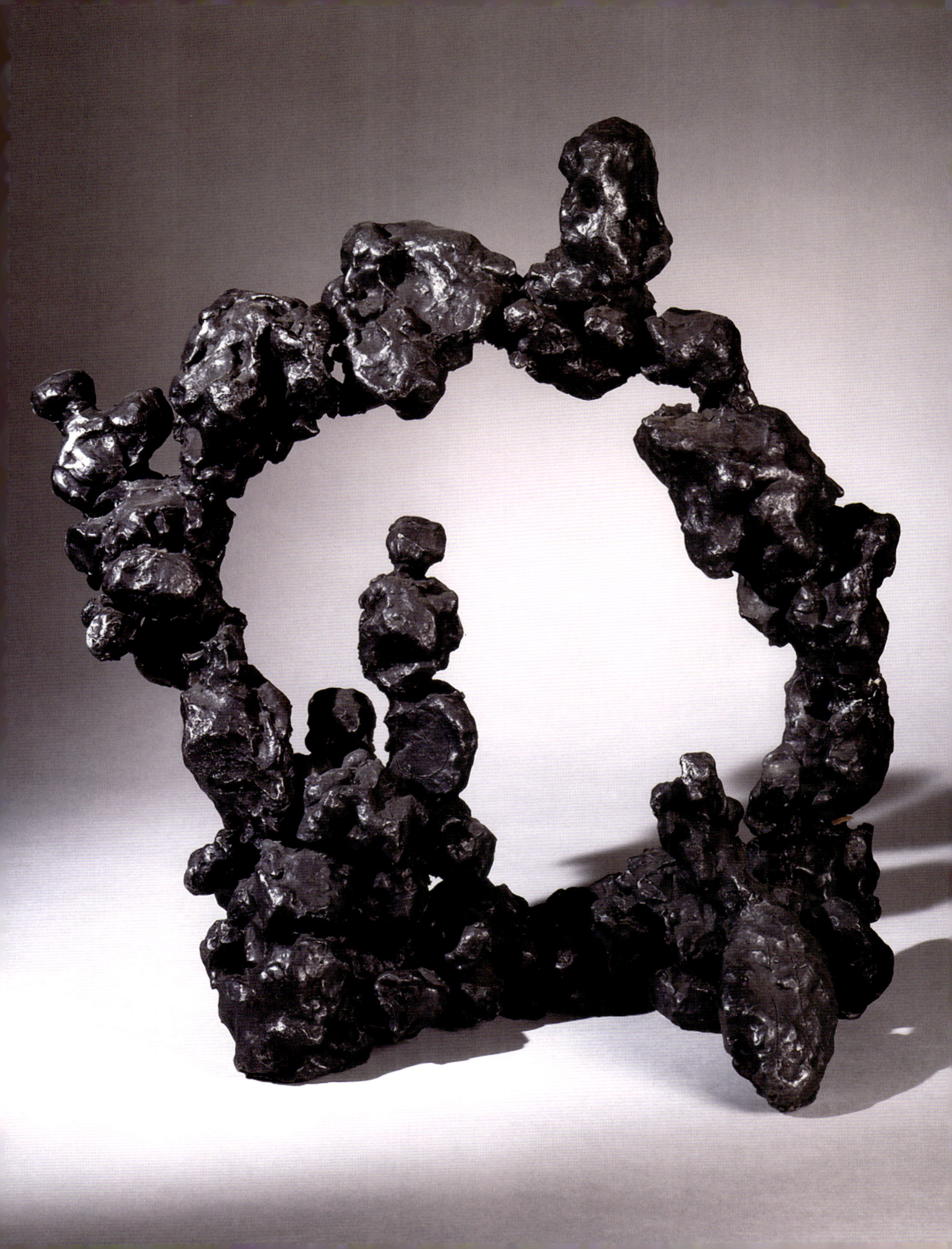

MOLDS AND SWARMS

Mid-twentieth-century art has been mapped according to strategies of seriality and geometric rationalization, on the one hand, and linguistic and photographic rhetorics of the document, on the other. Duchamp's erotic sculptures of the 1950s indicate an alternate or complementary tradition of the mold – an erotics of things – which, in different keys, resonates in the art of Jasper Johns, Eva Hesse, Lee Bontecou, Lucio Fontana, Marcel Broodthaers, Yayoi Kusama, Allan McCollum, and Robert Gober, to name only a few. But there is another extralinguistic formation that has arisen since *Female Fig Leaf* and its partners, a complement to the infra thin mold that Duchamp, nevertheless, failed to invent: the *swarm*, a principle of combination situated somewhere between the undoing of structural logic associated with Georges Bataille's *informe*[15] and the rule-based permutations of Minimalism. The swarm suggests an emergent order that arises out of immanent flows of matter. It is both unconscious and ordered, like a beehive or an anthill.[16] It finds its intersection with the mold in Marcel Broodthaers's fields of *moules* (mussels/molds), empty shells that press into and out of their deductive frames (a canvas, a casserole). These works emerge from the secreted shells of tiny bodies ingested or discarded, which are reanimated and redirected into new material flows. In Broodthaers's book, *Pense-Bête* (1964), published just before he began his artistic practice,[17] the following poem appeared:

> The Mussel [Moule]
> This clever thing avoided society's mold [moule].
> She's cast herself in her very own.
> Others, look-alikes, share with her the anti-sea.
> She's perfect.[18]

The swarm engulfs the mold as the mold articulates the swarm. The word is rubbed out,[19] making way for an erotics of things.

NOTES

1 This is clearly the ambition of *Part Object Part Sculpture*.

2 I am grateful to George Baker and his students at UCLA for expressing this objection during an informal presentation of my argument.

3 Michel Sanouillet and Elmer Peterson, *The Writings of Marcel Duchamp* (New York: Da Capo Press, 1973), 32.

4 This is one of Duchamp's terms for the upper section of *The Large Glass* devoted to the bride.

5 Katharine Kuh, "Marcel Duchamp," in *The Artist's Voice: Talks with Seventeen Artists* (New York: Harper and Row, 1960), 90.

6 See Thierry de Duve, "The Readymade and the Tube of Paint," *Artforum* 24 (May 1986): 110–21.

7 See my essay, "The Artist Readymade: Marcel Duchamp and the Société Anonyme," forthcoming in Jennifer R. Gross, ed., *The Société Anonyme: Modernism for America* (New Haven: Yale University Press, 2005), for a discussion of Duchamp's ambivalent relationship with the art market.

8 This term is drawn from Allucquère Rosanne Stone, *The War of Desire and Technology at the Close of the Mechanical Age* (Cambridge, Mass.: The MIT Press, 1995).

9 Gilles Deleuze and Félix Guattari, *A Thousand Plateaus: Capitalism and Schizophrenia*, trans. Brian Massumi (Minneapolis: University of Minnesota Press, 1987), 40–41.

10 *Marcel Duchamp Notes*, translated and arranged by Paul Matisse; preface by Anne d'Harnoncourt (Boston: G. K. Hall, 1983), unpaginated.

11 "The Western Round Table on Modern Art, San Francisco, 1949," in Bonnie Clearwater, ed., *West Coast Duchamp* (Miami Beach: Grassfield Press, 1991), 107.

12 Such an antilinguistic tendency may seem to run counter to the widespread adoption of text as a "medium" by practitioners of conceptual art. In fact, those artists who have deployed text from the late 1960s to the present have done as much to demonstrate its opacity as its transparency.

13 William S. Burroughs, *The Ticket That Exploded* (New York: Grove Press, 1962), 159; 49–50.

14 Ibid., 52.

15 For a very important discussion of *informe* as a procedure in modern art, see Yve-Alain Bois and Rosalind E. Krauss, *Formless: A User's Guide* (New York: Zone Books, 1997), especially Bois, "The Use Value of 'Formless,'" 13–40, and Krauss, "The Destiny of the *Informe*," 235–52.

16 See Kevin Kelly, "Hive Mind," in *Out of Control: The New Biology of Machines, Social Systems, and the Economic World* (Reading, Mass.: Perseus Books, 1994), 5–28.

17 In fact, he embedded unsold copies of this book in plaster as his first sculptural object.

18 Quoted in Michael Compton, "In Praise of the Subject," in Marge Goldwater, ed., *Marcel Broodthaers* (Minneapolis: Walker Art Center; New York: Rizzoli, 1989), 23.

19 It might be objected that Broodthaers often works with language, but, like Duchamp, he does so in such a way as to desublimate the word, interrupting its promise of transparency to signification.

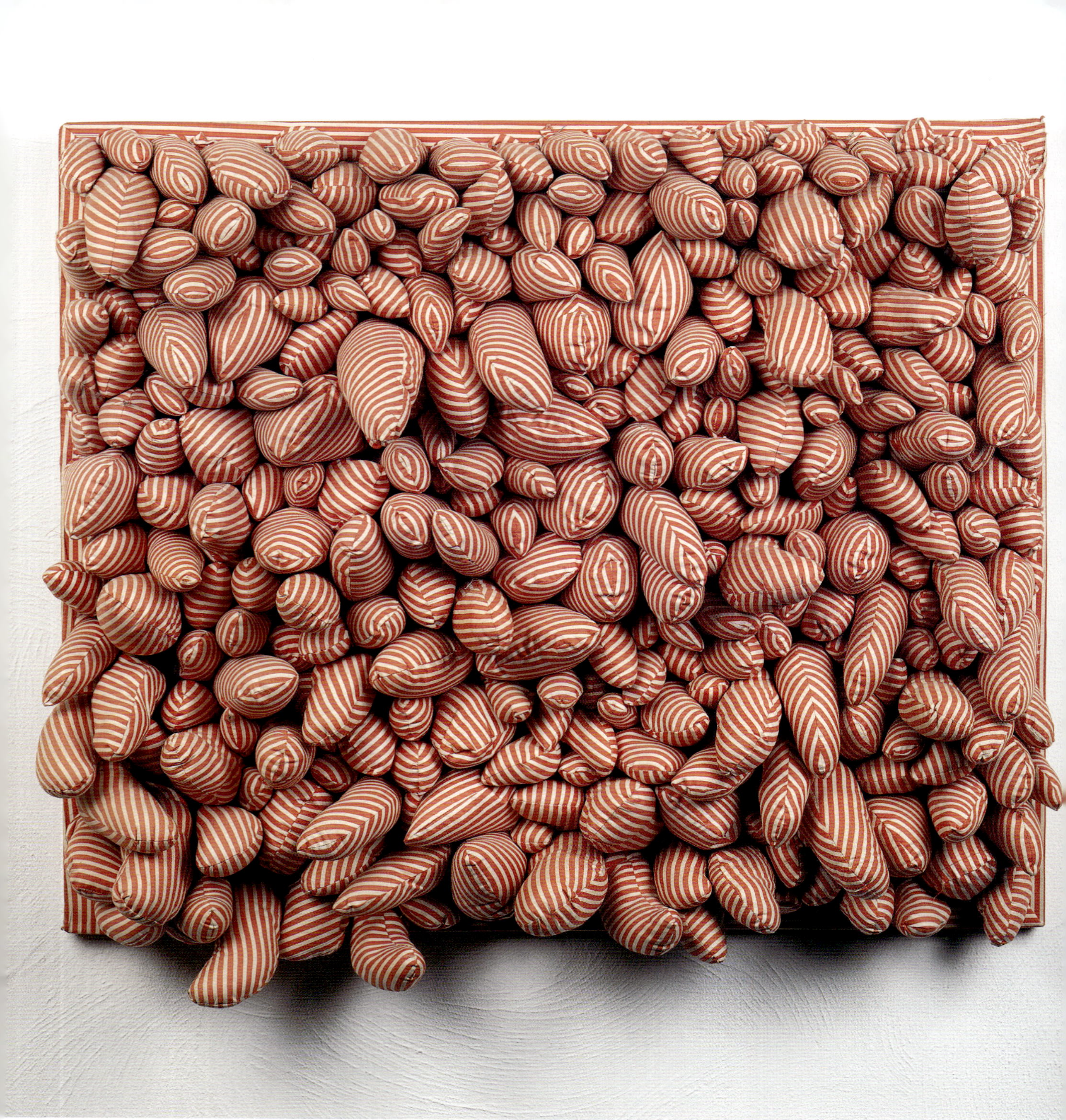

YAYOI KUSAMA 1929–

Yayoi Kusama arrived in New York from Japan in 1958. The timing of her arrival could not have been more auspicious, as she encountered a New York art world still in the throes of Abstract Expressionism's experimentation with the absorptive scale of all-over compositions and while at the same time feeling the nascent appeal of the everyday object, found in the work of Claes Oldenburg and Robert Rauschenberg. This was also a New York in which artists using seriality were increasingly visible. Kusama arrived well versed in abstraction, having already established her fundamental visual vocabulary of dots and veils or nets of paint. Given that she arrived with nearly two thousand small works on paper, we can assume that Kusama's interest in the problem of repetition may have already been active. Certainly her first New York exhibition of "Infinity Net" paintings, largely monochromatic works in which looping, heavily brush-worked skeins of paint cover the canvas from edge to edge, furthered both of these incipient interests.

By 1962, Kusama was to apply this all-over strategy in a new arena, covering household objects, starting with furniture, with monochromatically painted, sewn, stuffed-fabric phallic protrusions. *Accumulation II*, a sofa entirely enveloped in these protuberances, exaggerates the tactility of the three-dimensional object to ludicrous proportions, and the work has a kind of hilarious effect, underneath the laughter an almost electric flow of fear. This is the object world alive and pulsing, utterly animate, and its animateness is neither benign nor passive; these are not the whispering Personages of Louise Bourgeois. Rather, in photographs self-consciously staged by Kusama, we see her engaging with these objects in a physically literal way. She lies on *Accumulation II*, naked, except for a handful of dots painted on her body, looking up at the camera with a curious blend of defiance, boredom, and a blasé come-hither in her gaze. The images suggest that Kusama wanted the objects to retain their function, their status as objects, but also to have the full-fledged sensory capabilities of art. It also seems, however, that one of the effects of the swarming tactility of Kusama's encrusted objects is that of obliteration – an intensely radical dismissal not only of the boundaries between the world of objects and sculptures but also of persons and things. Reminiscent of Surrealist Roger Callois's essay on Legendary Psychoaesthenia, Kusama appears to produce wildly repetitive surfaces in an attempt to create a space wherein our relations to objects are utterly altered, such that the boundaries between bodies and objects and bodies and space are dissolved.

Sometimes Kusama's space is literally three-dimensional, as in her many rooms; sometimes it is merely representational, as in her collages or staged photographs. Sometimes the space is also intensely visual. In *Red Stripes* and *Blue Spots*, for instance, Kusama uses store-bought patterned fabric and covers rectangles of wood with myriad protrusions. Hung on the wall like paintings, these objects behave like sculptures, redolent with texture, dimensionality, and a vacillating mode of address, such that they shift dramatically based on the viewer's physical position in front of them. And yet the visual field of these objects pops and buzzes with a nearly vertiginous opticality. One is lost in a sea of apperceptions, as haptic and optic no longer seem demonstrably different from each other.

The intensity of this polymorphous pleasure has a dual engine. It is not only the tactility of the objects, or the bizarre and uncanny alteration of the everyday, that accounts for the sensations Kusama's work evokes – sensations, it's worth adding, that are deeply shared by artist and viewer alike. (Kusama is in many ways the ideal viewer of her own work. Her photographs act as instruction manuals of a sort for how to "engage" with or look at her work.) The concentration of the repetitiveness is also at stake here. Briony Fer recently described Kusama's work as one of cramming and stuffing the image, creating a "huge maximizing of surface area, a vastly expanded crust of surface, like a (now) brittle, white carapace."[1] The creation of this carapace, this protective shell, allows one, however counterintuitively, to lose sense of one's boundaries, in this case because of the obsessiveness of the repetition, both in Kusama's own handiwork and the never-ending repeat in the fabric patterns of polka dots or stripes. This repetition without content, repetition for its own sake, so to speak, propels the viewer to experience the kind of dispersal that is being enacted in the objects themselves.

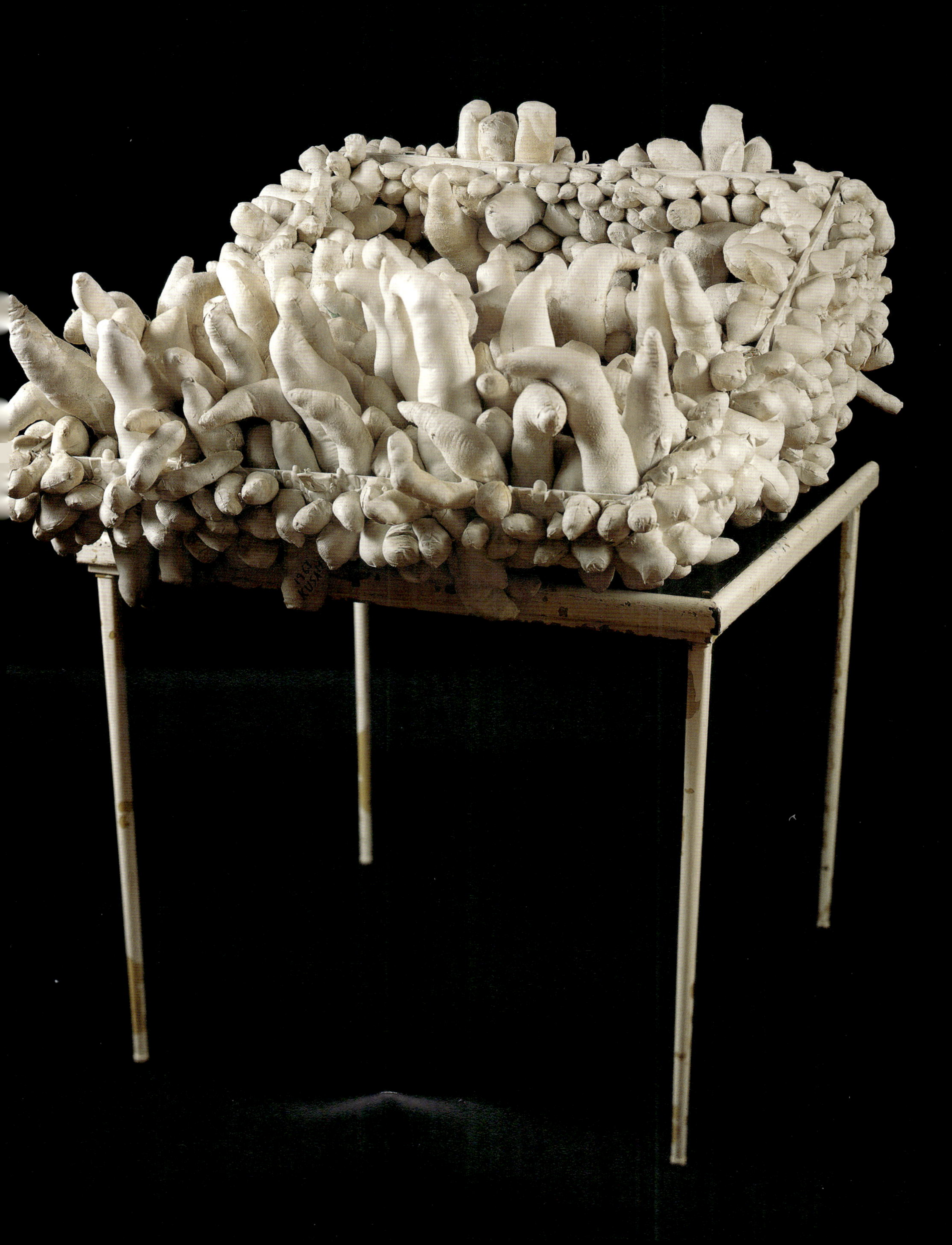

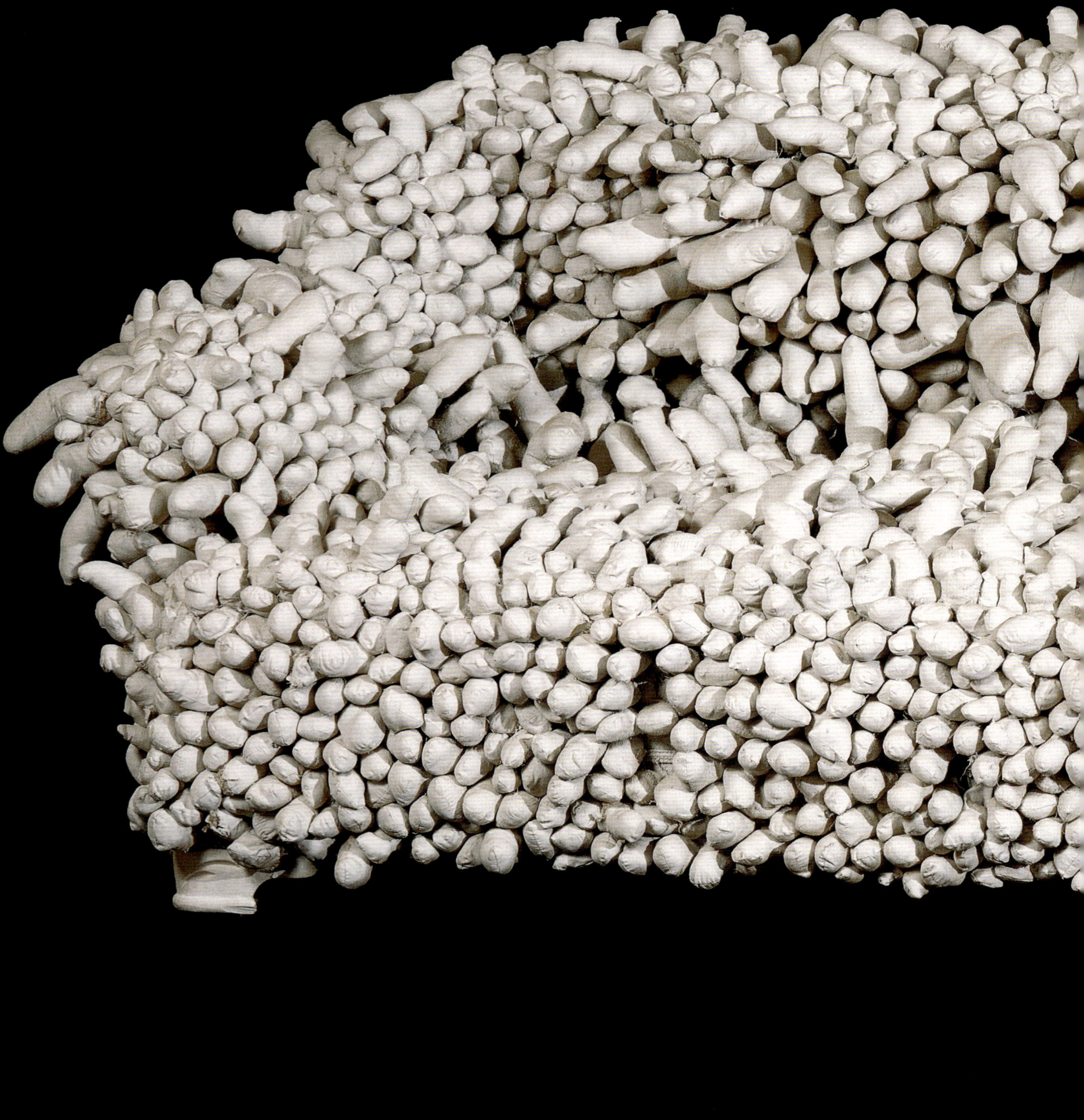

vious spread: left **Red Stripes**, 1965

vious spread: right **Suitcase**, 1963

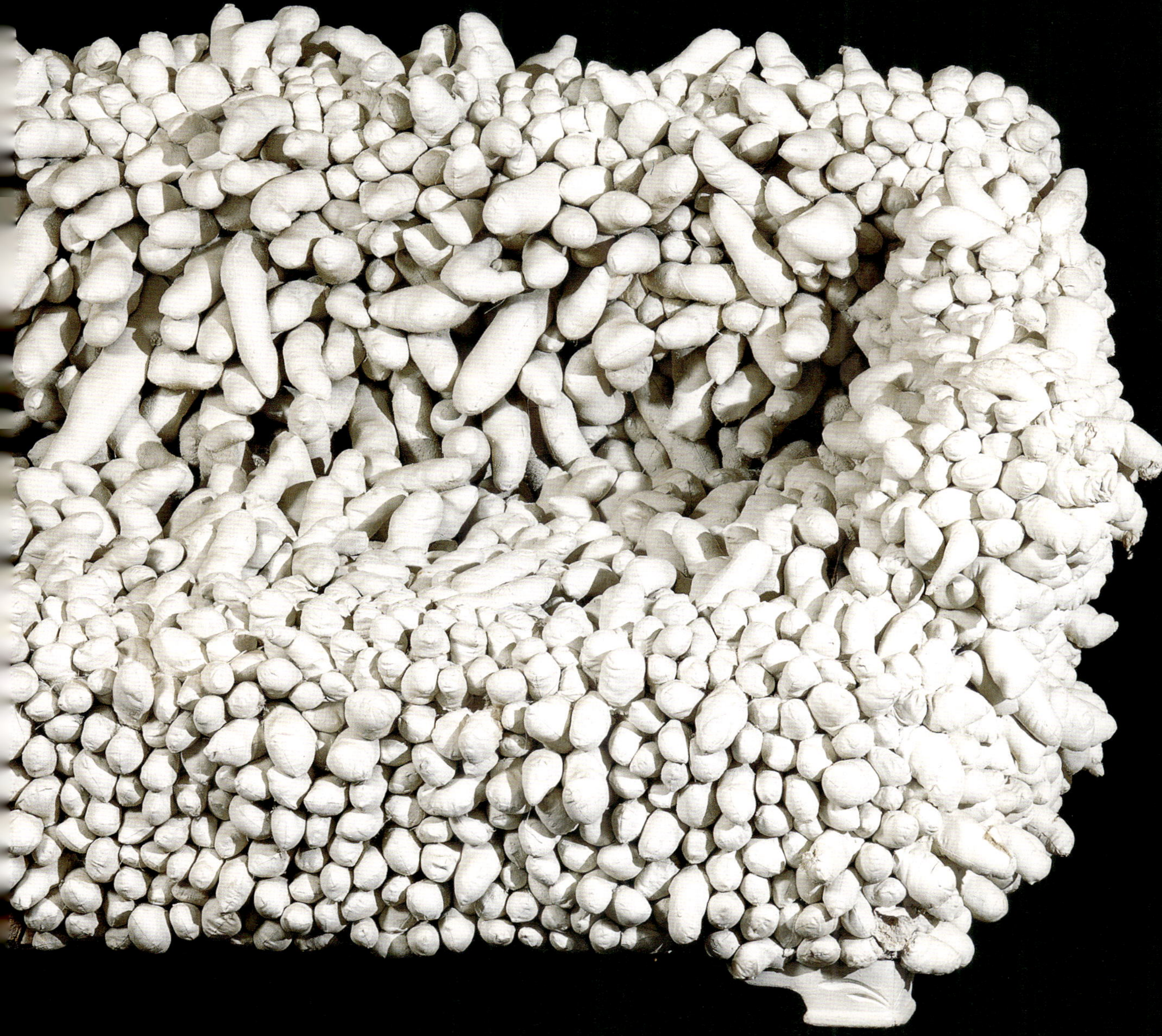

Accumulation II, 1962

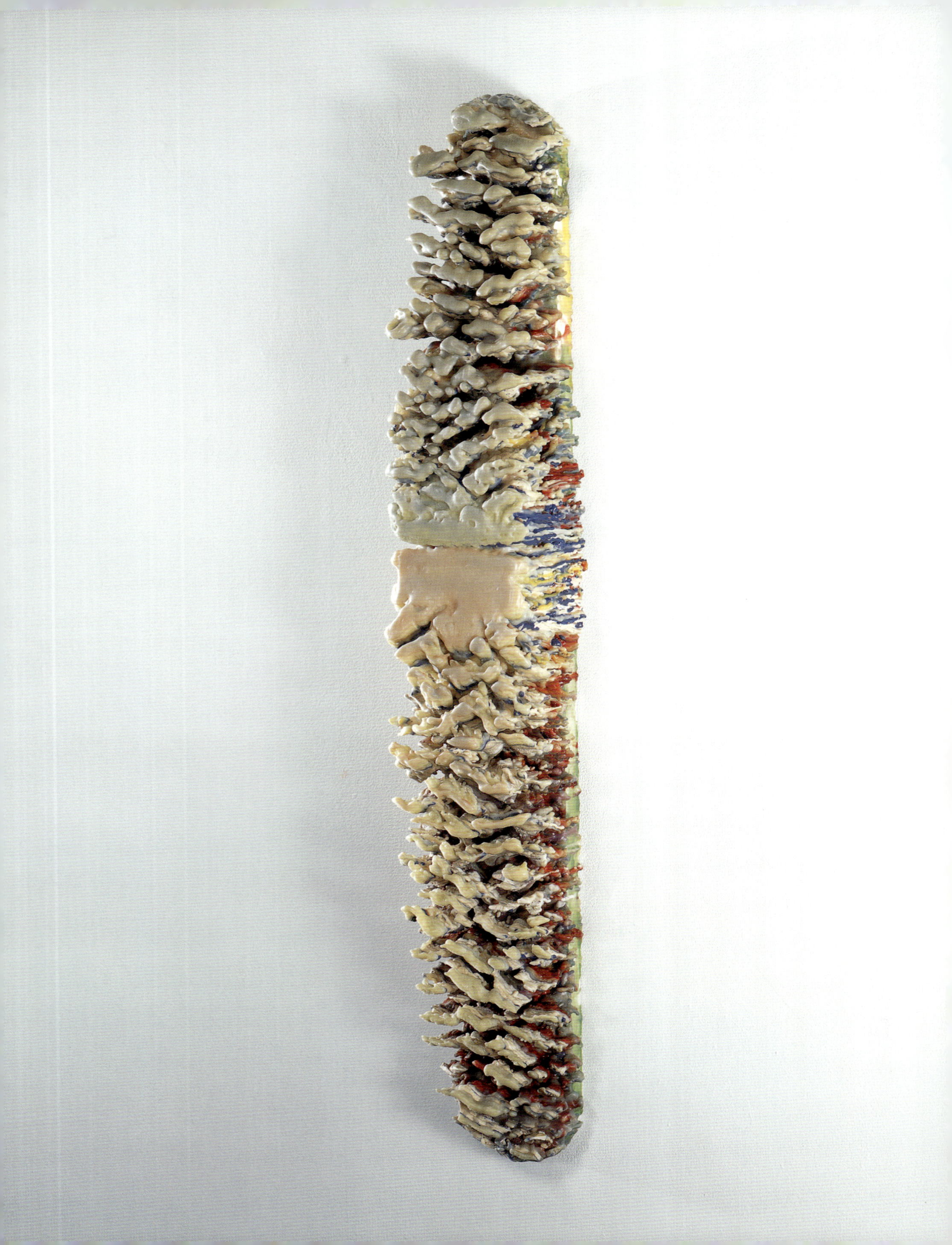

LYNDA BENGLIS 1941–

Interested in the expressivity and dynamic colors of Abstract Expressionism, Lynda Benglis arrived in New York when the art world was beginning its nascent love affair with sculpture. Benglis was to count among her friends avowed Minimalist sculptors such as Robert Morris, but she was also drawn to the tactility of artists such as Eva Hesse. After seeing Hesse's work through their mutual friend Sol LeWitt, Benglis was prompted to explore the use of latex in her own work. The result was a series of large latex pours, works Benglis produced by pouring large areas of overlapping color directly onto the floor in ways that problematized their identity as objects. Were the pours sculptures in the vein of Carl Andre or merely paintings that resided on the floor? Interested in such fundamental ambiguities, Benglis turned to the sculptural form of relief during the late 1960s. For many artists (consider the examples of Hesse, Burri, and Bontecou), the relief was a category of object that challenged the medium-based expectations of either painting or sculpture. Benglis's wax lozenges of the 1970s push this liminality even further, as their total abstraction eliminates any residual sense of a figure-ground relationship that might plague either a relief or a painting.

Instead, the lozenges combine the all-over composition of much Abstract Expressionist painting with the bodily scale of much post-Minimalist sculpture. Each lozenge approximates the length of Benglis's arm and hangs on the wall at a height that facilitates a direct address to the head and torso of the viewer. She felt that they were "highly surfaced and highly personal."[1] Despite the intense verticality of the images, they are subliminally addressed to things low and, in the spirit of French Surrealist Georges Bataille, *basesse*. Simultaneously phallic and vaginal, oral and pubic, humorous and eerie, abstract and vaguely figurative, the wax lozenges careen wildly along a dualistic register, offering a perpetual back-and-forth of meanings, allusions, and sensations. To Benglis: "The wax paintings were like masturbating in the studio, nutshell paintings dealing with male/female symbols, the split and the coming together. They are both oral and genital. But I don't want to get Freudian; they're also Jungian, Ying-Yang."[2] Even in her evocation of their theoretical parameters, she enumerates interpretive possibilities. But the slipperiness of fixing the meaning of the lozenges is also partly due to their powerfully organic nature. Benglis mixed her own pigments and integrated them directly into the wax, meaning that the pieces are devoid of any hint of industrially produced paints.[3] This is perhaps most evident in the rosy flesh tint of *Excess* (1971), and also in the sprightly verdant nature of *Karen* (1972). Benglis applied the wax in an equally laborious manner. Using a brush the same width as the Masonite base, she began in the center and pulled the wax out toward either edge, allowing the wax to build up and eventually drip over the edge and obliterate the support. This method not only creates an image of excess (I don't think it's an accident that one of the lozenges is entitled *Excess*), but also creates a work whose internal structure is one of doubling, as the two sides look as though they are symmetrical, as if they *could* have been made by folding one side over onto the other.

The internal doubling, the highly repetitive and worked nature of the surface, and the production of numerous lozenges all compound one another, suggesting that such a form is an infinitely repeatable one, same but different every time. This layering of repetitions may have seemed serial in nature, especially given the predominance of interest in seriality among New York artists at the time. But, according to Mel Bochner, seriality "is premised on the idea that the succession of terms (divisions) within a single work is based on a numerical or otherwise predetermined derivation…from one or more of the preceding terms in the piece."[4] Within this logical, even logarithmic version of seriality, Benglis's lozenges are an emotional wild card. While they have the appearance of seriality, in large measure because of their number and consistency, they are nothing if not organic in their proliferation, following the randomness of the material and the process through which the material is applied. Benglis's courting of the appearance of one thing while then providing the effect of another is part of the abiding interest in her work.

It is also interesting to register the similarity between the lozenges and Meret Oppenheim's infamous *Fur-Covered Cup, Saucer, and Spoon* (1936). Both works galvanize a host of bodily references, allowing a condensation of meanings and a radical slippage of coordinates to occur. And yet the effect of Oppenheim's extraordinary work is one of shock. The immediacy of the apprehension of the object is so intense, and the sexuality it calls into being is so visceral, that one holds both the object and one's response to it in the mind's eye as a whole and uninterrupted gestalt. Benglis's wax lozenges do not shock. Rather, every return to their visual and tactile field is rewarded by a propagation of small details that continually serve to scatter one's perception across the visual field. So too the repetition of the lozenges mitigates against the notion of shock. Instead, one experiences a kind of shattering as the reverberations between the dualistic poles continue over and over again.

LYNDA BENGLIS 1941–

interested in the expressivity and dynamic colors of Abstract Expressionism, Lynda Benglis arrived in New York when the art world was beginning its nascent love affair with sculpture. Benglis was to count among her friends avowed Minimalist sculptors such as Robert Morris, but she was also drawn to the tactility of artists such as Eva Hesse. After seeing Hesse's work through their mutual friend Sol LeWitt, Benglis was prompted to explore the use of latex in her own work. The result was a series of large latex pours, works Benglis produced by pouring large areas of overlapping color directly onto the floor in ways that problematized their identity as objects. Were the pours sculptures in the vein of Carl Andre or merely paintings that resided on the floor? Interested in such fundamental ambiguities, Benglis turned to the sculptural form of relief during the late 1960s. For many artists (consider the examples of Hesse, Burri, and Bontecou), the relief was a category of object that challenged the medium-based expectations of either painting or sculpture. Benglis's wax lozenges of the 1970s push this liminality even further, as their total abstraction eliminates any residual sense of a figure-ground relationship that might plague either a relief or a painting.

Instead, the lozenges combine the all-over composition of much Abstract Expressionist painting with the bodily scale of much post-Minimalist sculpture. Each lozenge approximates the length of Benglis's arm and hangs on the wall at a height that facilitates a direct address to the head and torso of the viewer. She felt that they were "highly surfaced and highly personal."[1] Despite the intense verticality of the images, they are subliminally addressed to things low and, in the spirit of French Surrealist Georges Bataille, *basesse*. Simultaneously phallic and vaginal, oral and pubic, humorous and eerie, abstract and vaguely figurative, the wax lozenges careen wildly along a dualistic register, offering a perpetual back-and-forth of meanings, allusions, and sensations. To Benglis: "The wax paintings were like masturbating in the studio, nutshell paintings dealing with male/female symbols, the split and the coming together. They are both oral and genital. But I don't want to get Freudian; they're also Jungian, Ying-Yang."[2] Even in her evocation of their theoretical parameters, she enumerates interpretive possibilities. But the slipperiness of fixing the meaning of the lozenges is also partly due to their powerfully organic nature. Benglis mixed her own pigments and integrated them directly into the wax, meaning that the pieces are devoid of any hint of industrially produced paints.[3] This is perhaps most evident in the rosy flesh tint of *Excess* (1971), and also in the sprightly verdant nature of *Karen* (1972). Benglis applied the wax in an equally laborious manner. Using a brush the same width as the Masonite base, she began in the center and pulled the wax out toward either edge, allowing the wax to build up and eventually drip over the edge and obliterate the support. This method not only creates an image of excess (I don't think it's an accident that one of the lozenges is entitled *Excess*), but also creates a work whose internal structure is one of doubling, as the two sides look as though they are symmetrical, as if they could have been made by folding one side over onto the other.

The internal doubling, the highly repetitive and worked nature of the surface, and the production of numerous lozenges all compound one another, suggesting that such a form is an infinitely repeatable one, same but different every time. This layering of repetitions may have seemed serial in nature, especially given the predominance of interest in seriality among New York artists at the time. But, according to Mel Bochner, seriality "is premised on the idea that the succession of terms (divisions) within a single work is based on a numerical or otherwise predetermined derivation . . . from one or more of the preceding terms in the piece."[4] Within this logical, even logarithmic version of seriality, Benglis's lozenges are an emotional wild card. While they have the appearance of seriality in large measure because of their number and consistency, they are nothing if not organic in their proliferation, following the randomness of the material and the process through which the material is applied. Benglis's courting of the appearance of one thing while then providing the effect of another is part of the abiding interest in her work.

It is also interesting to register the similarity between the lozenges and Meret Oppenheim's infamous *Fur-Covered Cup, Saucer, and Spoon* (1936). Both works galvanize a host of bodily references, allowing a condensation of meanings and a radical slippage of coordinates to occur. And yet the effect of Oppenheim's extraordinary work is one of shock. The immediacy of the apprehension of the object is so intense, and the sexuality it calls into being is so visceral, that one holds both the object and one's response to it in the mind's eye as a whole and uninterrupted gestalt. Benglis's wax lozenges do not shock. Rather, every return to their visual and tactile field is rewarded by a propagation of small details that continually serve to scatter one's perception across the visual field. So too the repetition of the lozenges mitigates against the notion of shock. Instead, one experiences a kind of shattering as the reverberations between the dualistic poles continue over and over again.

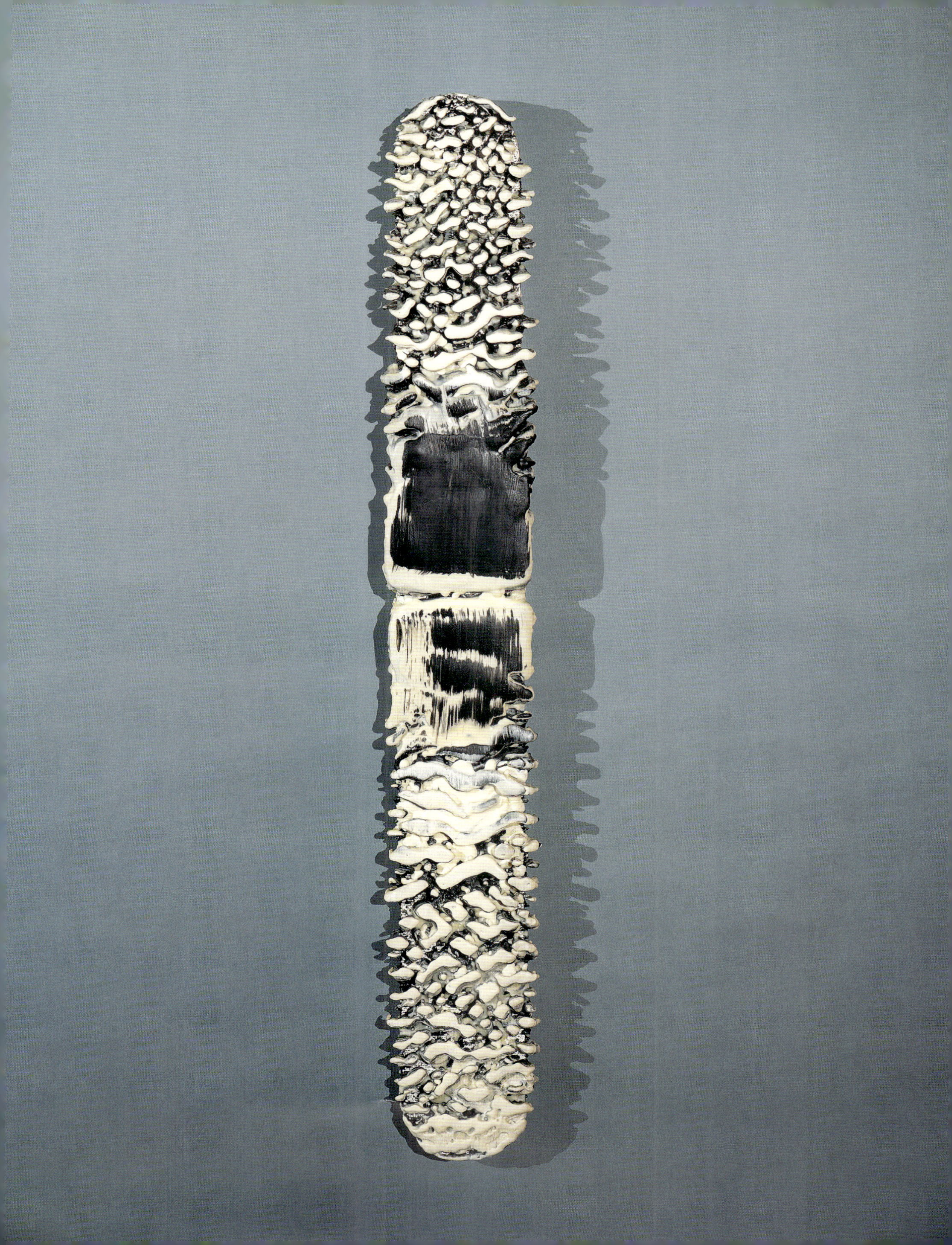

previous spread: left **Embryo II**, 1967

previous spread: right
Untitled from the Pinto Series, 1971

right **Excess**, 1971

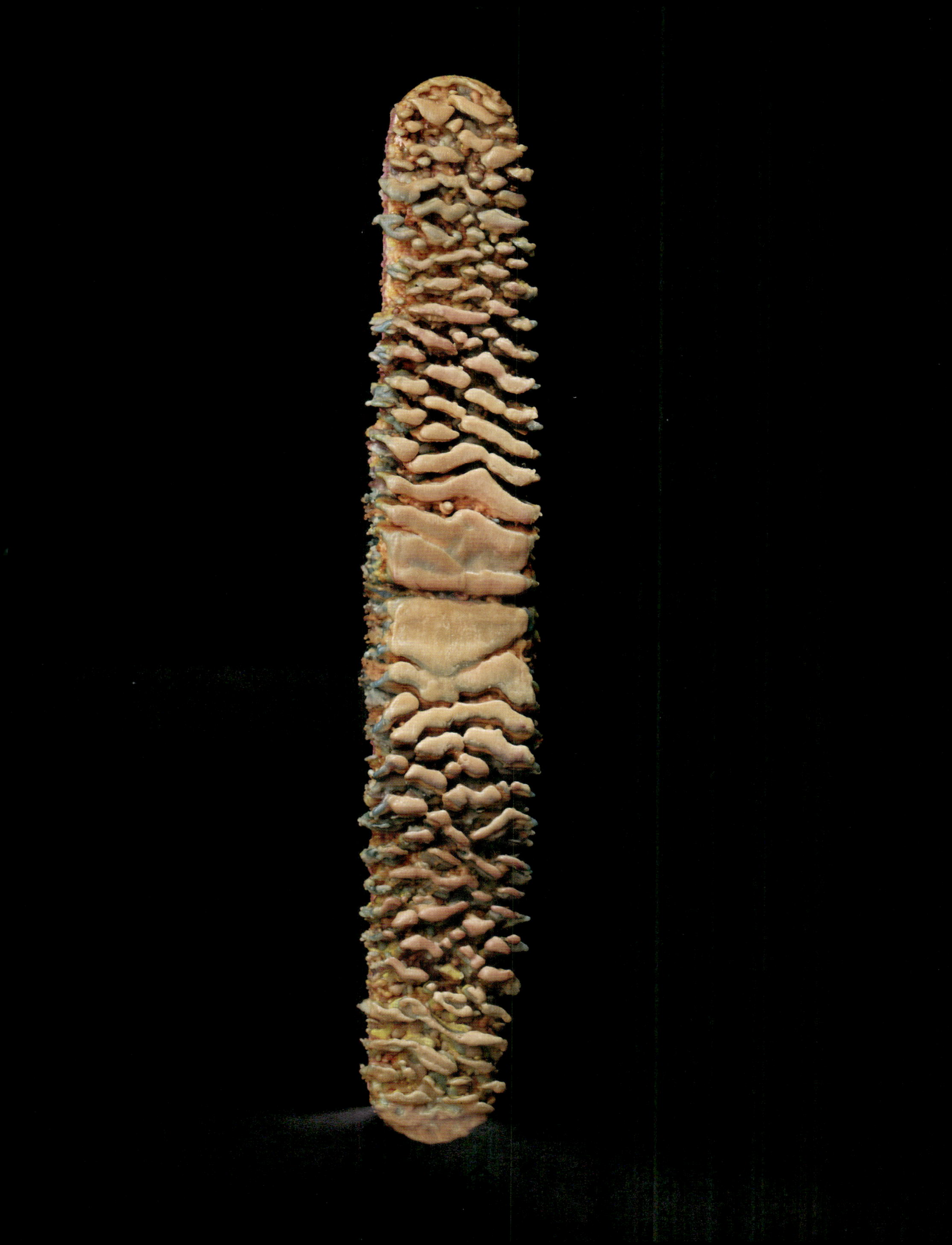

HELEN MOLESWORTH

DUCHAMP: BY HAND, EVEN

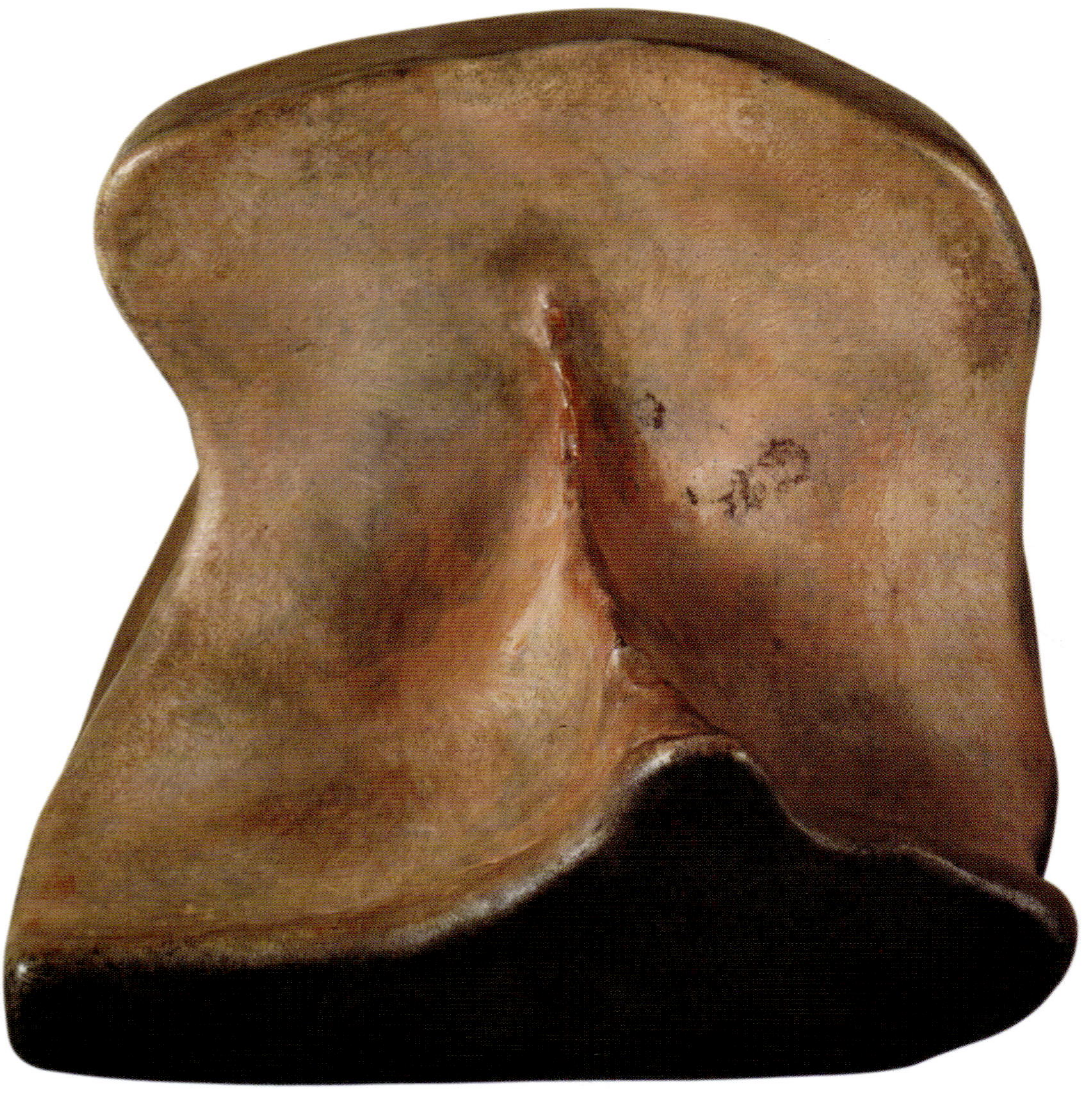

During the 1950s, Duchamp made three curious objects. Never mind that he had abandoned making art as early as 1921, they exist nonetheless. Each object is the scale of the human hand, strangely inert and oddly disturbing. They are often referred to as the three erotic objects. *Female Fig Leaf* looks like the inverse of a woman's vulva; its sensuous forms slope up into a ridgelike lip, the inverse of the opening on a real body, though no less alluring and provocative. The interplay between the smooth and rough surfaces lends it a palpable tactility. The object's haptic nature is heightened by its phantasmatic quality – both the fantasy of its making and the potential of its use. Duchamp made two copies of *Female Fig Leaf,* one for himself and one for his dear old friend Man Ray. A sexy joke between two boyish friends. It was also a gift borne of economic generosity, as Duchamp was to grant Man Ray the right to make an edition of ten of the sculptures for sale.

Objet-Dard had its debut at the Rose Fried Gallery in New York in 1953, and was shown alongside *Female Fig Leaf. Objet-Dard* is simultaneously phallic and scatological, flaccid and abject. Despite the object's nuanced psychological address, there is a whiff of the schoolboy snicker about it as well. Made of galvanized plaster, colored a dingy metallic brown, it prompted Francis Naumann's remark that it appears to be a cast, "but cast from what?"[1] Its title is similarly mutable; *dard* is French slang for penis as well as being a pun on the French *objet d'art,* indicating a slippage between sex and art as well as art and object. It too was reproduced, in an edition of eight. The *New York Times*'s Stuart Preston described it and *Female Fig Leaf* as "bizarre artifacts."[2] Who can blame him? Not quite sculpture, not quite objects, seemingly disconnected from Duchamp's other work on view, they must have been particularly hard to make sense of upon first viewing.

The last of the triumvirate is *Wedge of Chastity.* Inscribed "pour Teeny 16 Jan. 1954 Marcel," it was a wedding gift to Duchamp's bride, Teeny Matisse. Comprised of two pieces that fit snuggly together, hand in glove, the wedge is fashioned of plaster and the base is made from a handful of the material used to make dental impressions. Until now the interior of the object had never been photographed (although it bears a strong resemblance to a photograph of *Female Fig Leaf* that appeared on the cover of André Breton's magazine, *Le Surréalisme même*).[3] When the wedge is lifted, the rough edge gives way to a shocking pink interior that is an intensely intimate, loving, and erotic depiction of a pussy. Even the most personal of wedding presents was reproduced in an edition of eight.

Wedge of Chastity is a work for which touch is essential. Only through physical engagement with the object can the play between what is seen and unseen become evident. And even though there are no strictly defined anatomical parts, the dualistic nature of the work, its intense symbiosis, and its overwhelming implication of two bodies propose a particularly expansive version of the erotic. *Wedge of Chastity* offers an ineluctable mixture of the bodily and the nonbodily, a merging of two entities that nonetheless maintain their autonomy.

Marcel Duchamp
Feuille de Vigne Femelle
(Female Fig Leaf), 1950

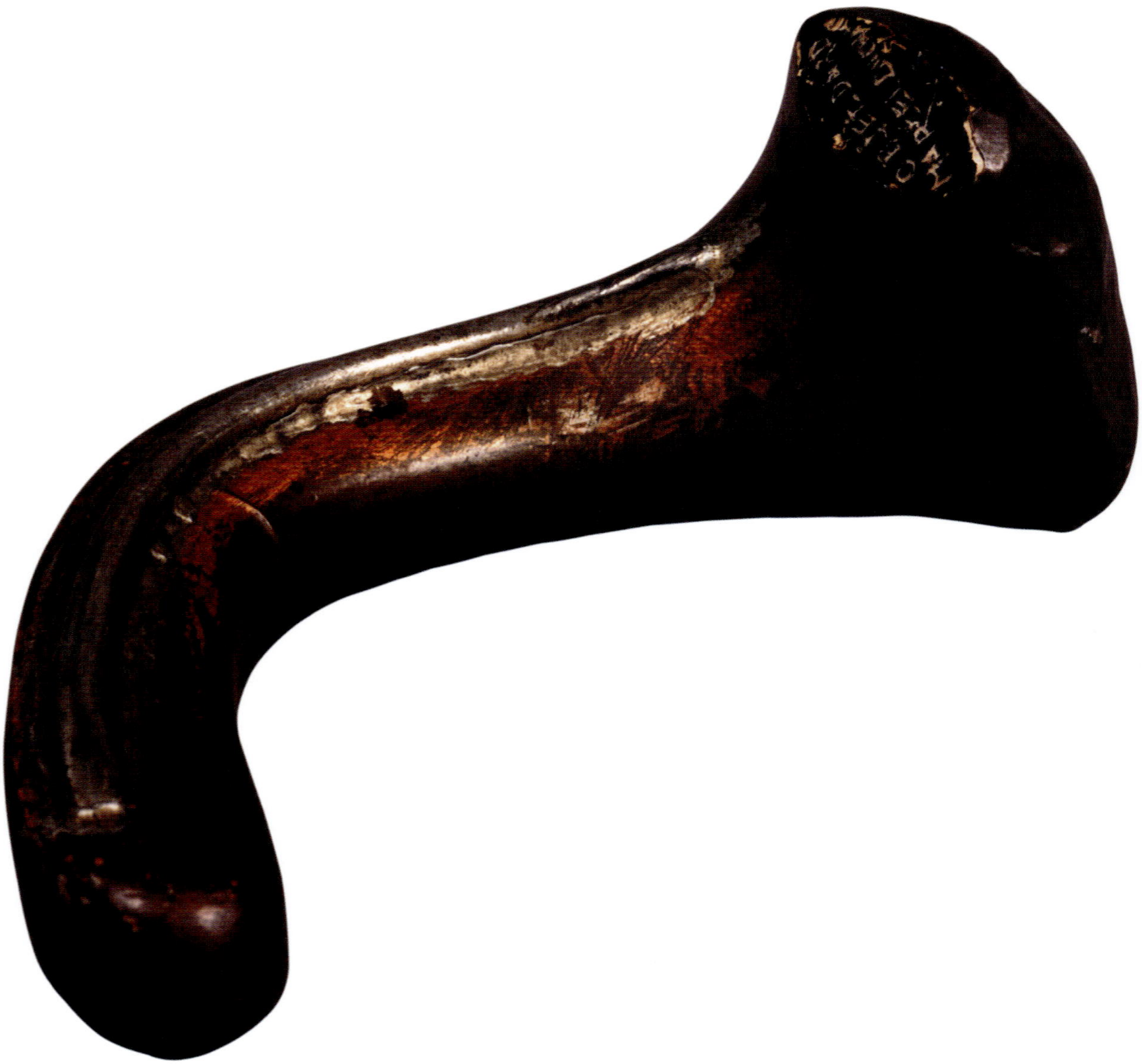

Marcel Duchamp
Objet-Dard (Dart-Object), 1951

right Marcel Duchamp
Coin de Chasteté (Wedge of Chastity), 1954

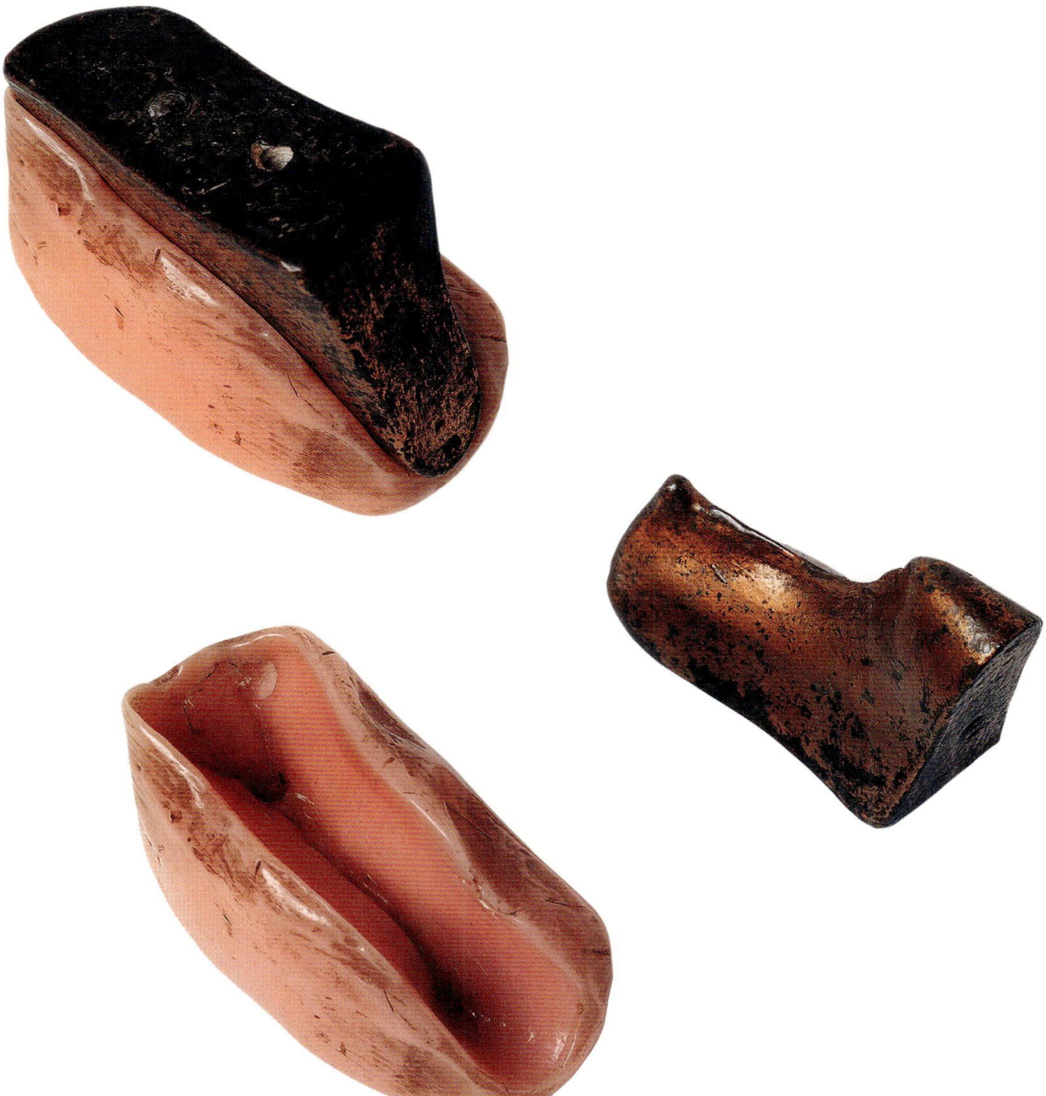

All in all, the three erotic objects instantiate what one art historian has called "the gap between what is presented and what is signified," inasmuch as in each sexuality, the body, and the strange reciprocity between bodies and objects is gestured toward but not demonstrated.[4]

The three erotic objects, and their subsequent editions, exert a strong appeal to our sense of touch. They employ a variety of nontraditional sculptural materials such as galvanized plaster and dental plastic. They explore the mold and casting as a form of sculptural production and reproduction. They establish a tabletop scale for sculpture – refusing both monumentality and the need for a base. And they constitute a field of play that is definitively erotic, harkening back to the explorations of eros and desire that figured so prominently in Duchamp's work of the teens and 1920s, most notably *The Bride Stripped Bare by Her Bachelors, Even* (1915–23). They were also exhibited quite a lot, both in the United States and in Europe, as the 1960s saw a rise in Duchamp exhibitions, and the three erotic objects were included in the most important of them.[5] This means that the erotic objects and the readymades – Duchamp's two important forays into the realm of sculpture – often appeared side by side, and indeed Duchamp considered them to be equally worthy of display.

The reappearance of the readymades in the 1960s is far from self-evident. In 1913 Duchamp invented the readymade by conceiving of the commodity object as an engine for making sculpture. During the teens, the mechanics of this operation were largely comprised of choice, purchase, and display. In other words, Duchamp allowed his artistic process to mime the relations and logic of the commodity world. As he strolled through the markets of Paris and the along the streets of New York looking for commodities to transform into art, he rehearsed one of Charles Baudelaire's famous complaints against sculpture – that it "suffers because it too easily becomes indistinguishable from a luxury object."[6] While one would be hard pressed to view the array of mundane and domestic objects chosen by Duchamp as luxury items (a hat rack, coat rack, bottle rack, and comb, for example), the problem of indistinguishability was acute, and, perhaps fittingly, most of the original readymades were lost, discarded, or simply went unnoticed. That is, until after World War II, when interest in Dada and Surrealism in general, and Duchamp in particular, became a hallmark of the postwar European and American art scene. As Hal Foster has argued, Duchamp becomes Duchampian only in the late 1950s and early 1960s, and in the blush of interest that accompanied his work the lost and discarded readymades – now known almost exclusively through photographs – were increasingly in demand.[7]

It is well documented, but not much discussed, that the Swedish curator Ulf Linde and the Italian art dealer Arturo Schwarz helped to meet this demand in the early 1960s by making handmade versions of the readymades.[8] In 1960 Linde made copies of *Bicycle Wheel* and *Fresh Widow* for a gallery exhibition of Duchamp's work in Stockholm. It appears that, at first, Duchamp was unaware of these copies. At Linde's beckoning, Duchamp traveled to Stockholm in 1961, where he was presented with Linde's copies, both of which he graciously

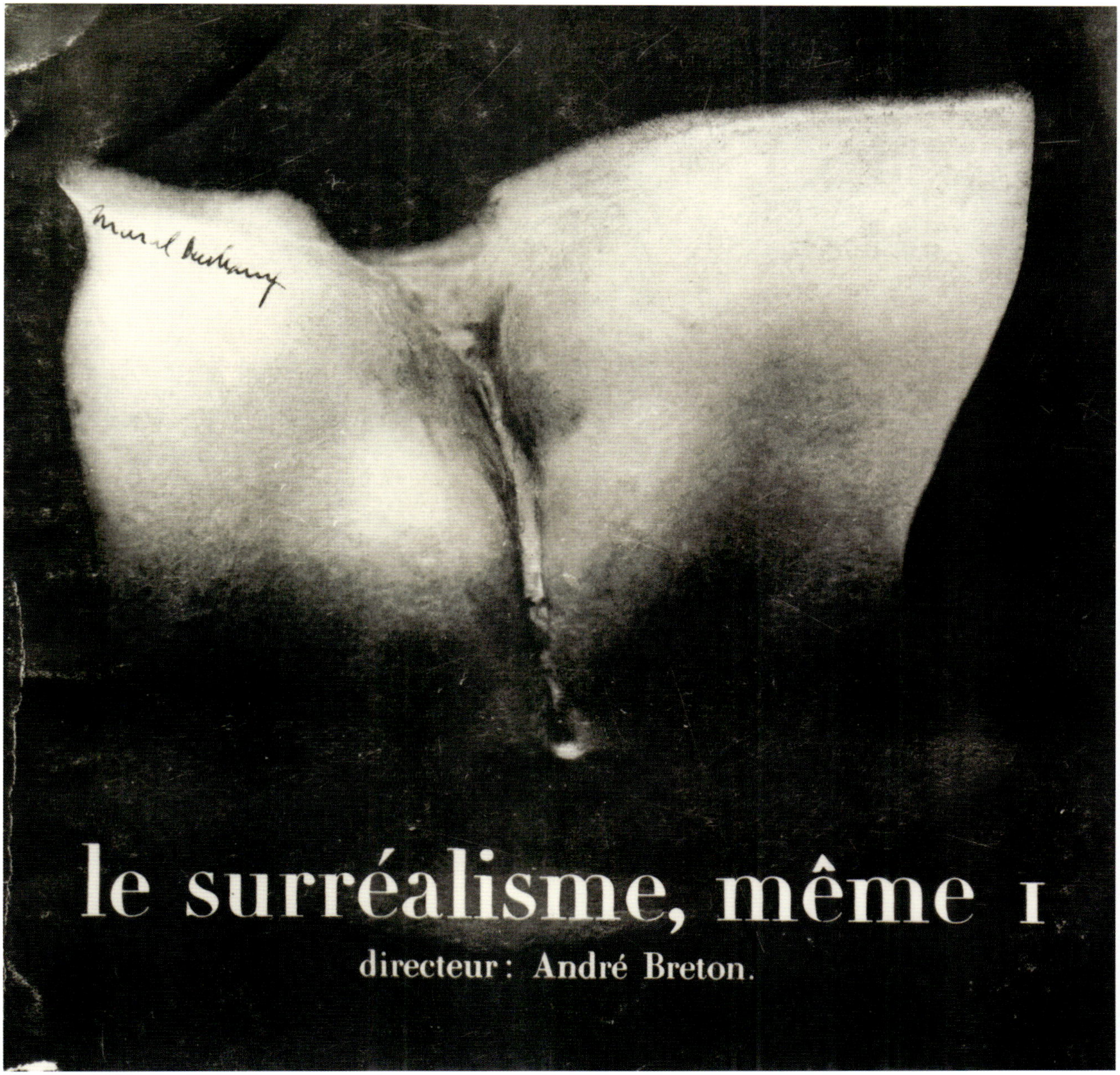

Marcel Duchamp
Cover for "Le Surréalisme, même," 1956

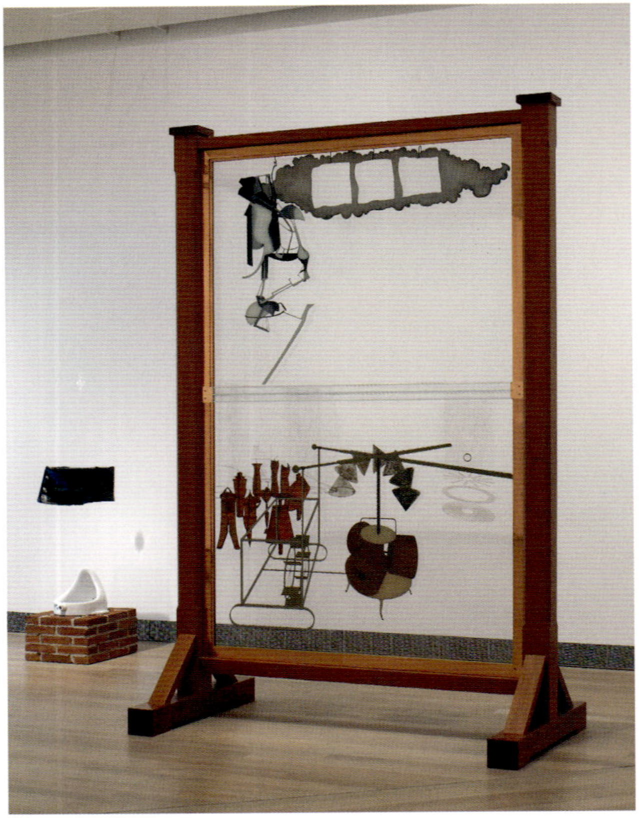

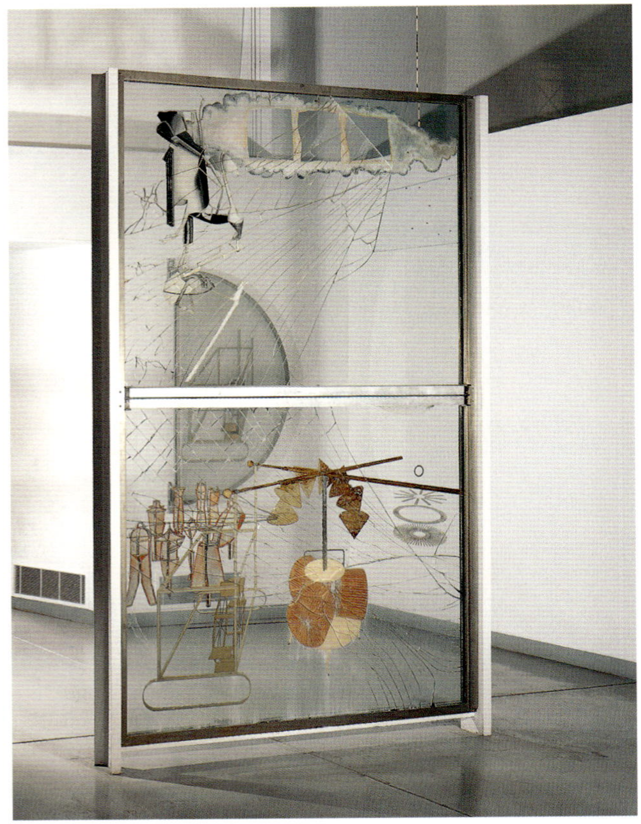

signed "copie conforme." Later, under the auspices of curator Pontus Hulten, the museum of modern art in Stockholm (the Moderna Museet) commissioned Linde to make a copy of *The Large Glass* as well as a complete set of readymades. This time Duchamp was aware of the project and requested that all the works be donated to the permanent collection of the museum. Working from photographs and the dimensions published in Robert Lebel's monograph, Linde fabricated some of the objects himself, some were produced by local craftspeople (*Paris Air*, for instance, was made by a local glassblower), and the Linde version of *Fountain* was purchased directly from a restaurant lavatory. The Linde replicas were to make two important public appearances. In 1963 Walter Hopps organized Duchamp's first retrospective exhibition at the Pasadena Museum. Four of Linde's readymades (*In Advance of a Broken Arm, Traveler's Folding Item, Paris Air,* and *Fresh Widow*) were on view, as was his replica of *The Large Glass*. This exhibition served as the first major introduction of Duchamp's work to American artists, and its catalogue clearly lists the readymade as Linde replicas: there was no hiding their replication.

The second important public viewing of Linde's replicas was in Arturo Schwarz's Milan gallery in an exhibition held there in 1963, precisely the moment Schwarz himself was beginning to remake a set of the lost readymades. Schwarz had already established an intense interest in Duchamp as early as 1957, when he began to collect materials for what would become the definitive catalogue raisonné of Duchamp's oeuvre. While Schwarz was singularly obsessed with Duchamp, he was also interested in Dada and Surrealism more broadly, and the Galleria Schwarz in Milan was an important conduit of these ideas for the post-war community of Italian artists. The precise details of how the Schwarz edition came to pass are not exactly known. Schwarz claims that Duchamp wanted to bring all of his works together – a desire that was evident in the *Boîte-en-Valise* ("Box in a Valise") – and was dismayed that the readymades were no longer extant.[9] Duchamp had already editioned the three erotic objects – indeed it was Schwarz who had issued *Objet-Dard* and *Wedge of Chastity*. In this regard, Duchamp's interest in casting and repetition was firmly in place. It was agreed that all the readymades would be editioned in groups of eight with two extra copies, one for Duchamp and one for Schwarz. Suffice it to say that the vast majority of people who have encountered a readymade in the second half of the twentieth century have seen one from the set Schwarz produced in 1964.

Unlike the Linde replicas, the Schwarz readymades were overseen by Duchamp at every turn, and accuracy was of the essence as Schwarz hired professional engineers to make blueprints of the readymades based on the photographs.[10] Only *Fountain* was not produced solely by a craftsman. A mold was made by a ceramicist and given to an Italian plumbing manufacturer, where, one evening, the factory line of mass production was halted as twelve *Fountain* sculptures were made instead.[11] Schwarz subsequently hired professional craftsmen to make the objects – a glassblower for *Paris Air,* a welder for the *Bottle Rack,* a carpenter for the *Hat Rack*. The dominant art-historical reception of the readymade

opposite: left Marcel Duchamp
La marieé mise a nu par ses célibataires, même (The Bride Stripped Bare by Her Bachelors, Even), 1915–23. Replica made by Ulf Linde c.1961

opposite: right Marcel Duchamp
La marieé mise a nu par ses célibataires, même (The Bride Stripped Bare by Her Bachelors, Even), (The Large Glass), 1915–23

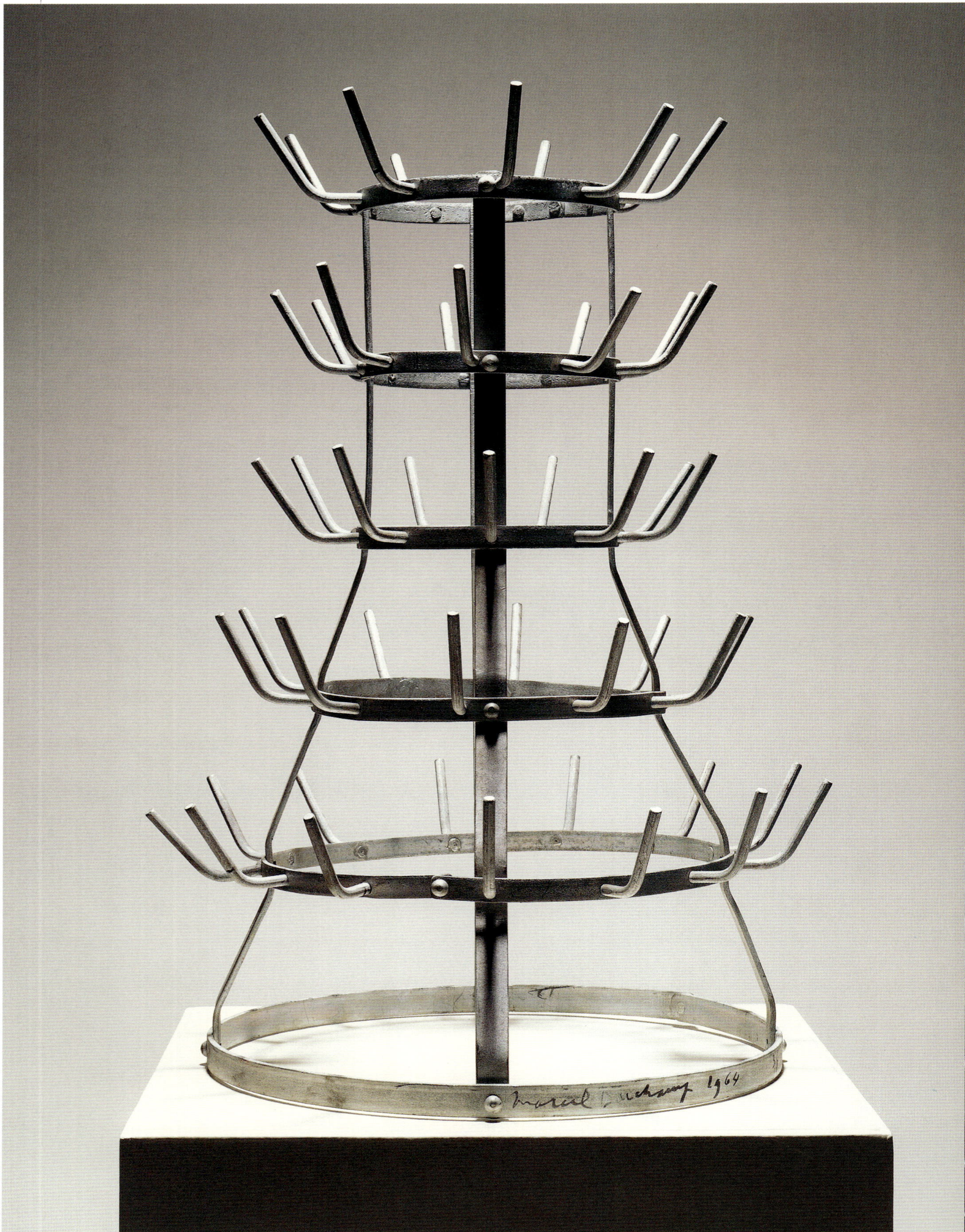

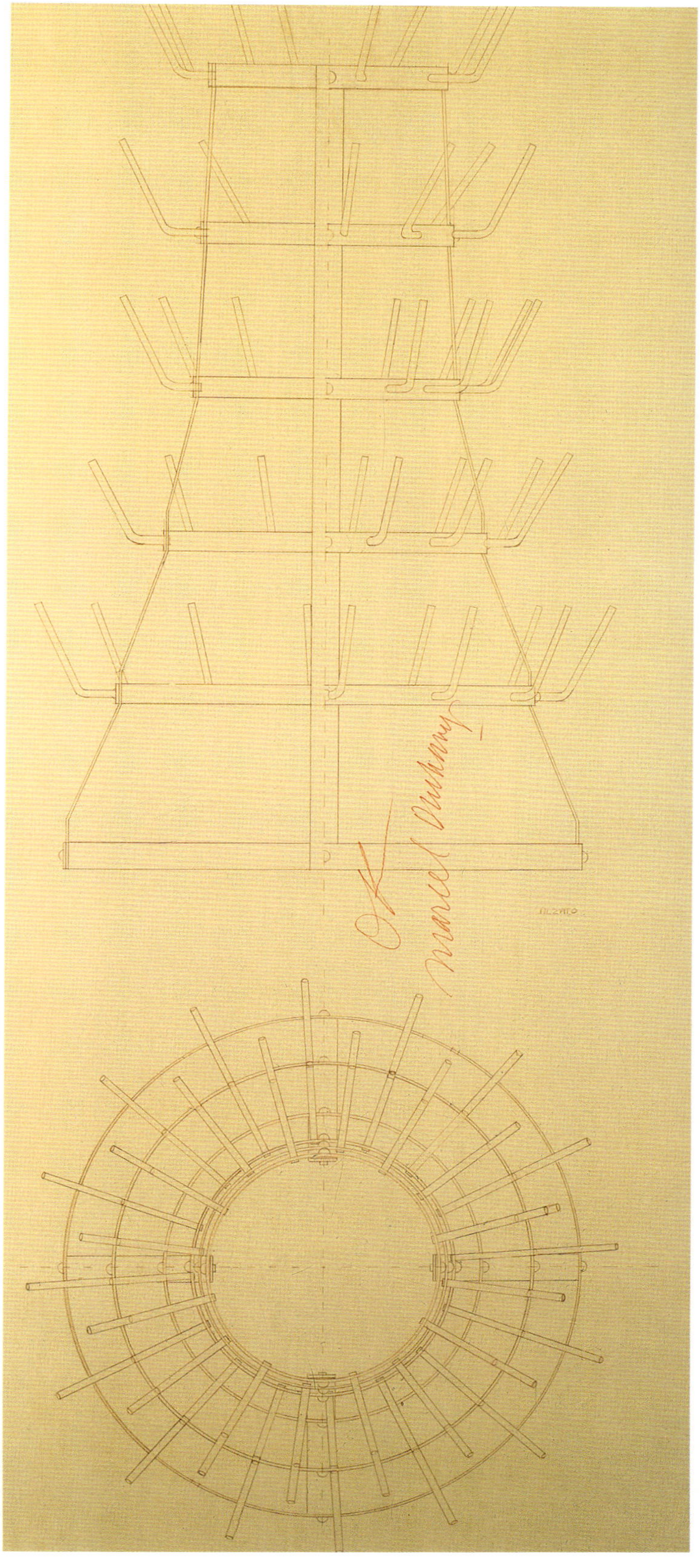

right Marcel Duchamp
Plan du Porte-bouteilles (Plan for Bottle Dryer), 1964

left Marcel Duchamp
Porte-bouteilles (Bottle Dryer), 1914, 5th version 1964

sees it as the agent that introduced the forces of mass production into the realm of art, yet this account too easily neglects the "handmade" wrinkle in the story. That Duchamp turned commodity production into a cottage industry, staffed by Swedish and Italian craftsmen, comes with all the requisite Duchampian irony. Yet if we look closely we might see the telltale evidence, traces of the handmade. *Bottle Rack* not only looks antiquated, but it lacks the polish of the assembly-line. *Paris Air*, originally made as a gift for Duchamp's New York patron Walter Arensberg, was an ampoule purchased from a Parisian pharmacy, broken and emptied, then filled with air and resealed. The 1964 *Paris Air*, by contrast, is seamless; there is no tear or break to suggest Duchamp's intervention or the abiding touch of friendship that suffuses the original object. And even the factory-produced *Fountain* prompted the following response from William Camfield, the art historian who has looked the most closely at all the versions of *Fountain*: "This replica seems more related to sculpture than to readymades, given its slight but perceptible modulations of surface which suggest its origin as handcrafted sculpture rather than an American assembly-line production."[12]

If the meaning of objects (aesthetic and otherwise) derives, in relatively equal measure, from their function and their production, then the handmade quality of the remade readymades, and Duchamp's explicit decision to have them refabricated in editions, seems wholly contradictory, certainly qualifying our sense of the "original" readymades. Given that Duchamp produced the three erotic sculptures of the 1950s by hand, it is possible they may offer some clues to the conundrum of the handmade readymades of the 1960s.

After Duchamp's death in 1968, it was revealed that more than merely making the erotic objects and the *Boîte-en-Valise*, he had also been at work, secretly, for nearly twenty years on the spectacular and mysterious *Etant donnés*. The work was donated to the Philadelphia Museum of Art so that it could be permanently on view and seen in relation to the largest collection of works by Duchamp in the world, including, importantly, *The Large Glass*. In a room all its own, the viewer comes upon a set of wooden doors, which contain two peepholes just below an average sight line. Bending forward, ever so slightly, to peer through them, one is confronted with a startling mise-en-scène: behind the doors, and then through an opening in a brick wall, one sees the prone figure of a white woman. Her face is obscured, although a bolt of blonde hair is visible just above her shoulder. The body is naked and splayed across a twig-filled landscape. She holds a flickering gas lamp in her left hand. In the background one can see a waterfall, complete with a mechanical simulation of moving water. These attributes are contained within the full title of the work, *Given: 1. The Waterfall 2. The Illuminating Gas*.

The mystery of *Etant donnés* is evidenced by how little has been written about it.[13] In the art-historical reception of Duchamp, it has largely been occluded by the invention of the readymades. Yet it looms large, and the relationship be-tween it and the three erotic objects may ultimately reconfigure our sense of the handmade readymades of the 1960s. All three of the erotic objects bear a strong relation to *Etant donnés*. *Objet-Dard* is a remainder from the process of breaking the mold for the woman's body in *Etant donnés,* specifically the part of the mold that supported an area under her breast. Similarly, *Female Fig Leaf* is cast from the figure's particularly mysterious genitals – which are not quite there, lacking in both pubic hair and proper placement. *Wedge of Chastity* shares an experiential dimension with *Etant donnés*. Obscure until seen, both *Wedge of Chastity* and *Etant donnés* splay open the female body, suggesting that desire and eros are the product of a gaze that is simultaneously scopophilic and haptic, voyeuristic and tactile.

Unlike *Etant donnés*, the three erotic objects are not fixed in space. They share a domestic scale, by which I mean that they all occupy the realm of things placed on top of tables and mantels, as opposed to floors and pedestals. Their modest scale gives them a migratory quality, which Duchamp acknowledged when discussing *Wedge of Chastity*: "We still have it on our table. We usually take it with us, like a wedding ring, no?"[14] I find the quickness of this elision quite telling, to think that an object as curious and oblique as *Wedge of Chastity* could so easily be held in relation to a ready-made (or luxury) object like a wedding ring. And it is precisely the relation between the erotic objects and the readymades that I would like to try to articulate, especially given the fact that by the late 1950s editions of the erotic objects had already begun to circulate. Schwarz exhibited them in Milan, where they were almost certainly seen by Lucio Fontana and Piero Manzoni.[15] Manzoni, in turn, showed *Female Fig Leaf* to Marcel Broodthaers; it was the first work by Duchamp he had seen.[16] By 1960 it appears that Jasper Johns owned a version of all three objects. I say this to indicate that the reception of Duchamp comes through these objects as much as through the readymades. Importantly, it was only *after* these intimate and cast objects were reproduced, and had begun to circulate, that Duchamp authorized Arturo Schwarz to fabricate a set of the then mostly lost readymades.

But why not simply go out and purchase a new urinal, a new bottle rack? After all, Duchamp had done just that when he first arrived in New York after leaving the original *Bicycle Wheel* in Paris.[17] Schwarz maintains that making the readymades by hand to the specifications of the photographs was a means to keep them looking as much like the originals as possible – the contemporaneous design of functional objects like hat racks and shovels had changed to such an extent that they apparently would no longer suffice. According to Schwarz, Duchamp "wanted a perfect reproduction of the original. The only way to do it perfectly was to do it by hand. There was no other way. How could he reproduce something that was manufactured over half a century before?"[18] Duchamp never quite addressed the issue head-on, although he maintained that readymades were chosen with "visual indifference." When asked by an interviewer in 1967 how a readymade should be looked at, Duchamp responded: "Ultimately, it should not be looked at. Through our eyes we get the notion that it exists. But we don't look at it the way we look at a painting. The idea of contemplation disappears completely. One simply notes that it's a bottle rack, or that it was a bottle

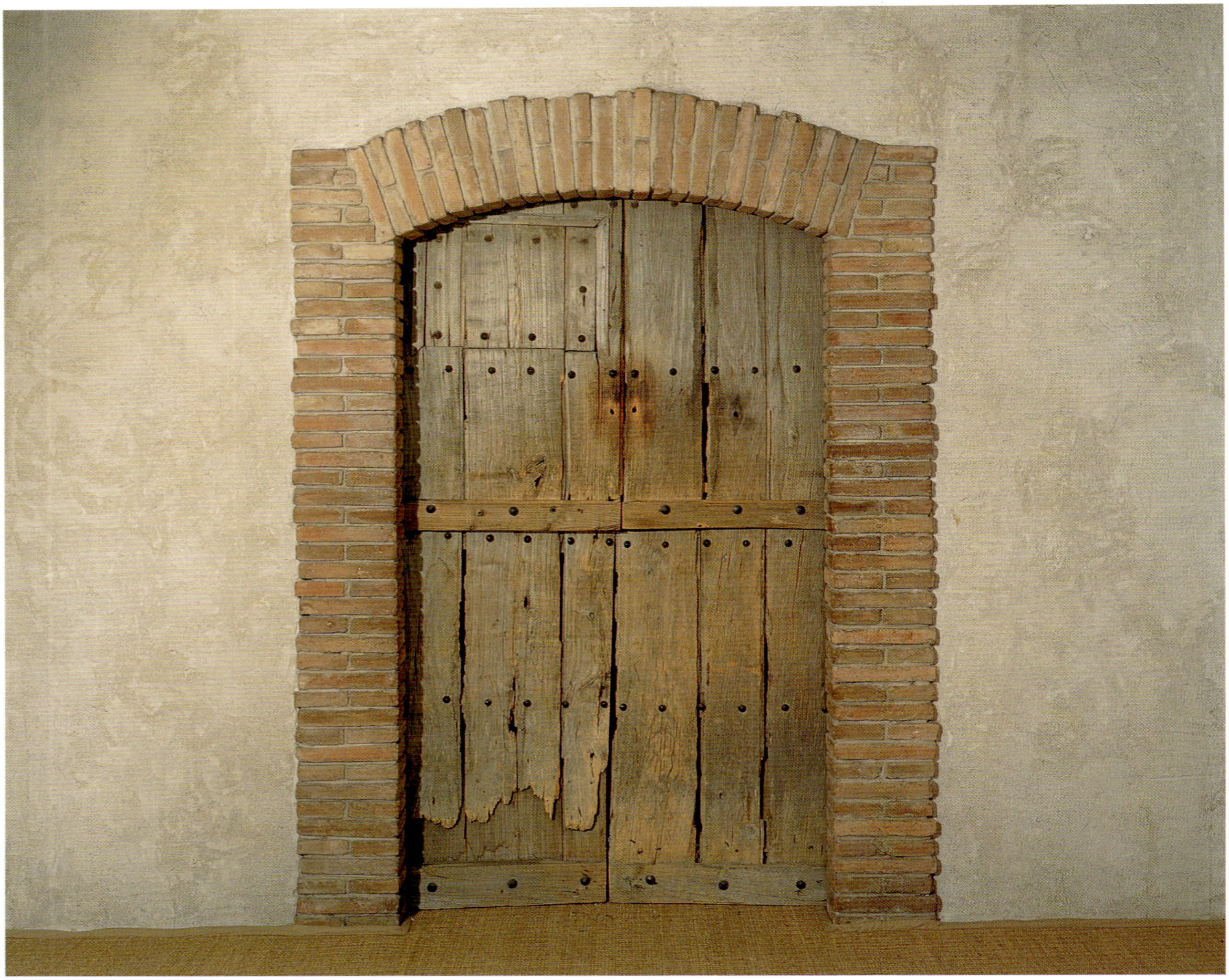

above and right Marcel Duchamp
Etant donnés: 1, La Chute d'Eau, 2, Le Gaz d'Eclairage (Given: 1. The Waterfall, 2. The Illuminating Gas), 1946–66

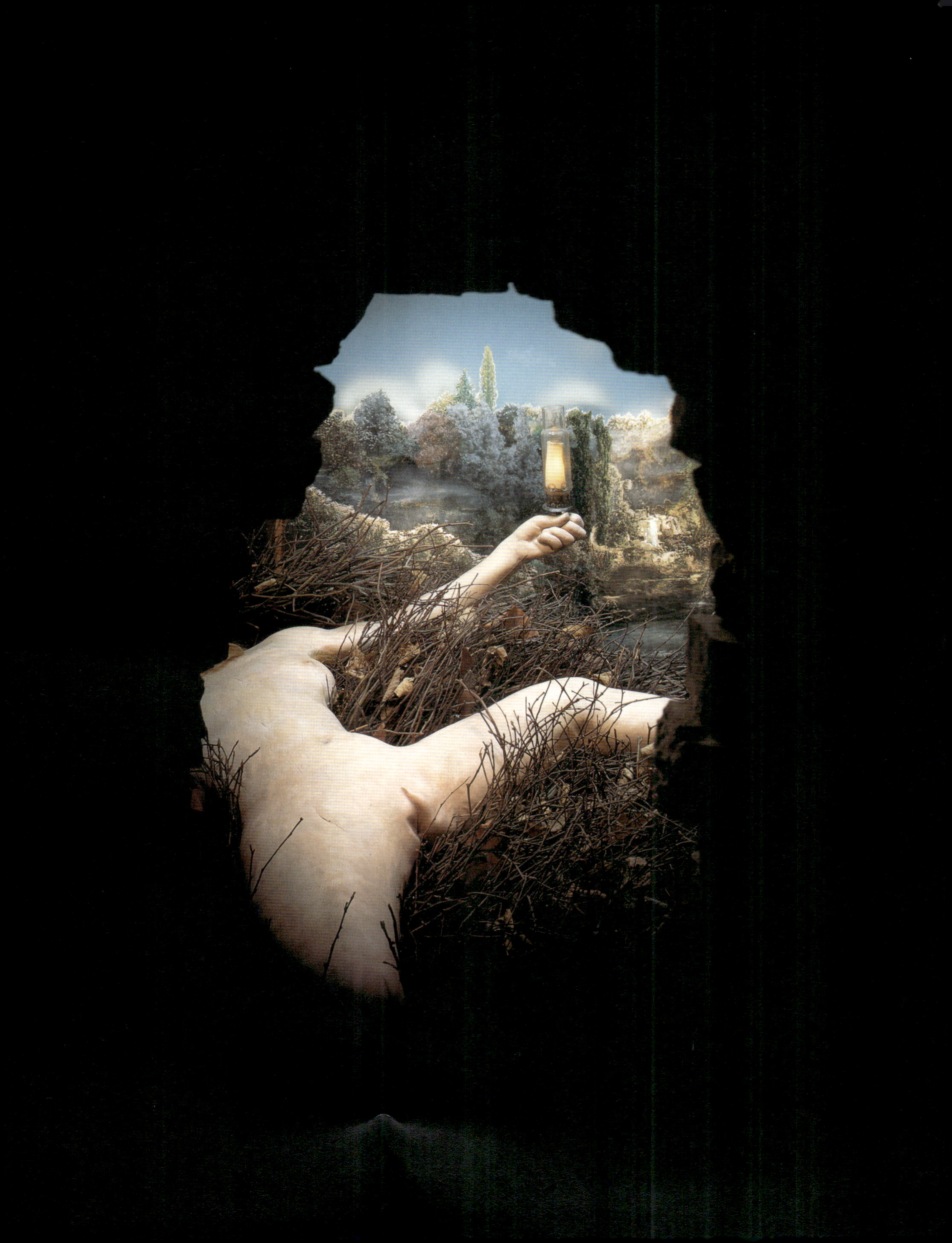

rack and has changed direction."[19] But if that's the case, then why go to all the trouble of having them remade by hand? Of course Duchamp had been going to the trouble of reproducing his oeuvre for quite some time, as the *Boîte-en-Valise* will attest. And it seems to go almost without saying that he was an artist deeply interested in the problem of reproduction and repetition. But making readymades by hand? What's that about?

I think the answer to this question is many sided. There is a prosaic answer, fitting in that Duchamp was nothing if not pragmatic. During the 1950s, Duchamp spent a prodigous amount of time and energy ensuring that his work was gathered and deposited in the right museums. He did this not only for his own benefit but also to ensure fair financial remuneration for his friends. He was nothing if not careful and calculated and generous in this regard.[20] This generosity extended to his newfound family as well, which has led many to surmise that Duchamp agreed to the Schwarz edition as a way to attend to the welfare of his wife and her children. However assiduously Duchamp had avoided the increasing pressures of a commercial art market, such a critique needed to be held in relation to the lived reality of family.[21]

Duchamp was far too intelligent and ethical an artist simply to make a thing or a set of things for money alone. He was an artist with a definitive set of interests, one worked out over time and in various media. The historical proximity of the intimately scaled and handmade erotic sculptures and the 1964 handmade edition of the readymades indicates there are connections to be made between the erotics of the body and the allure of the commodity object and further that Duchamp's sculptural practice is shaped by the relays between such different stagings of desire. To my way of thinking, the reproductions of the erotic objects created a sense of permission, or a field of possibility, for the production of handmade readymades. Handmade readymades offer a model of repetition that is more analogous to erotic or bodily modes of repetition, more similar to, as well, the model of repetition offered by casting than the mass production of the assembly line. (It was no mere expedient that the body of the woman in *Etant donnés* was made from a cast.) The erotic casts and the crafted readymades continue to maintain a difference, and a productive and structuring tension, between the forces of production that make commodities and the forces that make art. Both the handmade readymades and the erotic objects establish strong links between eros and objects. The mass-produced readymades of the teens offer the problem of reproduction and manufacture – the problem of the then relatively nascent assembly line – while the readymades of the 1960s offer us the problem of repetition and desire of and for lost objects, the quandary of how we negotiate difference (and hence our desire) in the field of overwhelming sameness and calcification.

I want to return to the temporal proximity of these two sets of objects. If the readymades were a conundrum, objects that resided in an uneasy place of legibility, inasmuch as they could not be regarded as *art* by those who first encountered them, then the cast objects are memory molds, fossils of psychic states. *Objet-Dard* is a remnant of a work of art – or, better yet, of the process of making a work of art. *Female Fig Leaf* is the memory of a body – albeit a fictional one. Both are also images of absence. *Objet-Dard* marks out the space underneath or around the breast of the figure in *Etant donnés*. *Female Fig Leaf* offers us the negative space of the figure's pudendum. The last of the triumvirate, *Wedge of Chastity*, memorializes the ineffable quality of the erotic encounter, and as such it offers the fantasy of each piece filling the other's void. *Wedge of Chastity* also functions as a mnemonic for intimacy and fidelity: "like a wedding ring." Perhaps Duchamp's desire to have *Wedge of Chastity* function "like a wedding ring" was a desire for it to be read along standard social conventions, for it to be *legible*, as well as portable.[22] One problem with the original readymades was that their legibility, their ability to be construed or understood as art, was compromised with every move – from Paris to New York, from the halls of the Independents Exhibition to Alfred Stieglitz's studio – in each instance they were discarded or misplaced, no longer available to perform the role of art. The irony here is pronounced, in that one of the foremost roles of art is to make things visible. It gives public form to thoughts and feelings, to ideas and bodies, to history and memory. Among the most important things the readymade did, and does, is to bestow this legibility upon the commodity – to its eccentricities and vagaries – to the deep peculiarity of objects, to the ways in which commodities trip us up or act as a trap, or precede us.

One way readymades render the commodity legible is in part by making the body legible. Bodies become legible in their encounters with readymades because they are either called into humorous action (go ahead, hang up your hat) or stymied by their inability to use a previously functional thing (the problem of an inverted urinal).[23] As we trip over *Trébuchet* in Duchamp's studio, or spin the *Bicycle Wheel*, or puzzle over what to do with *In Advance of a Broken Arm*, Duchamp's readymades of the teens set into motion an intense relay between bodies and things – each serving to make the other visible. It is no mistake that the little girl of *Apolinère Enameled* is painting her bedpost, marking it so that both she and it can been seen. In turn, however, no matter how newly animated bodies might have become in the face of the readymades as installed in Duchamp's studio (little machines for slapstick), the objects themselves were routinely thrown away, forgotten, or destroyed; the readymades were commodities that ceased to be legible, either as art or even as a commodity worth saving. In many ways, the readymades don't become truly visible until after the war, when people want to include them in exhibitions, and when Duchamp allows other people (like Sidney Janis) to purchase them for him. Yet it is precisely during *this* period that Duchamp began to make his erotic sculptures by hand, and when he was involved, in secret, with the beginnings of *Etant donnés*. And it was during this time that he began to imagine an edition of readymades made by hand, to the exact – or as exact as possible – specifications of the originals. And by making them by hand, they became legible as art – finally. No one will ever lose or misplace or discard or destroy a 1964 handmade readymade. They have

migrated off the floor, they have come down from the ceiling and sit properly on pedestals – like art, and as such they are as legible as a wedding ring.

There is one other intermediary step. When Duchamp "installed" the first miniature replicas of the readymades in the *Boîte-en-Valise*, he positioned them in league with *The Large Glass* – where they hang like a vertical predella explicating, and being explicated by in turn, the stalled machine of desire that is *The Bride Stripped Bare by Her Bachelors, Even.* (This installation was staged again by curator Walter Hopps in the 1963 Pasadena exhibition of Duchamp's work. It is also the installation of the Linde replicas at the Moderna Museet in Stockholm.) This pointed co-presentation is a way that Duchamp explored the relationships between the readymades and *The Large Glass* – between a set of objects that call the body into new ways of being and that exist at a liminal threshold between the commodity and something else – a readymade (if not a full-blown art object) and the kind of transformative but stymied erotic encounter imaged by *The Large Glass*. In other words, it was a way of talking about the effect of things on the body and the bodiliness of things.

This installation of the readymades helps to show us something about the corporeality of art and the potential reciprocity between the eroticism of the body and the sensuality of objects – art and otherwise. Here the commodity is shown to be a profoundly psychic object with erotic dimensions, as the readymades mirror the sexual division and frustration of *The Large Glass* – with *Paris Air* as an archetypal sinuous female form; *Traveler's Folding Item* as a simultaneous chaste protector and striptease waiting to happen; and finally *Fountain*, now turned upright – as if to offer at least some form of male release. Here, then, are the readymades presented as erotic objects. According to Walter Hopps, Duchamp used to call the readymades "my little pick-ups," a phrase that cannot refer only to his activity of shopping for them.[24] And just as there are three migratory commodities held in relation to *The Large Glass,* so too the three erotic objects are three clues to the as-yet-unveiled *Etant donnés*, snapshots of a picture not yet seen. If the 1964 set of readymades is the past reincarnated, then the three erotic objects are (or were) artifacts of the future.

Duchamp repeatedly stated that one aim of the readymade was to be antiretinal; indeed this has become an art-historical truism. And while I take Duchamp at his word, that the readymades are not necessarily about the visual as such, I don't think he ever meant for them to be anticorporeal. Rather, Duchamp's claims for the antiretinal can here be seen as having more to do with bodily modes of apprehension, memory, and legibility than ideas about art in the service of the mind. This is a way of looking at Duchamp as a purveyor of object relations that are in keeping with those of British psychoanalysts Melanie Klein and D. W. Winnicott. Kleinian object relations begin with the infant at her mother's breast. The breast stands alone, distinct and separate from the mother. It is the breast that is the satisfier of needs, creator of dependence. The child's fantasy life is formed around feelings toward the breast that are simultaneously loving and aggressive. The breast is an object that must be assimilated into the

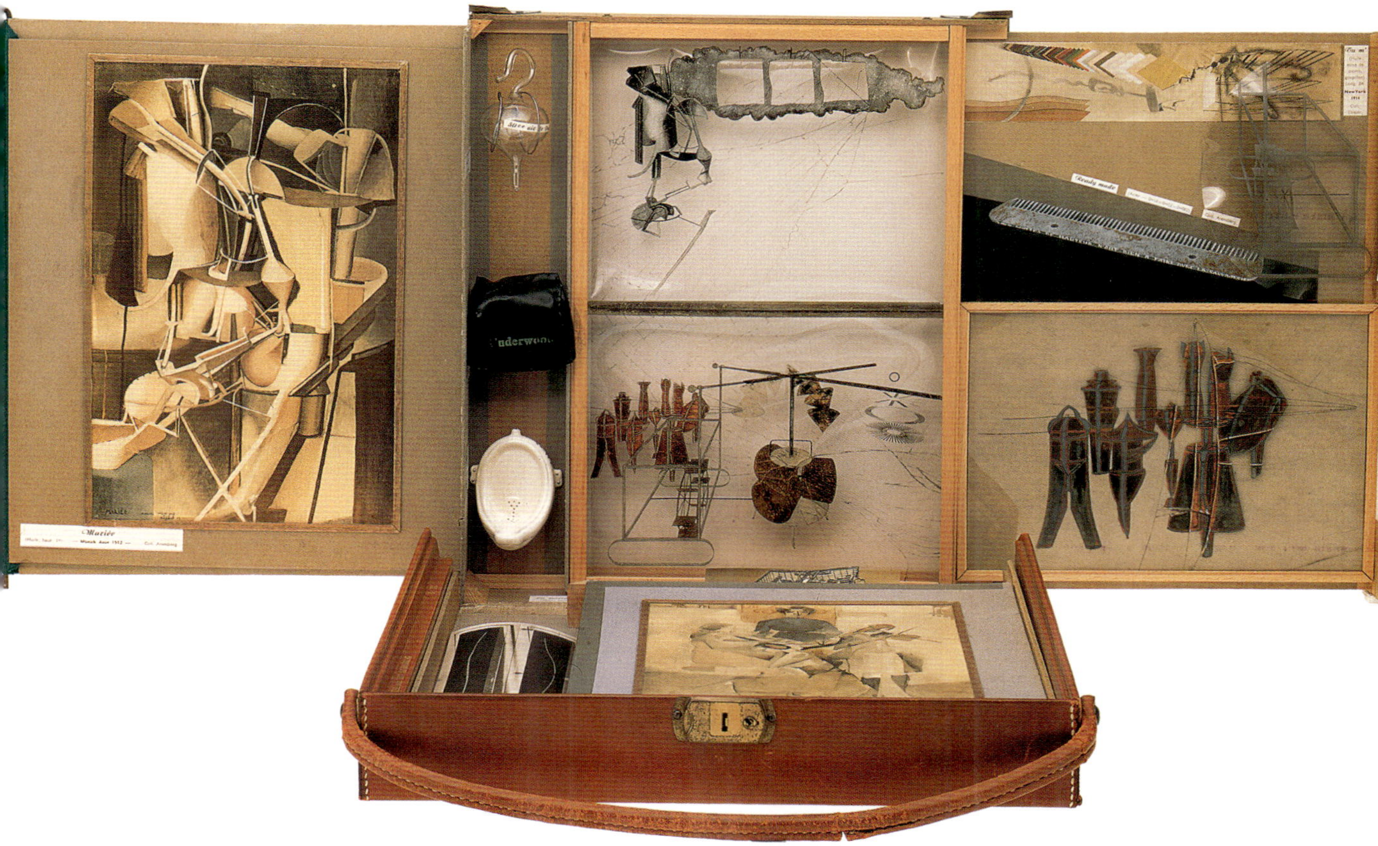

Marcel Duchamp
Boîte-en-Valise (The Box in a Valise),
1935–41

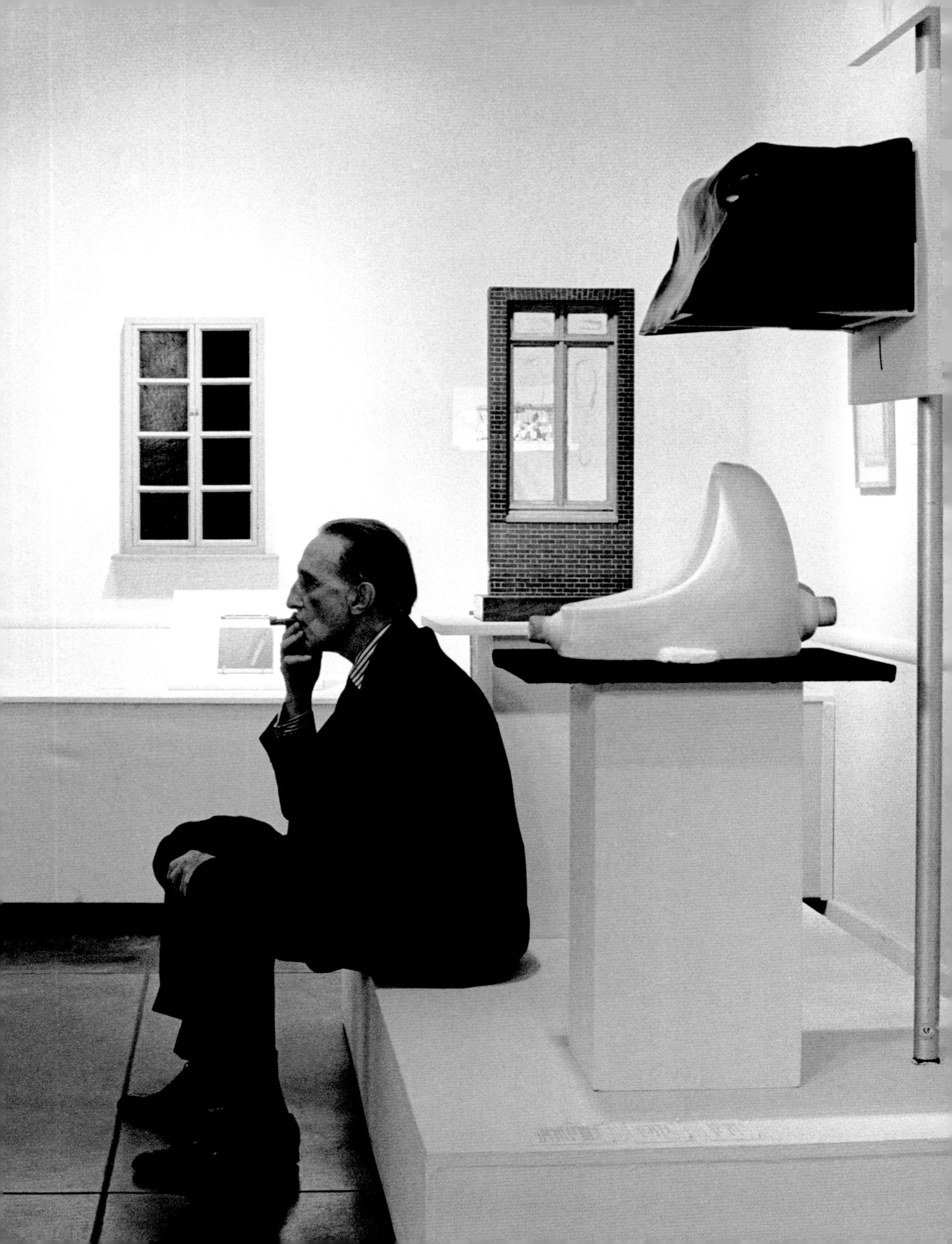

Julian Wasser
Marcel Duchamp in profile and Installation of Readymades for the Marcel Duchamp Retrospective, Pasadena, 1963

infant as well as rejected. In this model, the root of object relations is the child's struggle to understand the nature and existence of the boundaries between inside and outside, between "me" and "not me." This psychic and physical play between interior and exterior creates an intense cathexsis onto objects, as objects come to stand for persons and parts come to stand for wholes.

Often the child wishes to destroy the breast, particularly through the act of incorporation. Fantasies emerge in which the breast is devoured, absorbed into the child, which subsequently ignite equally strong fantasies around its expulsion. For Klein, these fantasies of destruction inevitably lead to feelings of guilt, provoking ensuing desires for reparation. Far from them being pathological, Klein sees "these conflicting feelings, together with the emotional and intellectual growth of the child, which enable him to find other objects of interest and pleasure result in the capacity to transfer love, replacing the first loved person by other people and things."[25] According to Klein, the child's navigation of its relation to the breast as a part object is constitutive of fantasy, of creativity, and even of love and emotion itself. The subject only comes into being through and with a relation to the world of objects – both real and phantasmatic.

It is tempting to see the three erotic objects of Duchamp as Kleinian part objects *par excellence*. All are fragmentary in relation to the "wholeness" of both *Etant donnés* and the marriage of two fully elaborated adults. They share an intense bodiliness that renders their fragmentary nature all the more psychically and physically charged. They are also residual products of a much larger space of fantasy – *Etant donnés* – a space that is consummately erotic and aggressive, a space in which the viewer is both lured to and repelled from. What is of interest, however, is the intensity of the abstraction of these objects, suggesting that Duchamp continued to be interested in the ways in which three-dimensional representations of love and eros mobilize the space of the visual, the tactile, and fantasy in ways that rhyme with the psychic processes of the ego. That he would quickly edition them, reproduce them, or, perhaps more precisely, *repeat* them intimates that there is no closure, no complete working through, no act of reparation that finalizes our pendulum swings from love to destruction; there are only countless small gestures and acts of reworkings.

If the replication of the erotic objects did indeed create a sense of permission for the 1964 readymades, then the terms of psychic engagement do not appear to be the same. Where the erotic objects are Kleinian part objects, the readymades are Winnicottian transitional objects. For Winnicott, the subject's relation to the object world is more readily demonstrable. As infants develop the capacity for recognizing objects as "not me," as they learn the various distinctions of inside and outside, they begin to constitute creative relationships to objects and phenomena. Such objects emerge as the mother adapts less and less to the infant's demands (this is the classic "good-enough mother" that predominates in Winnicott); importantly, the mother withdraws according to the infant's growing ability to deal with her failure (a failure I will to return to). Objects and phenomena enter into this growing space between the mother and child, and Winnicott

referred to these as "transitional objects." Distinctly unlike part objects, transitional objects do not reside largely in the fantasy life of the child but rather are actual objects – blankets, dolls – that function as psychic talismans – aids for easing anxiety, helping the child to sleep. Such objects are nothing if not deeply familiar. Indeed, they lack the intensity of the part object largely because they are not born of, or consigned to, the space of fantasy. Quite the opposite, the transitional object is:

> Gradually allowed to be decathected, so that in the course of the years it becomes not so much forgotten as relegated to limbo. By this I mean, in health the transitional object does not "go inside" nor does the feeling necessarily undergo repression. It is not forgotten and it is not mourned. It loses meaning, and this is because transitional phenomena have become diffused, have become spread out over the whole intermediate territory between "inner psychic reality" and "the external world as perceived by two persons in common," that is to say over the whole cultural field.[26]

The readymades are many things, but it seems they are also transitional objects of a sort. In their first iteration, they allowed Duchamp to move from painting to not-painting or from painting to not-art or from painting to object. (I prefer not to calcify this move; a lot is in limbo for Duchamp in the teens and 1920s.) Hence, these are the readymades that can be lost, misplaced, "de-cathected," and, far from such losses being mourned, they are instead "spread out over the whole intermediary territory" (which in this instance means their photographic reproductions, especially in the *Boîte-en-Valise*, as well as their belated reception as "foundational" for postmodernism).

Winnicott further argues that transitional objects do not have symbolic value; they possess *actual* value. In this scenario, a "blankie" is not symbolic of the lost breast (it is emphatically not a part object), it is a blankie, an object whose very actuality endows it with a kind of agency. Such a sense of the "realness" of the thing means that the term transitional object "gives room for the process of becoming able to accept the difference between difference and similarity."[27] If the readymades are transitional objects, then their actuality, their status as object *and* sculpture, seems particularly important – both a bottle rack and a sculpture – not a bottle rack symbolic of a sculpture or necessarily symbolic of art as a commodity. But rather they are objects in the process of accepting "the difference between difference and similarity." If the readymades of the teens and 1920s fail, inasmuch as they can never quite be assimilated into the field of art proper, then the readymades of the 1960s are "good enough" readymades, objects that accept the failure of the first go-around and deploy instead the strategy of the handmade as a way to ensure that the objects – part object, part sculpture – continue to have a kind of actuality, that they don't become "symbolic" of something else, that they continue not to be mourned, but rather to be comfortably (visually) neglected, thrown into the healthy limbo that is the "external world as perceived by two persons in common."

But it is the readymades of the teens that are the true transitional objects. To call the 1964 set of readymades "good enough" is not quite to address the problem of what kind of object they actually are. It is to dodge the bullet, once more, on saying why it is that they needed to be made by hand. For many, the idea of handmade readymades is a capitulation to a kind of fetishism of a lost original, an object that erases the difference between past and present, between loss and presence. In such a reading, the handmade readymades are nothing if not cynical. And yet, as ironic as the turn of events might be, I don't, in the end, think it is cynicism that motivated Duchamp to approve a set of handmade readymades. The 1964 readymades are sculptural and, as such, they make it clear that the readymades of the teens were precisely *not* sculpture. Just as the 1964 edition makes it clear that the readymades of the teens were not sculpture (that is, not legible as art), they also are a frank acknowledgment that the readymades of the teens are no longer extant, that they are, for the most part, lost objects. By having the original mass-produced and purchased readymades made by hand, Duchamp is actually insisting upon their identity as lost. Even though Duchamp deputized Sidney Janis to purchase a new urinal for his exhibition *Challenge and Defy* in 1950 and signed a *Bottle Rack* purchased by Robert Rauschenberg in 1960, it clearly wasn't satisfactory. To establish them as so readily available in the 1950s must have felt odd, for the readymades were never *found* objects in the sense of André Breton's *objet trouvé*. And it appears, although Duchamp experimented with the idea, they could not be reconstituted as found objects after the fact. Rather, the 1964 set of readymades firmly establishes the identity of the original readymades as *lost*, as though being nonlegible in the first instance had come to constitute their meaning. They were transitional objects, de-cathected, unrecognized, and gradually left behind; such objects are not, then, simply found by others, but rather exist in the realm of memory and come to constitute one's sense of embodiment. So too it is worth noting that a transitional object is not open to substitution as such; every mother knows one doesn't "replace" a fraying blankie with a new one. (This may be why when a precious object is lost or broken in adulthood its replacement with an exact replica often doesn't do the trick; it's not the point in the end.) In this regard, the 1964 readymades, by establishing their radical difference from the readymades of the teens, bring us back to Winnicott's sense that these are objects that help us to understand "the difference between difference and similarity" – the difference between art and not-art, between transitional and lost objects, between objects and sculpture, and all the permutations of the two.

Two sets of objects, each forming a constellation around another: the readymades framing the inscrutable screen of desire that is *The Large Glass* and the erotic objects orbiting around the massive spatialization of fantasy that is *Etant donnés.* Two sets of objects, each with its own model of repetition and strategy for reproduction. The erotic objects offer us repetitions of a bodily and psychic nature produced by the reproductive technique of casting, a process

redolent with metaphors for memory and loss. The readymades of 1964 seem to be structured by the repetitions of transition and transformation, produced by skilled craftsmen, all by hand, except *Fountain*. And their handmadeness points, ironically, to a certain kind of actuality of their objectness, no longer one commodity object plucked from an endless stream and asked to stand in for all the others, but a thing, made, limited, rare, serving the purposes of art, even.

Duchamp doesn't offer us *The Large Glass* and *Etant donnés* as static objects to be apprehended (or puzzled over) visually. Rather, their accompanying set of objects imply that when parts are taken for whole, objects are apprehended through a wide range of bodily modes that often supersede the visual. And just as the space of fantasy can evoke the most powerful of physical gestalts, so too objects often bear the brunt of an intense cathexis, one typically manifested in a demonstrably bodily and tactile fashion. In each instance, Duchamp's works propose that there is no adequate way to stage the problems of desire and repetition without recourse to a tactile relationship with the object world, and that it is precisely because our psychic lives become intricately bound up in things (whether commodities or art) that sculpture and its repetitions offer one of the most charged avenues into untying the knot of eroticism, repetition, and commodities that governs our daily lives.

An earlier version of this text, entitled "Eros and the Readymade," can be found in *The Lure of the Object*, ed. Stephen Melville (Williamstown, Mass.: Sterling and Francine Clark Art Institute, 2005).

NOTES

1 Francis M. Naumann, *Marcel Duchamp: The Art of Making Art in the Age of Mechanical Reproduction* (Ghent: Ludion Press, 1999; New York: Harry N. Abrams, 1999), 181.

2 As quoted in ibid., 181.

3 I was able to view the interior of *Wedge of Chastity* at the Marcel Duchamp Archive at Villiers-sous-Grez, December 19, 2003. The interior has been photographed for the first time for this catalogue.

4 Dawn Ades, Neil Cox, and David Hopkins, *Marcel Duchamp* (London: Thames and Hudson, 1999), 184.

5 There was the aforementioned gallery exhibition at Rose Fried Gallery in 1953. In the early 1960s things really heated up with retrospective exhibitions held at the Pasadena Museum in 1963 and at the Galleria Schwarz in Milan in 1964. *Omaggio a Marcel Duchamp*, the Schwarz exhibition, subsequently traveled to Bern, London, The Hague, Eindhoven, and Hannover. In New York, the Cordier and Ekstrom Gallery held a retrospective exhibition in 1965, as did the Tate Gallery in London in 1966.

6 As quoted in Alex Potts, *The Sculptural Imagination: Figurative, Modernist, Minimalist* (New Haven: Yale University Press, 2000), 63.

7 On the belatedness of the reception of Duchamp, see Hal Foster, "What's Neo about the Neo Avant-Garde?" in Potts, *The Sculptural Imagination*.

8 The two notable exceptions are William Camfield's *Marcel Duchamp/Fountain* (Houston: Houston Fine Art Press, 1989) and David Joselit's unpublished lecture, "The Belated Career of the Readymade."

9 Letter from Schwarz to William Camfield, cited in Camfield, *Marcel Duchamp/Fountain*, 91–92.

10 Ulf Linde asserts that the blueprints were actually made from his replicas. Conversation with the author, April 19, 2004, Stockholm.

11 This information is based on a conversation between the author and Schwarz, December 16, 2003, Milan. Memory is mutable, however, so in Calvin Tomkins's biography of Duchamp he states that only a ceramicist was involved. See *Duchamp: A Biography* (New York: Henry Holt, 1996), 427. In addition to the edition of eight, plus the two – one for Duchamp and one for Schwarz – two additional copies of *Fountain* were made for exhibition purposes. According to William Camfield, they "do not bear Duchamp's signature or the metal plaque found on the edition of ten." Camfield, *Marcel Duchamp/Fountain*, 93.

12 Camfield, *Marcel Duchamp/Fountain*, 94.

13 The notable exceptions are Jean-François Lyotard, *Duchamp's Transformers: A Book* (Venice, Calif.: Lapis Press, 1990), and Molly Nesbit, "Marcel Duchamp: *Etant Donnés*," *Artforum International* 32 (September 1993): 158–59.

14 Pierre Cabanne, *Dialogues with Marcel Duchamp* (New York: Da Capo Press, 1979), 88.

15 There is a photograph of Fontana and Duchamp at a Schwarz gallery opening, and Manzoni's knowledge of Duchamp's work is well documented.

16 On the relations between Broodthaers and Manzoni, see Rachel Haidu, "Marcel Broodthaers, 1963–1972, or The Absence of Work" (Ph.D. diss., Columbia University, 2003).

17 When Duchamp moved to New York from Paris in 1915, he left the *Bicycle Wheel* (1913) behind in his Paris studio. In 1951 he remade the work with a wheel and fork that Sidney Janis brought back from Paris for an exhibition entitled "Climax in Twentieth-Century Art, 1913," held at the Sidney Janis Gallery.

18 Conversation with the author, December 16, 2003, Milan.

19 "Marcel Duchamp Talking about Readymades: Interview by Philippe Collin, Galerie Givaudan, Paris, 21 June, 1967," in *Marcel Duchamp*, exh. cat., Museum Jean Tinguley Basel (Ostfildern-Ruit: Hatje Cantz, 2002), 38.

20 A major instance of this generosity can be seen in Duchamp's correspondence with Henry Pierre Roche regarding the possible sale of works of Duchamp owned by Roche that were wanted by American collections. See *Affectionately, Marcel: The Selected Correspondence of Marcel Duchamp*, ed. Francis M. Naumann and Hector Obalk, trans. Jill Taylor (Ghent: Ludion Press, 2000), 310–24.

21 This argument can be found in Calvin Tomkins's biography. Curator Walter Hopps told me this in conversation, as did art historian Molly Nesbit.

22 On notions of transportability and Duchamp, see T. J. Demos, "Duchamp Homeless? The Avant-Garde and Post-Nationalism" (Ph.D. diss., Columbia University, 2000).

23 On the physicality of the readymades, see Helen Molesworth, "Slapstick and Laziness: The Everyday Life of Marcel Duchamp's Readymades," *Art Journal* (January 1999): 50–61.

24 Conversation with Walter Hopps, April 2, 2004, Houston.

25 Melanie Klein, "Love, Guilt, and Reparation," in *Love, Hate, and Reparation*, two lectures by Melanie Klein and Joan Riviere (London: Hogarth Press, 1937), 91.

26 D. W. Winnicott, "Transitional Objects and Transitional Phenomena," in *Playing and Reality* (New York: Basic Books, 1971), 5.

27 Ibid., 6.

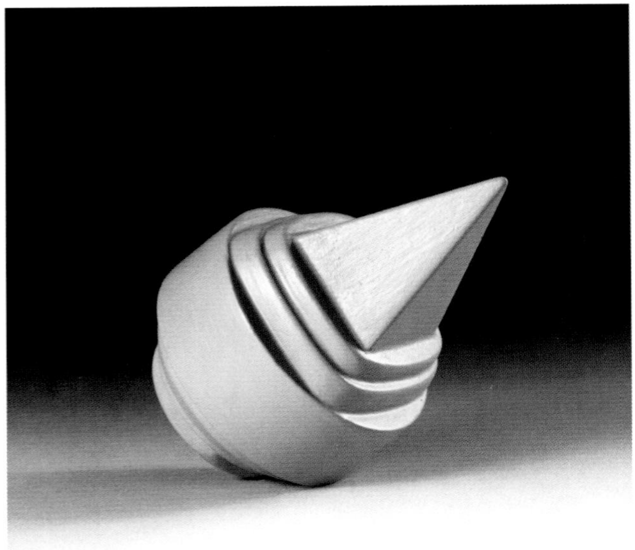

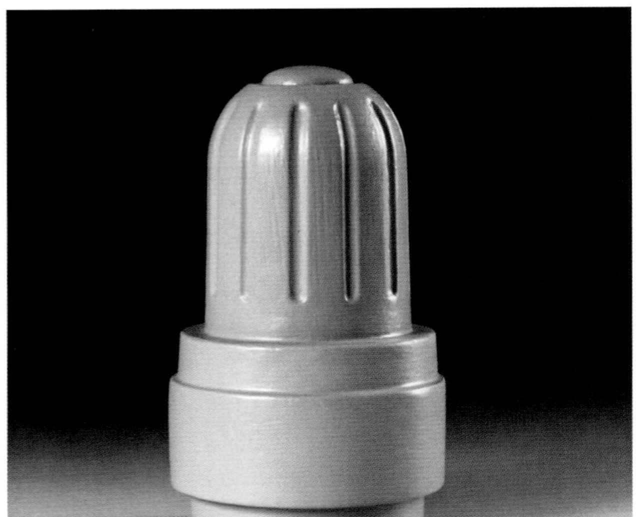

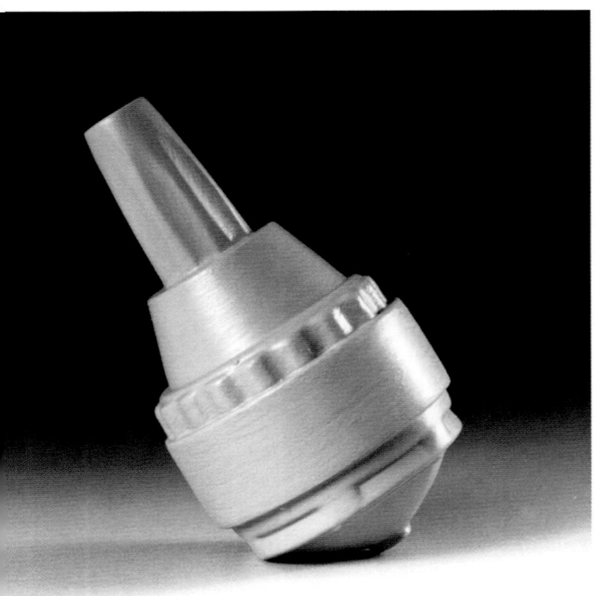

ALLAN McCOLLUM 1944–

Allan McCollum first made his *Perfect Vehicles* in 1985. Sitting atop plinths,the standard mode for the display of sculpture, the groupings ranged from five to twenty-five generic cast-plaster vases. The shape of the vase was that of an antique Chinese ginger jar, a shape made ubiquitous by centuries of its reproduction. The *Perfect Vehicles* came in a range of colors, such that even though each vase was identical in shape, no two groupings were alike based on quantity and color. Radically dysfunctional (they are solid and could never be used actually to hold anything), they nonetheless perform their domestic role as decoration. In so doing, they conflate the art object proper with its lesser partner, the *objet d'art*, suggesting that the shared function of the two categories is their presentation of taste and wealth within the domestic interior.

In subsequent iterations of the *Perfect Vehicles*, McCollum played with issues of scale. Maintaining the same shape, he enlarged the vases to human scale. This monumentalization of an everyday object had the strange effect of anthropomorphizing it. The shape took on both male and female characteristics, looking, on the one hand, like a plump and proud member of the bourgeoisie (they have always reminded me of Ingres's infamous portrait of *Louis-François Bertin*, 1832), and on the other, miming the sensuous curves of the female body. While the works connote the bodies of the living, they also recall funerary urns and as such bring death and its memorializations into the space of the gallery.

McCollum's use of casting is the structuring formal element of his work. For him, the cast is intimately connected with the representation of death. In a 1991 interview, he said:

> Now it is probably evident in my work that I suffer some preoccupation with absence, and with death, and with how the objects we produce and the objects we collect work to defer our knowledge of death, displace our fears of it and so forth. All artists know how every symbolic object exists in some way to re-present that which is not present, that which is absent, that which is gone, that which is beyond recall. And I think that making as many molds and casts as I've made has worked symbolically for me as a kind of attempt to master my own apprehensions about death and absence. I've come to feel that a cast object quite automatically functions as a symbol for an absent original model, for instance, in a way that is especially visceral.[1]

If the *Perfect Vehicles* imply death through their form as well as through the process by which they are made, then *Over Ten Thousand Individual Works* does something slightly different. More than ten thousand objects lay on top of a mammoth table. All of a size to fit comfortably into the palm of the hand, they lie in seemingly endless rows, and while each is different, the effect is of a uniform mass, a totality. The work is produced from "hundreds of small shapes casually collected from peoples' homes, supermarkets, hardware stores, and sidewalks: bottle caps, jar lids, drawer pulls, salt shakers, flashlights, measuring spoons, cosmetic containers, yogurt cups, earrings, push buttons, candy molds, garden hose connectors, paperweights, shade pulls, Chinese teacups, cat toys, pencil sharpeners, and so on."[2] This list of fragmentary readymades, unluxurious, mass-produced, and inherently quotidian, is a list of part objects and of lost objects. Replicas of these objects were made from casts and thus assembled according to a numerical system that ensures that each object is indeed individual. On the face of it, their individuality is assured, by the title, by a cursory glance at a corner of the table. One quickly senses, however, that attempting to verify this individuality could easily descend into madness. Despite the simplicity of the mathematical system, its very rationality appears irrational in the face of the infinitesimal differences of the individual objects.

Over Ten Thousand Individual Works presents a spatialization of the reciprocity between bodies and things. The incommensurate nature of our lived reality as individual beings that have nonetheless been rendered equivalent to one another – we are interchangeable within the work place, within the market, as an audience for the mass media – is played out in the proliferation of mathematical difference that produces an effect of overwhelming similarity. That humans then adopt that similarity as a protective device is perhaps yet another thing we learn from the very objects we desire. If the *Perfect Vehicles* are imbued with a sense of death, a death that pervades our relationship to objects that threaten to outlast us, then the *Individual Works* are suffused with the struggle between reification and the experience of individuality that is a hallmark of daily life under capitalist mass production.

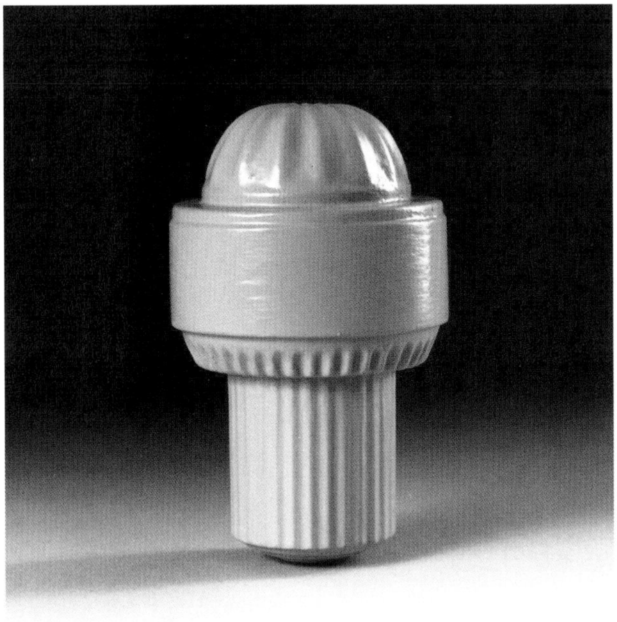

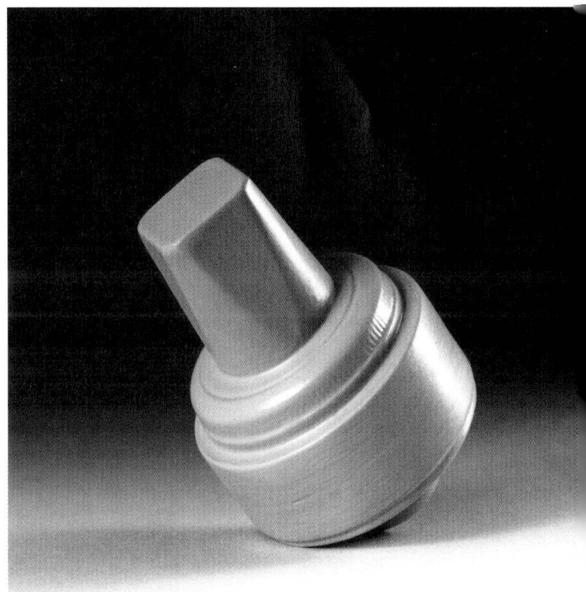

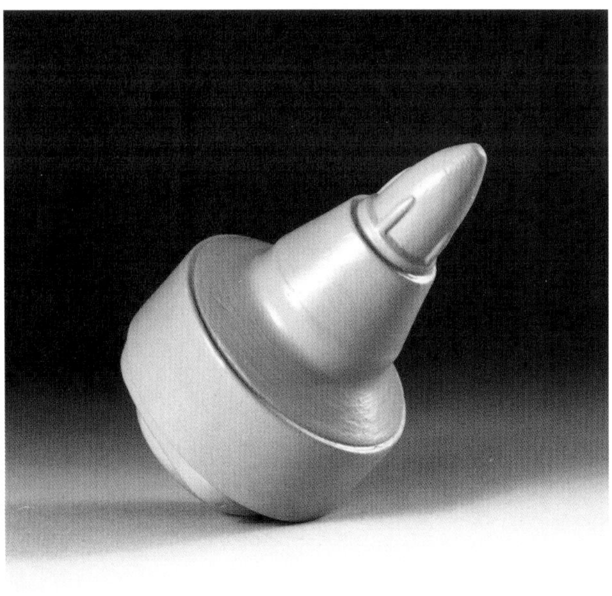

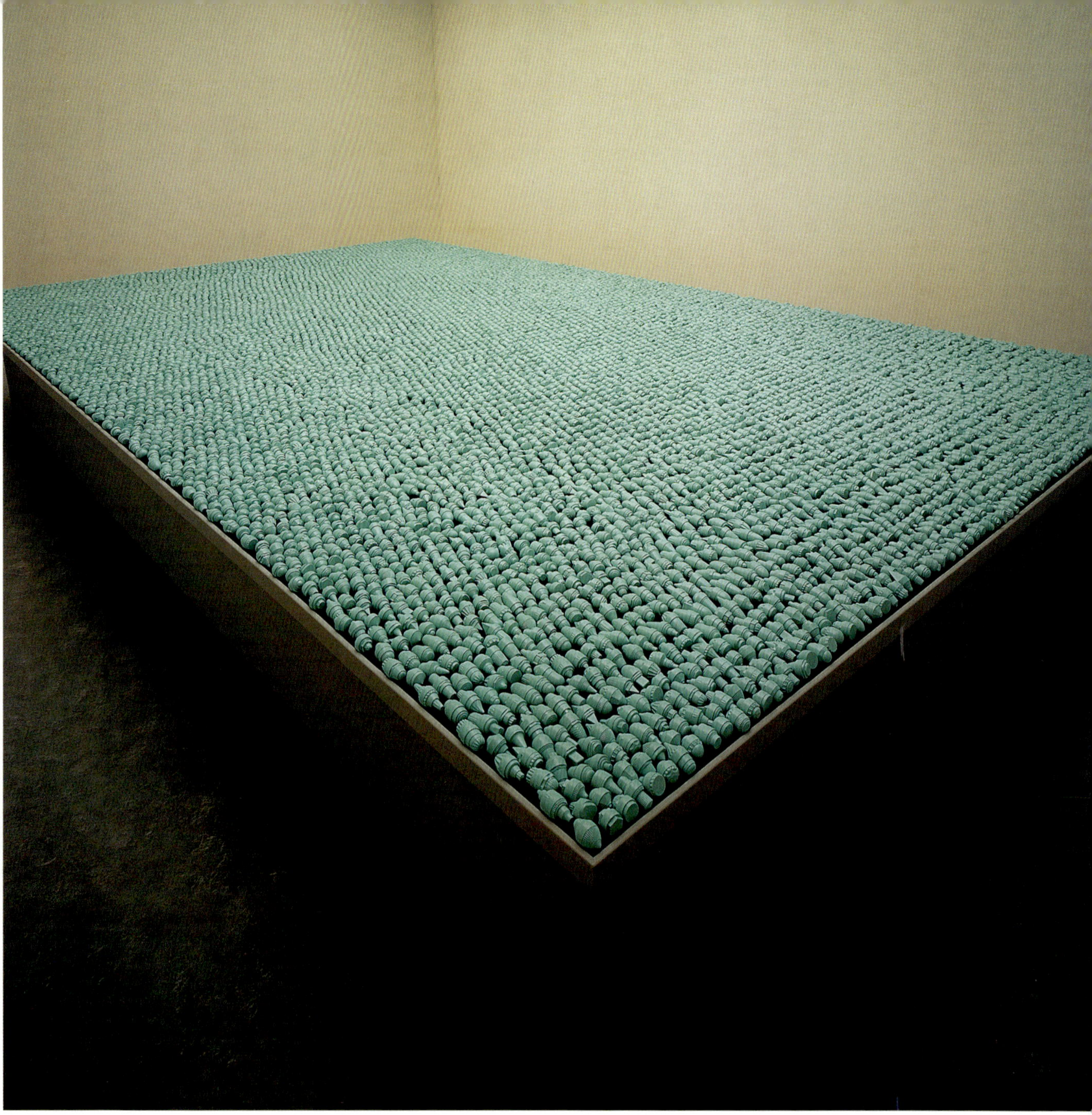

all images previous and current spread:
Over Ten Thousand Individual Works,
1987/88

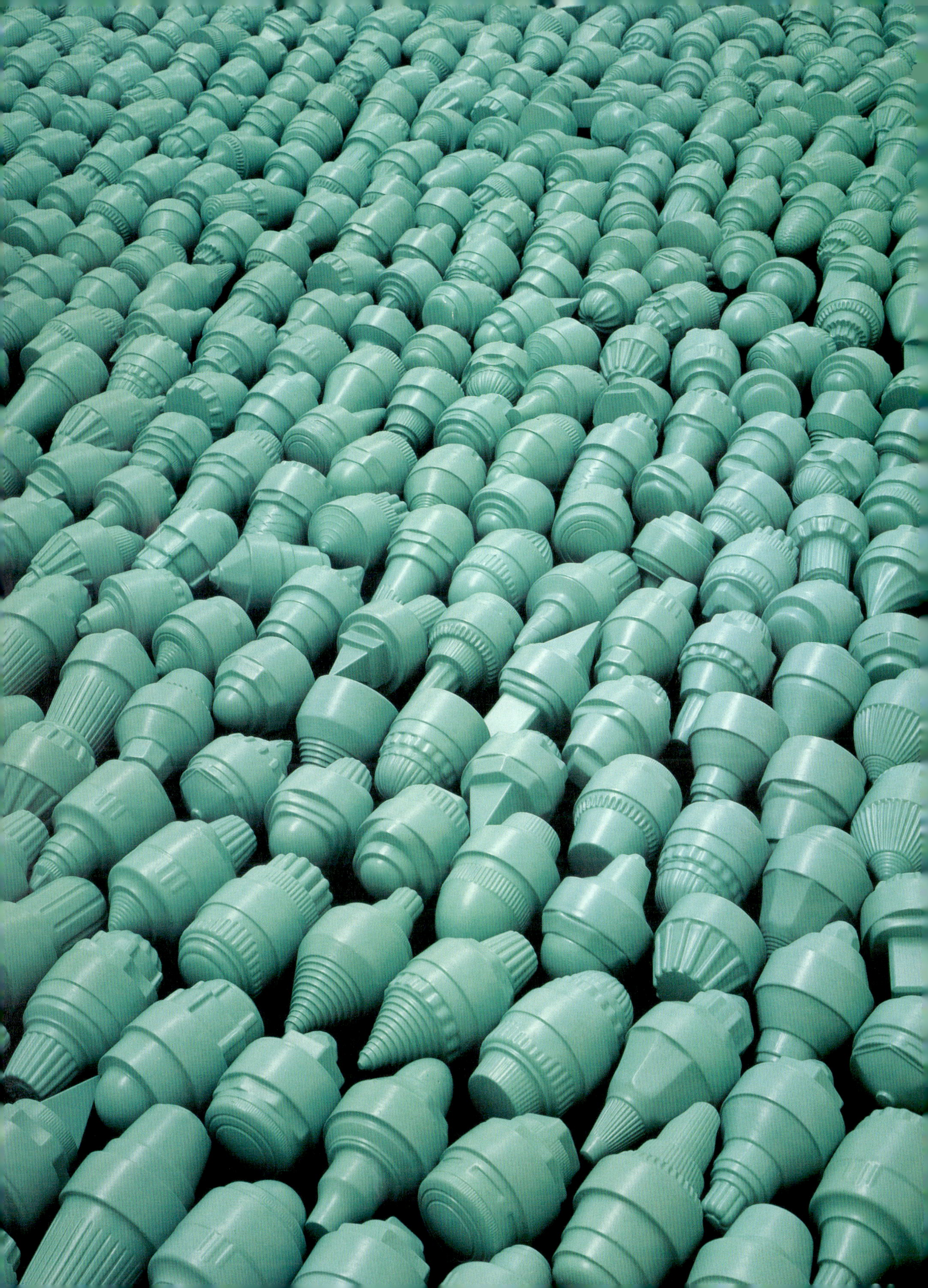

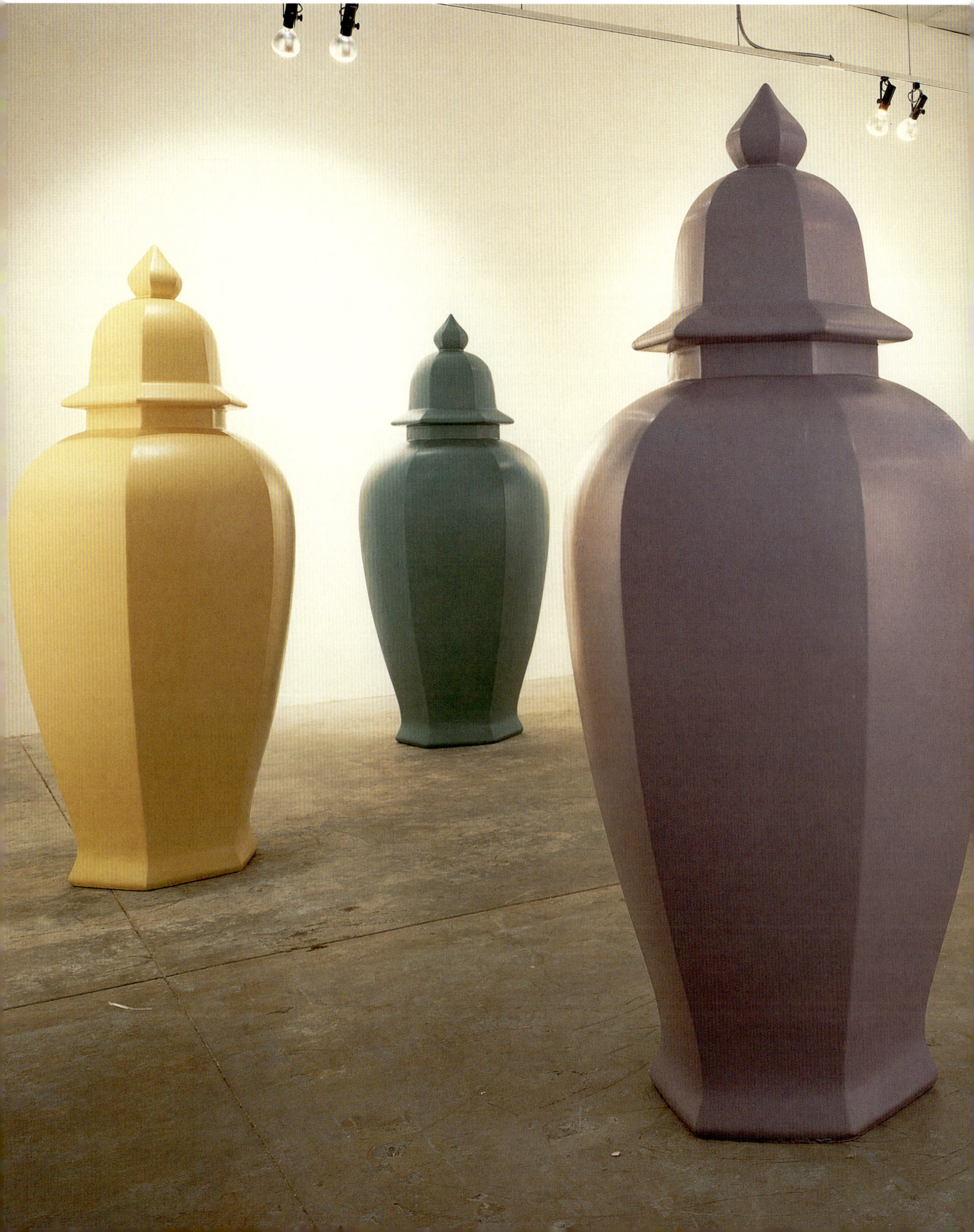

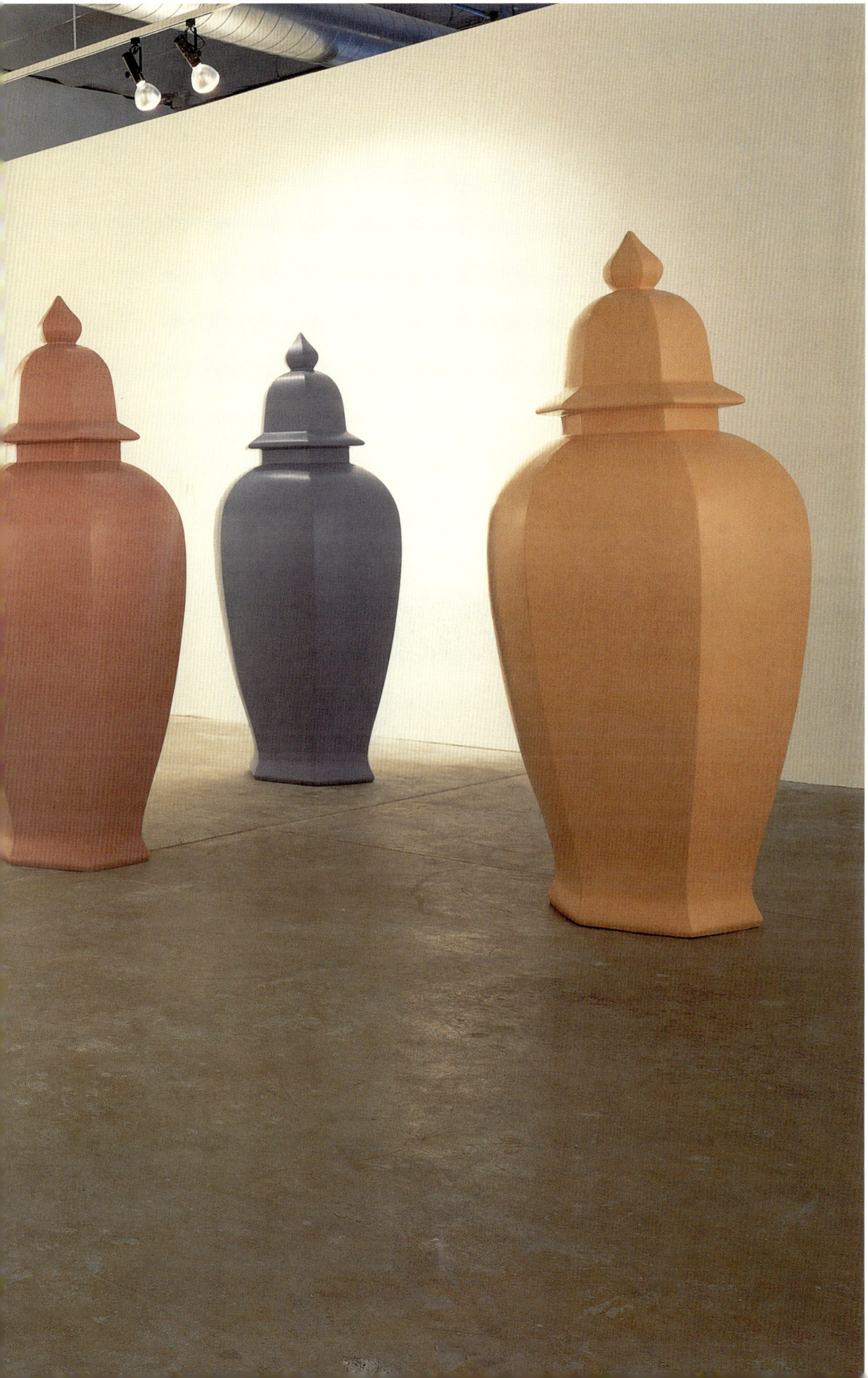

Perfect Vehicles, 1988/89

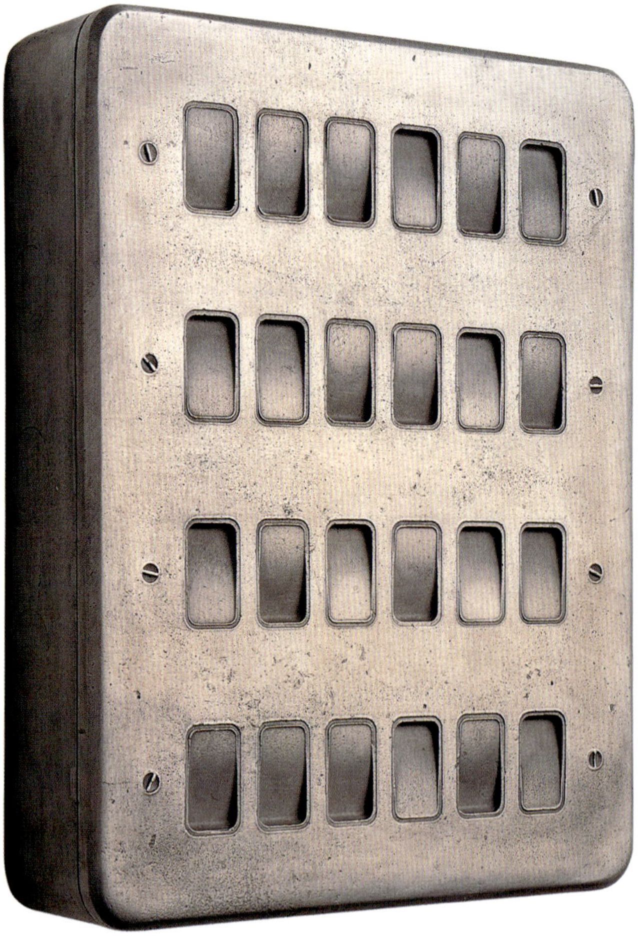

Untitled (Twenty-four Switches), 1998

right **Untitled** (Yellow Bed, Two Parts), 1991

RACHEL WHITEREAD 1963–

From the outset of her career, Rachel Whiteread has tested the resources of casting. Casting is a time-honored form of making both sculpture and everyday objects, speaking equally to the world of bronze sculptures and assembly-line gewgaws. However, under the aesthetic regime of modernism, casting came to be denigrated because it was presumed to offer the repetition of an existing form, or to enable the production of identical forms – both of which were seen to be antithetical to the privileging of the sculptural object as unique. In this regard, Whiteread's exploration of casting takes part in a larger challenge to modernist sculpture, situating her in the company of such artists as Bruce Nauman and Allan McCollum, both of whom used repetition and casting as engines for making sculpture precisely because of its proximity to bodily modes of production (birth, defecation) as well as commodity production (the endless stream of identical objects of the assembly line). Whiteread revalues the act of casting, removing it from the charge of inauthenticity or kitsch, seeing casting instead as a liminal practice that straddles the world of both objects and bodies.

Whiteread almost always casts the spaces as well as the objects of domestic life – and almost always at their actual scale. Mattresses, floorboards, closets, bathtubs, bookshelves, tombstones, and entire rooms – all are spaces of and for the body. One effect of this mirror image of domesticity in the public space of the museum is a distinct sense of the uncanny, the familiar made strange; the homey made *unheimlich*. These all-too-familiar and banal objects are now rendered doubly strange in that they both eerily resemble their "originals" and are in decidedly the "wrong" place. Their simultaneous easy recognizability and their dramatically disjointed sense of placement evoke the classic mode of displacement and condensation in dreams. Through displacement, the casts deliver an emotional impact far in excess of that aroused by the original, ordinary object. Hence, a bank of light switches appears loaded with meaning that supersedes itself, a meaning that can only have come from elsewhere. So too Whiteread's casts often feel like the act of condensation, inasmuch as the classic example of condensation is the dreamer's inability to verbalize the dream for others. In the recounting, the object or narrative falls away, for far too many attributes have been compressed or condensed into one image or word. In the process of describing Whiteread's cast objects, the bed is a bed, a coffin, a tomb, a medical gurney, a plateau, an art object, a sculpture, a thing made of plaster. All are correct, but none is enough, as the object appears to sag under the weight of its condensed meanings.

The heavy, almost lugubrious quality of Whiteread's objects, both psychically and physically, is occasionally compounded by her exploitation of repetitious forms, whether the proliferation of switches in *Untitled (Twenty-four Switches)* or the plethora of books in the bookcases. This is particularly the case in *Untitled (Yellow Bed, Two Parts)*. Here the mirroring aspect of casting is doubled as the cast of the mattress leans against the cast of the mattress support. The pair functions in tandem; the casts are interdependent. Two parts form a whole and yet are also slightly out of synch, as if one looked in the mirror and saw the reflection of someone other than oneself. The anthropomorphic quality of the sculpture is variously heightened by the fact that the mattress has been cast with a sheet on it, leaving "wrinkles all over the surface like an old person's skin,"[1] as well as the yellow staining, which simultaneously evokes the seepages of the body in both life and death, youth and old age, and all the more so as it is a single bed – the nearly exclusive province of the young and the very old.

In the context of *Part Object Part Sculpture*, Whiteread's decision to cast *Yellow Bed* from dental plaster, the material Duchamp used for his seductive and oblique *Wedge of Chastity*, demands at least one comment. For both artists, casting functions not as mere replication, but rather as an indexical process that records marks of individual identity – dental records, like thumbprints, offer the insignia of our uniqueness – even as it produces an inert object. For the most part, Whiteread fashions unique sculptures through a process generally employed to make multiple copies of an original. This gesture speaks to the tension in her work between individual experience and memory (my bed, the room of my childhood, the specificity of my bookshelf) and the homogeneity of the readymade objects that carry individuals through those experiences. Art is the space and casting the process through which Whiteread explores the bodiliness of things as they straddle the divide between object and sculpture.

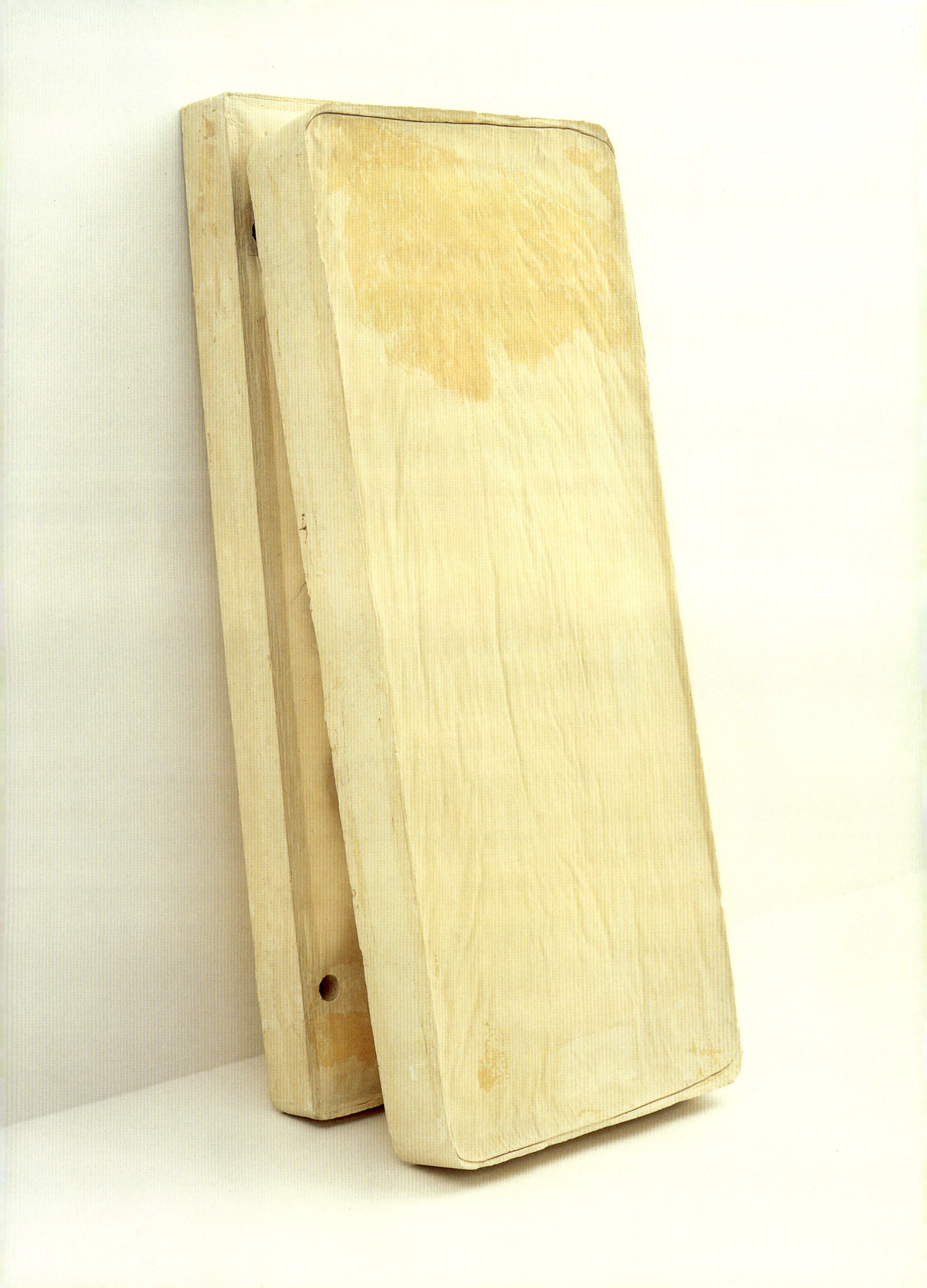

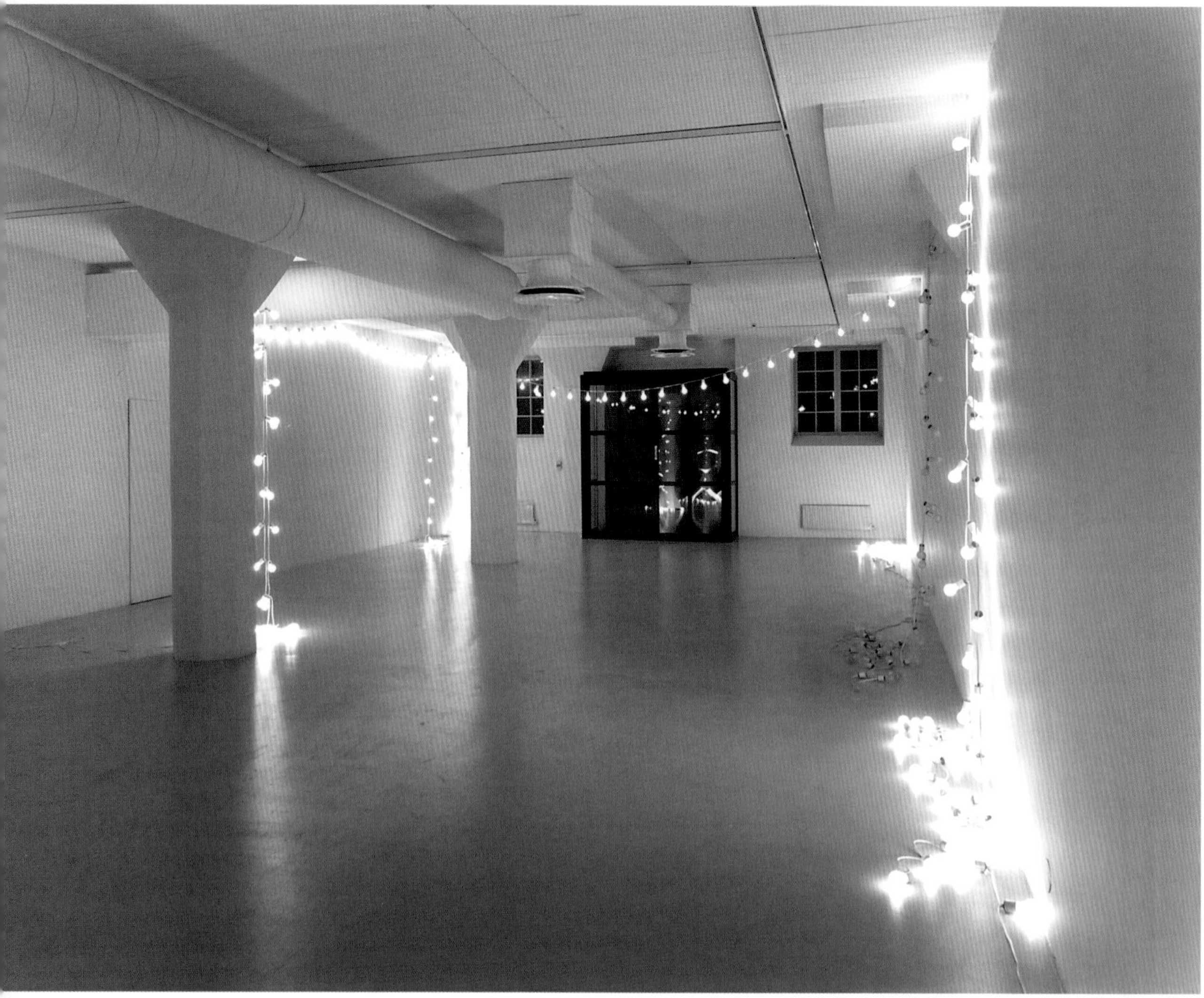

FELIX GONZALEZ-TORRES 1957–1996

Felix Gonzalez-Torres's artistic career was brief, his life cut ridiculously short from AIDS. During his brief career, the simple gestures in his work did much to complicate and revitalize the legacy of Minimalist sculpture.

The 1990s were marked by an interest in theories and politics of identity that rethought the hegemonic status of Minimalist sculpture for postwar art. Traditionally, the spectator of Minimalist sculpture was posited as an abstract body, who, through an interaction with art in the public spaces of the gallery and museum, discovered a phenomenological awareness of their bodies. Yet, for artists who came of age during the 1990s, the abstraction of Minimalist sculpture was matched by a similar abstraction of the viewer, where the body of the viewer was imagined to be devoid of gender, sexuality, race, class, or place. For artists interested in politics and identity, such a position became untenable.

Gonzalez-Torres's work was at the forefront of this generation of artists, and his unique quality was that he would critique Minimalism in part by paying homage to it. Gonzales-Torres's work was made exclusively from industrially produced materials. His stacks of candies and posters mimed the logic of mass production at the same time that they resembled the stark geometric forms of Minimalist objects. Yet, a viewer's interaction with this work – whether or not to take a candy, or whether to preserve or throw away a poster – opened up questions of personal preference and taste that disallowed the neutrality of the viewer. This effect was also partly achieved by the prevailing sense of loss and memory that saturates Gonzalez-Torres's work. Made during the peak years of the AIDS crisis in the United States, the effervescent, ever-disappearing nature of his work, combined with his light touch in handling everyday materials, produced works of art whose emotional effect was one of loss and mourning.

Gonzalez-Torres's ability to transform industrially produced materials into emotionally charged objects was in part the result of his unique deployment of repetition. In an early essay about the artist's work, critic David Deitcher suggested that French sociologist Henri Lefebvre's account of repetition in industrialized societies helped to unpack what is so distinct about Gonzalez-Torres's work. For Lefebvre, advanced cultures are marked by two forms of repetition – one linear and industrial and one cyclical and rooted in nature. Industrial models of repetition, according to Deitcher, "mask and crush the more differentiated, cyclical patterns of organic life."[1] Even though Gonzalez-Torres gathered his materials from linear and industrial repetition, he nonetheless used that repetition "to create works that communicate the greater complexity of everyday life as it is lived: at the intersection of both linear and cyclical structures."[2]

A large part of how this seemingly magical transformation occurred is through the open-ended installation of his work – of which the light sculptures are the most emblematic. There are nearly twenty of them, all fashioned from the same equipment: fifteen-watt light bulbs, porcelain light sockets strung on electrical cords, and extension cords. Each work is unique because each is comprised of a different number of bulbs and strands. More important, however, is that each work may be installed in any configuration by the owner or exhibitor, so that every time the work is exhibited it has the radical potential to be completely new.

The ability of the light sculptures to straddle different models of repetition does not derive only from the mutability of their presentation. Nearly all the light sculptures have place names in their titles. On the one hand, this gesture indicates a memorable specificity – there is no other place *like* Stockholm, for instance. Indeed it can be argued that light is one of the hallmarks of the uniqueness of place – the northern light of Stockholm, the much written about light of Los Angeles, the less well known sky at dusk in the Midwest – all are indelible and differentiating aspects of place. Naming the light sculptures after places gestures toward this kind of organic and experiential specificity. And yet the light emanating from the sculptures is to a large degree utterly homogenous and devoid of such markers of place: a string of fifteen-watt bulbs gives off a relatively even glow no matter where or how it is installed. To this end, the works articulate the potentially crushing aspects of the homogenizing and efficient logic of industrial production. But the interpretive turn doesn't stop there. Even though the bulbs emit the same amount of light, the space they illuminate has the potential to be different. As the works move – and are reconfigured – from one site to another, they help to create the specificity of that site anew. While "Untitled" (North) (1993) and "Untitled" (For Stockholm) (1992) are on view at the Wexner Center for the Arts, they will contain the metaphoric residue of other places, all the while carving out the unique parameters of a Columbus, Ohio, viewer's experience.

FELIX GONZALEZ-TORRES 1957–1996

Felix Gonzalez-Torres's artistic career was brief; his life cut ridiculously short from AIDS. During his brief career, the simple gestures in his work did much to complicate and revitalize the legacy of Minimalist sculpture. The 1990s were marked by an interest in theories and politics of identity that rethought the hegemonic status of Minimalist sculpture for postwar art. Traditionally, the spectator of Minimalist sculpture was posited as an abstract body, who, through an interaction with art in the public spaces of the gallery and museum, discovered a phenomenological awareness of their bodies. Yet, for artists who came of age during the 1990s, the abstraction of Minimalist sculpture was matched by a similar abstraction of the viewer, where the body of the viewer was imagined to be devoid of gender, sexuality, race, class, or place. For artists interested in politics and identity, such a position became untenable.

Gonzalez-Torres's work was at the forefront of this generation of artists, and his unique quality was that he would critique Minimalism in part by paying homage to it. Gonzales-Torres's work was made exclusively from industrially produced materials. His stacks of candies and posters mimed the logic of mass production at the same time that they resembled the stark geometric forms of Minimalist objects. Yet, a viewer's interaction with this work – whether or not to take a candy, or whether to preserve or throw away a poster – opened up questions of personal preference and taste that disallowed the neutrality of the viewer. This effect was also partly achieved by the prevailing sense of loss and memory that saturates Gonzalez-Torres's work. Made during the peak years of the AIDS crisis in the United States, the effervescent, ever disappearing nature of his work, combined with his light touch in handling everyday materials, produced works of art whose emotional effect was one of loss and mourning.

Gonzalez-Torres's ability to transform industrially produced materials into emotionally charged objects was in part the result of his unique deployment of repetition. In an early essay about the artist's work, critic David Deitcher suggested that French sociologist Henri Lefebvre's account of repetition in industrialized societies helped to unpack what is so distinct about Gonzalez-Torres's work. For Lefebvre, advanced cultures are marked by two forms of repetition – one linear and industrial and one cyclical and rooted in nature. Industrial models of repetition, according to Deitcher, "mask and crush the more differentiated, cyclical patterns of organic life." Even though Gonzalez-Torres gathered his materials from linear and industrial repetition, he nonetheless used that repetition "to create works that communicate the greater complexity of everyday life as it is lived: at the intersection of both linear and cyclical structures."

A large part of how this seemingly magical transformation occurred is through the open-ended installation of his work – of which the light sculptures are the most emblematic. There are nearly twenty of them, all fashioned from the same equipment: fifteen-watt light bulbs, porcelain light sockets strung on electrical cords, and extension cords. Each work is unique because each is comprised of a different number of bulbs and strands. More important, however, is that each work may be installed in any configuration by the owner or exhibitor, so that every time the work is exhibited it has the radical potential to be completely new.

The ability of the light sculptures to straddle different models of repetition does not derive only from the mutability of their presentation. Nearly all the light sculptures have place names in their titles. On the one hand, this gesture indicates a memorable specificity – there is no other place like Stockholm, for instance. Indeed it can be argued that light is one of the hallmarks of the uniqueness of place – the northern light of Stockholm, the much written about light of Los Angeles, the less well known sky at dusk in the Midwest – all are indelible and differentiating aspects of place. Naming the light sculptures after places gestures toward this kind of organic and experiential specificity. And yet the light emanating from the sculptures is to a large degree utterly homogenous and devoid of such markers of place: a string of fifteen-watt bulbs gives off a relatively even glow no matter where or how it is installed. To this end, the works articulate the potentially crushing aspects of the homogenizing and efficient logic of industrial production. But the interpretive turn doesn't stop there. Even though the bulbs emit the same amount of light, the space they illuminate has the potential to be different. As the works move – and are reconfigured – from one site to another, they help to create the specificity of that site anew. While "Untitled" (North) (1993) and "Untitled" (For Stockholm) (1992) are on view at the Wexner Center for the Arts, they will contain the metaphoric residue of other places, all the while carving out the unique parameters of a Columbus, Ohio, viewer's experience.

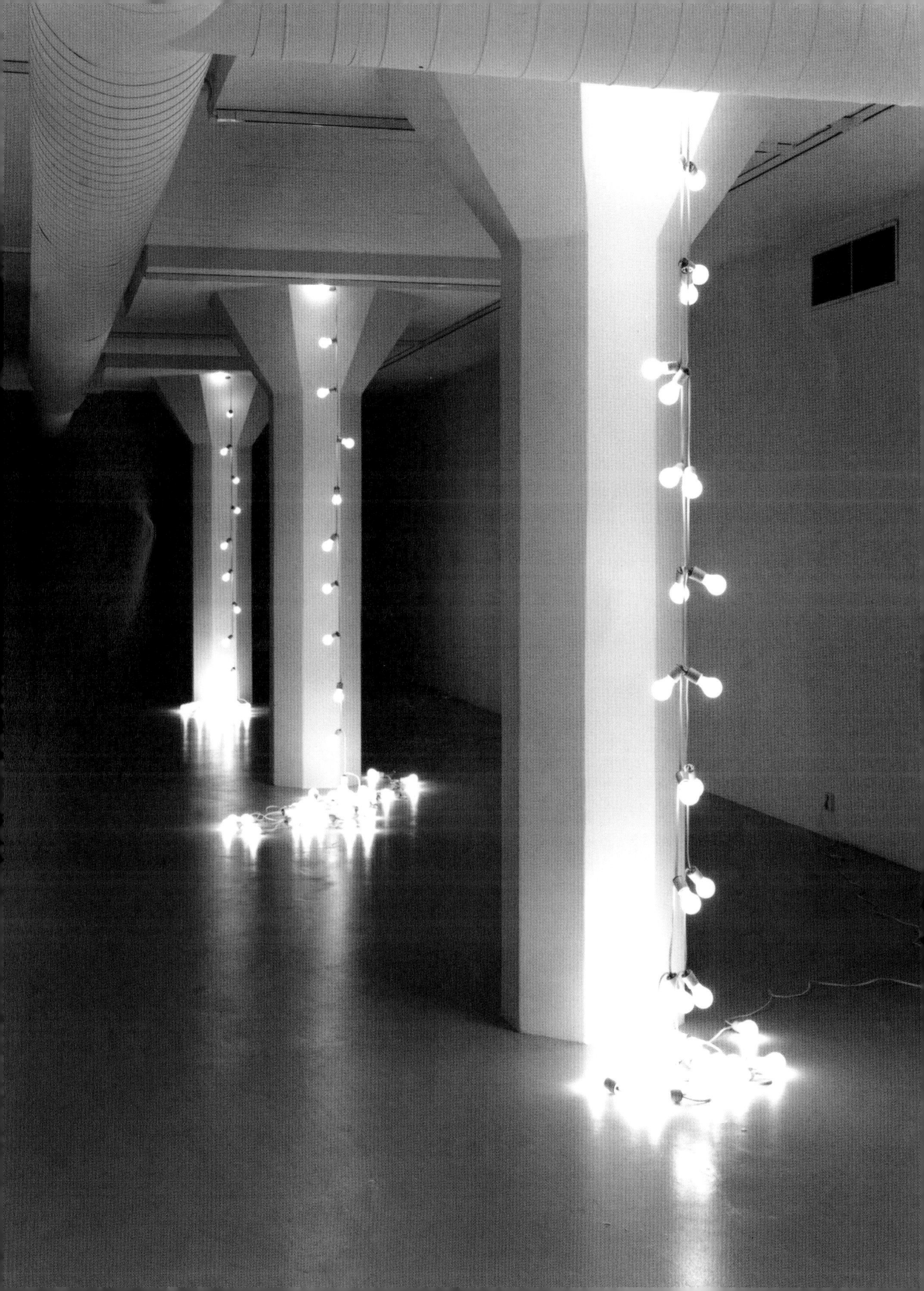

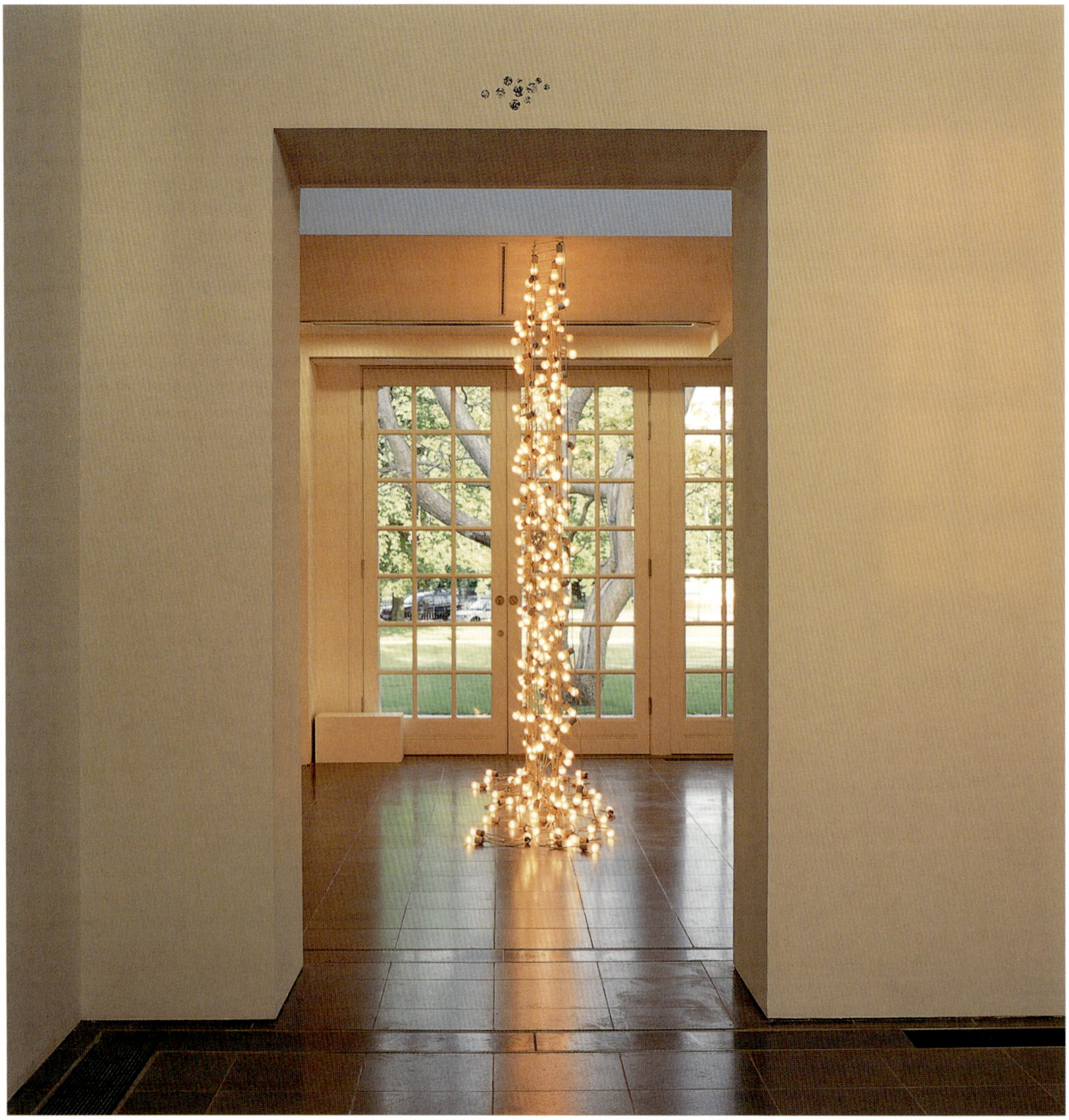

previous spread: left and right
"Untitled" (For Stockholm), 1992

current spread: left and right
and following spread
"Untitled" (North), 1993

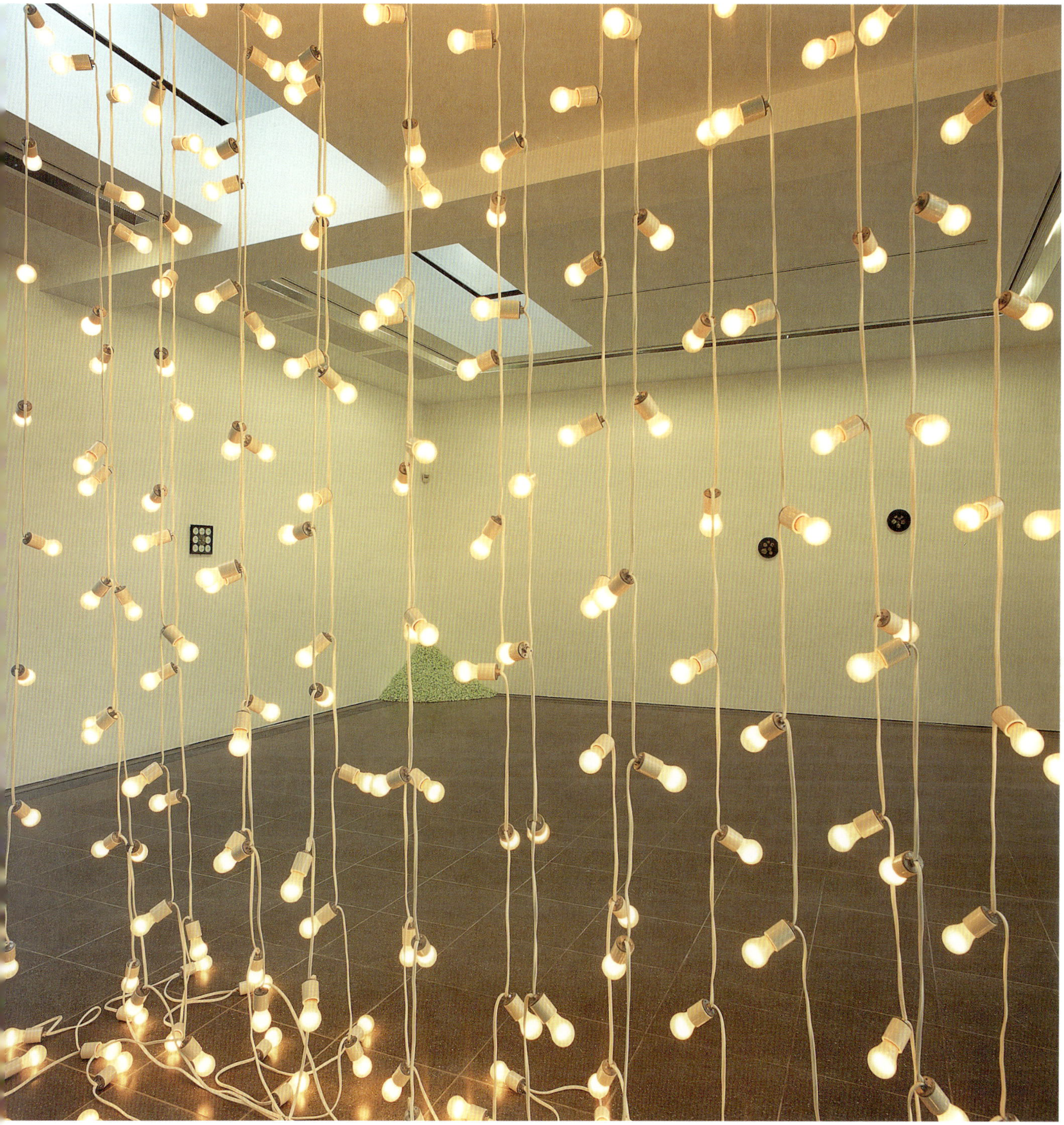

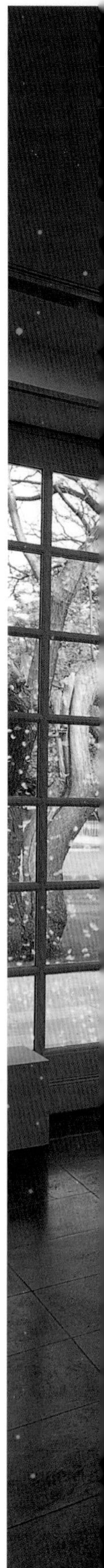

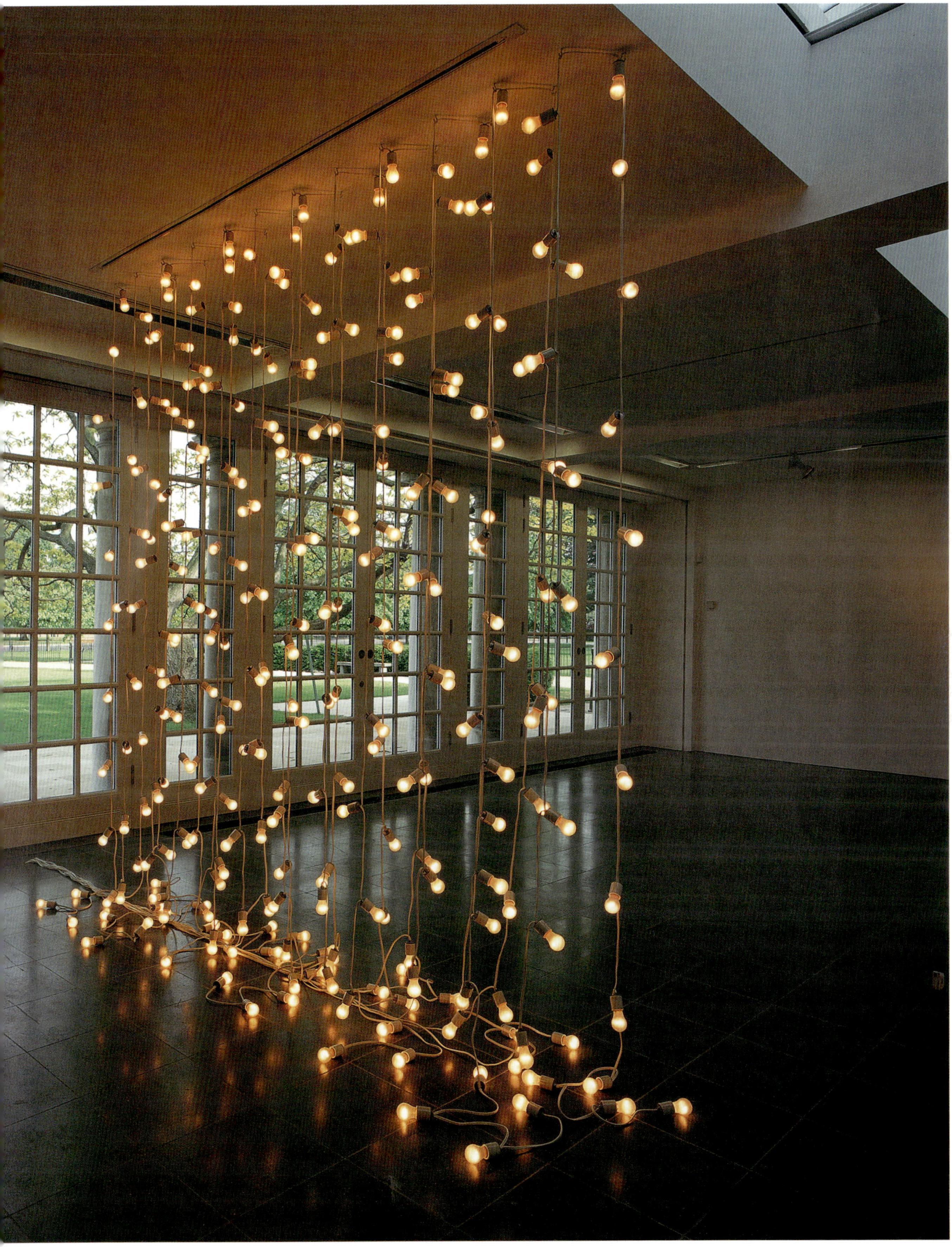

BRIONY FER

THE SCATTER:
SCULPTURE AS LEFTOVER

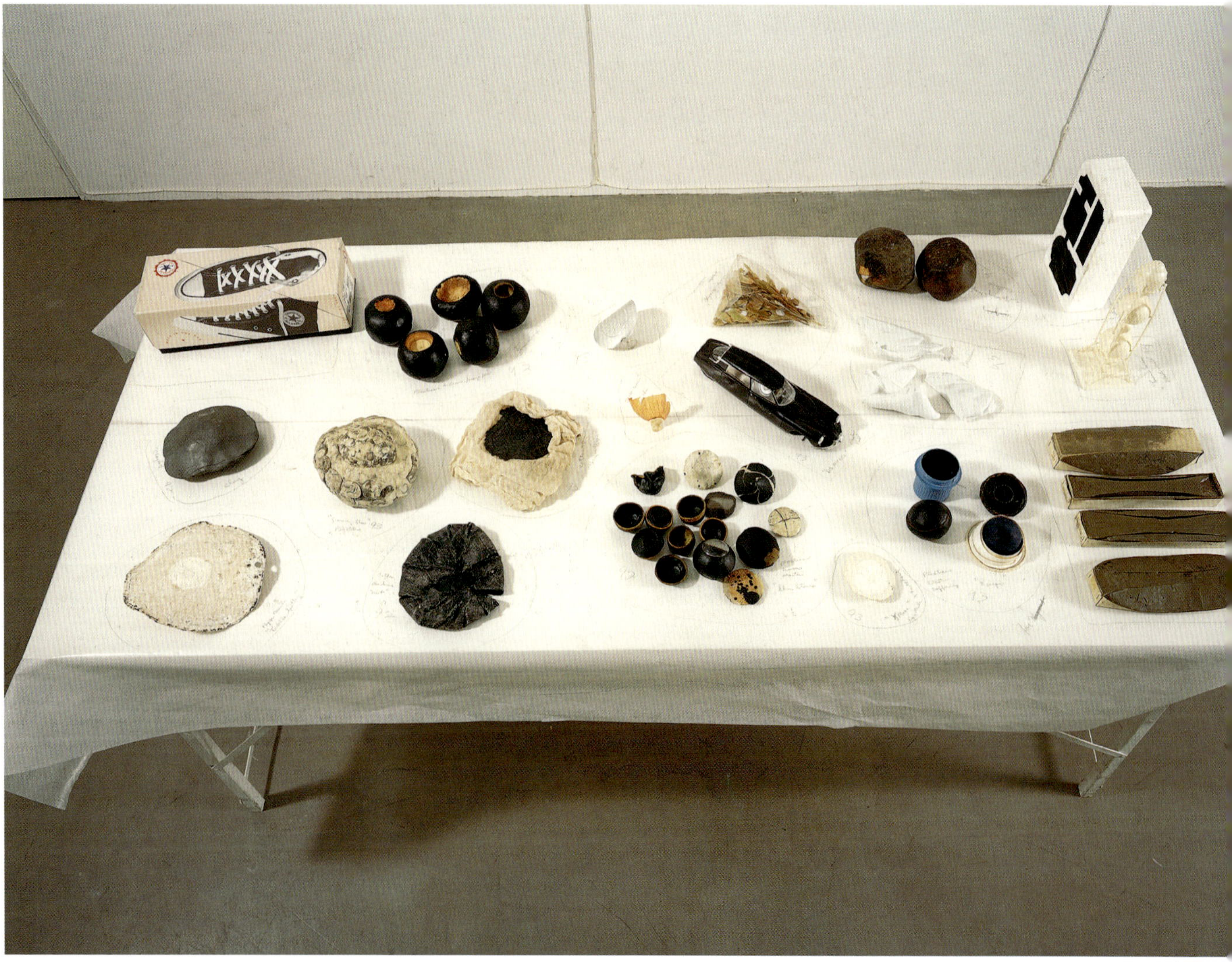

How freely the air circulates around your objects!
DIDEROT ON CHARDIN

Gabriel Orozco showed his first *Working Table* in Zurich in 1996. He conceived of it as something like a "work in progress," arranged with objects drawn from three or four years of work. The objects themselves were laid out unlike sculpture and more like tools on a workshop bench – or at least tools for thinking, enabling him to experiment with different materials and combinations and arrangements, as well as, he said, "generating some kind of thinking process for each material."[1] Laid out on the table was a diverse range of objects – a small toy DS car near the center, things made of plaster, papier-mâché, and plasticine, a Converse shoebox, and other found objects. Some are containers, like the shoebox, or receptacles made of fabric or lids filled with black plasticine, and in the end the table becomes a big container holding a lot of diverse things.

Parts and wholes are relative. Seeing the table as some kind of container is very different from seeing it as a whole that is contained. Except, of course, the table *is* contained. It is contained by a room. We could go on, imagining the world in the manner of a child reeling off an address as if it were an ever-expanding series of circles: a table is part of a room, a room is part of a building, a building is part of a street, a street is part of a town – and so on, ending up with the world, the universe. Does this make one feel big or small? Close or far? Scale and distance become unstable. Galaxies fold back into everyday life. The *Working Table* may not be the largest container of all, then, but like a universe it has its galaxies and constellations – the groups of objects clustered and scattered across it. This train of thought may seem an absurd inflation, but the vaulting and veering, between small and large, micro and macro, is very much part of our engagement with Orozco's work.

The *Working Table* provides a temporary container in which part-to-part relations and thing-to-thing connections never add up to a whole. The photograph shows pencil-drawn circles and notes on materials mapping out the arrangement on the white paper cloth as a series of zones. Some of the pencil circles touch and overlap, isolating the objects in little "islands" of drawing at the same time as they "attract" and connect with other objects. The intervals between things are as important as the things themselves. This is reminiscent of the way a tabletop, in still-life paintings, is only apparently a neutral space but is actually a highly charged one. In the most interesting still-life painting, the spaces between things, rather than the things themselves, trigger an extreme mobility. It often happens that the "stiller" the still life, the more mobile the *psychic* effect in the imagination (think of Chardin). Although we might think of still-life painting as testing the limits of composition, it often contains either a single or several highly disruptive elements that break out of its self-imposed limits, like a knife balanced on the edge of a table. Anthony Caro's small table sculptures from the 1960s, balancing precariously over an edge, are neither sculptures nor pictures.

Gabriel Orozco
Various Models, 1992-1995

They tap into a neglected but significant history of still-life sculpture within modernism, which, for example, in Picasso's small painted and stippled bronzes of a glass had broken down the distinction between the pictorial and the sculptural, the image and the object.

Orozco has made several working tables since the first one he made for Zurich.[2] The same things often reappear in new combinations; and new things appear that make the old things look quite different. If it were the same table, you could see it as a recycling plant. But the tables change too, sometimes large simple rectangular platforms (it would be misleading to call them plinths), sometimes trestles or other found versions. Orozco's thinking process seems to involve spreading things out, arranging and rearranging them: "They became like my landscape with all my objects."[3] Putting the tables on display plots that process, alongside the photographs he takes of pieces as he works on them. He has said: "Some pieces are more like finished sculptures, like the socks or the heart, and some of them are like models, like the car, the small DS or the little *Yielding Stone* which is the first one I ever made. Then some of them are totally ready-made like the box of soap or the shoebox. Some of them are failed sculptures, models that didn't work out but have interesting possibilities for the future, like nice leftovers."[4] This constellation of terms is curious: failed sculptures, models, nice leftovers. They all refer to things you might throw out, but to Orozco they seem to be more interesting than some of the things you might keep. They are not quite waste products. They are kept on "standby," as Orozco has put it, for future use.[5] They are left on hold rather than abandoned completely.

A leftover is a piece of something that has been remaindered – a part of something that has become detached and is now surplus to requirements or redundant. It is the flip side to the new commodity (the box for shoes, but no shoes). Leftovers have a history. The rise of the commodity had always gone hand in hand in the modernist imagination with the ragpickers picking over the debris of the city. As a cornucopia of the obsolete, the flea markets of Paris had fueled the dreamworld of the Surrealists. The discarded could be generative and even celebrated. Robert Morris's roomful of detritus could hail antiform and process art. But for Orozco, I think, "process" means something quite different from what it meant for the post-Minimalists, even though he shares an antipathy to the "specificity" and "finish" of Minimalism. Against a "specific object" is set an indeterminate one in a permanent state of incompletion. Material process is a thought process, not a product, let alone a *finished* product. Conversely, thought is manifested as material. Thinking occurs through things, where material things are a necessary condition of thought. This suggests that we do not think *about* things so much as *through* things.

From this point of view, three-dimensional models take on a new vividness because they are ideas in formation – whether or not they succeed as finished work. Rather than preparatory work, models encapsulate an idea or thought in a concise way and usually on a small scale. The photographs Orozco takes of some of the objects being made – a papier-mâché cast of a stretched cotton glove drying on a radiator, pliable plasticine through which peeps a small ball of cotton wool, an orange encased in plasticine gradually shriveling – are both part of the work and the work itself, just as the tables are. There is a sense in all of this that the most interesting work may be the work you might be about to throw out. The "nice leftovers" are the things you put aside but don't jettison completely. All these small objects are stored in boxes and are brought out periodically. If they once seemed unworkable, they may now get recycled and reused. Small things, cut adrift from their histories, are made to look not like a museum display but "more like an organic world that was working, that you could mentally play."[6]

Orozco likes tables because they are what he calls "platforms for an action" – they are both found and made.[7] They are absolutely not vitrines or glass boxes. But we could certainly compare them to Eva Hesse's glass pastry cases filled with small test pieces. These are small landscapes of things. Some were also experiments with materials, but they also become something else once they are arranged, sometimes next to each other, sometimes overlapping, like the shriveled latex sleeves and the pleated concertina of rubber tubes strewn across the top tier of *Untitled* (1968). It was Sol LeWitt who first collected the little objects that Hesse gave him as gifts in one of these ready-made glass cases similar to the kind Claes Oldenburg used for his fake papier-mâché "fancies." Hesse took up the idea and made several. The fact that they have an ambiguous relation to her other works is partly the point: it is as if the things in her glass cases *are* in limbo in some way. The word "process" never did justice to Hesse's work, even at the time, when it seemed perhaps the most vivid way to describe the resistance to a certain kind of finish that had become associated with Minimalism.

Part objects focus attention on the body and on a bodily topography. The strange, uncanny landscapes of Hesse's glass cases are an alien material world, all the more so because the intimate bodily textures, like wrinkled latex, invite us to imagine and project. They also make us think of all the other large-scale works she made – her expanding "body" of work. Lateral connections proliferate in a freefall of metonymic chains running through a variety of materials – latex, foam rubber, plaster, wax – and through a variety of techniques, such as threading, piercing, embedding, and wrapping. They are often visceral, and when the latex was new it would have glistened as if wet, like the inside of a bodily orifice or, for that matter, like the shiny dental plastic of Duchamp's *Wedge of Chastity* (1954), which Hesse would have seen at the exhibition of his small erotic objects in Bern in 1964. Hesse's way of mapping the body changed pretty radically after her return from Germany at the end of 1964. The machine drawings that she had made in Europe reveal her engagement with the pumping, directional flows of a Duchampian body, diagrammatically rendered as a line that inflates and deflates, with details of joints and articulations often blown up out of all proportion. When she later makes a work like *Compass,* she is no longer interested in those kinds of articulations; instead, she brings together the small

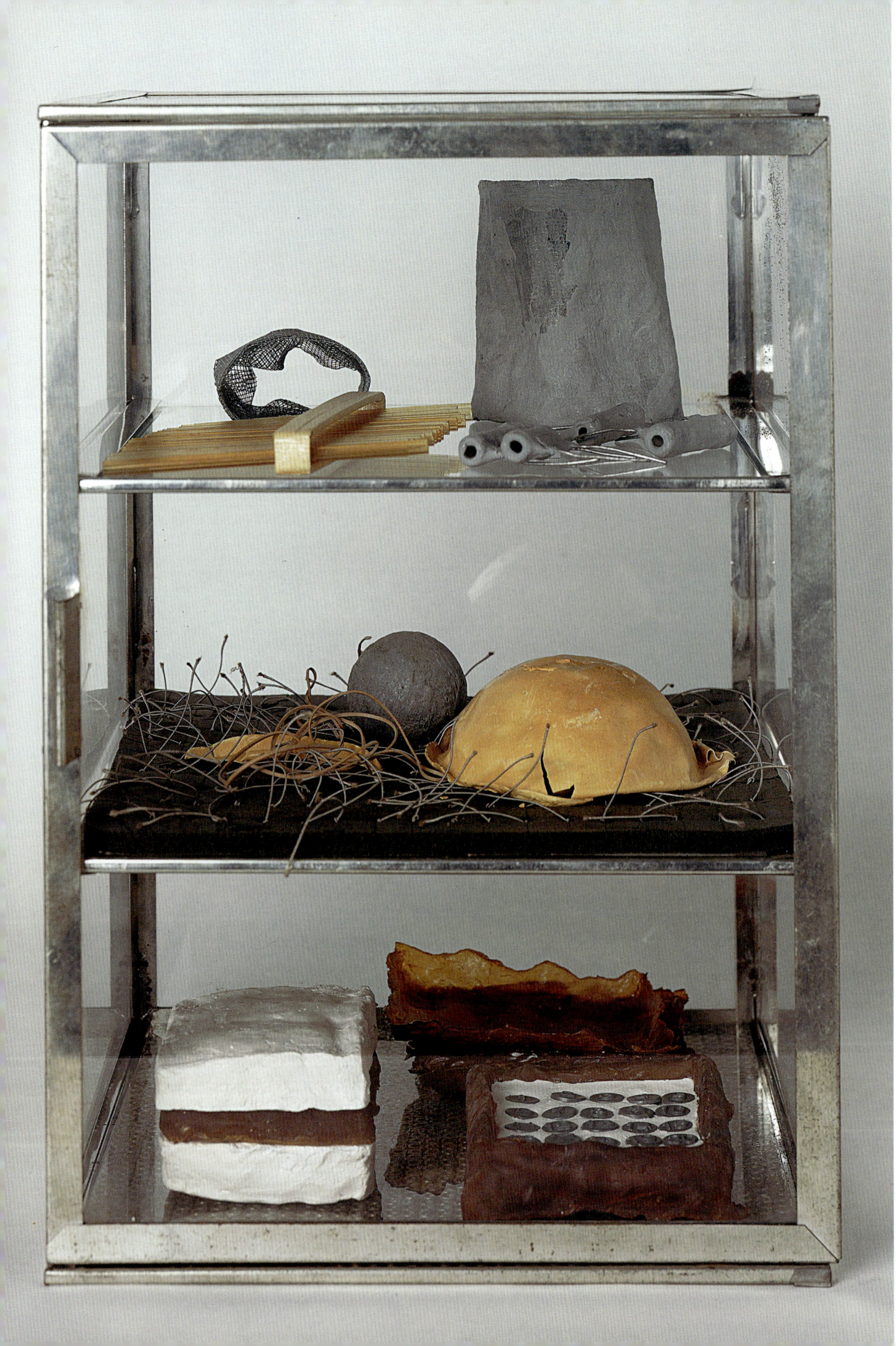

washers as a repetition of tiny parts to make an intricate and uneven grid. Now she prefers to join things without joints, it seems, but that is not to say that they add up to a whole. Rather, the joins and connections that interest her seem to be simple, variable, and often temporary placements.

Mel Bochner once called the small pieces Hesse put in cases "the more scatological things she made…the side of her work that alludes to the body as a sewer system."[8] In a way, it is precisely this *systemic* approach to the visceral that is so striking. Making them *work* together: part object to part object; or as Annette Michelson put it, "Part object to art object."[9] They are both working parts and leftovers of other works, like relics without aura. Some were simply experiments with materials, but the ones Hesse kept obviously intrigued her as something more than technical experiments, or potentially so when placed together with other things. Little experimental latex hemispheres can seem like negative craters in a strange material terrain; remaindered from other work, they get recycled here. We run the gamut of her material, in miniature, both readymade like the washers or handmade like latex painted over mesh or cheesecloth. The question is how to encompass rather than unify such disparity. The vitrine or glass case heightens the effect through concentration, but also by the invitation to the viewer to look through the glass sides onto a series of miniature scapes.

Orozco's tables invite a different kind of looking, one that is spread out, dispersed, one that scans across the kind of surface – a table – that we think we know and that in some ways is highly conventionalized but is culturally variable. In a way, this is part of Orozco's attempt to avoid references (especially, he has said, references to Duchamp).[10] And I think it is striking that Orozco's tables precisely do not inventorize or archive his work. They do not operate as Duchamp's *Boîte-en-Valise* to provide either an ideal catalogue or a working manual, but a *working table,* where things are made or partly made or arranged or rearranged, where things are *handled.* There is an appeal to touch. The bodiliness of these textures can be imagined. But, as with Hesse's work too, a bodily address through the tactile is mental rather than literal – anticipated rather than actual, if no less affective for that.

At work here is a dynamic series of circuits. The turnover of objects is reminiscent of what Karl Marx called the "*perpetuum mobile* of circulation." The artist who most vividly encapsulates that absolute mobility of capital is Piero Manzoni, who offers another historical trajectory for Orozco – one that he has frequently spoken of. It was Manzoni who most directly brought together the circuits of the body and the circuits of capital. He packaged breath as well as shit. He once criticized contemporary painters for their gymnastics: "They paint a line in, step back, look at their work with head on one side and half closed eye, then jump forward again and add another line of colour."[11] He took some delight in caricaturing the painter as an extravagant, posturing gymnast, filling up a painting as if it were a receptacle with "artificial meanings." Why, he asked, "shouldn't this receptacle be emptied?" He set himself the task with his "achromes," which hung on the wall as paintings but behaved as objects would. In this way his gymnastics would be different – he would turn somersaults with the object of art itself.

Eva Hesse
Untitled, 1968

In 1954 Arturo Schwarz opened his gallery cum bookshop in Milan with an exhibition entitled "Homage to Marcel Duchamp," comprising publications and some of the small erotic objects he had recently made. According to Schwarz, Manzoni was a frequent visitor. Schwarz's own reading of Duchamp, promoted in his capacity as writer and *galleriste*, was of Duchamp the alchemist, reading his intricate and cryptic symbolic language as one of alchemical transformation. Manzoni was exposed to this heady mixture of alchemy and commerce – and some of its vocabulary seeps into his – but he seems to have turned it to his own ends. In 1959, he covered a coat hook with kaolin (his answer to Duchamp's *Trébuchet*, or *Trap*) and so made it part of the vast array of objects that he called his "achromes." In some of the earliest of these, kaolin, a white slip used in the production of ceramic glazes, petrifies their pleats and folds of canvas as they were stretched across the frame. The kaolin slip also froze or calcified the object – like materialist counterparts to Schwarz's reading of the alchemical Duchamp. Such objects seem petrified, but the more "frozen" they appear, the greater the mobility that is set up in the connections between disparate materials and things. And the materials Manzoni preferred were far from old or obsolete but tended to be synthetic and contemporary, like the polystyrene balls used for stuffing furniture but siphoned off from functional use to drift and scatter across an air-filled synthetic terrain. The aeration of his materials links back to breath, the air the body inhales and exhales. In his delirious and comic gesture, breath, in his *Corpo D'Ario* series, is material, expelled from the mouth into a balloon, expelled from the balloon as it shrinks to nothing, leaving an abject remainder of *pure* body. Duchamp had already invoked the orality of breath when he talked of smoke exhaled in tobacco-breath as the "olfactory infrathin."[12] This is air thickened by body. Manzoni's breath is another body-product, like a phantasmatic object expulsed from the body.

Manzoni presents one historical trajectory for thinking about Orozco's "organic world"; Hesse presents another. They share a pursuit of circuits in which parts do not add up to a whole so much as circulate in perpetual motion. The pattern is no longer even part-to-part so much as *part-circuiting-part* in a series of temporal rhythms. This is an organicity where things are generated and degenerate in time as well as space. There is a systemic relation between things, where the intervals between things become mobile and animated, and where even a breath or something as immaterial as the air that circulates around things can be transformed into matter. Leftovers come to stand not for what once has been but what will be. They suggest forever-fluctuating possibilities. What is kept as important and what is cast out as unimportant have always been mutually dependent, and, needless to say, have been subject to radical historical changes over time. Focusing attention on the leftover puts in question the value of what we choose to keep. The things that seem important at first end up being abandoned, and what is at first abandoned ends up being the most productive. Chance often works this way, when something that has been cast aside breaks through to something new.

right Piero Manzoni
Achrome, 1960

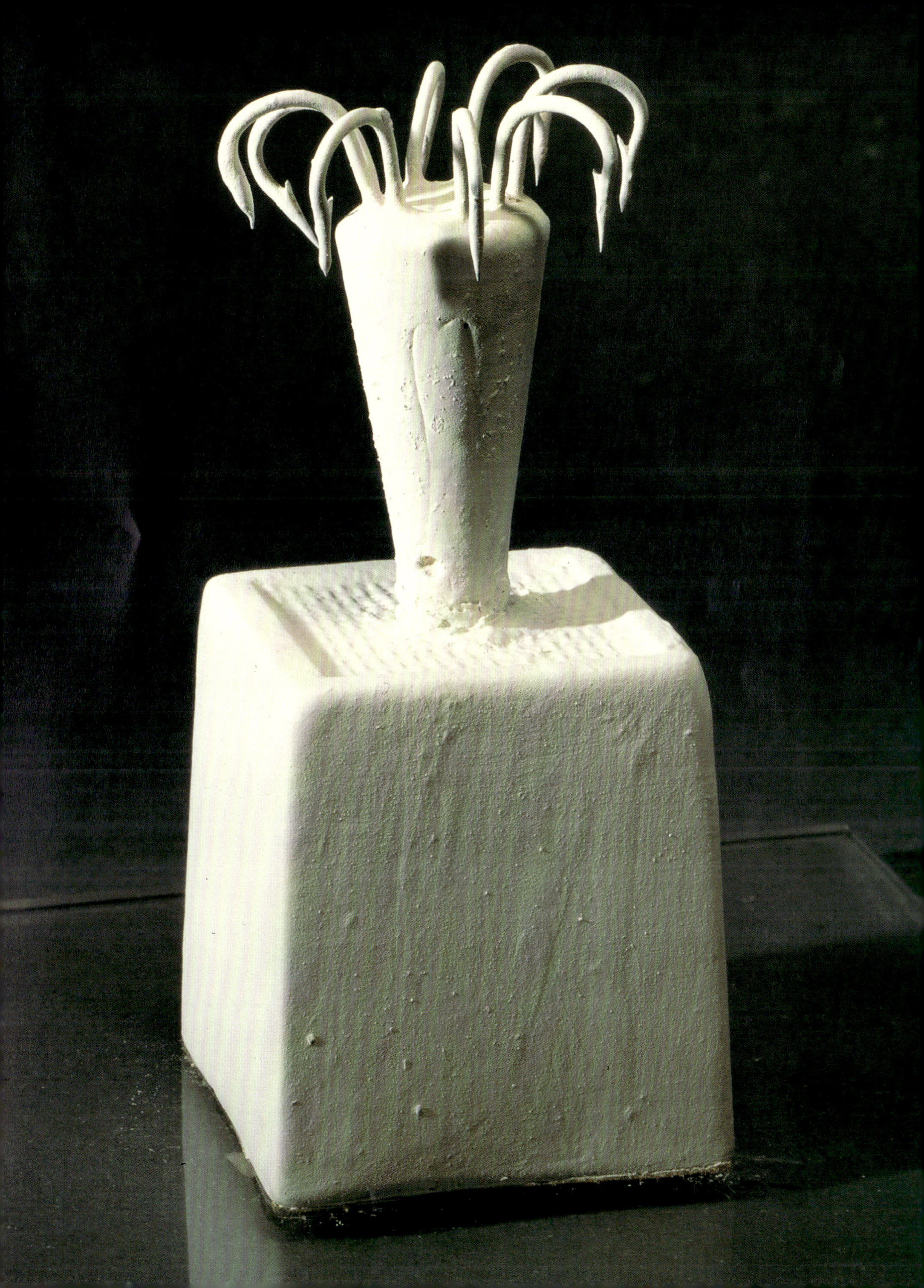

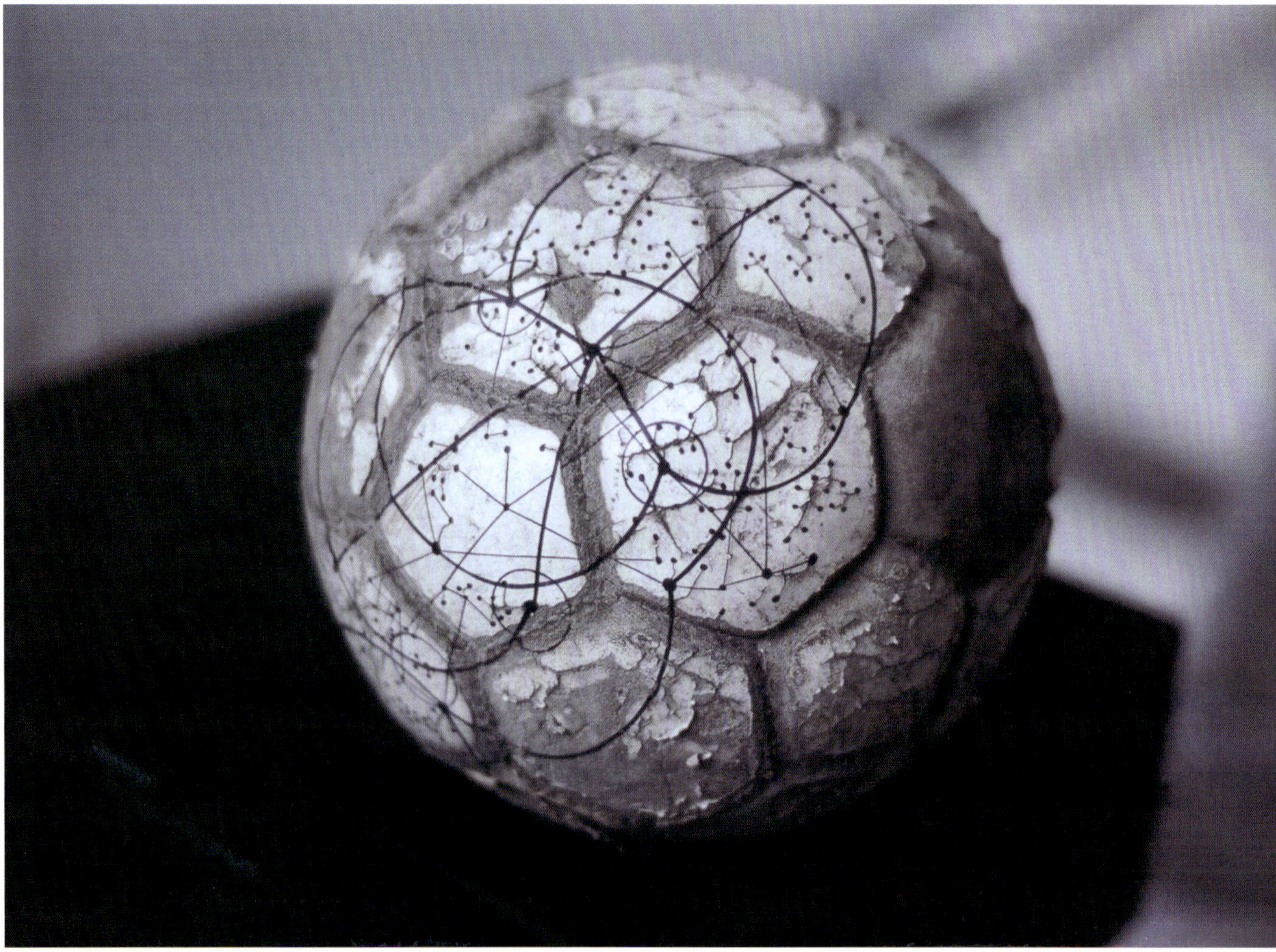

In 2003 Orozco worked with polyurethane, a highly toxic material used as insulation in building construction. He made a series of hanging works called *Spumes*, by pouring the polyurethane into a stretched-out latex sheet, its weight causing the latex to bear down. Like lava, it ran its course and quickly dried, uncannily fixing the form of its movement. Full of tiny bubbles of air, this is how air moves – the most immaterial of vapors made palpably material. In other works he made at this time, he poured the foam through mesh. Orozco experimented with the polyurethane in different containers and receptacles, pouring it into a range of different kinds of trays for fruit, the kind found on the street after an open-air market. A cardboard melon tray buckles under the expansive synthetic foam. In another, a polystyrene apple tray, it squeezes through the slits that he has cut in a kind of rough-and-ready grid. These are neither strictly cast nor molded and the foam necessarily exceeds its support. They are not strictly experiments either but are more like exercises or improvisations. They now reappear on a table in a new set of relations, having in the meantime been stored away. Leftovers, but also proto-objects: they are no longer redundant as they once were, but neither have they quite become something else, yet. A term Duchamp coined, "indefinity," seems appropriate here.[13]

Leftovers are part objects in time rather than space. Leftovers suggest fractured rather than continuous time. They are cut off from both a past and a future. This cutting adrift is more violent than we might at first imagine. This is neither an archive nor a memory bank of things. If memories are stirred by some objects, they are quickly cancelled by being dislodged from the circuits they normally inhabit. They leapfrog from one to another, temporary residents in a different space. A kind of violent dispersal is at work, a dispersal that generates a tissue of shifting relations.

One point remains to be made: Orozco's economy of leftovers differs from an economy of collecting. After all, both involve groups and arrangements of objects that have been deliberately removed from functional use. Walter Benjamin once described the hidden motive of a person who collects as the "struggle against dispersion. Right from the start, the great collector is struck by the confusion, by the scatter, in which things in the world are found." However bizarre collections of objects might be, the drive is "to overcome the wholly irrational character of the object's mere presence at hand" through integrating it into a classifiable system as a "form of practical memory."[14] Orozco's working tables seem to me to be an anticollection of objects that seeks out "the object's mere presence at hand" – the accident by which it happens to be there. Given the inertia and stasis of contemporary cultural life, to insist on the "scatter" is to insist again on the sensual encounter with the world *at hand*. The "scatter" includes the spaces between things, the air surrounding things, as at least as material, at least as bodily, at least as "left over" as the things on a table.

On one of Orozco's tables sits a soccer ball, scruffy and frayed, with circular shapes excised from its surface. Slightly deflated, the ball echoes any number of spheres: a shrunken peel from half an orange covered in plasticine

Gabriel Orozco
Soccer Ball, 2002

nearby or a spinning world. On its surface is drawn a small constellation, like a stellar constellation charting the vast intervals between the stars in a miniature diagram. To call this drawing the scatter is to emphasize the role of chance; to call it a constellation is to emphasize the systemic. The friction between these two creates maximum mobility.

NOTES

1 Gabriel Orozco interviewed by Benjamin Buchloh, in *Clinton Is Innocent*, exh. cat. (Paris: Musée d'Art Moderne de la Ville de Paris, 1998), 127.

2 Also shown at the Whitney Biennial.

3 Orozco interviewed by Benjamin Buchloh, 127.

4 Ibid.

5 Gabriel Orozco, in conversation with the author, Paris, November 2004.

6 Orozco interviewed by Benjamin Buchloh, 127.

7 Ibid.

8 Mel Bochner interviewed by Joan Simon, 1992, reprinted in *Eva Hesse*, ed. Mignon Nixon (Cambridge, Mass.: October Files MIT, 2002), 42.

9 Annette Michelson, "'Where is your rupture?" Mass Culture and the *Gesamtkunstwerk*" *October* 56 (Spring 1991): 48. Mignon Nixon discusses Michelson's claim in her fine essay on Eva Hesse, "Ringaround Rosie: 2 in 1," in *Eva Hesse*, 195–218.

10 Orozco interviewed by Benjamin Buchloh. Unusually, and partly for practical reasons, Orozco used vitrines in his recent exhibition in the Palacio de Cristal at the Museo Nacional Centro de Arte Reina Sofía in Madrid in 2005. However, I think the radical point of difference still holds–arguably, glass vitrines in a glass house do not operate like a vitrine in a conventional building. The open, scattering effect was, if anything, enhanced by the installation.

11 Manzoni, in Germano Celant, *Piero Manzoni*, exh. cat. (London: Serpentine Gallery, 1998), 130.

12 See discussion of the "infrathin" in the Marcel Duchamp entry in this volume.

13 *In the Infinitive*, a typotranslation by Richard Hamilton and Ecke Bonk of Marcel Duchamp's "White Box" (Northend: Typosophic Society, 1999), 76.

14 Walter Benjamin, *The Arcades Project*, trans. Howard Eiland and Kevin McLaughlin (Cambridge, Mass.: Belknap Press of Harvard University Press, 1999), 211.

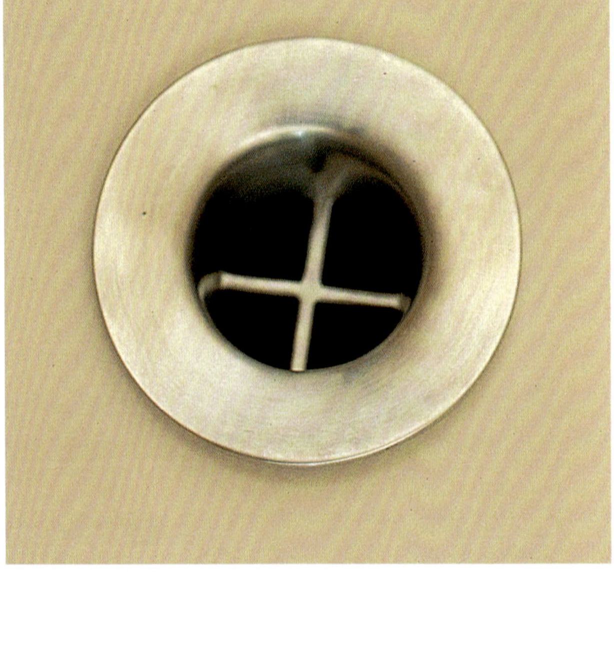

Drains, 1990

right **The Floating Sink**, 1986

ROBERT GOBER 1954–

Robert Gober makes things by hand. Sinks, drains, bags of cat litter, human torsos, all manner of things that are not normally, nor need to be, made by hand. In this regard his oeuvre can be understood as a rejection of the implications of Duchamp's readymades. Inasmuch as Gober could have purchased his sinks and drains already made, he chose not to. Of course, by laboriously making such objects by hand, Gober taints them with features of failure and vulnerability – the sinks have no faucets, the drains are inserted directly into the wall – that undermine the very imperviousness to the world that constitutes the allure of the mass-produced commodity object. Nonetheless these moments of failure, or better yet, impossibility, are an extension of a less-examined part of Duchamp's practice. Indeed Gober's dialogue with the Duchampian readymade sheds a new light upon it: Gober's nonusable sinks highlight how Duchamp has rendered the functionality of his readymades null and void through his placement of them. Additionally, the delayed reaction most people experience when looking at a Gober sink–as they slowly realize the sink is in fact *not* one, but is rather a handmade representation of a sink – harkens back to the original aesthetic failure of Duchamp's readymades, as they went largely unseen by the general public and unrecognized as art at their first showings.[1] Gober permits the emotive ramifications of the readymades to generate his sculptural practice. In doing so, his handmade readymades acknowledge the crafted quality of Duchamp's postwar oeuvre – from the *Boîte-en-Valise*, to the erotic objects and *Etant donnés*, to the 1960s handmade readymades.

Gober's work isn't only to be held in relation to Duchamp's, however. One of the most important sculptors of the postwar period, his work articulates a space outside the hegemonic concerns of Minimalism. Gober's sinks of the mid-1980s were numerous, and yet no two are alike. In contrast to the overarching sameness of much Minimalist sculpture, Gober continually played with the notion of difference. The work is repetitive but infinitely varied. The variation is in the permutations of the sinks themselves, but it also emerges from the trace of the handmade on all of them. Although they gleam with porcelain whiteness, they are in fact made of plaster and coated with a semigloss enamel paint. Hence, they are fabricated from the stuff of domestic space (they share more with the average construction of bedroom walls than they do with mass-produced sinks) and as such are ever so slightly lumpy, their "imperfections" betraying at every turn the body that made them.

The cool exterior of the sinks and drains differs demonstrably from Gober's use of wax. Noted for its malleability and softness, wax also takes on pigment in such a way that it appears as if light is emanating from within it. This is undoubtedly why Gober chose it as a medium for both a suspended light bulb, in *Untitled, Lightbulb* (1990) and his renderings of the human form. In *Untitled* (1990), a nude male torso sits directly on the floor, propped up against a wall. The history of sculpture took a dramatic turn when Brancusi eliminated sculpture's reliance upon a base; even so, the harshness of the juxtaposition of this truncated human form and the museum floor is shocking. More troubling, however, is that the torso shares its shape with the sculpted rendition of a bag of cat litter. The transposability of a person and a thing is simultaneously disturbing and pathetic, as the sagging male form is no more energetic than the inert cat litter. This juxtaposition heightens the shared attributes between them – a formless interior held together by a protective outer casing, each a repository for waste and a commodity predestined for disposal.

Gober's sense of the go-between between bodies and things, the intense reciprocity that people have with commodity objects, is not only marked by the sadness and reification noted above. In *Untitled* (1997), the viewer approaches an open suitcase, placed directly on the floor. As always in Gober's work, the suitcase is entirely handmade, and, unlike the gleaming sinks, it harkens back to another time – the hard leather cases of the 1950s and 1960s, the suitcase of an old man. Defying expectation, the suitcase is not filled with pressed white shirts and ties but instead contains a running tidepool. As water moves and swirls in the bottom of the case, it glimmers over reproductions of shells and seaweed. And at an oblique angle, one can see the naked legs of a man holding a small child, whose legs dangle between the man's.

Untitled (1997) is an extraordinary feat of trompe l'oeil (everything looks absolutely real) and a diorama of utter fantasy and desire (in my grandfather's or my father's suitcase resides he and I, an image, a memory of care, and human touch). If Duchamp's *Boîte-en-Valise* offered his world in miniature, a traveling museum dedicated to the work of one person, Gober's suitcase offers a space where objects contain memories and fantasies and desires. The memories may be untenable, the fantasies magical, and the desires unrequited, but the ability of the object both to enclose and present them makes it utterly indispensable.

ROBERT GOBER 1954–

Robert Gober makes things by hand. Sinks, drains, bags of cat litter, human torsos, all manner of things that are not normally, nor need to be, made by hand. In this regard his oeuvre can be understood as a rejection of the implications of Duchamp's readymades. Inasmuch as Gober could have purchased his sinks and drains already made, he chose not to. Of course, by laboriously making such objects by hand, Gober taints them with features of failure and vulnerability – the sinks have no faucets, the drains are inserted directly into the wall – that undermine the very imperviousness to the world that constitutes the allure of the mass-produced commodity object. Nonetheless these moments of failure, or better yet, impossibility, are an extension of a less-examined part of Duchamp's practice. Indeed Gober's dialogue with the Duchampian readymade sheds a new light upon it. Gober's nonusable sinks highlight how Duchamp has rendered the functionality of his readymades null and void through his placement of them. Additionally, the delayed reaction most people experience when looking at a Gober sink – as they slowly realize the sink is in fact not one, but is rather a handmade representation of a sink – harkens back to the original aesthetic failure of Duchamp's readymades, as they went largely unseen by the general public and unrecognized as art at their first showings.[1] Gober permits the emotive ramifications of the readymades to generate his sculptural practice. In doing so, his handmade readymades acknowledge the crafted quality of Duchamp's postwar oeuvre – from the Boîte-en-Valise, to the erotic objects and Étant donnés, to the 1960s handmade readymades.

Gober's work isn't only to be held in relation to Duchamp's, however. One of the most important sculptors of the postwar period, his work articulates a space outside the hegemonic concerns of Minimalism. Gober's sinks of the mid-1980s were numerous, and yet no two are alike. In contrast to the overarching sameness of much Minimalist sculpture, Gober continually played with the notion of difference. The work is repetitive but infinitely varied. The variation is in the permutations of the sinks themselves, but it also emerges from the trace of the handmade on all of them. Although they gleam with porcelain whiteness, they are in fact made of plaster and coated with a semigloss enamel paint. Hence, they are fabricated from the stuff of domestic space (they share more with the average construction of bedroom walls than they do with mass-produced sinks) and as such are ever so slightly lumpy, their "imperfections" betraying at every turn the body that made them.

The cool exterior of the sinks and drains differs demonstrably from Gober's use of wax. Noted for its malleability and softness, wax also takes on pigment in such a way that it appears as if light is emanating from within it. This is undoubtedly why Gober chose it as a medium for both a suspended light bulb, in *Untitled, Lightbulb* (1990) and his renderings of the human form. In *Untitled* (1990), a nude male torso sits directly on the floor, propped up against a wall. The history of sculpture took a dramatic turn when Brancusi eliminated sculpture's reliance upon a base; even so, the harshness of the juxtaposition of this truncated human form and the museum floor is shocking. More troubling, however, is that the torso shares its shape with the sculpted rendition of a bag of cat litter. The transposability of a person and a thing is simultaneously disturbing and pathetic, as the sagging male form is no more energetic than the inert cat litter. This juxtaposition heightens the shared attributes between them – a formless interior held together by a protective outer casing, each a repository for waste and a commodity predestined for disposal.

Gober's sense of the go-between between bodies and things, the intense reciprocity that people have with commodity objects, is not only marked by the sadness and reification noted above. In *Untitled* (1997), the viewer approaches an open suitcase, placed directly on the floor. As always in Gober's work, the suitcase is entirely handmade, and, unlike the gleaming sinks, it harkens back to another time – the hard leather cases of the 1950s and 1960s, the suitcase of an old man. Defying expectation, the suitcase is not filled with pressed white shirts and ties but instead contains a running tidepool. As water moves and swirls in the bottom of the case, it glimmers over reproductions of shells and seaweed. And at an oblique angle, one can see the naked legs of a man holding a small child, whose legs dangle between the man's.

Untitled (1997) is an extraordinary feat of trompe l'oeil (everything looks absolutely real) and a diorama of utter fantasy and desire (in my grandfather's or my father's suitcase reside he and I, an image, a memory of care, and human touch). If Duchamp's Boîte-en-Valise offered his world in miniature, a traveling museum dedicated to the work of one person, Gober's suitcase offers a space where objects contain memories and fantasies and desires. The memories may be untenable, the fantasies magical, and the desires unrequited, but the ability of the object both to enclose and present them makes it utterly indispensable.

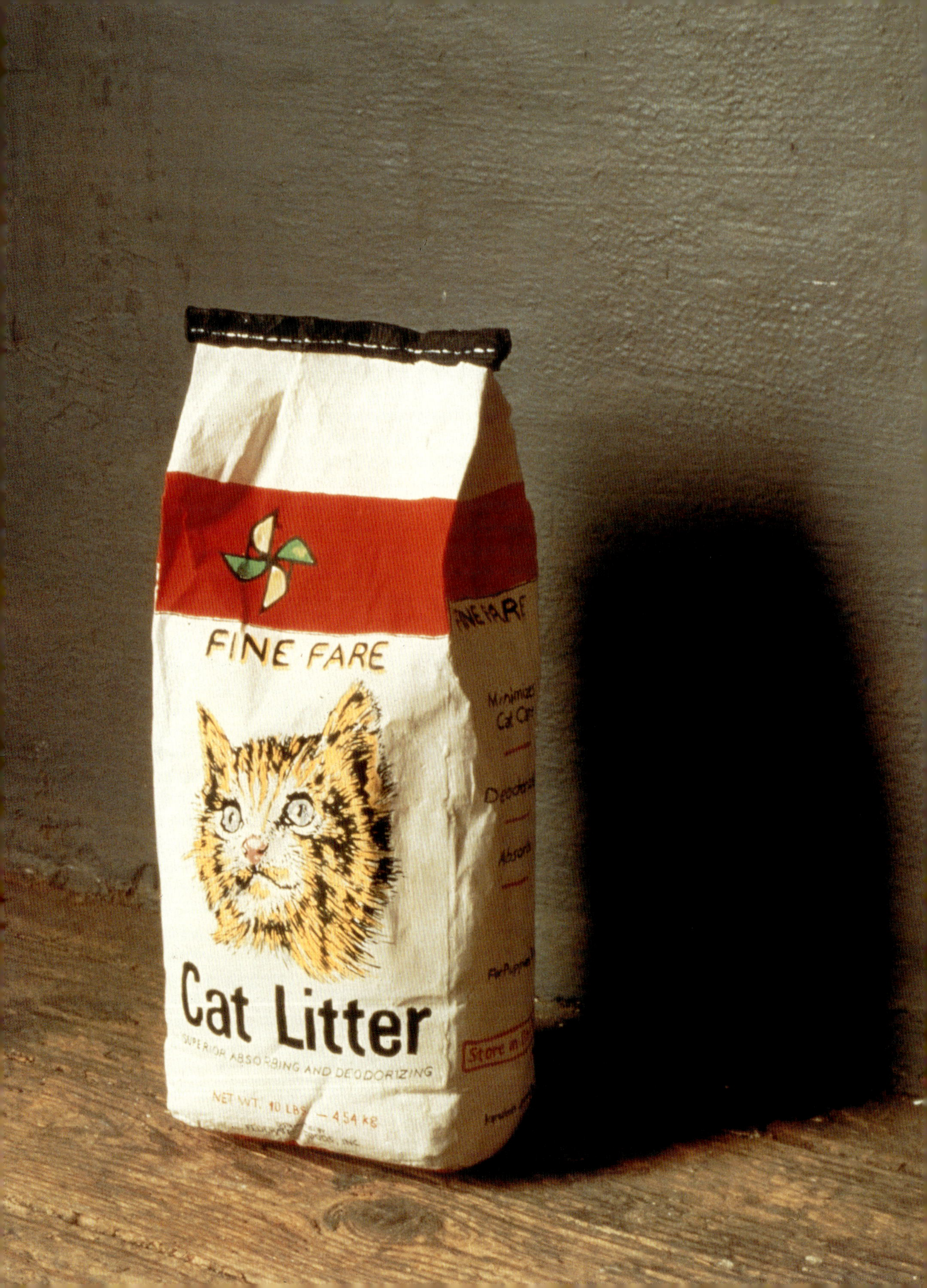
FINE FARE
Cat Litter
SUPERIOR ABSORBING AND DEODORIZING
NET WT. 10 LBS — 4.54 KG

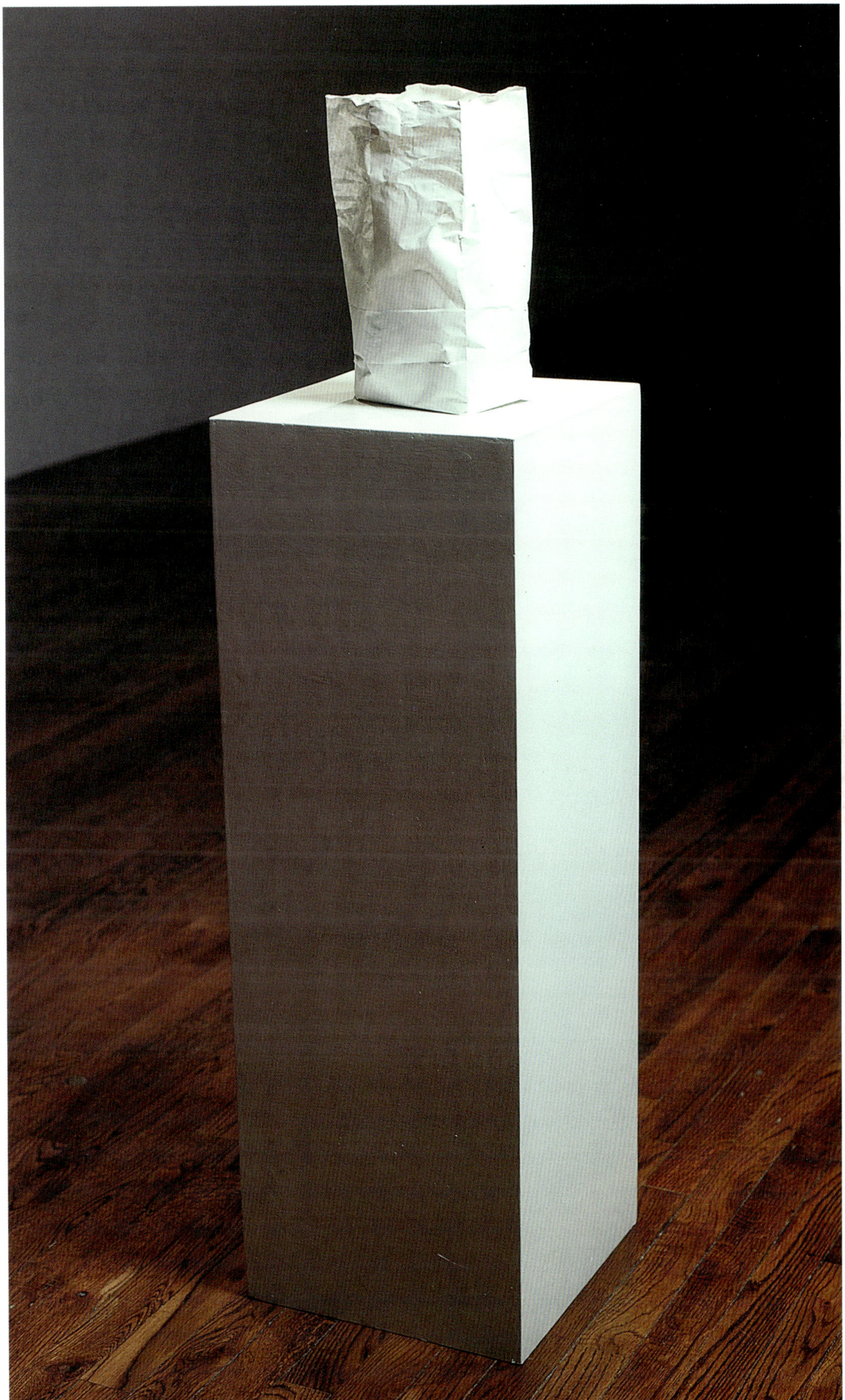

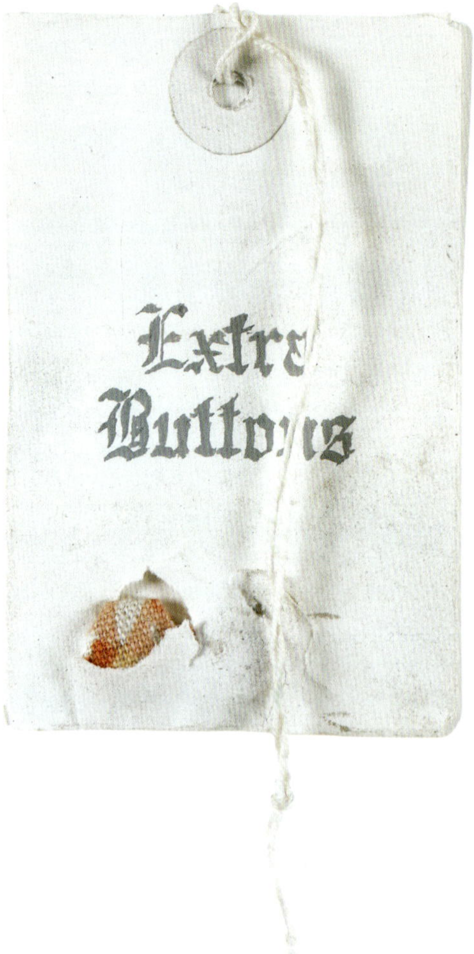

previous spread: left **Cat Litter**, 1989

previous spread: right **Bag of Donuts**, 1989

above **Untitled**, 1994

Untitled, 1990

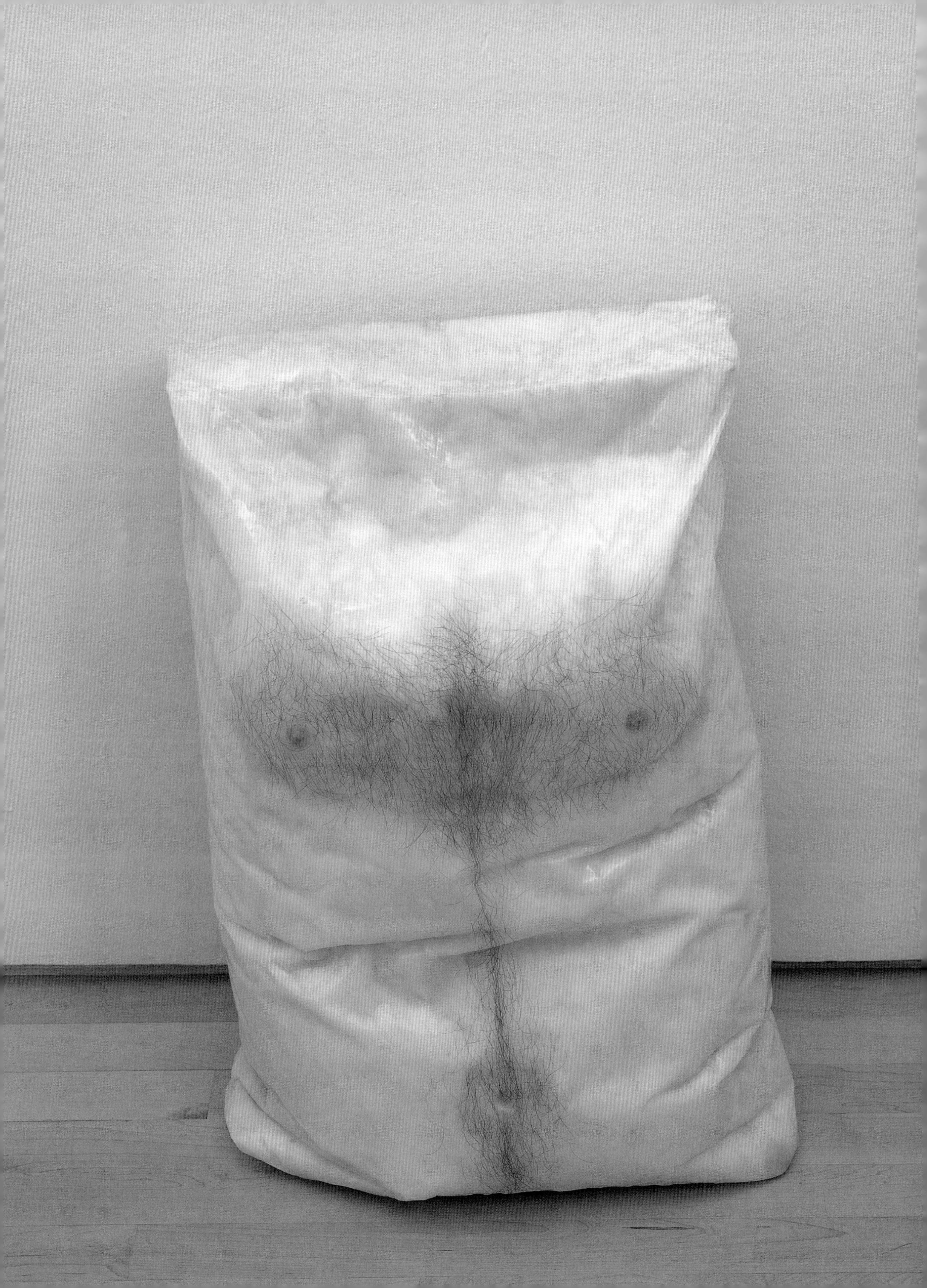

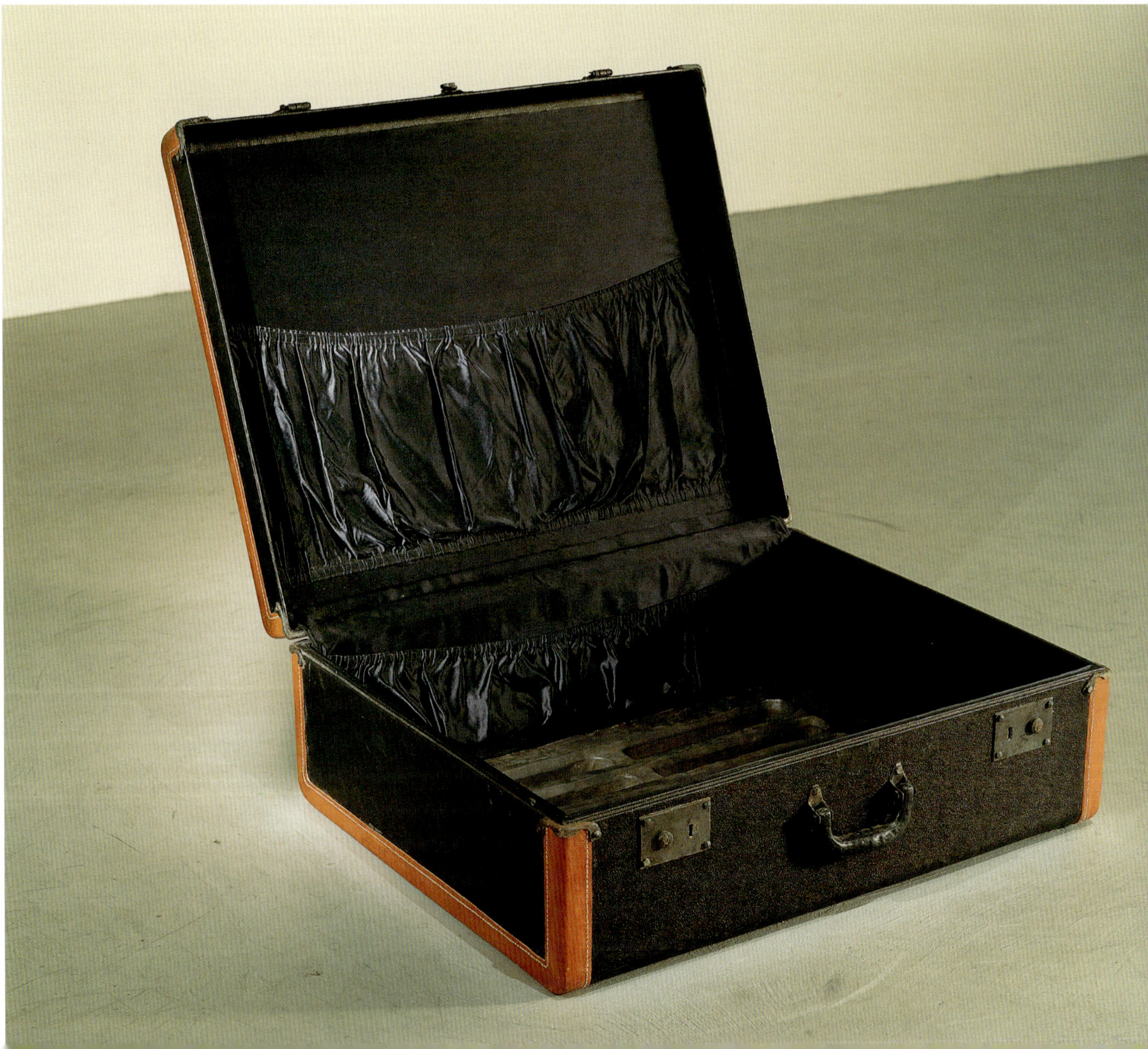

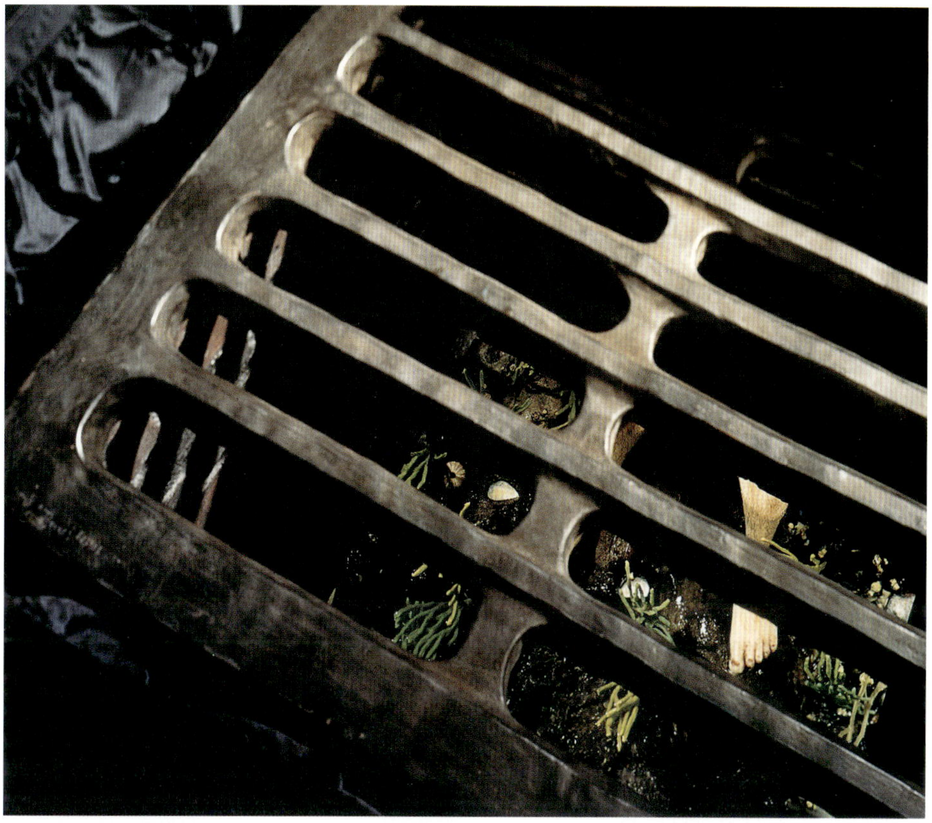

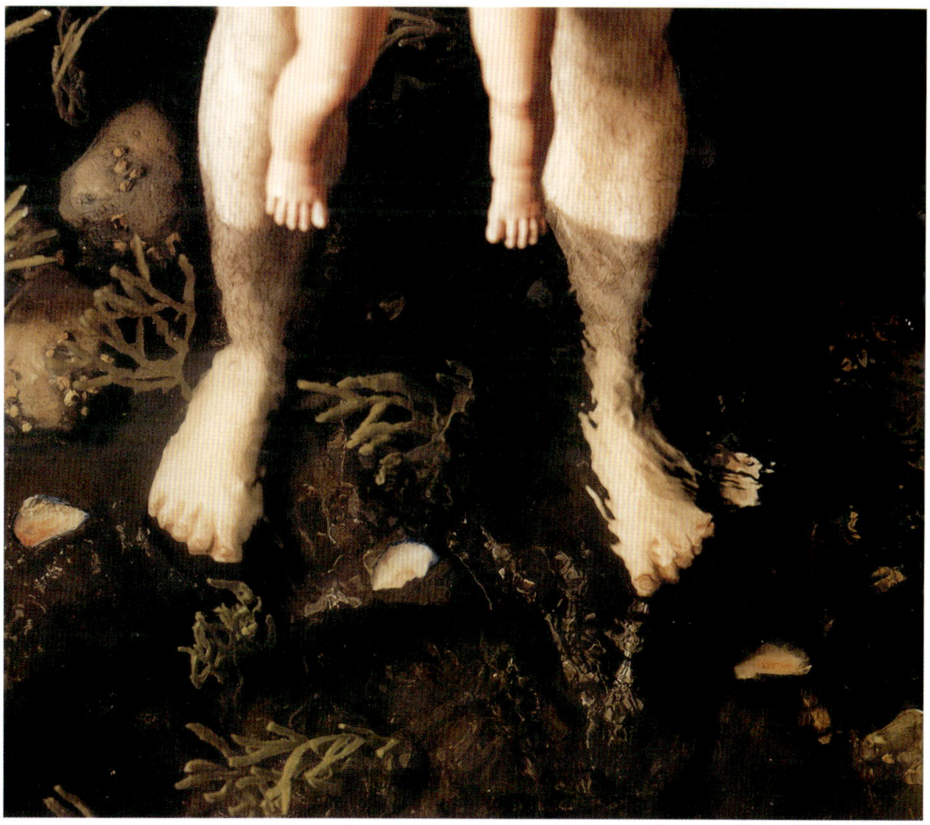

all and following spread
Untitled, 1997

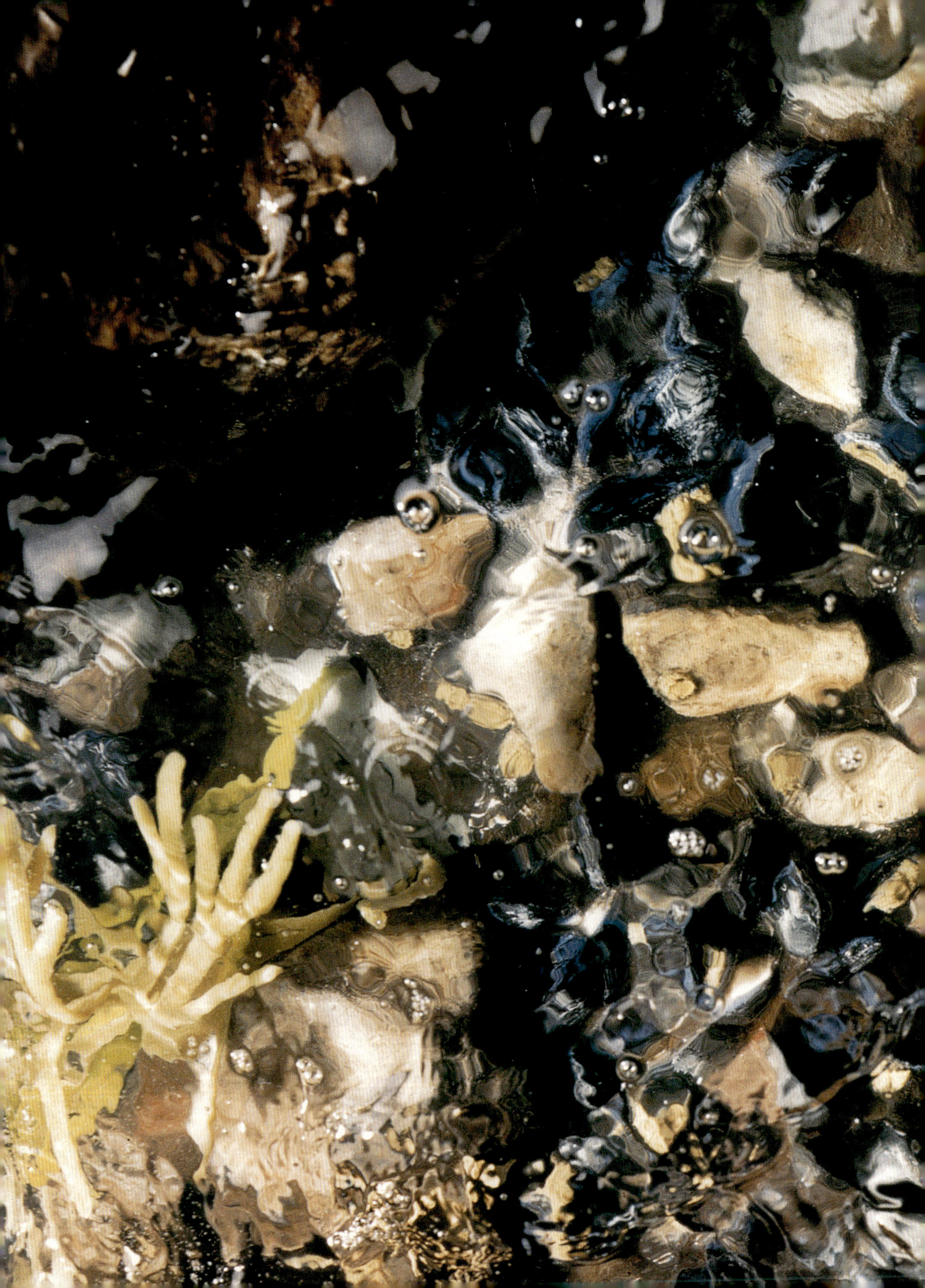

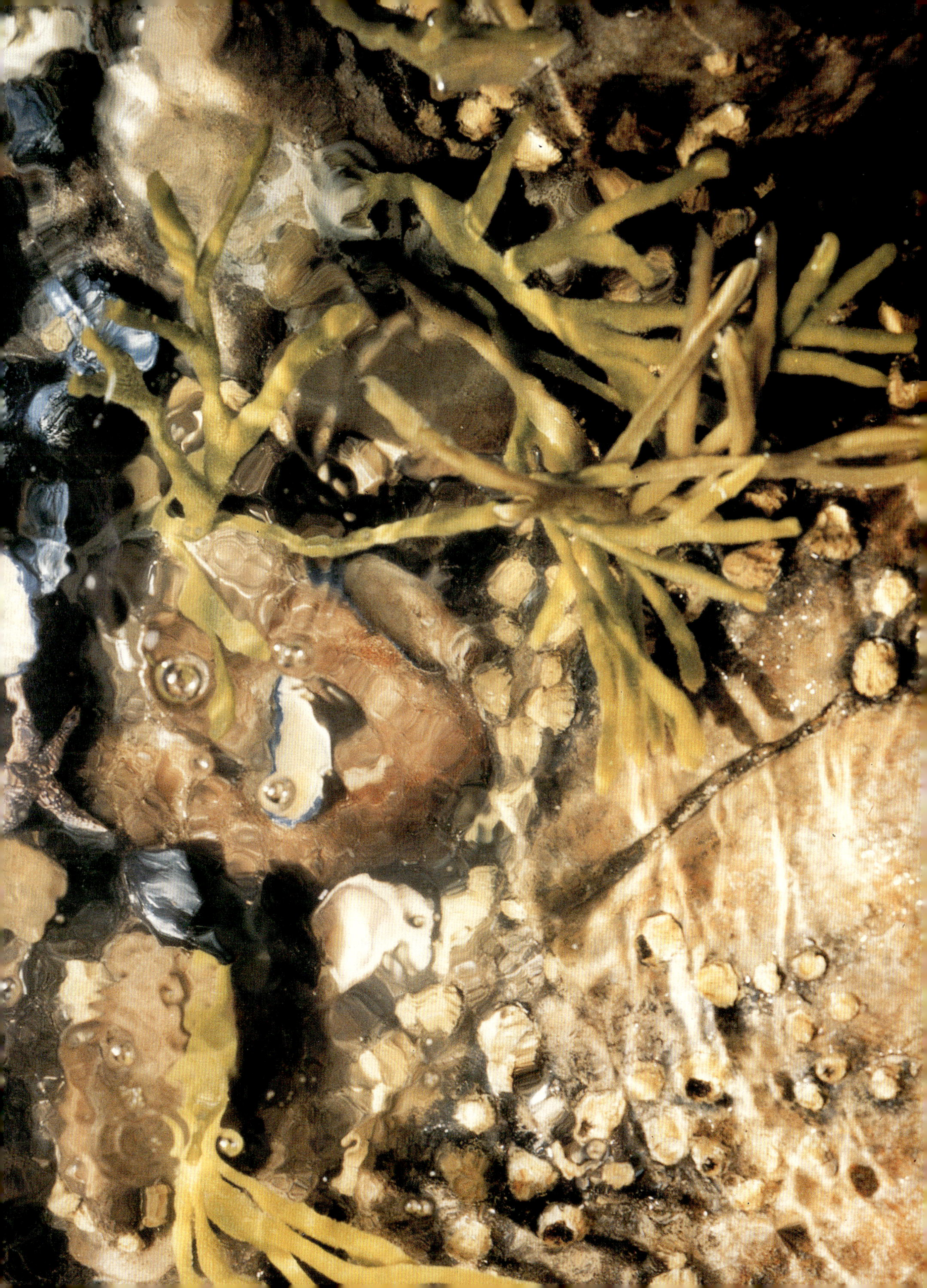

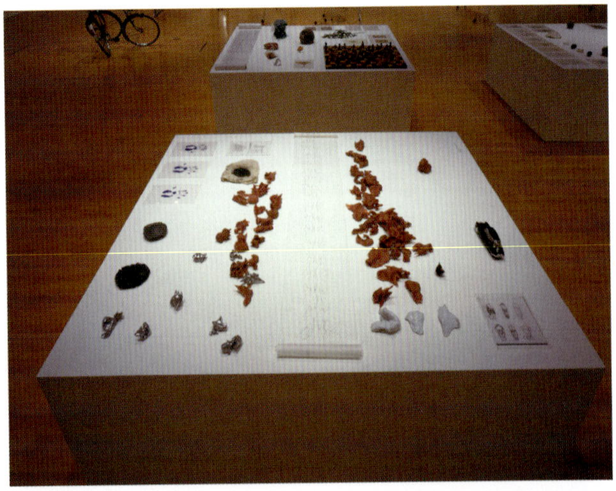
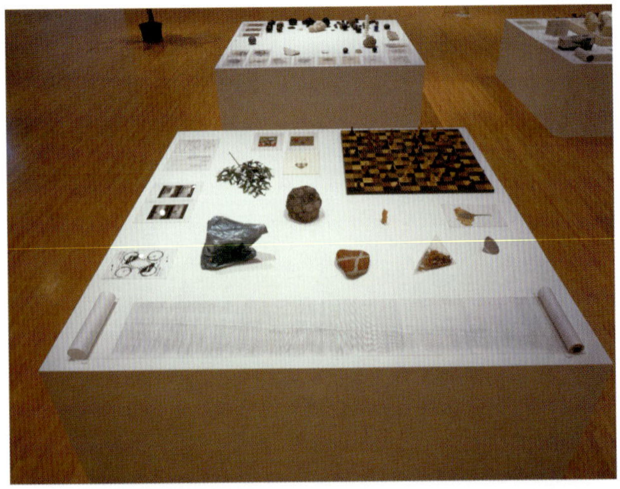
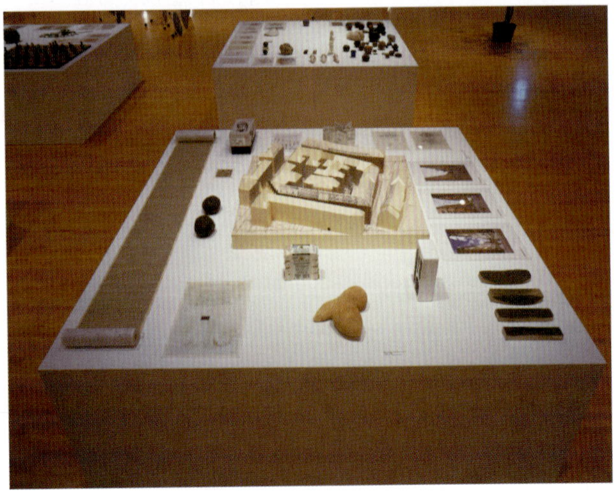
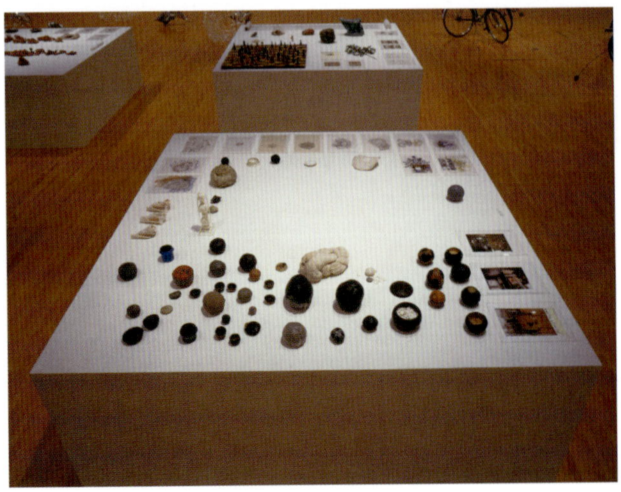

GABRIEL OROZCO 1962–

On a low platform, the height of a table as opposed to a traditional plinth, one encounters an array of heterogeneous objects. Some are clearly made by hand, plasticine pressed and molded into forms. Others are readymade, an empty shoebox, a light bulb with small press-type letters applied to it. And some are derived from the natural world: oranges, their skin delicately opened, their contents removed and reformed. The tables are Gabriel Orozco's *Working Tables (Mesas de Trabajo)*. An ongoing project, the tables have become a mystic writing tablet for his oeuvre. One set, owned by the Centre Pompidou in Paris, contains objects made over a ten-year period. All of them function as a repository of memory, a miniature staging of a creative decade, especially since many of the objects on the tables are models for Orozco's larger-scale objects. Both magical and sly, the Pompidou tables have the feel of Duchamp's *Boîte-en-Valise*. They smuggle an artist's retrospective exhibition into the space of the museum – sans curator, sans official sanctioning.

Orozco's tables don't stop here in either their address to the legacy of Duchamp or in their restaging of Orozco's own oeuvre. The tables are ongoing; they can be convened and staged with the objects of a given time period. Orozco is continually making the types of objects that find their way onto his tables. Notoriously peripatetic (he lives and works in New York, Paris, and Mexico City), Orozco makes these hand-scaled objects partly out of an acknowledgment of a deeply nonstudio practice. This is the art of kitchen tables, of objects made with the materials at hand, made while on the move, made to be tucked away in a drawer or in a pocket, to be saved for later, to be taken to the next place. This is sculpture at the scale of the daily, the intimate, and the domestic, rather than of the timeless or the monumental and public. Continuously made anew, covered with the latest crop of objects, the tables bear comparison to the space of the unconscious once described by Freud as a mystic writing pad. For Freud, this simple child's toy, upon which one writes on a transparent sheet attached to a base of a dark, sticky substance, is a model for the unconscious. When the sheet is lifted, the words disappear, but the base retains their imprint forever. Freud's metaphor of the unconscious as a palimpsest hovers around the *Working Tables* as Orozco makes and presents his found and made objects, then packs them up and puts them away. They are a continual spatial layering of ideas and activities even as one set endlessly supplants another.

Orozco's *Working Tables* also occupy the space of the horizontal, and, as such, recall critic Leo Steinberg's early assessment of Robert Rauschenberg's dramatic challenge to the vertical sanctity of traditional easel painting in his landmark essay "Other Criteria." For Steinberg, what differentiated Rauschenberg from his historical predecessors (so much so that the phrase "post modern" would be used for the first time in art criticism) was his use of the "flat bed picture plane," the horizontal space of work – of printing and writing, of newspaper assembly, and the work of a wood shop – rather than the vertical space of traditional easel painting. Rauschenberg's formal contiguity with these spaces of labor allowed the works to truly act in the gap between art and life that he had so famously announced was his arena. Orozco also moves deftly between the realms of art and life. His steady exploration of the object world, his manipulations of the handmade and the readymade, reduces the nettlesome aspects of the commodity object to a sculptural problem of solid and void – a series of infinite permutations in which objects are either full or empty. In doing so, Orozco neuters distinctions between the handmade and the machine made, as if the full/empty binary were merely a mathematical code.

This sense of the code in Orozco utterly lacks the logarithmic nature of the code in Conceptual art or the serial progression of Minimalism. Rather, in the *Working Tables* this code is offered as ludic, a mental gamesmanship of form, a perpetual play between the past and the future – as the objects function both as mnemonics for works already made and models of works to come – as well as being utterly part of the present, part of the dailyness of their making, the steady domesticity of their nomadic production. All these binary engines – solid and void, memory and presentness, model and actuality, play and work, handmade and machine made, nature and commodity, conscious and unconscious – propel us into the space of part object and part sculpture.

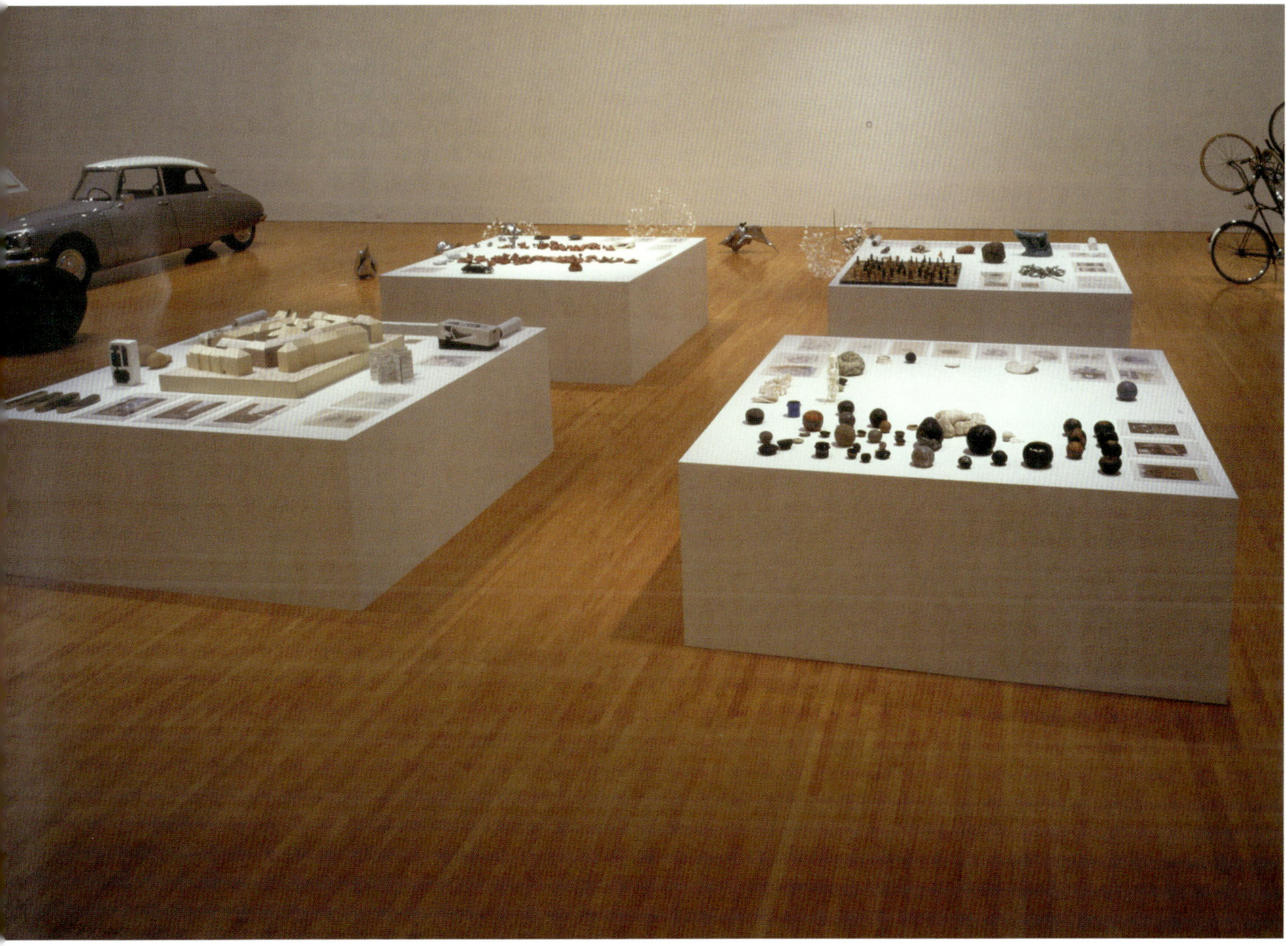

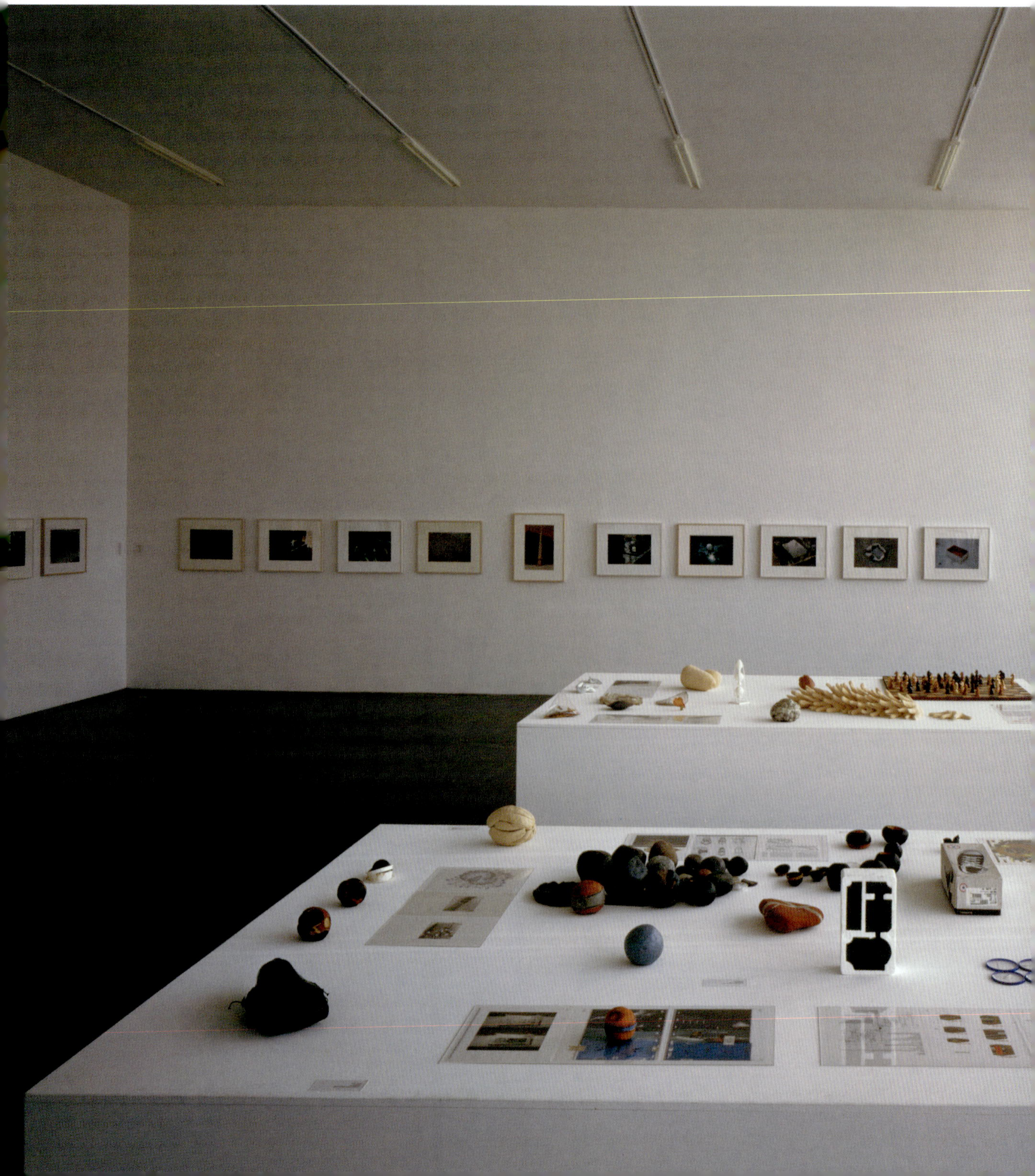

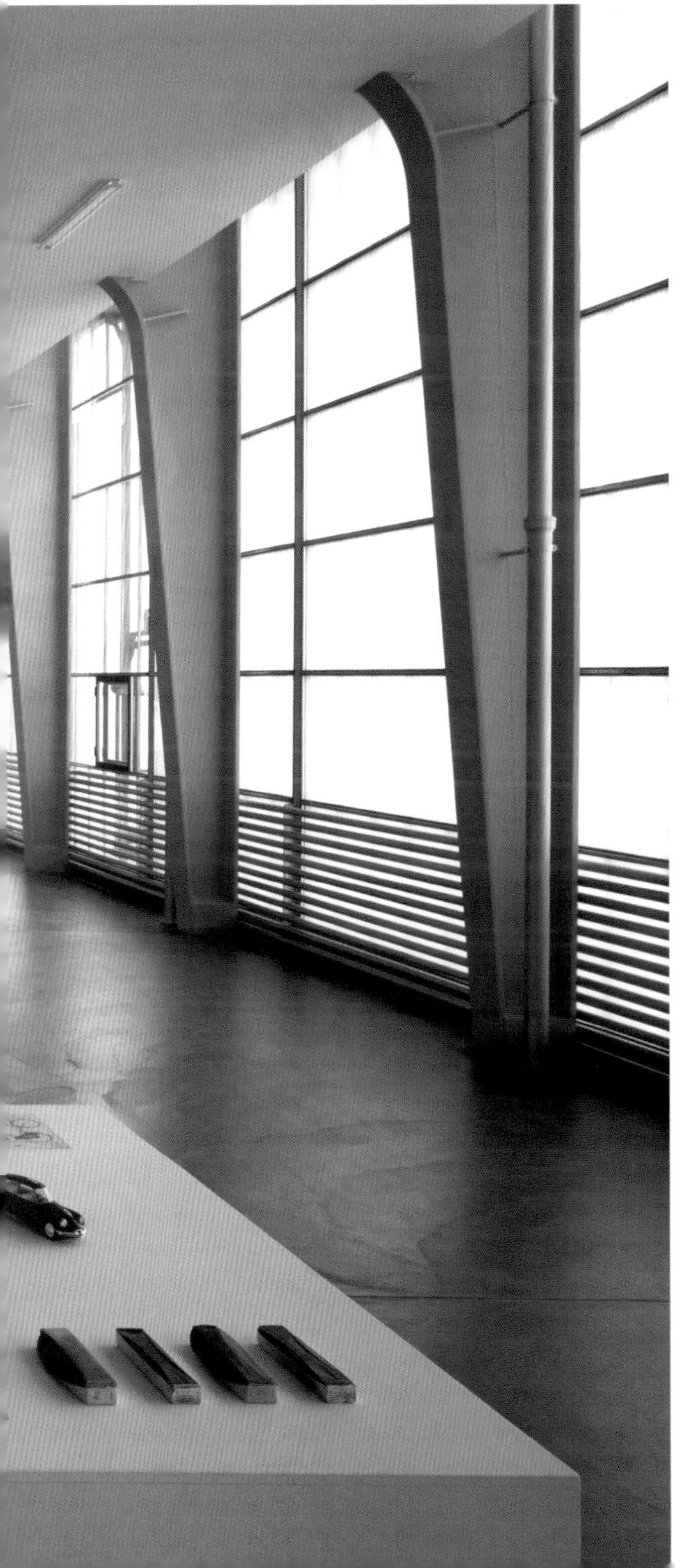

previous spread: left and right
Working Tables (Mesas de trabajo), 2000

left **Working Tables** (Mesas de trabajo), 1996

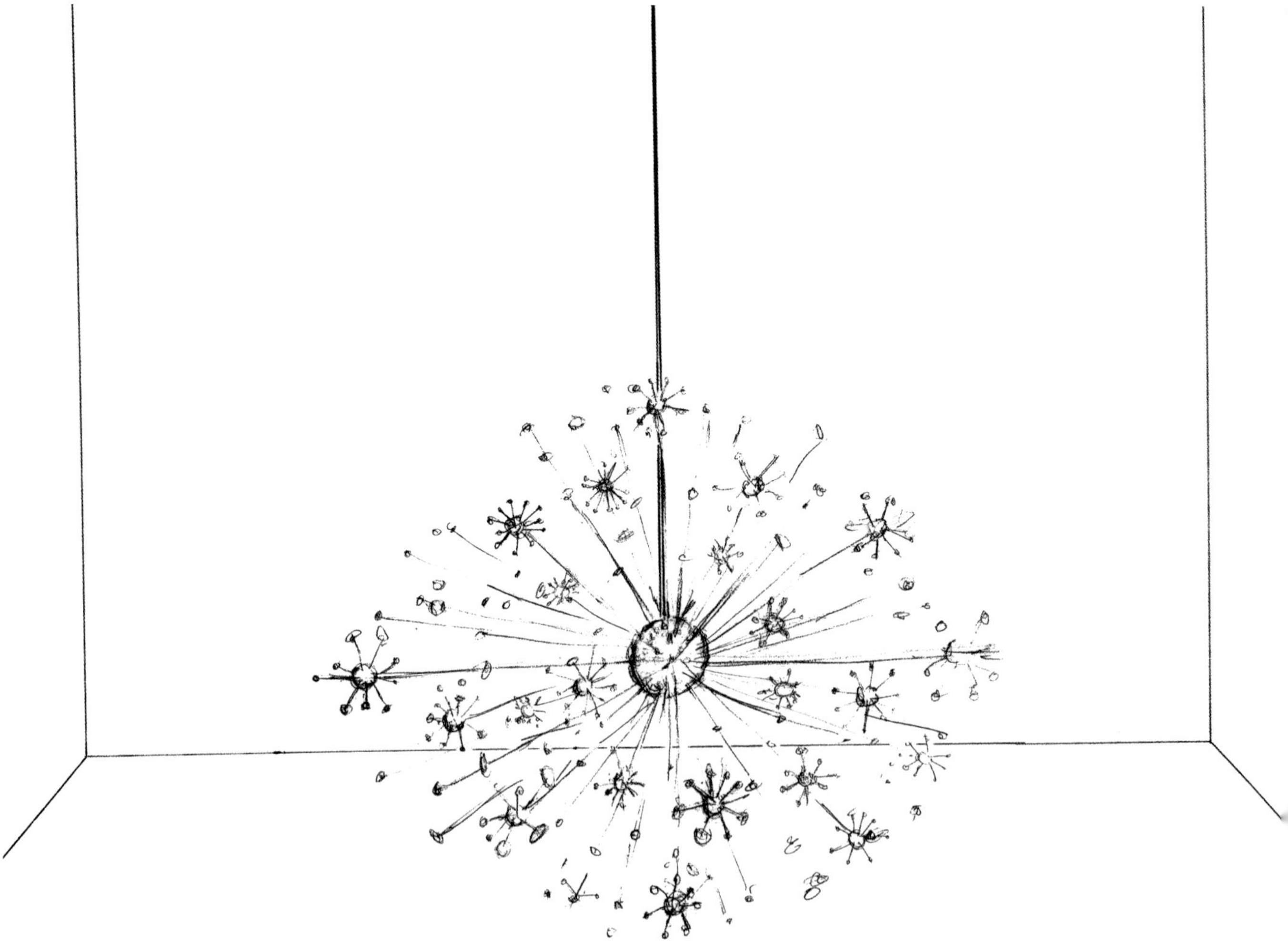

JOSIAH McELHENY 1966–

Josiah McElheny's work exists in the tremulous terrain between object and sculpture, craft and art, applied arts and design, memory and history, narrative and fact, and opacity and translucence. Despite the fluidity of these intellectual and artistic parameters, the work is emblematically solid, consisting of blown-glass objects that the artist himself has blown, often configured in vitrines or on tables and shelves. McElheny learned this craft by apprenticing himself to master glassblowers Lino Tagliapietra, Jan-Erik Ritzman, Ronald Wilkinson, and Sven-Åke Carlsson. What makes McElheny's work exceptional is the way in which it bypasses the dichotomy between art and craft through his engagement with modernism, which is evidenced by the conceptual finesse of his adaptation of museum practices of display as well as his sustained interest in the legacies of Marcel Duchamp and Adolf Loos.

McElheny's work is wide-ranging in its exploration, from the trope of the mirror in the fiction of Jorge Luis Borges to the geometric explorations of Renaissance perspective. These disparate interests are bound together in his work by a keen belief in the ability of objects to transmit history. For McElheny, the made world, the everyday objects that surround us, are the physical embodiments of ideas, narrative, memory, and history. Glass, amorphous until shaped and hardened into final form, serves as McElheny's prime metaphor for the flow of concepts into objects.

An Historical Anecdote about Fashion (1999) is an elegant glass vitrine made from two separate glass containers delicately perched on a tablelike base accompanied by photographs and drawings. Within each container we see beautifully colored vases, although on closer inspection the representation of the female form is undeniable. The objects are not simply generic female bodies. The bottles are imagined renderings of dress forms, but dresses of a particular nature. The installation purports to be a remnant of the 1952 Venice Biennale. As part of that Biennale, glassblowers from the famed Venini company displayed a group of vases based on the French couture dresses worn by the factory owner's wife. Translated into glass, the hourglass silhouette of Christian Dior, an excessive display of wealth in the culture of scarcity in postwar Italy, speaks of longing from a distance transformed into a palpable object that not only can be made but indeed can be possessed.

For *Part Object Part Sculpture*, the Wexner Center for the Arts commissioned two new works from McElheny. In *An End to Modernity*, McElheny created an enormous chandelier, 15 feet wide by 10 feet high, modeled on Lobmeyr's design for the chandeliers in the lobbies and main concert hall of Lincoln Center in New York City. Ironically, these ultimate Sixties-era objects, complete with the utopian sensibility of space exploration that suffused so much of mid-century design, were produced the same year the Big Bang Theory was officially accepted in the scientific community. That both modernist design and the Big Bang Theory were invented at the turn of the century, only to reach their apotheosis during the post–World War II period, is a historical coincidence and convergence that McElheny's sculpture seeks to explore. A film documenting historical images of the Big Bang, McElheny's first *Conceptual drawings for a chandelier*, will accompany this magical object.

Working with Ohio State University astronomer David Weinberg, McElheny fashioned a chandelier that is as accurate as possible a visual representation of the Big Bang. Suspended from the ceiling, but hanging only six inches off the floor, the chandelier both literalizes and transforms the magical aura of the original object. McElheny's chandelier is illuminated and hence fully functional, but by bringing the object down into the sphere of the viewer's body it no longer casts light from above. Rather, it occupies the traditional space of art, making it consummately part object part sculpture. Through this mode of display, the viewer can examine the hundreds of component parts, each fabricated by the artist. Individually they share the diminutive scale of so many of the objects in the exhibition, yet here the part-object status that scale has represented in the other works in *Part Object Part Sculpture* preceding *An End to Modernity* is no longer the case. Here, the vast network of component pieces is not forever fragmentary; instead, the pieces coalesce into a whole. Yet the whole is illusory and remains a whole that we can never fully comprehend, or even apprehend. Indeed the very status of the chandelier as a *model* points to the kind of impossibility of representation's ability to render adequately or accurately the totality of the universe as imagined by modernity – and yet it was, and remains, part of modernism's wish to provide such an image. In McElheny's version of the Big Bang, which is simultaneously his version of modernism's love affair with the object, part and whole merge and collide, coalesce and disintegrate, forever staging the problem of the part object part sculpture while offering the image of the birth of the universe as one of modernism's many penultimate objects.

JOSIAH McELHENY 1966–

Josiah McElheny's work exists in the tremulous terrain between object and sculpture, craft and art, applied arts and design, memory and history, narrative and fact, and opacity and translucence. Despite the fluidity of these intellectual and artistic parameters, the work is emblematically solid, consisting of blown-glass objects that the artist himself has blown, often configured in vitrines or on tables and shelves. McElheny learned this craft by apprenticing himself to master glassblowers Lino Tagliapietra, Jan-Erik Ritzman, Ronald Wilkinson, and Sven-Åke Carlsson. What makes McElheny's work exceptional is the way in which it bypasses the dichotomy between art and craft through his engagement with modernism, which is evidenced by the conceptual finesse of his adaptation of museum practices of display as well as his sustained interest in the legacies of Marcel Duchamp and Adolf Loos.

McElheny's work is wide-ranging in its exploration, from the trope of the mirror in the fiction of Jorge Luis Borges to the geometric explorations of Renaissance perspective. These disparate interests are bound together in his work by a keen belief in the ability of objects to transmit history. For McElheny, the made world, the everyday objects that surround us, are the physical embodiments of ideas, narrative, memory, and history. Glass, amorphous until shaped and hardened into final form, serves as McElheny's prime metaphor for the flow of concepts into objects.

An Historical Anecdote about Fashion (1999) is an elegant glass vitrine made from two separate glass containers delicately perched on a tablelike base accompanied by photographs and drawings. Within each container we see beautifully colored vases, although on closer inspection the representation of the female form is undeniable. The objects are not simply generic female bodies. The bottles are imagined renderings of dress forms, but dresses of a particular nature. The installation purports to be a remnant of the 1952 Venice Biennale. As part of that Biennale, glassblowers from the famed Venini company displayed a group of vases based on the French couture dresses worn by the factory owner's wife. Translated into glass, the hourglass silhouette of Christian Dior, an excessive display of wealth in the culture of scarcity in postwar Italy, speaks of longing from a distance transformed into a palpable object that not only can be made but indeed can be possessed.

For *Part Object Part Sculpture*, the Wexner Center for the Arts commissioned two new works from McElheny. In *An End to Modernity*, McElheny created an enormous chandelier, 15 feet wide by 10 feet high, modeled on Lobmeyr's design for the chandeliers in the lobbies and main concert hall of Lincoln Center in New York City. Ironically, these ultimate Sixties-era objects, complete with the utopian sensibility of space exploration that suffused so much of mid-century design, were produced the same year the Big Bang Theory was officially accepted in the scientific community. That both modernist design and the Big Bang Theory were invented at the turn of the century, only to reach their apotheosis during the post–World War II period, is a historical coincidence and convergence that McElheny's sculpture seeks to explore. A film documenting historical images of the Big Bang, McElheny's first conceptual drawings for a chandelier, will accompany this magical object.

Working with Ohio State University astronomer David Weinberg, McElheny fashioned a chandelier that is as accurate as possible a visual representation of the Big Bang. Suspended from the ceiling, but hanging only six inches off the floor, the chandelier both literalizes and transforms the magical aura of the original object. McElheny's chandelier is illuminated and hence fully functional, but by bringing the object down into the sphere of the viewer's body it no longer casts light from above. Rather, it occupies the traditional space of art, making it consummately part object part sculpture. Through this mode of display, the viewer can examine the hundreds of component parts, each fabricated by the artist. Individually they share the diminutive scale of so many of the objects in the exhibition, yet here the part-object status that scale has represented in the other works in *Part Object Part Sculpture* preceding *An End to Modernity* is no longer the case. Here, the vast network of component pieces is not forever fragmentary; instead, the pieces coalesce into a whole. Yet the whole is illusory and remains a whole that we can never fully comprehend, or even apprehend. Indeed the very status of the chandelier as a *model* points to the kind of impossibility of representation's ability to render adequately or accurately the totality of the universe as imagined by modernity – and yet it was, and remains, part of modernism's wish to provide such an image. In McElheny's version of the Big Bang, which is simultaneously his version of modernism's love affair with the object, part and whole merge and collide, coalesce and disintegrate, forever staging the problem of the part object part sculpture while offering the image of the birth of the universe as one of modernism's many penultimate objects.

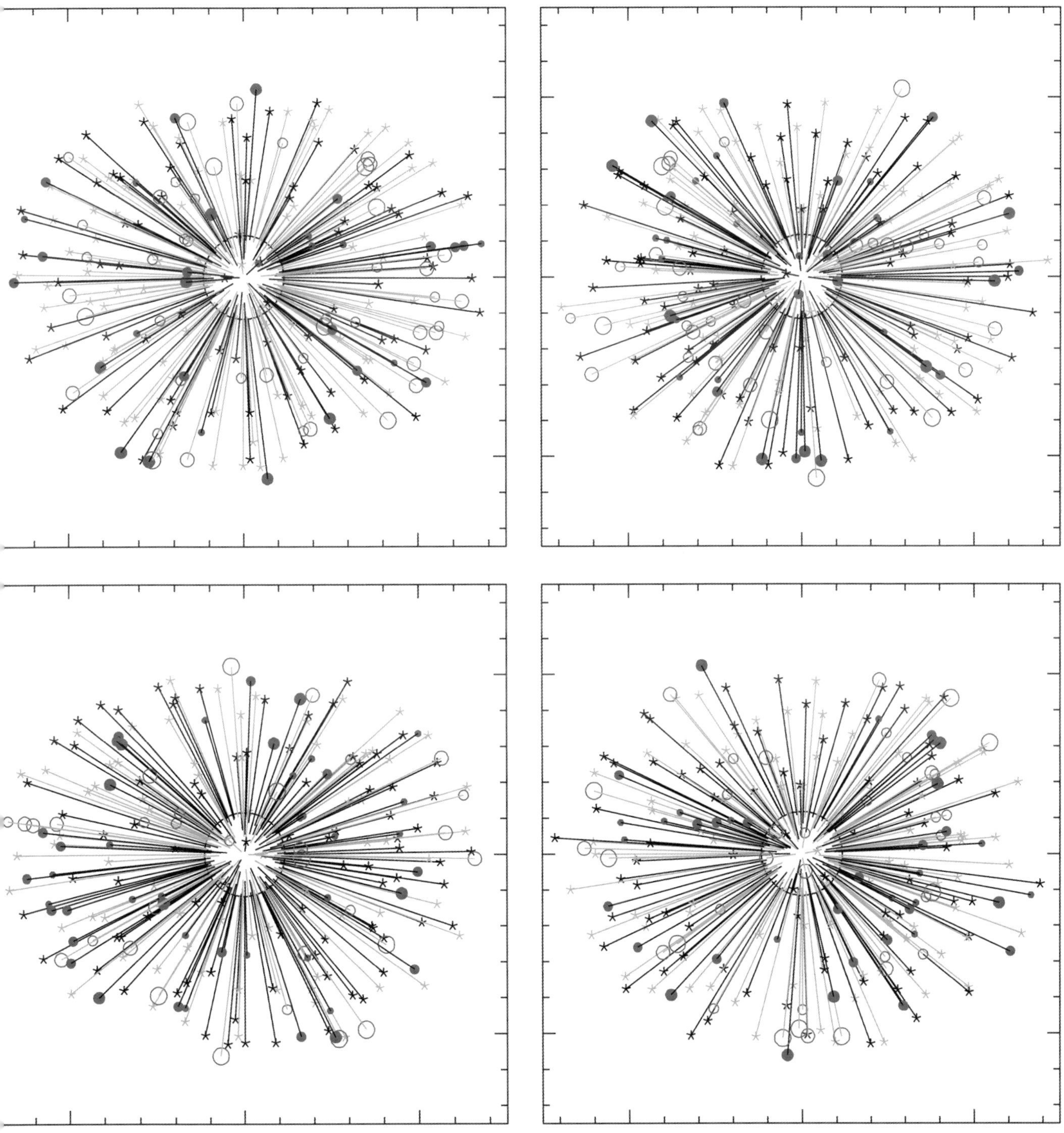

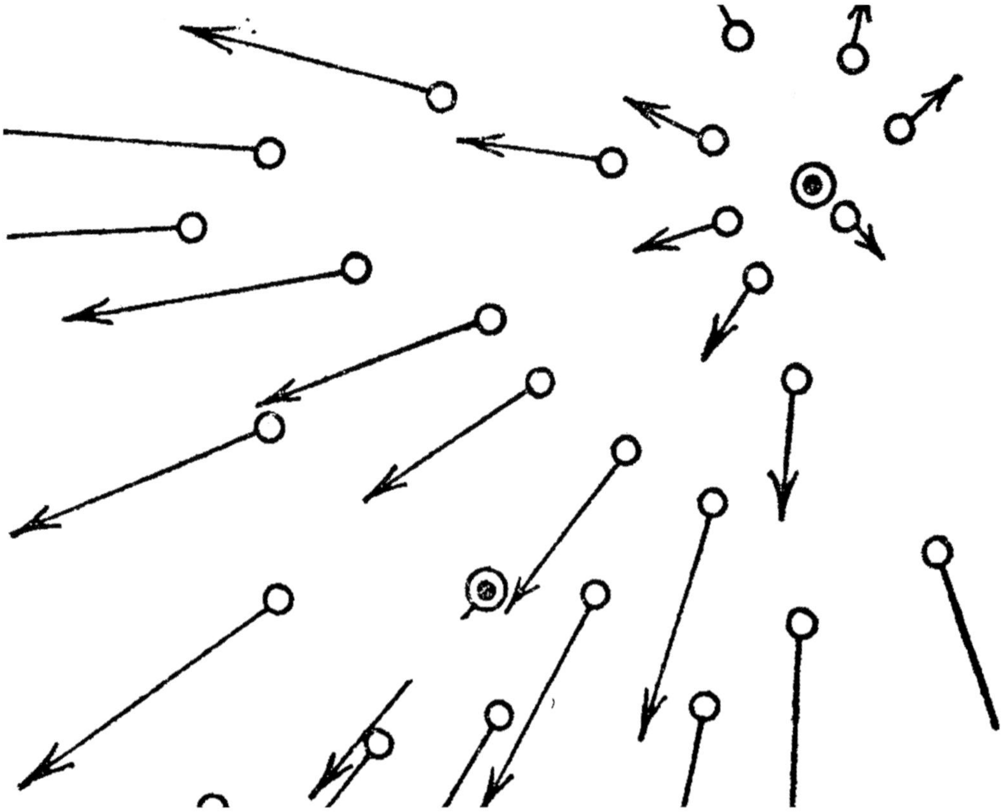

previous spread: left Early sketch for **An End to Modernity**, 2005

previous spread: right Conceptual drawing for **An End to Modernity**, 2005

Preliminary drawing for **Conceptual drawings for a chandelier, 1965**, 2005

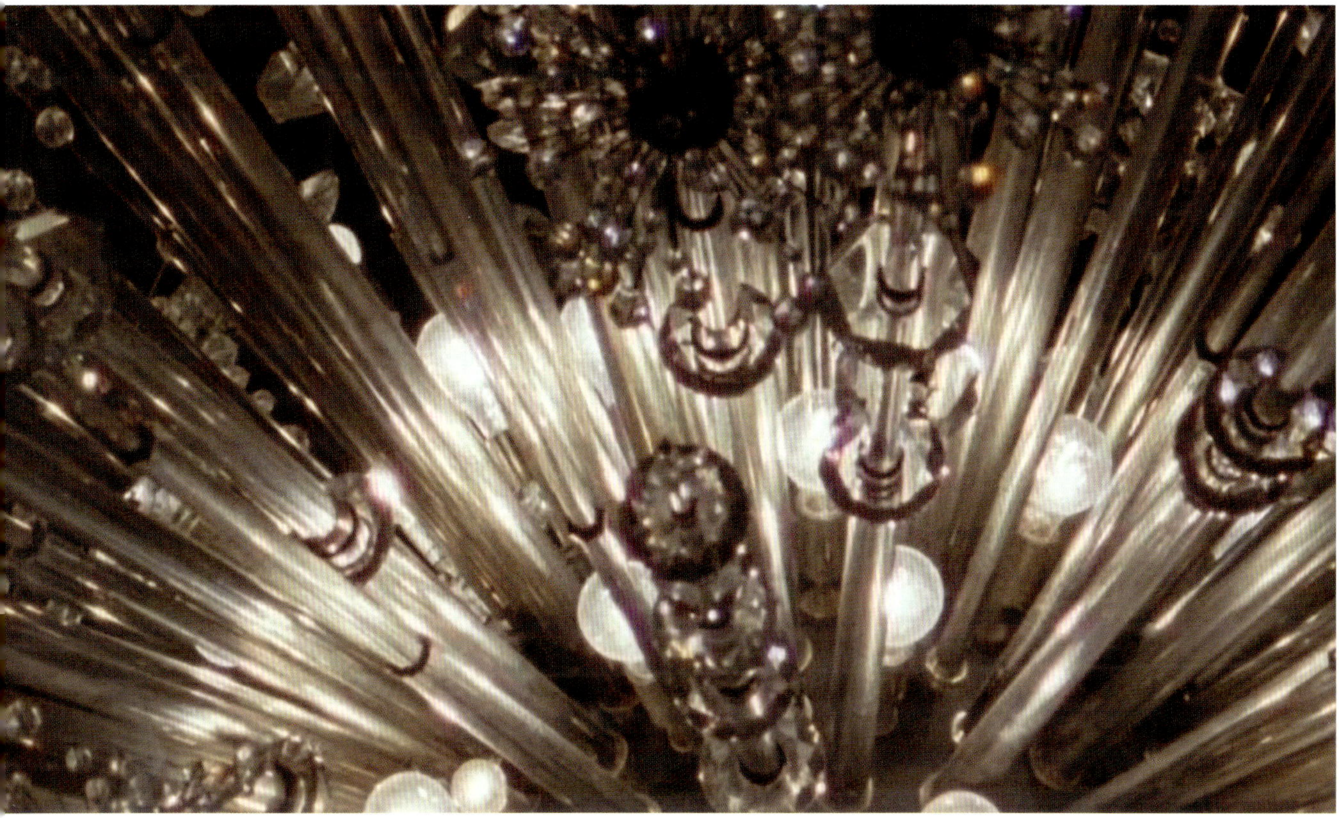

Production still from **Conceptual drawings for a chandelier, 1965**, 2005

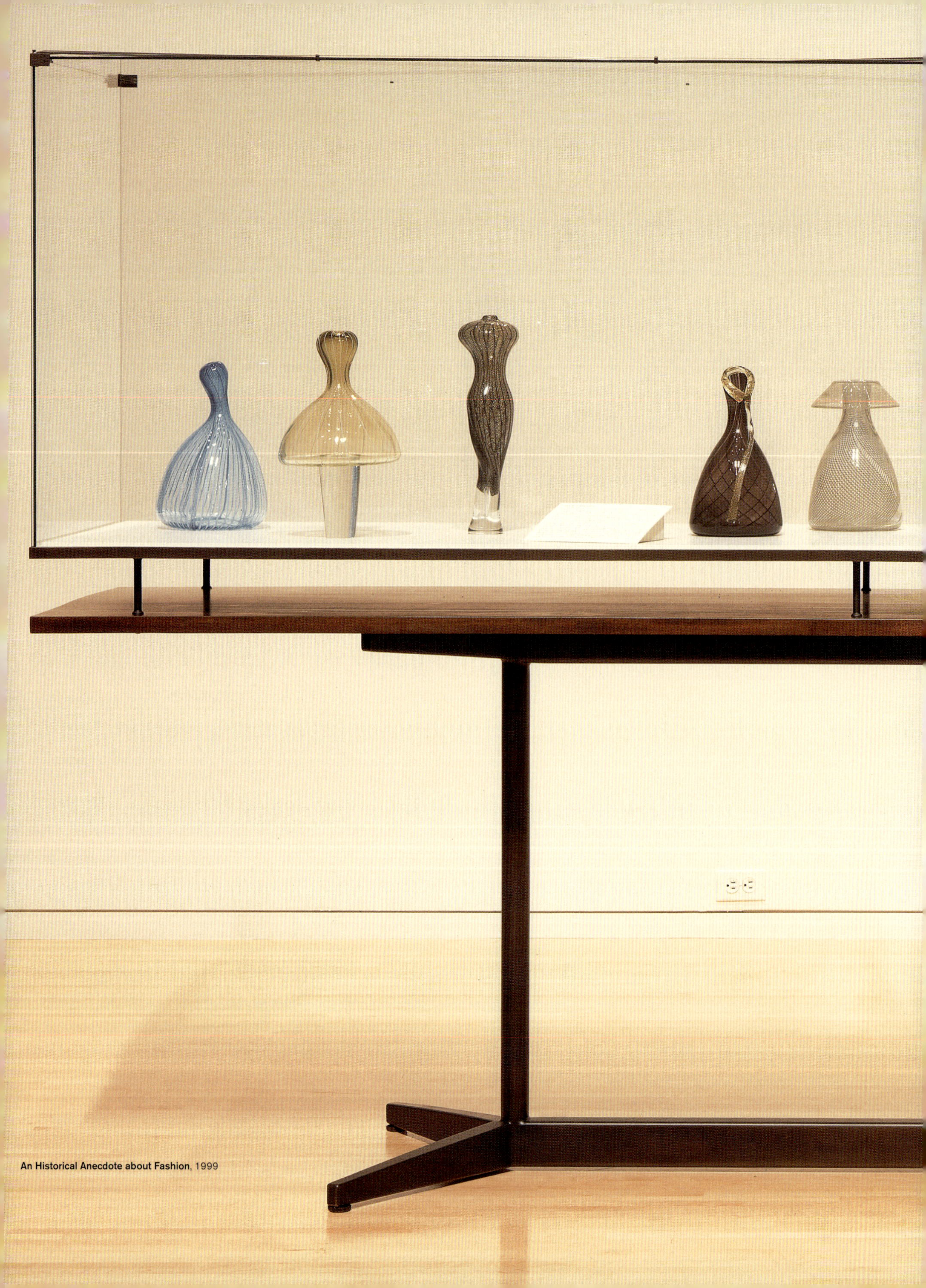

An Historical Anecdote about Fashion, 1999

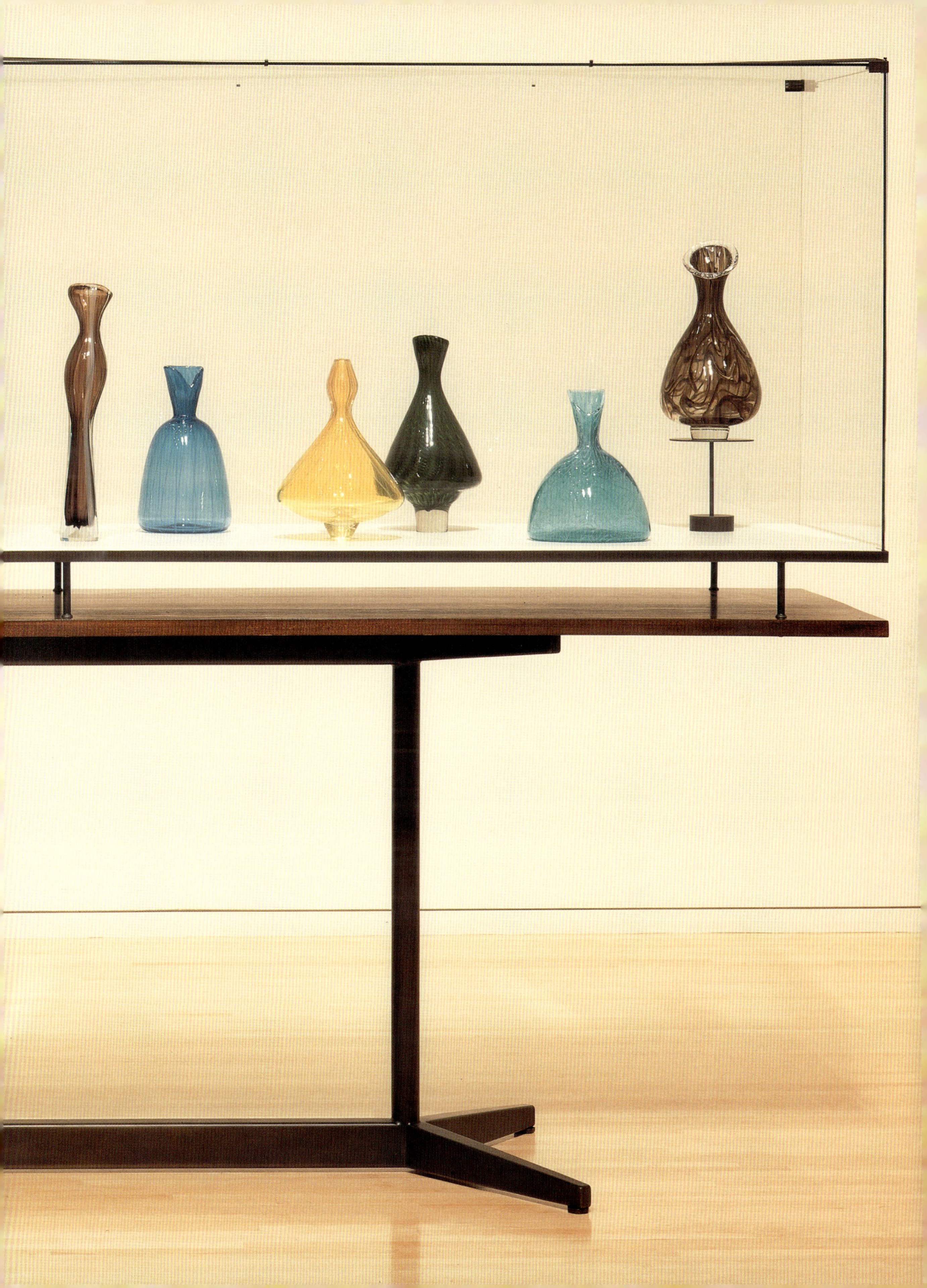

MOLLY NESBIT

PARTS IMPLY WHOLES AND WHOLES ARE SOCIAL

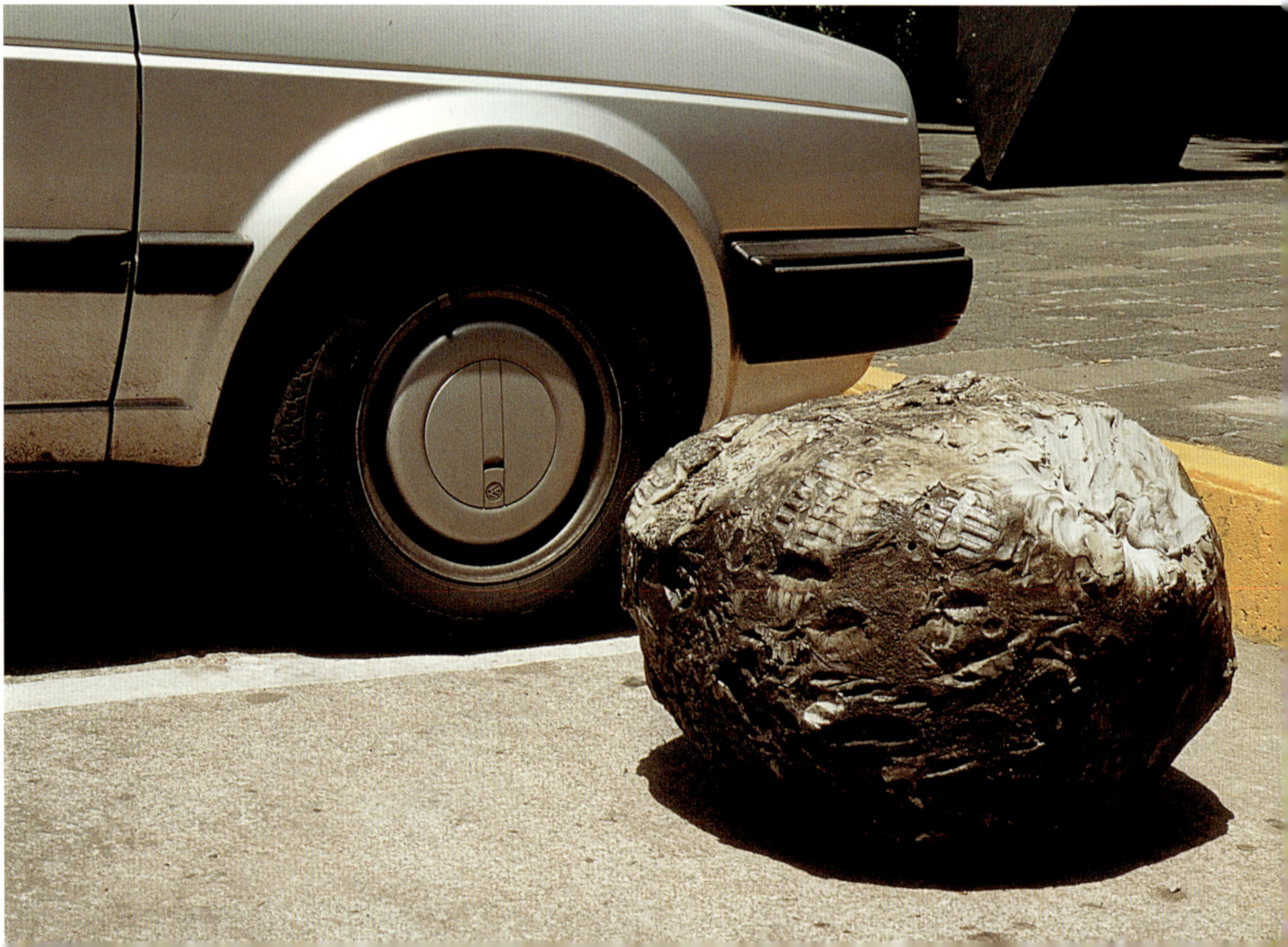

In 1966 Michel Foucault began *The Order of Things* with a passage from Jorge Luis Borges about a Chinese encyclopedia where the animals are divided into fourteen categories:

> (a) those that belong to the emperor, (b) embalmed ones, (c) those that are trained, (d) suckling pigs, (e) mermaids, (f) fabulous ones, (g) stray dogs, (h) those that are included in this classification, (i) those that tremble as if they were mad, (j) innumerable ones, (k) those drawn with a very fine camel's-hair brush, (l) others, (m) those that have just broken a flower vase, (n) those that resemble flies from a distance.[1]

Foucault had laughed out loud when he first read this. Was it sane? Was it insane? He kept laughing. His eruption had the odd effect of turning him back to philosophy. He began describing the spaces that separated these figures of knowledge from one another. Were they bound by anything? or by an idea of something?

It would not be utopia, Foucault wrote. A utopia would have produced some consolation, even though it was, like all utopias, unreal: it would have provided smooth, marvelous grounds, beautifully planted gardens, wide avenues, sweet dreams. It would not even be a heterotopia, the kind of space that opens up alongside, opting out, disturbing plans. He considered other models. He noted that even Lautréamont's famous combination of the-umbrella-and-the-sewing-machine-on-the-operating-table had that operating table holding matters together. The Chinese encyclopedia did not come with a table, but, he remarked, the day would be saved by the Chinese origin of this encyclopedia, for China was known in the West for being a reservoir of utopias.[2] On inspection, however, this list of Borges stood on nothing known. Call it a list without legs.

Utopia would become a low tone, always available, ready to return. Its returns, its changes and disappearances, seem to be provoked by seismic shifts in historical events. 1989, for example, was a watershed. That year saw the fall of the Berlin Wall, the disintegration of the Soviet bloc, the end of the Cold War, the repression of the student demonstrations for democracy in Bejing's Tiananmen Square, and the U. S. invasion of Panama. In 1990 the South African government released Nelson Mandela from prison and began the undoing of apartheid. In 1991 the world saw the first Gulf War when Iraq invaded Kuwait. Consciousness of the AIDS epidemic increased exponentially. The European Union was coming into being. A new wave of immigration pushed labor and culture into new configurations around the globe. As did the quantum advance of the new technologies, since none of these factors was isolated from the others. This was another world picture. But was it a picture? And how could all this be thought? The question of the whole, plainly a social whole, was put forward unceasingly. It eclipsed the existing fetishes in parts.

A two-hundred-year-old theater of bourgeois culture was closing down: there would be new definitions of the social actor. The neoliberal economy unleashed by the flood of opportunity for capital expansion required a different symbolic form. Would this be the revenge of the machines? As this turn of events was taking place, Gilles Deleuze was writing one last book with Félix Guattari.

Gabriel Orozco
Yielding Stone (Piedra que cede), 1992

They went back to first questions; the title of the book starting the interrogation right away. *What Is Philosophy?* This was the context for their return to the word utopia:

> Actually, *utopia is what links* philosophy with its own epoch, with European capitalism, but also already with the Greek city. In each case it is with utopia that philosophy becomes political and takes the criticism of its own time to its highest point. Utopia does not split off from infinite movement: etymologically it stands for absolute deterritorialization but always at the critical point at which it is connected with the present relative milieu, and especially with the forces stifled by this milieu. *Erewhon*, the word used by Samuel Butler, refers not only to no-where but also to now-here. What matters is not the supposed distinction between utopian and scientific socialism but the different types of utopia, one of them being revolution. In utopia (as in philosophy) there is always the risk of a restoration, and sometimes a proud affirmation, of transcendence, so that we need to distinguish between authoritarian utopias, or utopias of transcendence, and immanent, revolutionary, libertarian utopias.[3]

At this point they footnoted Ernst Bloch, whose three-volume *Principle of Hope*, written in exile in America in the middle of the century, remains the great twentieth-century meditation on all preceding utopias. Bloch began his book with a section entitled "We Start Out Empty."[4] Deleuze and Guattari were not starting out empty. They invoked revolution.

> But to say that revolution is itself utopia of immanence is not to say that it is a dream, something that is not realized or that is only realized by betraying itself. On the contrary, it is to posit revolution as plane of immanence, infinite movement and absolute survey, but to the extent that these features connect up with what is real here and now in the struggle against capitalism, relaunching new struggles whenever the earlier one is betrayed. The word utopia therefore designates *that conjunction of philosophy, or of the concept, with the present milieu* – political philosophy (However, in view of the mutilated meaning public opinion has given to it, perhaps *utopia* is not the best word).[5]

Utopia was not capable of enough empirical grind and was too freighted with cliché to stand on its own. Reduced to a no-place, a nameless no-place, however, it remained, still a low tone, a low plane, from which one could come and go.

At this point a new generation of travelers emerged. They plunged into their own epoch. Some of them would see the interest in finding altogether new ground for the things they would bring or make or leave. The ground itself was imbricated – both an actual geographical place and a no-place, newly conceived (the events of 1989 and the early 1990s had washed it fairly clean). The travelers were searching outside the usual marketplaces for art, outside the museum, outside psychoanalysis and the purchase of the state. A number of these people were artists. They were travelers, not nomads but explorers; nowadays they are usually called immigrants. It was not possible to englobe their work or name it.[6] Those who watched them and saw what they were doing to be sculpture invoked Marcel Duchamp.

Duchamp was by then taken to be as much a climatic condition as anything else, partly because of the challenges his work had posed. Was he hot? Was he cold? Was he lukewarm when in 1913 he took a few objects of everyday life because they left him indifferent, and held them apart, eventually naming them readymades? Duchamp called these things distractions and did not ask them to be anything. Certainly they were not to be called works of art. They should be looked at like a fire in the fireplace, he said about the bicycle wheel, or like a peach in a corner, if you like peaches.[7] He was setting up a field defying categories, characterized by nothing. He and his friend the poet Walter Arensberg played a game called "Concept of Nothing" that produced some inscriptions for the readymades, like "in advance of the broken arm" and "3 ou 4 gouttes d'hauteur n'ont rien à faire avec la sauvagerie."[8]

Those who could not withdraw to the point of absolute indifference would recast the supra-human nothingness in which Duchamp set his work, a nothingness very few could understand, and fewer could accept, a nothingness that, in spite of Duchamp's admonitions, most would want to civilize by casting it as art alone. The story of the readymade is now so twisted into this opposite reaction that it seems condemned to exist in most minds as a permanent lie. Yet after 1989 the readymade's very nothingness was being mistaken in various new ways. Parts imply wholes. The no-place of the unrealized, unthought utopia began to reposition and even supplant the readymade of fruit, fire, and wheel.

In Cachoeira, Brazil, one evening in 1991, Gabriel Orozco found an empty market with its crowd of tables and a pile of unsold, rotting oranges. He laid an orange on each table, arranged them like points in the day's wake, took a photo of this field of points, a hitherto unseen latent plane, and moved on. The Brazilians watching laughed and called him a crazy tourist. He smiled too and did not dispute them. He later said that this was his work in reality. Not on reality, not with reality, but in reality, his way of traveling in reality.[9] The next year, in Monterrey, Mexico, he measured out his weight in black plasticine and rolled the result into a large ball which was then rolled out into the street. Plasticine never hardens and the ball yielded to whatever surface it found. Small things stuck to it, so did dust. This *Yielding Stone* grew dirtier as it moved and grew older.

The physical no-places were also opening up spaces between books. By the time Orozco got to Brazil, the books of John Cage and Borges were like pole stars to him. John Cage gave a celebrated lecture on nothing in New York in 1949 in which he said simply, "A structure is like a bridge from nowhere to nowhere and anyone may go on it: noises or tones, corn or wheat."[10] Borges once wrote that every novel is an ideal place inserted into the realm of reality.[11] But neither could provide the traveler or the artist with a world picture suited to the new times. Still, their observations were instructive. Cage launched a story in midstream: " – in his ear where he will find a metal ball, to toss it on the road in front of them, so that, as the horse goes on to say, we may be led by it. This, too, given himself and his quest up to the aimless rolling of a metal ball, the hero, unquestioningly does. They proceed thus, by chance, by no will of their own,

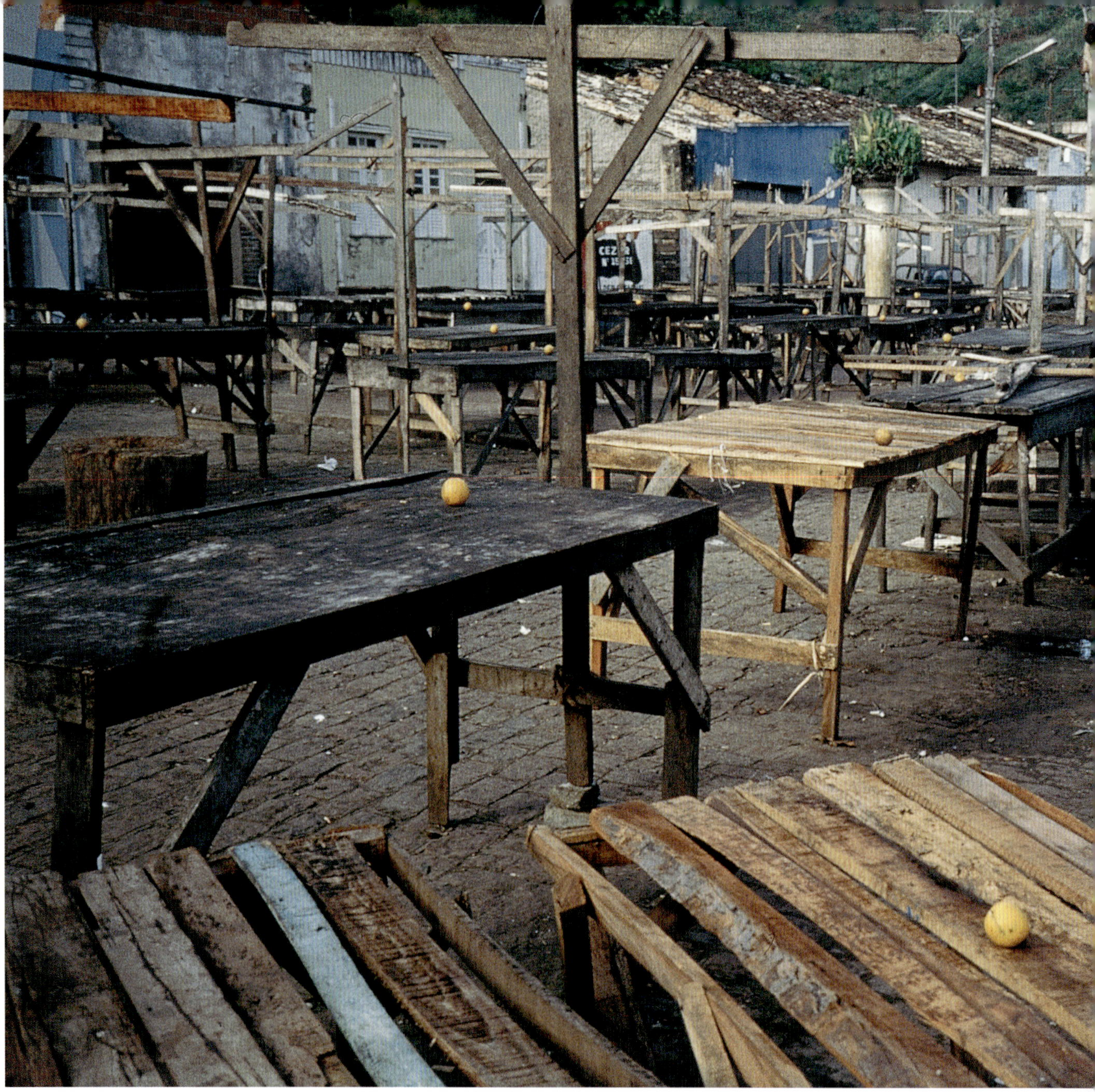

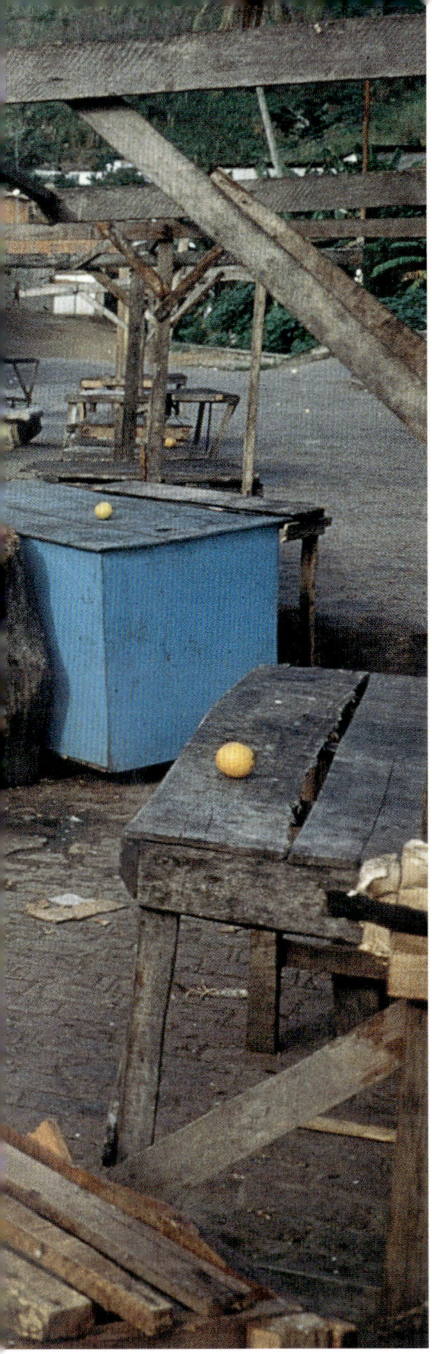

passing safely through many perilous situations. At the end of the journey, when success is almost in view, the horse, to whom the hero now knows he is most utterly indebted, asks the hero to kill him. This causes some hesitation on the hero's part but he finally acquiesces, and Lo, and behold, the horse turns into a Prince, who except for the acquiescence of the hero would have had to remain a miserable shaggy nag."[12] At the end Cage announced that all this led to his sense that there was no split between spirit and matter, and yet things had their differences: "a vacant lot, a piece of string and a sunset, possessing neither, each acts."[13]

These ideas come close to the lists in Borges. The most inclusive of them was poured out in "The Aleph" at the moment when Borges sees the Aleph, a point in space from which all other points can be seen, in other words a point from which the entire universe appears. But the universe appeared as small things; he listed forty-eight of them, including the teeming sea, daybreak and nightfall, the multitudes of America, a silvery cobweb in the center of a pyramid, a splintered labyrinth that turned out to be London, all the mirrors on earth, none of which reflected our new hero, who kept looking. He saw bunches of grapes, snow, tobacco, lodes of metal, steam, convex equatorial deserts and each one of their grains of sand. He saw his own dark blood. He came away with the unimaginable universe. He did not call it utopia. He began to forget it.[14]

Orozco also did not use utopia as a point or plane of reference to mark the ground between all things and nothing, between markets and time. He preferred to call the no-place reality. When his work in reality was first shown inside the museum, he found a way to stress the outside. He exhibited reality as photographs so that reality did not become confused with museum hygiene. For his project show at the Museum of Modern Art in 1993, he took fresh oranges to a neighboring apartment building and asked the residents to put single oranges in their windows looking over the sculpture garden of the museum. He called the work "Home Run," as if the oranges were enchanted baseballs hit out of the park, passing like ghosts through the glass. Later he would be led to make tables.

The tables made for exhibition in the museum were themselves objects – large solid blocks of white, enough like proverbial white cubes, the shorthand figure by which the modern gallery and museum space is known, to become themselves microcosm and reference. On these tables Orozco arranged some of the small models from which his larger work was made. He would come to include drawings and small things in the mix. These too would construct planes of points. The things placed on these tables were not consistent from exhibition to exhibition. The only aspect that remained constant was their placement: they sat on top, on the outside surface of the white cube, transition points to a space of the outside, a present, that had grazed them, just as they had grazed it. The cube neither contains nor controls the no-place that dusts it. The cube is made to yield to a permanent revolution in a world that will not sum itself up.

Someone asked Orozco a question about the earth. "You know the earth before it was called a planet," Orozco replied, "it was called a wandering

Gabriel Orozco
Crazy Tourist, 1991

star. Before, there were only stars, there were no planets. We didn't know that there were planets and some of these stars were moving in a weird way, so they were called 'wandering stars' and after that they were called planets. So the idea of a wandering star, the idea of wandering, the idea of constant movement, and the movement of erosion, exposition to erosion, or the body that is moving and is getting eroded – that is a planet. So the *Yielding Stone*, for example, you can consider it as a planet, wandering. When I took a picture of the rotating field, it was because of the scale, it was this little cute thing with marbles like God. And then it was a whole field full of yielding stones, bottles, geometry, nature, a game. I don't know if that answers your question, but [there is] that connection with our planet and the landscape, like in 'Island in an Island,' I like to work in different levels."[15]

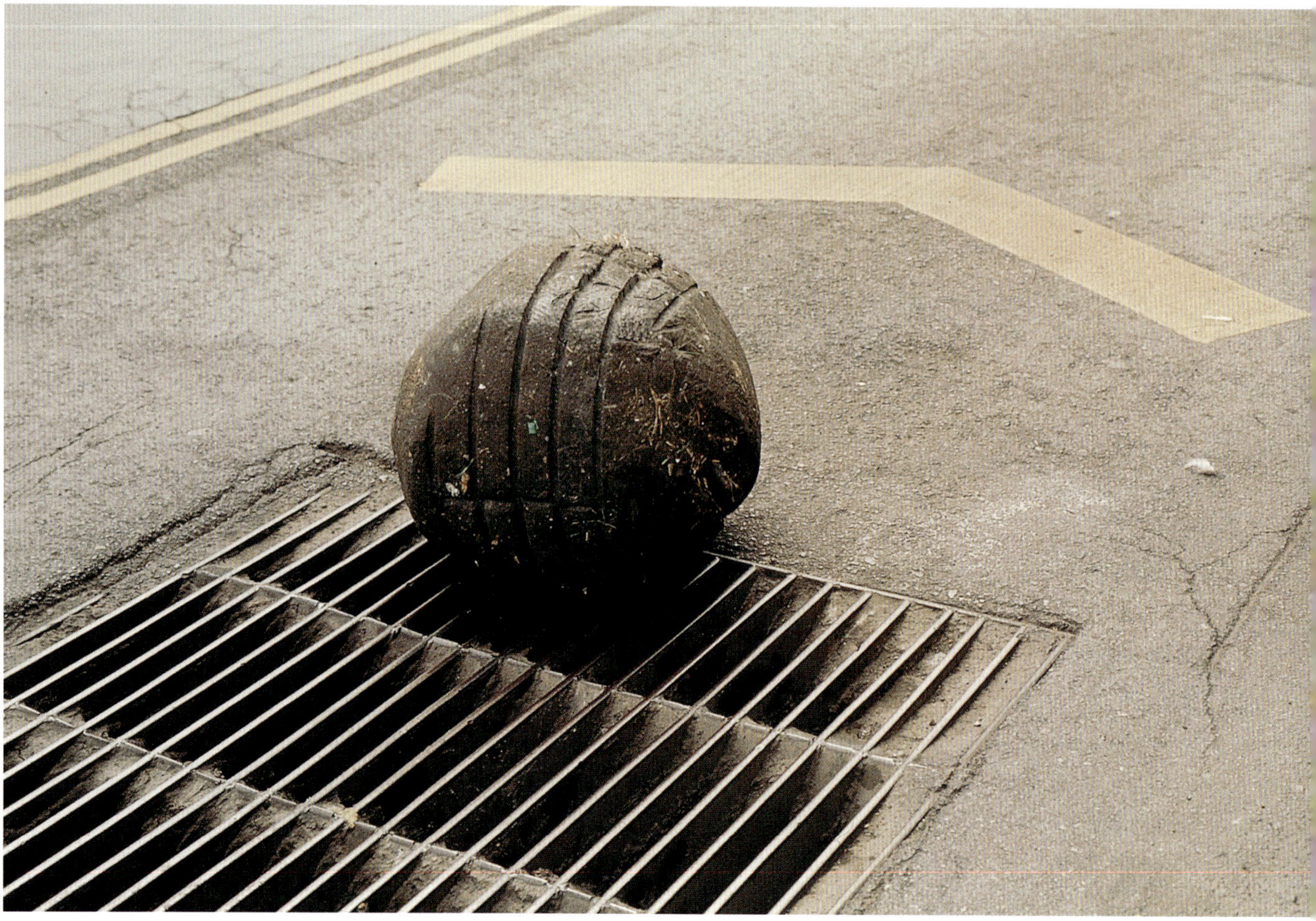

This is reality. Neither "Island in an Island" nor the landscape it mimicked in trash has survived intact. Outside art, events wreak their havoc on all the levels. No rotation rises above them. Where does it end? There is no end to the no-place, now earth, now sky. It helps to watch the stars. Some call the no-place a good night.

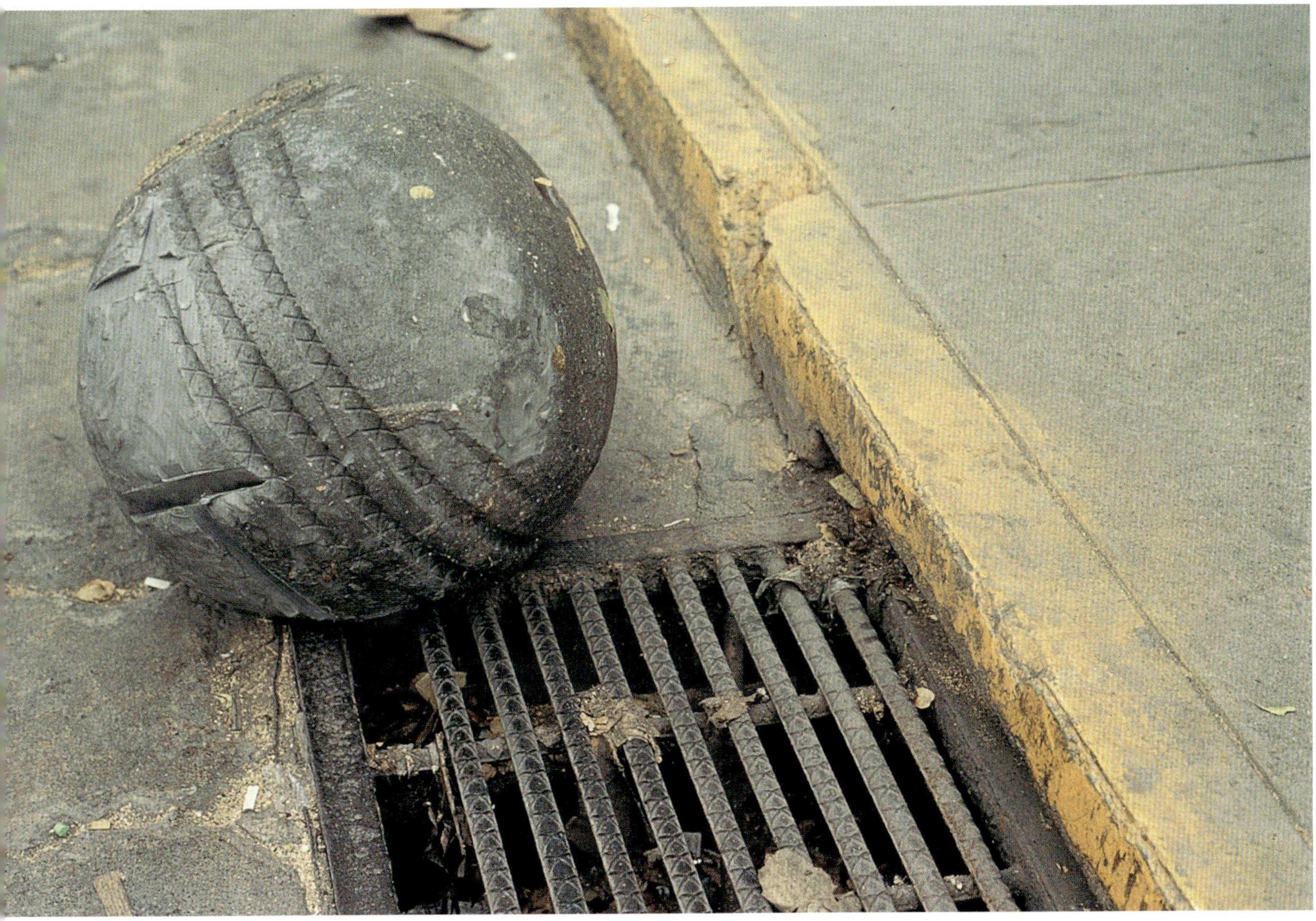

above and left Gabriel Orozco
Yielding Stone (Piedra que cede), 1992

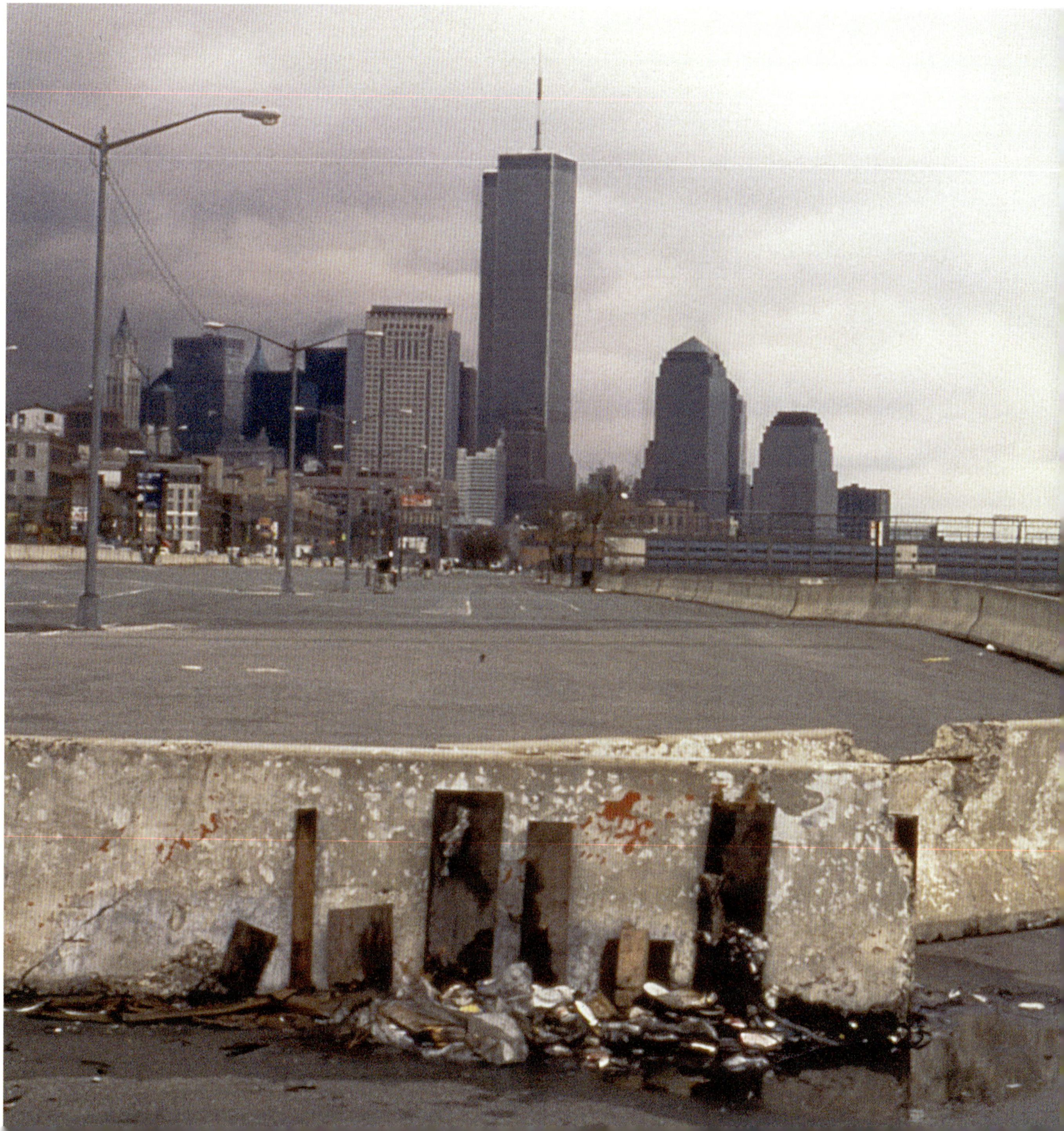

NOTES

1 Jorge Luis Borges, "The Analytical Language of John Wilkins," in *Borges, a Reader: A Selection from the Writings of Jorge Luis Borges*, ed. Emir Rodriguez Monegal and Alastair Reid (New York: E. P. Dutton, 1981), 142 (trans. Ruth L. C. Simms).

2 Michel Foucault, *The Order of Things* (New York: Vintage, 1973), preface. French edition, *Les mots et les choses*, 1966.

3 Gilles Deleuze and Félix Guattari, *What Is Philosophy?* trans. Hugh Tomlinson and Graham Burchell (New York: Columbia University Press, 1994; French edition 1991), 99–100.

4 Ernst Bloch, *The Principle of Hope*, 3 vols., trans. Neville Plaice, Stephen Plaice, and Paul Knight (Cambridge: The MIT Press, 1986), 1:21.

5 Deleuze and Guattari, *What Is Philosophy?* 99–100. See also 110: "Utopia is not a good concept because even when opposed to History it is still subject to it and lodged within it as an ideal or motivation. But becoming is the concept itself. It is born in History and falls back into it, but is not of it. In itself it has neither beginning nor end but only a milieu."

6 Nicolas Bourriaud would write an important series of essays in the mid-1990s that bracketed the work under the term "relational aesthetics." The essays have been collected in *Esthétique relationelle* (Paris: Les Presses du réel, 1998). In their catalogue *Formless: A User's Guide* (New York: Zone Books, 1997), Yves-Alain Bois and Rosalind Krauss redress the techniques of formalism and psychoanalytic criticism, generally structuralist techniques, in order to set up a genealogy for the ongoing collapse in bourgeois form. They present the collapse as textual, following Roland Barthes, who declared in his seminar "Comment Vivre Ensemble" at the Collège de France in1977 that the idea of utopia he was pursuing, an idiorrhythmic one, was not social. See *Comment Vivre Ensemble*, ed. Claude Coste (Paris: Seuil, 2002), 177. The no-place is an implicit structuring structure informing the work of the great documenta exhibitions of Catherine David in 1997 and Okwui Enwezor in 2002. The best summary of the art of the 1990s is to be found in their work.

7 Duchamp often compared the bicycle wheel to a fire in the fireplace. See, for example, his interview with Richard Hamilton on the BBC program "Monitor" (September 27, 1961). The comparison to peaches was made in another interview, with Richard Hamilton, R. Kitaj, Robert Melville, and David Sylvester, June 19, 1966, in Hamilton's London studio, p. 29. The transcript credits the Arts Council of Great Britain.

8 Anyone interested in pursuing the question of the readymade will do well to read Duchamp's interviews carefully. See, especially, Georges Charbonnier, "Six entretiens avec Marcel Duchamp," *France-Culture*, December 9, 1960–January 13, 1961, published as *Entretiens avec Marcel Duchamp* (Marseilles: André Dimanche, 1994); Hamilton interview, BBC "Monitor"; "Apropos of Readymades," Art of Assemblage symposium, October 19, 1961, was first published in *Art and Artists*1 (July 1966):47, and is included in the English edition of Michel Sanouillet, *Duchamp du signe: Écrits*; Francis Roberts, "I Propose to Strain the Laws of Physics – Interview with Marcel Duchamp (October 1963)," *Art News* 67 (December 1968): 46–47, 62–64; Hamilton, Kitaj, Melville, and Sylvester, interview, June 19, 1966; Pierre Cabanne, *Entretiens avec Marcel Duchamp* (Paris: Pierre Belfond, 1967). I have written at length on this topic in Nesbit, *Their Common Sense* (London: Black Dog, 2000).

9 Reality was a constant topic in Orozco's unpublished Agnes Rindge Claflin lecture at Vassar College, Poughkeepsie, New York, September 23, 2002. These arguments follow from those developed in my essays on Orozco's work: "The Tempest," in *Gabriel Orozco*, curated by Alma Ruiz (Los Angeles: Museum of Contemporary Art, 2000), 121–71; "Location, Location, Location! by Gabriel Orozco," *trans* 7 (2000): 25–50; "Walking to Work," for Gabriel Orozco, *Trabajo* (Cologne: Walther König and Galerie Chantal Crousel, 2003), cxxiii–cxxxiii.

10 John Cage, "Lecture on Nothing," *Silence* (Hanover, N.H.: Wesleyan University Press, 1961), 124.

11 Borges, "Partial Magic in the Quixote," in *Labyrinths*, ed. Donald A. Yates and James E. Irby (New York: New Directions, 1964), 194.

12 John Cage, "Julliard Lecture," *A Year from Monday* (Middletown, Conn.: Wesleyan University Press, 1967), 102–3. (The lecture was given in 1952.)

13 Ibid., 111.

14 Borges, "The Aleph," in *Borges, a Reader*, 154–63 (trans. N. T. di Giovanni).

15 The question came up during his lecture at Vassar College, September 23, 2002.

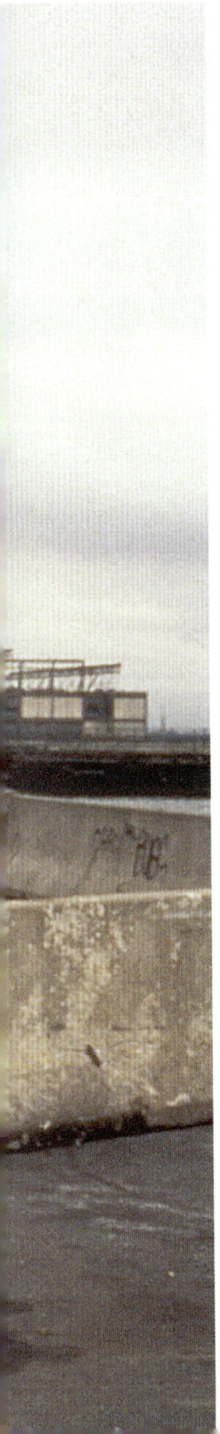

Gabriel Orozco
Island in an Island, 1993

ENDNOTES

MARCEL DUCHAMP

1 *Marcel Duchamp, Notes,* arranged and translated by Paul Matisse (Boston: G. K. Hall, 1983), n. 33, unpaginated.

2 Ibid., n. 18.

LOUISE BOURGEOIS

1 Jeremy Strick, *The Personages* (Saint Louis: Saint Louis Art Museum, 1994), 14.

2 M. G. in *Art News* 48 (October 1949), 46, quoted in ibid.

3 Stuart Preston, "Modern Masters," *New York Times,* October 9, 1949, 9.

4 Interview between Jeremy Strick and Louise Bourgeois as quoted in Strick, *The Personages,* 26.

5 Susi Bloch, "An Interview with Louise Bourgeois," *The Art Journal* 35 (Summer 1976), 373.

6 Numerous photographs were taken of the Personages in their various "poses." For more on these photographs, see Josef Helfenstein, *Louise Bourgeois: The Early Work* (Champaign, Ill.: Krannert Art Museum, 2002).

7 Ibid., 19.

ALBERTO BURRI

1 See Elizabeth A. T. Smith, "All Freedom in Every Sense," in *Lee Bontecou: A Retrospective* (Chicago: Museum of Contemporary Art; Los Angeles: UCLA Hammer Museum; New York: Harry N. Abrams, 2003), 173.

2 Donald Judd, "Specific Objects," *Arts Yearbook* 8 (1965), reprinted in James Meyer, ed., *Minimalism* (London: Phaidon Press, 2003), 210.

3 For more on Burri's influence on American artists, particularly Rauschenberg and Twombly, see Carolyn Christov Bakargiev, "Alberto Burri: The Surface at Risk," in *Burri, Opere, 1944–1995* (Milan: Electa, 1996); Germano Celant, *Roma–New York, 1948–1964,* trans. Joachim Neugroschel (Milan: Edizioni Charta, 1993); and Robert Storr, "Seek and Hide," in *Lee Bontecou: A Retrospective* (Chicago: Museum of Contemporary Art; Los Angeles: UCLA Hammer Museum; New York: Harry N. Abrams, 2003).

LEE BONTECOU

1 See the catalogue entries on Alberto Burri and Robert Rauschenberg for an elaboration of this point.

2 See Maria Grazia Tolomeo, "Burri's Beginnings: 'There is much that can be made into matter,'" in *Burri: Opere, 1944–1995* (Milan: Electa, 1996), 83.

3 As quoted in ibid., 83.

4 Mario Perinola, "Burri and Esthetics," in *Burri: Opere*, 105.

LUCIO FONTANA

1 See Yve-Alain Bois, "Fontana's Base Materialism," *Art in America,* vol. 77 (April 1989), as well as the catalogue for the exhibition on *l'informe* that he did with Rosalind Krauss: *Formless: A User's Guide* (New York: Zone Books, 1997), 51–62. Both *l'informe* and "base materialism" are terms borrowed from Georges Bataille, the de facto leader of a group of dissident Surrealists who gathered around the journal *Documents.*

2 Bois, entry on Fontana and Manzoni, in Hal Foster, Rosalind Krauss, Yve-Alain Bois, and Benjamin Buchloh, *Art Since 1900* (New York: Thames and Hudson, 2005), 411.

3 The *Wedge of Chastity (Coin de chasteté)* was made in 1954, a wedding gift from Duchamp to his bride, Teeny Matisse.

4 Many critics have remarked on the implicit violence of Fontana's holes, which he obviously produced by actually puncturing the canvas; but the *Wedge* seems hardly less aggressive in nature, even if the orthodontic connotation of the material (*vagina dentata* indeed!) implies a certain reciprocity in regard to that aggression. Interestingly, in speaking of the *Wedge,* Duchamp referred to "le sens du coin qui s'enfonce" ("the meaning of the wedge hammered in"), where the verb, *s'enfoncer,* is precisely that used for a nail or other implement of the sort used to produced Fontana's *Buchi.*

5 Such configurations are especially conspicuous in Fontana's 1962–64 series, *The End of God*; see especially Sarah Whitfield, *Lucio Fontana* (London: Hayward Gallery, 1999), 44.

6 Sigmund Freud, "The Antithetical Sense of Primal Words," trans. M. N. Seal, in Freud, *Character and Culture,* ed. Philip Rieff (New York: Collier Books, 1963).

7 Fontana first met Miró in 1937, during a trip to France arranged around a visit to the Sèvres porcelain factory.

8 Michel Leiris, "Joan Miró," *Documents* (Paris), vol. 1, no. 5 (1929): 264. Quoted in Rosalind Krauss, "Miró's Base Seduction," in Agnes de Beaumelle, ed., *Joan Miró, 1917–1934* (Paris: Éditions du Centre Pompidou, 2004), 77.

9 Fontana himself referred to the works in this series as *Pietre* (Stones), although the actual material used is glass—in this case, covered with paint.

10 Similar in this regard is Duchamp's (literally) seminal *Paysage fautive* (Wayward Landscape), which accompanied the *Boîte-en-Valise* given to the Brazilian sculptor Maria Martins; reputedly it was she who served as the model for Duchamp's *Etant donnés.* The dried pool of semen constituting the "medium" of Duchamp's "landscape" closely resembles the sort of biomorphic figures that populate Miró's Surrealist "dream" canvases. Of the latter, Duchamp wrote in 1946, the very year he produced the *Paysage fautive,* that Miró had managed to express "a new two-dimensional cosmogony without the least tie to abstraction"—a statement that might apply as well to both Duchamp's own *Landscape* and to much of Fontana's later work. For Duchamp's quotation, see Lucy Lippard, ed., *Surrealists on Art* (Englewood Cliffs, N.J.: Prentice-Hall, 1970), 116.

PIERO MANZONI

1 Briony Fer, *The Infinite Line: Remaking Art After Modernism* (New Haven: Yale University Press, 2004), 36. Manzoni himself, in referring to the *Achromes,* described them as "unfinishable, repeatable to infinity, and [with] a continuity that remains unresolved." See his "Libere dimensione," *Azimuth,* no. 2 (Milan, 1960): 130–34; translated as *Free Dimension,* in Germano Celant, ed., *Piero Manzoni* (London: Serpentine Gallery, 1998).

2 Later, working with a chemist, Klein would develop and patent a particular shade of ultramarine, International Klein Blue (IKB), which the artist described as the supreme "representation of the immaterial, the sovereign liberation of the spirit."

3 "Libere dimensione," 130–34; translation in Celant, *Piero Manzoni,* 130–32.

4 On the notion of modernism's "unconscious," see Rosalind Krauss, *The Optical Unconscious* (Cambridge, Mass.: The MIT Press, 1993).

5 For a discussion of the relation of the *Achromes* to the monochrome and the grid, see Jaleh Mansoor, "Piero Manzoni: We Want to Organicize Disintegration," *October* 95 (Winter 2001): 28–53. For a more general examination of Manzoni's relation to modernism, see Yve-Alain Bois's entry, "Base Materialism," in Bois and Krauss, *Formless: A User's Guide* (New York: Zone Books, 1997), 51–62.

6 Jon Thompson, "Piero Manzoni: Out of Time and Place," in Celant, *Piero Manzoni,* 39.

ROBERT RAUSCHENBERG

1 For more on the potential reciprocity between Burri and Rauschenberg, see Germano Celant, *Roma–New York, 1948–1964,* trans. Joachim Neugroschel (Milan: Edizioni Charta, 1993).

2 This exhibition statement is reproduced in Walter Hopps, Robert Rauschenberg: *The Early 1950s* (Houston: The Menil Collection: Houston Fine Arts Press, 1991), 252.

3 This recollection can be found in Carolyn Christov-Bakargiev, "Alberto Burri: The Surface at Risk," in *Burri: Opere, 1944–1995* (Milan: Electa, 1996), 114.

4 Hopps, *Robert Rauschenberg,* 252.

5 Ibid., 160.

CY TWOMBLY

1 Katharina Schmidt, *Cy Twombly: Die Skulptur* (Ostfildern-Ruit: Hatje Cantz, 2001), 37.

2 Charles Olson, "Cy Twombly," *Olson: The Journal of the Charles Olson Archives* 8 (Fall 1977): 14, quoted in ibid., 45.

JASPER JOHNS

1 Jasper Johns, letter to Helen Molesworth, November 29, 2004.

2 Interview with David Sylvester, *Jasper Johns Drawings* (London: Arts Council of Great Britain, 1974), 7–8.

3 Alan R. Solomon, *Jasper Johns* (New York: The Jewish Museum, 1964), 8.

4 Ibid., 18.

EVA HESSE

1 See Maurice Berger, "Objects of Liberation: The Sculpture of Eva Hesse," in Helen A. Cooper, *Eva Hesse: A Retrospective*, ed. Leslie K. Baier (New Haven: Yale University Art Gallery: Yale University Press, 1992); Renate Petzinger, "Thoughts on Eva Hesse's Early Work, 1959–1965," in *Eva Hesse*, ed. Elizabeth Sussman (San Francisco: San Francisco Museum of Modern Art; New Haven: Yale University Press, 2002); and Sabine Folie, "Just Substitute Painting–That Is All," in *Eva Hesse: Transformations: The Sojourn in Germany 1964/65* (Cologne: Walther König, 2004).

2 As quoted in Berger, "Objects of Liberation," 130.

MARCEL BROODTHAERS

1 The title is a pun. The whole phrase *pense-bête* refers to a mnemonic device–a knot in a handkerchief, a brief note written on one's hand–reminding one of a task yet to be completed. The sense of the phrase clearly derives from the adjective "*bête*," which means "lacking in intelligence" (thus *pense-bête* = "stupid thought"). But "*bête*" also means "animal," and so seems wholly appropriate to a collection of poems that comprises a bestiary, in the tradition of La Fontaine.

2 The full text reads:

I, too, wondered whether I could not sell something and succeed in life. For some time I had not been good at anything. I am forty years old....

Finally the idea of inventing something insincere crossed my mind, and I set to work at once. At the end of three months I showed what I had produced to Philippe Eduoard Toussaint, the owner of Galerie St Laurent. "But it is art" he said "and I will gladly exhibit all of it." "Agreed" I replied. If I sell something, he takes 30%. It seems these are the usual conditions, some galleries take 75%.

What is it? In fact it is objects.

3 See Dieter Schwarz, "'Look! Books in Plaster!' On the First Phase of the Work of Marcel Broodthaers," *October*, no. 42 (Fall 1987): 60–62.

4 Broodthaers quoted in *Piero Manzoni*, exh. cat. (Brussels: Galerie des Beaux-Arts, 1987), and cited by Michael Compton, "In Praise of the Subject," in Marge Goldwater, ed., *Marcel Broodthaers* (Minneapolis: Walker Art Center; and New York: Rizzoli, 1989), 21.

5 See Buchloh's entry on Broodthaers in Hal Foster, Rosalind Krauss, Yve-Alain Bois, and Benjamin Buchloh, *Art Since 1900* (New York: Thames and Hudson, 2005), 549–53.

BRUCE NAUMAN

1 Cited in Coosje van Bruggen, *Bruce Nauman* (New York: Rizzoli International, 1988), 109.

2 See Neal Benezra, "Surveying Nauman," in *Bruce Nauman*, exh. cat. (Minneapolis: Walker Art Center, 1994), 24.

3 For more on the importance of the body in Duchamp, see, "Duchamp: By Hand, Even," in this volume.

YAYOI KUSAMA

1 Briony Fer, *The Infinite Line: Remaking Art After Modernism* (New Haven: Yale University Press, 2004), 93–94.

LYNDA BENGLIS

1 Interview with Ned Rifkin, *Early Work* (New York: New Museum, 1982), 10.

2 Robert Pincus-Witten, "The Frozen Gesture," *Artforum* 13 (November 1974): 55.

3 This is quite different from her use of Day-Glo colors in the latex pours.

4 Mel Bochner, "Serial Art, Systems, Solipsism," revised version of the article "Serial Art, Systems, Solipsism," which appeared in *Arts Magazine* (Summer 1967), reprinted in Gregory Battcock, ed., *Minimal Art: A Critical Anthology* (Berkeley and Los Angeles: University of California Press, 1995), 100.

ALLAN McCOLLUM

1 Excerpt from an interview with Lynne Cooke [online]. New York, May 31, 1991 [cited March 5, 2005]. Available from World Wide Web: (http://home.att.net/~allanmcnyc/Lynne_Cooke_Carnegie.html).

2 As described in William S. Bartman, ed., *Allan McCollum: Interview by Thomas Lawson* (Los Angeles: A.R.T. Press, 1996), 58.

RACHEL WHITEREAD

1 Charlotte Mullins, *Rachel Whiteread* (London: Tate Publishing: 2004), 26.

FELIX GONZALEZ-TORRES

1 David Deitcher, "The Everyday Art of Felix Gonzalez-Torres, in *Felix Gonzalez-Torres*, exh. cat., Magasin 3 Stockholm Konsthall, October 1992–February 1993, unpaginated.

2 Ibid.

ROBERT GOBER

1 See "Duchamp: By Hand, Even" in this volume for an expansion of this point.

LIST OF ILLUSTRATIONS

MOLESWORTH **INTRODUCTION**

Yayoi Kusama
Blue Spots, 1965
Sewn stuffed fabric on wood
32 5/8 x 27 1/2 x 5 1/8 in. (83 x 70 x 13 cm)
Becht Collection, Naarden, The Netherlands

Lucio Fontana
Concetto spaziale (Spatial Concept), 1956
Oil, glass on canvas
30 3/4 x 25 1/4 x 1 1/2 in. (78 x 64 x 4 cm)
Darwin and Geri Reedy, Dellwood, Minnesota

Louise Bourgeois
Untitled, 1950
Painted Wood
57 1/2 x 12 x 12 in. (146 x 30.5 x 30.5 cm)
Collection Jerry Gorovoy, New York
Courtesy of Cheim & Read, New York

Lynda Benglis
Karen, 1972
Purified pigmented beeswax, damar resin and gesso on Masonite
36 x 5 x 3 in. (91.4 x 12.7 x 7.6 cm)
Collection of Howard Read

Eva Hesse
Compass, 1967
Steel washers and sculp-metal on wood
10 x 10 x 1 in. (25.4 x 25.4 x 2.5 cm)
Hauser & Wirth Zürich London

Robert Gober & Sherrie Levine
Untitled, Lightbulb, 1990
Enamel paint, beeswax, rope
8 x 3 x 3 in. (20.3 x 7.6 x 7.6 cm)
Private collection, New York

Jasper Johns
Light Bulb II, 1958
Sculp-metal
5 x 8 x 4 in. (12.7 x 20.3 x 10.2 cm)
Collection of the artist, on loan to the Philadelphia Museum of Art

Alberto Burri
Nero Plastica, 1961
Plastic, fabric, vinyl, burning on canvas
39 3/8 x 25 1/2 in. (100 x 65 cm)
Fondazione Palazzo Albizzini "Collezione Burri," Città di Castello

FER **COLOR-IN-PIECES**

Alberto Burri
Rosso Plastica, 1964
52 x 46 in. (132 x 117 cm)
Courtesy Fondazione Palazzo Albizzini "Collezione Burri"

Ugo Mulas
Photograph of Fontana at work

Piero Manzoni
Achrome, 1961
Artificial fibers
12 5/8 x 11 3/8 in. (32 x 29 cm)
Private collection

Marcel Duchamp
Cover for deluxe edition Le Surréalisme en 1947 "Prière de Toucher" "(Please touch)"
1947 New York
Modified Readymade: collage of foam-rubber breast and velvet on board, 10 x 9 inches (25 x 22.8 cm) Inscribed bottom center, on metal plate: PRIERE DE TOUCHER
Inscribed lower right in pencil: Marcel Duchamp 1947

KRAUSS **OBJET (PETIT) a**

Constantin Brancusi
The Newborn (version I, 1920, close to the marble of 1915)
Bronze
5 3/4 x 8 1/4 x 5 3/4 in. (14.6 x 21 x 14.6 cm)
The Museum of Modern Art, New York
Acquired through the Lillie P. Bliss Bequest

Torso of a Kouros
From Miletos. Greek (Archaic), c. 480 BCE
Louvre, Paris

Auguste Rodin
Female torso (Iris)
Musée Rodin, Paris, France

Jacques Lacan
Schema L
From Jacques Lacan, **Écrits: A Selection**. New York: W. W. Norton, 1997
p. 193.

Eva Hesse
Accession II, 1967
Galvanized steel with plastic tubing
30 3/4 x 30 3/4 x 30 3/4 in. (78.1 x 78.1 x 78.1 cm)
Detroit Institute of Arts, Founders Society Purchase, Friends of Modern Art Fund and Miscellaneous Gifts Fund

HAIDU **LAUGHTER**

Marcel Broodthaers
Fémur de la Femme Française (Bone of a French Woman), 1965
Painted human thigh bone
3 9/16 x 16 15/16 x 3 1/2 in. (9 x 43 x 8.9 cm)
Sonnabend Collection

Marcel Broodthaers
Panneau de Moules (Panel of Mussels), 1966
Mussel shells, resin, and paint on panel
45 3/4 x 48 x 5 1/2 in. (116 x 122 x 14 cm)
National Gallery of Art, Washington, D.C.
Gift of the Collectors Committee

Piero Manzoni
Achrome, 1962
Bread rolls and kaolin
9 1/2 x 15 3/8 in. (24 x 39 cm)
Collection Paolo Consolandi, Milan

JOSELIT **MOLDS AND SWARMS**

Marcel Duchamp
Fontaine (Fountain), 1917, 5th version 1964
Glazed ceramic white ware with black oil paint
14 1/8 x 18 7/8 x 24 in (36 x 48 x 61 cm)
displayed flat on its back
National Gallery of Canada, Ottawa, Purchased 1971

Marcel Duchamp
Moule à pièces pour Feuille de Vigne Femelle (Mold for Female Fig Leaf), 1950/1951
Plaster
5 1/4 x 10 5/8 x 9 1/4 in. (13.5 x 27 x 23.5 cm)
Centre Georges Pompidou, Paris, France

Marcel Duchamp
Feuille de Vigne Femelle (Female Fig Leaf), 1950
Painted plaster
3 9/16 x 5 1/2 x 4 15/16 in. (9 x 14 x 12.5 cm)
Private Collection

Marcel Duchamp
Not a Shoe, 1950
Galvanized plaster
2 3/4 x 2 x 1 in. (7 x 5.1 x 2.5 cm)
Centre Georges Pompidou, Paris, France

Lucio Fontana
Concetto spaziale, Scultura nera (Spatial Concept, Black Sculpture), 1947
Bronze
22 1/2 x 20 1/8 x 9 1/2 in. (57 x 51 x 24 cm)
The Lucio Fontana Foundation, Milan

Marcel Broodthaers
Moules Sauce Blanche (Mussels with White Sauce), 1967
Oil and shellac on mussel shells and painted metal casserole
19 1/2 x 15 1/2 x 13 in. (49.5 x 39.4 x 33 cm)
Private collection, New York

MOLESWORTH **DUCHAMP: BY HAND, EVEN**

Marcel Duchamp
Feuille de Vigne Femelle (Female Fig Leaf), 1950
Painted plaster
3 9/16 x 5 1/2 x 4 15/16 in. (9 x 14 x 12.5 cm)
Private Collection

Marcel Duchamp
Objet-Dard (Dart-Object), 1951
Galvanized plaster with inset lead rib
2 15/16 x 7 15/16 x 2 3/8 in. (7.5 x 20.1 x 6 cm)
Private Collection

Marcel Duchamp
Coin de Chasteté (Wedge of Chastity), 1954
2 pt. sculpture: galvanized plaster for the wedge and dental plastic for the lower base
2 3/16 x 3 3/8 x 1 5/8 in. (5.6 x 8.6 x 4.2 cm)
Private Collection

Marcel Duchamp
Cover for "Le Surréalisme, même," Winter 1956

Installation shot from the collections of Moderna Museet, Stockholm, with works by Marcel Duchamp:

La mariée mise a nu par ses céliba-taires, même (The Bride Stripped Bare by Her Bachelors, Even), 1915–23
111 3/8 x 74 3/8 in. (283 x 189 cm)
Oil and lead on glass

Air de Paris (Paris Air), 1919
6 7/8 x 2 3/4 in. (17.5 x 7 cm)
Glass, replica by Ulf Linde and Vilgot Ahlqvist)

...pliant ...de voyage (Traveler's Folding Item), 1917
9 7/8 x 16 7/8 x 13 in. (25 x 43 x 33 cm)
Oilcloth, replica by Ulf Linde 1963, signed by Marcel Duchamp in Milan 1964

Fontaine (Fountain), 1917
13 x 16 1/2 x 20 1/2 in. (33 x 42 x 52 cm)
Porcelain, replica by Ulf Linde 1963

Marcel Duchamp
The Bride Stripped Bare by Her Bachelors, Even (The Large Glass), 1915–23
109 1/4 x 69 1/4 in. (277.5 x 175.9 cm)
Oil, varnish, lead, foil, lead wire, and dust on two glass panels
Philadelphia Museum of Art: Bequest of Katherine S. Dreier

Marcel Duchamp
Etant donnés: 1, La Chute d'Eau, 2, Le Gaz d'Eclairage (Given: 1. The Waterfall, 2. The Illuminating Gas), 1946–66
95 ½ x 70 in. (242.6 x 177.8 cm)
Mixed media Assemblage: wooden door, bricks, velvet, wood, leather stretched over an armature of metal, twigs, aluminum, iron, glass, Plexiglas, linoleum, cotton, electric lights, gas lamp (Bec Auer type), motor, etc.
Philadelphia Museum of Art: Gift of the Cassandra Foundation, 1969

Marcel Duchamp
Etant donnés: 1, La Chute d'Eau, 2, Le Gaz d'Eclairage (Given: 1. The Waterfall, 2. The Illuminating Gas), 1946-66
95 ½ x 70 in. (242.6 x 177.8 cm)
Mixed media assemblage
Philadelphia Museum of Art: Gift of the Cassandra Foundation

Marcel Duchamp
Boîte-en-Valise (The Box in a Valise)
de ou par Marcel Duchamp ou Rrose Sélavy (by or of Marcel Duchamp or Rrose Sélavy)
1935-41 (box); 1938 (collotype)
Brown leather valise with handle containing sixty-nine miniature replicas and printed reproductions and one original, Virgin (No. 2), 1938, hand-colored collotype
Valise (closed): 16 x 14 ¾ x 4 ¼ in. (40.6 x 37.5 x 10.8 cm)
Philadelphia Museum of Art: The Louise and Walter Arensberg Collection

Julian Wasser
Marcel Duchamp in profile and Installation of Readymades for the Marcel Duchamp Retrospective, Pasadena, 1963

Marcel Duchamp
Porte-bouteilles (Bottle Dryer), 1914, 5th version 1964
Galvanized steel bottle dryer
24 ¾ x 15 ¼ in. (63 x 38.8 cm)
National Gallery of Canada, Ottawa, Purchased 1971

Marcel Duchamp
Plan du Porte-bouteilles (Plan for Bottle Dryer), 1964
Working drawing, heliographic paper
46 ½ x 19 ¼ in. (118 x 49 cm)
The Berardo Collection – Sintra Museum of Modern Art

FER **THE SCATTER**

Gabriel Orozco
Various Models, 1992-95
Mixed Media
Courtesy Marian Goodman Gallery, New York

Eva Hesse
Untitled, 1968
Glass and metal display case
Metal, latex, plaster, paint, string, tape and plastic
14 ⅝ x 10 ¼ x 10 ¼ in. (37 x 26 x 26 cm)
Private Collection, Courtesy Annely Juda Fine Art, London

Piero Manzoni
Achrome, 1960
Wood, steel, kaolin
1 ⅝ x 1 ⅝ x 3 ⅞ in. (4 x 4 x 10 cm)
Torino, Collection Christian Stein

Gabriel Orozco
Soccer Ball, 2002
Cut out soccer ball
11 ¾ in. (30 cm) diameter
Courtesy: kurimanzutto, Mexico City

NESBIT **PARTS IMPLY WHOLES**

Gabriel Orozco
Yielding Stone (Piedra que cede), 1992
Plasticine and dust
132.2 lb (60 kg)
Courtesy Marian Goodman Gallery, New York

Gabriel Orozco
Crazy Tourist, 1991
C-Print, Edition of 5
16 x 20 in. (40.6 x 50.8 cm)
Courtesy Marian Goodman Gallery, New York

Gabriel Orozco
Yielding Stone (Piedra que cede), 1992
Plasticine and dust
132.2 lb (60 kg)
Courtesy Marian Goodman Gallery, New York

Gabriel Orozco
Yielding Stone (Piedra que cede), 1992
Plasticine and dust
132.2 lb (60 kg)
Courtesy Marian Goodman Gallery, New York

Gabriel Orozco
Island in an Island, 1993
Cibachrome
16 x 20 in. (40.6 x 50.8 cm)
Courtesy Marian Goodman Gallery, New York

ROBERT RAUSCHENBERG

p. 100
Robert Rauschenberg
Soles, 1953
Painted wood box containing six objects (2 dirt balls, stone, glass shard, polished blue stone, and Roman fresco fragment), individually wrapped in fabric and string
4 ½ x 17 x 3 in. (11.4 x 43.2 x 7.6 cm)
Collection of Jasper Johns

BRUCE NAUMAN

p. 150
Bruce Nauman
Eating My Words (from the portfolio **Eleven Color Photographs**), 1966–1967/1970
Chromogenic color print
19 ⅜ x 23 ³⁄₁₆ in. (49.2 x 60.5 cm)
Collection Museum of Contemporary Art, Chicago
Gerald S. Elliot Collection

p. 153
Bruce Nauman
Self-Portrait as a Fountain (from the portfolio **Eleven Color Photographs**), 1966–1967/1970
Chromogenic color print
19 ⅞ x 23 ¾ in. (50.9 x 60.3 cm)
Collection Museum of Contemporary Art, Chicago
Gerald S. Elliot Collection

ALLAN McCOLLUM

pp. 202 and 205
Allan McCollum
Over Ten Thousand Individual Works, 1987/88
Enamel on Hydrocal
2 in. (5.1 cm) diameter each, length variable, each unique
Collection of the artist

pp. 206–207
Allan McCollum
Over Ten Thousand Individual Works, 1987/88
Enamel on Hydrocal
2 in. (5.1 cm) diameter each, length variable, each unique
Installation: Stedelijk Van Abbemuseum, Eindhoven, 1989
Collection of the artist

pp. 208–209
Allan McCollum
Perfect Vehicles, 1988/89
Acrylic enamel on cast glass-fiber-reinforced concrete
78 x 36 in. (198.1 x 91.4 cm)
Installation: Richard Kuhlenschmidt Gallery, Santa Monica, California, 1989
Courtesy of the artist and Friedrich Petzel Gallery, New York

FELIX GONZLAEZ-TORRES

pp. 214 and 217
Felix Gonzalez-Torres
"Untitled" (For Stockholm), 1992
15-watt light bulbs, extensions cords, porcelain light sockets
Overall dimensions vary with installation
Twelve parts: 62 feet (18.9 m) in length each
Installation at Magasin 3, Stockholm Konsthall, Stockholm, 1992

pp. 218 and 221
Felix Gonzalez-Torres
"Untitled" (North), 1993
15-watt light bulbs, extension cords, porcelain light sockets
overall dimensions vary with installation
Twelve parts: 42 ½ feet (13 m) in length each
Installation view of "Felix Gonzalez-Torres" at Serpentine Gallery, London, 2000

p. 219
front to back:
Felix Gonzalez-Torres
Detail of "Untitled" (North), 1993
15-watt light bulbs, extension cords, porcelain light sockets
overall dimensions vary with installation
Twelve parts: 42 ½ feet (13 m) in length each
and
"Untitled" (Rossmore II), 1991
Green candies individually wrapped in cellophane, endless supply
Overall dimensions vary with installation
Ideal weight: 75 lbs (34 kg)
and
A selection of early work
Installation view of "Felix Gonzalez-Torres" at Serpentine Gallery, London, 2000

GABRIEL OROZCO

pp. 246 and 249
Gabriel Orozco
Working Tables (Mesas de trabajo)
Installation View
The Museum of Contemporary Art, Los Angeles, 2000
Courtesy Marian Goodman Gallery, New York

pp. 250–251
Gabriel Orozco
Working Tables (Mesas de trabajo)
Installation View
Kunsthalle Zürich,1996
Courtesy Marian Goodman Gallery, New York

Complete information for all other works appears in the Checklist of the Exhibition.

CHECKLIST OF THE EXHIBITION

LYNDA BENGLIS

Embryo II, 1967
Purified pigmented beeswax, damar resin, and gesso on Masonite
36 x 5 x 5 in. (91.4 x 12.7 x 12.7 cm)
Courtesy of the artist and Cheim & Read, New York

Excess, 1971
Purified beeswax, damar resin, and pigments on Masonite and wood
36 x 5 x 4 in. (91.4 x 12.7 x 10.2 cm)
Collection Walker Art Center, Minneapolis Art Center Acquisition Fund, 1972

Untitled from the Pinto Series, 1971
Pigmented beeswax, damar resin, and gesso on Masonite and wood
36 x 5 x 1¾ in. (91.4 x 12.7 x 4.5 cm)
New Orleans Museum of Art: gift of Mr. and Mrs. Leonard Glade, 81.98

Karen, 1972
Purified pigmented beeswax, damar resin, and gesso on Masonite
36 x 5 x 3 in. (91.4 x 12.7 x 7.6 cm)
Collection of Howard Read
Courtesy of Cheim & Read, New York

LEE BONTECOU

Flit, 1959
Welded iron, canvas, wire, and black velvet
65 x 65 x 7½ in. (165.1 x 165.1 x 19.1 cm)
Anonymous gift, courtesy of the Herbert F. Johnson Museum, Cornell University

Untitled, 1959–60
Welded iron, canvas, wire, and velvet
58 x 99 x 15 in. (147.3 x 251.5 x 38.1 cm)
Collection of Maxine and Stuart Frankel Foundation for Art

Untitled, 1961
Welded steel, canvas, black fabric, copper wire, and soot
80¼ x 89 x 34¾ in. (203.6 x 226 x 88 cm)
The Museum of Modern Art, New York, Kay Sage Tanguy Fund, 1963

LOUISE BOURGEOIS

Listening One, 1947–49
Bronze, painted white
80 x 20 x 20 in. (203. 2 x 50.8 x 50.8 cm)
Collection of the artist
Courtesy of Cheim & Read, New York

Observer, 1947–49
Painted wood
76½ x 24 x 12 in. (194.3 x 61 x 30.5 cm)
Constance Caplan, Baltimore, Maryland

Untitled, 1950
Painted Wood
57½ x 12 x 12 in. (146 x 30.5 x 30.5 cm)
Collection Jerry Gorovoy, New York
Courtesy of Cheim & Read, New York

Janus Fleuri, 1968
Bronze with golden patina
10⅛ x 12½ x 8⅜ in. (25.7 x 31.7 x 21.2 cm)
Collection of the artist
Courtesy of Cheim & Read, New York

MARCEL BROODTHAERS

Portemanteau aux Moules (Coat Hanger with Mussels), 1965
Coat hanger with four branches in wire painted in pink, six mussels shells hung up with metallic clothes pegs
17⅛ x 16⅞ in. (43.5 x 43 cm)
Musées royaux des Beaux-Arts de Belgique, Bruxelles – Koninklijke Musea voor Schone Kunsten van België, Brussel

289 Coquilles d'oeufs, 1966
Eggshells and oil paint on canvas
78¾ x 39⅜ in. (200 x 100 cm)
Stedelijk Museum voor Actuele Kunst (Municipal Museum of Contemporary Art), Ghent

Grande Casserole de Moules (Large Casserole of Mussels), 1966
Casserole pan, mussel shells, and paint
25⅝ x 29½ x 27½ in. (65 x 75 x 70 cm)
Stedelijk Museum voor Actuele Kunst (Municipal Museum of Contemporary Art), Ghent

Panneau de Moules (Panel of Mussels), 1966
Mussel shells, resin, and paint on panel
45¾ x 48 x 5½ in. (116 x 122 x 14 cm)
National Gallery of Art, Washington, Gift of the Collectors Committee

Moules Sauce Blanche (Mussels with White Sauce), 1967
Oil and shellac on mussel shells and painted metal casserole
19½ x 15½ x 13 in. (49.5 x 39.4 x 33 cm)
Private collection, New York

Valise avec Alphabet (Suitcase with Alphabet), 1973
Gray suitcase with pressed paper and painting
8 x 28 x 17 in. (20.3 x 71.1 x 43.2 cm)
Collection of Marie Puck Broodthaers
Courtesy of Marian Goodman Gallery, New York

ALBERTO BURRI

Sacco, 1952
Sack, canvas, oil, and vinyl on canvas and sack
33⅞ x 39⅜ in. (86 x 100 cm)
Fondazione Palazzo Albizzini "Collezione Burri," Città di Castello

Legno e rosso 3 (Wood and Red 3), 1956
Painted canvas covered with lacquered bark
62½ x 34½ in. (158.75 x 87.63 cm)
Courtesy of the Fogg Art Museum, Harvard University Art Museums, Gift of Mr. G. David Thompson, in memory of his son G. David Thompson, Jr., Class of 1958

Martedi Grasso (Fat Tuesday), 1956
Collage, paint, and rags on canvas
59½ x 98½ in. (151.1 x 250.2 cm)
Carnegie Museum of Art, Pittsburgh; Patrons Art Fund: Gift of G. David Thompson, 1957

Grande Sacco: Congo Binga, 1961
Burlap and canvas
62 x 100¾ in. (157.5 x 255.9 cm)
The Museum of Fine Arts, Houston

Nero Plastica, 1961
Plastic, fabric, vinyl, burning on canvas
39⅜ x 25½ in. (100 x 65 cm)
Fondazione Palazzo Albizzini "Collezione Burri," Città di Castello

MARCEL DUCHAMP

Boîte-en-Valise (The Box in a Valise), 1935–41
Series E of seven series, lettered A – G
Edition of 30 unnumbered boxes
68 miniature replicas and color reproductions of works by Marcel Duchamp contained in a dark green imitation leather covered cardboard box, signed in blue ballpoint pen Marcel Duchamp, assembled by Jacqueline Matisse Monnier, 1963.
15¾ x 14¾ x 3½ in. (40 x 37.5 x 8.9 cm)
Barbara and Aaron Levine, Washington D.C.

Feuille de Vigne Femelle (Female Fig Leaf), 1950
Painted plaster
3 9/16 x 5½ x 4 15/16 in. (9 x 14 x 12.5 cm)
Private Collection

Objet-Dard (Dart-Object), 1951
Galvanized plaster with inset lead rib
2 15/16 x 7 15/16 x 2⅜ in. (7.5 x 20.1 x 6 cm)
Private Collection

Coin de Chasteté (Wedge of Chastity), 1954
2-part sculpture: galvanized plaster for the wedge and dental plastic for the lower base
2 3/16 x 3⅜ x 1⅝ in. (5.6 x 8.6 x 4.2 cm)
Private Collection

...pliant...de voyage (Traveler's Folding Item), 1917 / 1963
Replica of Readymade fabricated by Ulf Linde 1963, signed by Marcel Duchamp in Milan 1964
9⅞ x 16⅞ x 13 in. (25 x 43 x 33 cm)
Moderna Museet, Stockholm
Gift 1965 from the Friends of Moderna Museet

Plan du Porte-bouteilles (Plan for Bottle Dryer), 1964
Working drawing, heliographic paper
46½ x 19¼ in. (118 x 49 cm)
The Berardo Collection – Sintra Museum of Modern Art

Porte-bouteilles (Bottle Dryer), 1914, 5th version 1964
Galvanized steel bottle dryer
24¾ x 15¼ in. (63 x 38.8 cm)
National Gallery of Canada, Ottawa, Purchased 1971

Fontaine (Fountain), 1917, 5th version 1964
Glazed ceramic white ware with black oil paint
14 ⅛ x 18 ⅞ x 24 in (36 x 48 x 61 cm)
National Gallery of Canada, Ottawa,
Purchased 1971

Porte-chapeaux (Hat Rack), 1917, 2nd version 1964
Wood hat rack
9 x 17 ⅓ x 13 in. (23 x 44 x 33 cm)
National Gallery of Canada, Ottawa,
Purchased 1971

Trébuchet (Trap), 1917, 2nd version 1964
Coat rack with oak panel and steel hooks
7 ½ x 39 ⅜ x 4 ½ in. (19 x 100.1 x 11.6 cm)
National Gallery of Canada, Ottawa,
Purchased 1971

Air de Paris (Paris Air), 1919 / 1964
Replica fabricated by Ulf Linde and glassblower Vilgot Ahlqvist, 1974, After lost version of 1964
6 ⅞ x 2 ¾ in. (17.5 x 7 cm)
Moderna Museet, Stockholm
Gift 1965 from the Friends of Moderna Museet

LUCIO FONTANA

Concetto spaziale, Scultura nera, 1947
Bronze
22 ½ x 20 ⅛ x 9 ½ in. (57 x 51 x 24 cm)
Fondazione Lucio Fontana, Milan

Concetto spaziale, 1956
Oil and glass on canvas
30 ¾ x 25 ¼ x 1 ½ in. (78 x 64 x 4 cm)
Darwin and Geri Reedy, Dellwood, Minnesota

Concetto spaziale, Natura, 1959–60
Terracotta with deep hole
16 ½ x 22 ⅞ x 15 ¾ in. (42 x 58 x 40 cm)
Fondazione Lucio Fontana, Milan

Concetto spaziale, Natura, 1959–60
Terracotta with deep hole
15 ¾ x 18 ⅞ x 15 ¾ in. (40 x 48 x 40 cm)
Fondazione Lucio Fontana, Milan

Concetto spaziale, Natura, 1959/60
Cast bronze
23 x 29 x 31 ½ in. (58.4 x 73.7 x 80 cm)
Collection of Maxine and Stuart Frankel, Bloomfield Hills, Michigan

Concetto spaziale, 1962
Oil, lacerations, and scratches on canvas
57 ½ x 44 ⅞ in. (146 cm x 114 cm)
Fondazione Lucio Fontana, Milan

ROBERT GOBER

The Floating Sink, 1986
Plaster, wire lath, and semigloss enamel paint
25 x 25 x 24 in. (63. 5 x 63.5 x 61 cm)
Private collection

Bag of Donuts, 1989
Acid-free hand-cut paper, dough, and synthetic resin
11 x 6 ½ x 6 in. (27.9 x 16.5 x 15.2 cm)
Collection of the artist

Cat Litter, 1989
Plaster, ink, and latex paint
16 ½ x 7 ¾ x 4 ½ in. (41.9 x 19.7 x 11.4 cm)
Stefan T. Edlis Collection

Drains, 1990
Cast pewter
3 ¾ in. diameter x 1 ¾ in. (9.5 x 4.4 cm)
Collection of the artist

Untitled, 1990
Beeswax, pigment, and human hair
23 ¾ x 17 ½ x 11 ¼ in. (60.3 x 44.5 x 28.6 cm)
San Francisco Museum of Modern Art
Purchased through Rita and Toby Schreiber, by exchange, Various Donors, the Members Accessions Fund, the Lenore and Ira Gershwin Fund, and the Accessions Committee Fund: gift of Carla Emil and Rich Silverstein, Lisa and John Miller, Helen and Charles Schwab, Norah and Norman Stone, Danielle and Brooks Walker, Jr., and Robin Wright

Robert Gober & Sherrie Levine
Untitled, Lightbulb, 1990
Enamel paint, beeswax, and rope
8 x 3 x 3 in. (20.3 x 7.6 x 7.6 cm)
Private collection, New York

Untitled, 1994
Paper, string, acrylic paint, and fabric
3 ½ x 2 ½ in. (8.9 x 6.4 cm)
Ron and Ann Pizzuti, Columbus, Ohio

Untitled, 1997
Leather, wood, forged iron, cast plastics, bronze, silk, satin, steel, beeswax, human hair, brick, fiberglass, urethane, paint, lead, motors, and water
Overall: 122 ½ x 104 x 75 in.
(311.1 x 264.2 x 190.5 cm)
Above Ground: 35 ½ x 35 ½ x 40 in.
(90.2 x 90.2 x 101.6 cm)
Below Ground: 87 x 104 x 75 in.
(221 x 264.2 x 190.5 cm)
Collection of the artist

FELIX GONZALEZ-TORRES

"Untitled" (For Stockholm), 1992
15-watt light bulbs, extensions cords, porcelain light sockets
Overall dimensions vary with installation
Twelve parts: 62 feet (18.9 m) in length each
Collection Magasin 3 Stockholm Konsthall

"Untitled" (North), 1993
15-watt light bulbs, extension cords, porcelain light sockets
overall dimensions vary with installation
Twelve parts: 42 ½ feet (13 m) in length each
Marieluise Hessel Collection, on permanent loan to the Center for Curatorial Studies, Bard College, Annandale-on-Hudson, New York

EVA HESSE

Eighter from Decatur, 1965
Tempera, enamel, cord, rope, found object, particle board, wood
27 ⅛ x 21 ¼ x 7 ½ in. (68.9 x 54 x 19 cm)
Museum Wiesbaden, Germany

Legs of a Walking Ball, 1965
Varnish, tempera, enamel, cord, metal on Masonite
17 ¾ x 26 ⅜ x 5 ½ in. (45.1 x 67 x 14 cm)
Leeum Samsung Museum of Art

Oomamaboomba, 1965
Paint, varnish, cord, metal, saw dust and glue on Masonite
22 x 25 ⅝ x 5 ⅛ in. (56 x 65 x 13 cm)
Hauser & Wirth Collection, Switzerland

Ringaround Arosie, 1965
Graphite, enamel, varnish, ink, cord, papier-mâché on Masonite
26 ⅝ x 16 ¾ x 4 ½ in. (67.5 x 42.5 x 11.4 cm)
The Museum of Modern Art, New York, Fractional and promised gift of Kathy and Richard S. Fuld, Jr., 2005

Accession II, 1967
Galvanized steel and plastic tubing
30 ¾ x 30 ¾ x 30 ¾ in. (78.1 x 78.1 x 78.1 cm)
Detroit Institute of Arts, Founders Society Purchase, Friends of Modern Art Fund and Miscellaneous Gifts Fund

Compass, 1967
Steel washers and sculp-metal on wood
10 x 10 x 1 in. (25.4 x 25.4 x 2.5 cm)
Hauser & Wirth Zürich London

JASPER JOHNS

Flashlight II, 1958
Papier-mâché and glass
3 x 8 ¾ x 4 in. (7.6 x 22.2 x 10.2 cm)
Collection of Robert Rauschenberg

Light Bulb II, 1958
Sculp-metal
5 x 8 x 4 in. (12.7 x 20.3 x 10.2 cm)
Collection of the artist, on loan to the Philadelphia Museum of Art

Do It Yourself (Target), 1960
Pencil with paint brush and dry watercolor cakes, and wood frame
7 ¾ x 5 ½ in. (19.7 x 14 cm)
Sonnabend Collection

Light Bulb, 1960
Painted bronze, edition 4 of 4
4 ¼ x 6 x 4 in. (10.8 x 15.2 x 10.2 cm)
Collection of the artist, on loan to the Philadelphia Museum of Art

Bronze, 1960–61
Bronze, edition #2/2 cast in 1979
3 ½ x 11 ½ x 6 ½ in. (8.3 x 29.2 x 15.9 cm)
Collection of the artist

YAYOI KUSAMA

Accumulation II, 1962
Sewn stuffed fabric, plaster, and paint on sofa frame
35 x 88 x 40 ¼ in. (88.9 x 223.5 x 102.2 cm)
Hood Museum of Art, Dartmouth College, Hanover, New Hampshire;
Gift of Mr. and Mrs. Harry L. Tepper

Suitcase, 1963
Mixed media
39 x 32 x 20 in. (99.1 x 81.3 x 50.8 cm)
Des Moines Art Center Permanent Collections; Gift of Hanford Yang, New York, 1971.7

Blue Spots, 1965
Sewn stuffed fabric on wood
32 ⅝ x 27 ½ x 5 ⅛ in. (83 x 70 x 13 cm)
Becht Collection, Naarden, The Netherlands

Red Stripes, 1965
Sewn stuffed fabric on wood
27 ½ x 32 ⅝ x 7 ⅞ in. (70 x 83 x 20 cm)
Becht Collection, Naarden, The Netherlands

PIERO MANZONI

Achrome, 1960–61
Polystyrene on canvas
28¾ x 20⅞ in. (73 x 53 cm)
Courtesy Sperone Westwater, New York

Achrome, 1962
Cotton on board
14½ x 12½ in. (37 x 32 cm)
Courtesy Michael Werner Gallery, New York and Cologne

Achrome, 1962
Pebbles, kaolin on canvas
31½ x 25⅝ in. (80 x 65 cm)
Constance Caplan, Baltimore

ALLAN McCOLLUM

Perfect Vehicles, 1988/2004
Acrylic enamel on cast glass-fiber-reinforced concrete
78 x 36 in. (198.1 x 91.4 cm)
Courtesy of the artist and Friedrich Petzel Gallery, New York

Over Ten Thousand Individual Works, 1987/91
Enamel on Hydrocal
2 in. (5.1 cm) diameter each, length variable
Collection of the artist

JOSIAH McELHENY

An Historical Anecdote about Fashion, 1999
Mixed media installation with glass objects; Fabricated (glass, metal, and wood)
98 ½ x 120 x 27 in. (250.2 x 304.8 x 68.6 cm) (display case size)
Henry Art Gallery, University of Washington, Seattle, purchased with funds from the Kayla Skinner Fund and Henry Contemporaries Acquisition Fund, Jodi Green and Dr. Mike Halperin, Edie Adams and courtesy of Donald Young Gallery, Chicago

An End to Modernity, 2005
Nickel plated aluminum, electric lighting, handblown glass, steel cable and rigging
Approximately 180 x 180 x 150 in. (457.2 x 457.2 x 381 cm)
Commissioned by the Wexner Center for the Arts at The Ohio State University
Courtesy of Donald Young Gallery, Chicago and Andrea Rosen Gallery, New York

Conceptual drawings for a chandelier, 1965, 2005
Super 16 mm color film and digital animation with soundtrack, projected on digital video
Music and sound composition by Beth Coleman and Howard Goldkrand
Running time: approximately 5 minutes
Commissioned by the Wexner Center for the Arts at The Ohio State University
Courtesy of Donald Young Gallery, Chicago and Andrea Rosen Gallery, New York

BRUCE NAUMAN

Eleven Color Photographs, 1966–1967/1970
Chromogenic development prints
Each approximately: 19 11/16 x 23⅝ in. (50 x 60 cm)
Collection Museum of Contemporary Art, Chicago, Gerald S. Elliott Collection

GABRIEL OROZCO

Working Table (Mesa de trabajo)
Mixed media
Dimensions variable
Courtesy of the artist and Marian Goodman Gallery

ROBERT RAUSCHENBERG

Untitled (Scatole Personali), 1951
Painted wood box with lid, containing wood beads, fabric, dirt, pebbles, and insect
1¾ x 13¼ x 3¾ in. (4.4 x 33.7 x 9.5 cm)
Collection of Ruth and Donald Saff

Nine Untitled Hanging Assemblages, 1952
Gelatin silver print
13 x 15 in. (33 x 38.1 cm)
Collection of the artist

Untitled (Scatole Personali), 1952
Painted wood box with lid, containing painted fabric, thorns, and snail shells
4 15/16 x 5⅜ x 5⅜ in. (12.5 x 13.7 x 13.7 cm)
Collection of Jasper Johns

Untitled Hanging Assemblage, 1952
Gelatin silver print
14¾ x 14¾ in. (37.5 x 37.5 cm)
Collection of the artist

Thirty Scatole Personali, 1953
Gelatin silver print
12 x 15 in. (30.5 x 38.1 cm)
Collection of the artist

Untitled (Gold Painting), circa 1953
Gold and silver leaf on fabric, newspaper, paint, wood, paper, glue and nails on wood, in wood-and-glass frame
10½ x 11½ x 1⅜ in. (26.7 x 29.2 x 3.5 cm)
Collection of the artist

Johanson's Painting, 1962
Oil, fabric, wood, metal, string and mixed media on canvas combine painting
56 5/16 x 48 x 7 in. (143 x 121.9 x 17.8 cm)
Sonnabend Collection

CY TWOMBLY

Untitled, Lexington, 1948
Wood, porcelain knobs, metal curtain tie-back, cloth, and house paint
14⅛ x 10½ x 12 in. (35.8 x 26.7 x 30.5 cm)
Private collection

Untitled, New York, 1953
Wood, wire, twine, nails, house paint, and wax on cloth
15⅜ x 10 x 4 in. (39.1 x 25.4 x 10.2 cm)
Collection of Robert Rauschenberg

Untitled, New York, 1955
Wood, cloth, twine, and house paint
22¼ x 5⅝ x 5⅛ in. (56.5 x 14.3 x 13 cm)
Collection of the artist
Courtesy of the Gagosian Gallery, New York

RACHEL WHITEREAD

Untitled (Twenty-four Switches), 1998
Aluminum
10¼ x 8 x 2⅜ in. (26.3 x 20.3 x 6 cm)
Collection of Peggy and Ralph Burnet, Wayzata, Minnesota

Untitled (Yellow Bed, Two Parts), 1991
Dental plaster
Overall (as installed): 66 x 27½ x 28 in. (167.6 x 69.8 x 71.1 cm)
Part A : 66 x 27¼ x 6¾ in. (167.6 x 69.2 x 17.1 cm)
Part B : 66 x 27 x 7½ in. (167.6 x 68.6 x 19.1 cm)
Hirshhorn Museum and Sculpture Garden, Smithsonian Institution, Museum Purchase, 1993

SELECTED BIBLIOGRAPHY

Ades, Dawn, Neil Cox, and David Hopkins. *Marcel Duchamp.* London: Thames and Hudson, 1999.

Affectionately, Marcel: The Selected Correspondence of Marcel Duchamp. Edited by Francis M. Naumann and Hector Obalk. Translated by Jill Taylor. Ghent: Ludion Press, 2000.

Alberto Burri: A Retrospective View, 1948–77. Los Angeles: Frederick S. Wight Art Gallery, University of California, 1977.

Alberto Burri: Galleria Nazionale d'Arte Moderna, Roma, 15 Gennaio–14 Marzo 1976. Edited by Giovanna De Feo. Rome: De Luca Editore, 1976.

Alberto Burri: October 16 to December 1, 1963. Houston: The Museum of Fine Arts, 1963.

Allan McCollum: Interview by Thomas Lawson. Edited by William S. Bartman. Los Angeles: A.R.T. Press, 1996.

Assemblage. Edited by Kristine Bell and Greg Lulay. New York: Zwirner and Wirth, 2003.

Barrette, Bill. *Eva Hesse Sculpture.* New York: Timken Publishers, 1989.

Bernadac, Marie-Laure. *Louise Bourgeois.* Translated by Deke Dusinberre. Paris and New York: Flammarion, 1996.

Bersani, Leo. *The Freudian Body: Psychoanalysis and Art.* New York: Columbia University Press, 1986.

Bois, Yve-Alain, and Rosalind E. Krauss. *Formless: A User's Guide.* New York: Zone Books, 1997.

Bruce Nauman. Edited by Joan Simon. Minneapolis: Walker Art Center, 1994.

Burri. Edited by Chiara Sarteanesi. Citta di Castello: Petruzzi Editore, 2001.

Burri: Opere, 1944–1995. Edited by Carolyn Christov-Bakargiev and Maria Grazia Tolomeo. Milan: Electa, 1996.

Cabanne, Pierre. *Dialogues with Marcel Duchamp.* New York: Da Capo Press, 1979.

Calvesi, Maurizio. *Alberto Burri.* Translated by Robert Erich Wolf. New York: Harry N. Abrams, 1975.

Camfield, William. *Marcel Duchamp/Fountain.* Houston: Houston Fine Art Press, 1989.

Celant, Germano, and Anna Costantini. *Roma–New York: 1948–1964: An Art Exploration.* Translated by Joachim Neugroschel. Milan and Florence: Edizioni Charta, 1993.

Cy Twombly: Die Skulptur / The Sculpture. Translated by Fiona Elliot, David Britt, and Eileen Walliser. Edited by Katharina Schmidt. Ostfildern-Ruit: Hatje Cantz, 2000.

Deitcher, David. "The Handmade Readymade." In *Post-Pop Art,* edited by Paul Taylor. Cambridge, Massachusetts: The MIT Press, 1989.

Demos, T. J. "Duchamp Homeless? The Avant-Garde and Post-Nationalism." Ph.D. diss., Columbia University, 2000.

Eva Hesse. Valencia: IVAM Center Julio González, 1993.

Eva Hesse. Edited by Elisabeth Sussman. San Francisco: San Francisco Museum of Modern Art; New Haven: Yale University Press, 2002.

Eva Hesse: A Retrospective. Edited by Leslie K. Baier. New Haven and London: Yale University Art Gallery: Yale University Press, 1992.

Eva Hesse: Paintings from 1960 to 1964. New York: Robert Miller Gallery, 1993.

Eva Hesse: Transformationen=Transformations/Kalendernotizen 1964–65= Datebooks 1964–65. Edited by Kunsthalle Wien. Cologne: Walther König, 2004.

Felix Gonzalez-Torres. Edited by Dietmar Elger. Ostfildern-Ruit: Hatje Cantz, 1997.

Felix Gonzalez-Torres. Stockholm: Magasin 3 Stockholm Konsthall. October 1992–February 1993.

Fer, Briony. *The Infinite Line: Remaking Art After Modernism.* New Haven and London: Yale University Press, 2004.

Fontana. Edited by Enrico Crispolti. Milan: Charta, 1999.

Fontana: Catalogo Generale, Vols. 1 and 2. Edited by Enrico Crispolti. Milan: Edizioni Electa, 1986.

Gumpert, Lynn, Ned Rifkin, and Marcia Tucker. *Early Work: Lynda Benglis, Joan Brown, Luis Jimenez, Gary Stephan, Lawrence Weiner.* New York: New Museum, 1982.

Haidu, Rachel. "Marcel Broodthaers, 1963–1972, or The Absence of Work." Ph. D. diss., Columbia University, 2003.

Helfenstein, Josef. *Louise Bourgeois: The Early Works.* Champaign, Illinois: Krannert Art Museum, 2002.

Hopps, Walter. *Robert Rauschenberg: The Early 1950s.* Houston: Menil Foundation and Houston Fine Art Press, 1991.

Jasper Johns: Drawings. London: The Arts Council of Great Britain, 1974.

Jasper Johns. Edited by Alan R. Solomon. New York: The Jewish Museum, 1964.

Jasper Johns: The Sculptures. Edited by Penelope Curtis. Leeds: The Henry Moore Institute, 1996.

Johnson, Ellen H. *Modern Art and the Object: A Century of Changing Attitudes.* London: Thames and Hudson, 1976.

Josiah McElheny. Edited by Centro Galego de Arte Contemporanea. A Coruna: Xunta de Galicia, 2002.

Klein, Melanie, and Joan Riviere. *Love, Hate, and Reparation: Two Lectures.* London: Hogarth Press, 1937.

Krauss, Rosalind E. *The Optical Unconscious.* Cambridge, Massachusetts, and London: The MIT Press, 1993.

———. *The Originality of the Avant-Garde and Other Modernist Myths.* Cambridge, Massachusetts, and London: The MIT Press, 1985.

Kusama, Yayoi, and Laura Hoptman. *Yayoi Kusama.* London: Phaidon, 2000.

Laplanche, Jean. *Life and Death in Psychoanalysis.* Translated by Jeffrey Mehlman. Baltimore and London: The Johns Hopkins University Press, 1976.

Lee Bontecou: A Retrospective. Chicago: Museum of Contemporary Art; Los Angeles: UCLA at the Armand Hammer Museum of Art and Cultural Center; New York: Harry N. Abrams, 2003.

Lippard, Lucy R. *Changing: Essays in Art Criticism.* New York: Dutton, 1971.

———. *Eva Hesse.* New York: New York University Press, 1976.

Louise Bourgeois: Sculptures, Environments, Designs, 1938–1995. Paris: –Paris-Musées, Editions des musées de la Ville de Paris, Editions de la Tempete, 1995.

Louise Bourgeois: The Personages. Edited by Mary Ann Steiner. Saint Louis: The Saint Louis Art Museum, 1994.

Louise Bourgeois: The Personages. New York: C & M Arts, 2001.

Love Forever: Yayoi Kusama, 1958–1968. exh. cat. Los Angeles: Los Angeles County Museum of Art, 1998.

Lucio Fontana. Paris: Editions du Centre Georges Pompidou, 1987.

Lucio Fontana, 1899–1968. Edited by Centre Culturel de la Fundacio Caixa de Pensions. Barcelona: Fundacio Caixa de Pensions, 1988.

Lynda Benglis. New York: Cheim & Read Gallery, 2004.

Lynda Benglis: Dual Natures. Edited by Susan Krane. Atlanta: High Museum of Art, 1991.

Lynda Benglis: Early Work. New York: New Museum, 1982.

L'empreinte. Edited by Georges Didi-Huberman. Paris: Centre Georges Pompidou, 1997.

Marcel Broodthaers. London: Tate Gallery, 1980.

Marcel Broodthaers. Edited by Walker Art Center. Minneapolis: Walker Art Center; and New York: Rizzoli, 1989.

Marcel Broodthaers: Korrespondenzen/Correspondences. Zurich: Galerie Hauser & Wirth; New York: David Zwirner Gallery; and Stuttgart: Oktagon Publishers, 1995.

Marcel Duchamp. Edited by The Museum Jean Tinguely Basel. Ostfildern-Ruit: Hatje Cantz, 2002.

Marcel Duchamp, Notes. Translated by Paul Matisse. Boston: G. K. Hall, 1983.

Marcel Duchamp, Pasadena Art Museum: A Retrospective Exhibition, October 8 Through November 3, 1963. Pasadena: Pasadena Art Museum, 1963.

Marcel Duchamp: Dans les Collections du Centre Georges Pompidou, Musée National d'Art Moderne. Edited by Didier Ottinger. Paris: Editions du Centre Georges Pompidou, 2001.

Marcel Duchamp: The Box in a Valise: De ou par Marcel Duchamp ou Rrose Selavy. Translated by David Britt. Edited by Ecke Bonk. New York: Rizzoli, 1989.

Minimal Art: A Critical Anthology. Edited by Gregory Battcock. Berkeley and Los Angeles: University of California Press, 1995.

Minimalism. Edited by James Meyer. London: Phaidon, 2003.

Mullins, Charlotte. *Rachel Whiteread*. London: Tate Publishing, 2004.

Naumann, Francis. *Marcel Duchamp: The Art of Making Art in the Age of Mechanical Reproduction*. Ghent: Ludion Press, 1999.

Nemser, Cindy. *Art Talk: Conversations with 12 Women Artists*. New York: Scribner, 1975.

The New Decade: 22 European Painters and Sculptors. Edited by Andrew Carnduff Ritchie. New York: The Museum of Modern Art, New York, 1955.

New Sculpture: Robert Gober, Jeff Koons, Haim Steinbach. Chicago: The Renaissance Society at The University of Chicago, 1986.

Panza: The Legacy of a Collector, the Panza Di Biumo Collection at the Museum of Contemporary Art, Los Angeles. Los Angeles: Museum of Contemporary Art, 1999.

Piero Manzoni. Edited by Germano Celant. Milan: Charta; London: Serpentine Gallery, 1998.

Potts, Alex. *The Sculptural Imagination: Figurative, Modernist, Minimalist*. New Haven: Yale University Press, 2000.

Rachel Whiteread. London: Haunch of Venison Gallery, 2002.

Rachel Whiteread: Shedding Life. Edited by Fiona Bradley. New York: Thames and Hudson, 1997.

Robert Rauschenberg. Edited by Branden W. Joseph. Cambridge, Massachusetts, and London: The MIT Press, 2002.

Robert Rauschenberg: A Retrospective. New York: Guggenheim Museum Publications, 1997.

Schwarz, Arturo. *The Complete Works of Marcel Duchamp*. Revised and expanded paperback edition, vol. 1: The Text. New York: Delano Greenridge Editions, 2000.

Singular Forms (Sometimes Repeated): Art from 1951 to the Present. Edited by the Solomon R. Guggenheim Foundation. New York: Guggenheim Museum Publications, 2004.

Soby, James Thrall, and Alfred H. Barr Jr. *Twentieth-Century Italian Art*. New York: The Museum of Modern Art, 1949.

Tomkins, Calvin. *Duchamp: A Biography*. New York: Henry Holt and Company, 1996.

Varnedoe, Kirk. *Jasper Johns: A Retrospective*. New York: The Museum of Modern Art, 1996.

Winnicott, D. W. *Home Is Where We Start From: Essays by a Psychoanalyst*. Edited by Clare Winnicott, Ray Shepherd, and Madeleine Davis. New York: Penguin Books, 1986.

———. *Playing and Reality*. New York: Basic Books, 1971.

Younger European Painters: A Selection: December 2, 1953 to February 21, 1954. New York: The Solomon R. Guggenheim Foundation, 1953.

INDEX

WEXNER CENTER FOR THE ARTS

PHOTO CREDITS

In addition to the individuals and institutions credited in the List of Illustrations and Checklist of the Exhibition, we gratefully acknowledge the contributions of the following photographers, collectors and institutions whose works are reproduced herein:

Lynda Benglis: Art © Lynda Benglis/Licensed by VAGA, New York, NY. Christopher Burke, Courtesy Cheim & Read, New York, pages 23 and 172; Courtesy New Orleans Museum of Art, page 175; Courtesy Walker Art Center, page 177. Lee Bontecou: All works Copyright © Lee Bontecou / courtesy Knoedler & Company, New York. Digital Image © The Museum of Modern Art / Licensed by SCALA / Art Resource, NY, page 44; Courtesy Herbert F. Johnson Museum, Cornell University, page 47; Courtesy Maxine and Stuart Frankel Foundation for Art, pages 48-49. Louise Bourgeois: Courtesy Louise Bourgeois Studio, page 14; Christopher Burke, Courtesy the artist, pages 22, 41 and 43; Peter Bellamy, Courtesy Cheim & Read, New York, page 38. Constantin Brancusi: © 2005 Artists Rights Society (ARS), New York / ADAGP, Paris, Digital Image © The Museum of Modern Art / Licensed by SCALA / Art Resource, NY, page 84. Marcel Broodthaers: All works © 2005 Artists Rights Society (ARS), New York / SABAM, Brussels. Courtesy Sonnabend Collection, page 131; Image © 2005 Board of Trustees, National Gallery of Art, Washington, pages 132 and 144-145; Courtesy Musées royaux des Beaux-Arts de Belgique, Bruxelles, page 140; Courtesy the lender, page 143; Dirk Pauwels, Courtesy Stedelijk Museum voor Actuele Kunst (Municipal Museum of Contemporary Art), Ghent, pages 146 and 147; Courtesy Marian Goodman Gallery, New York, page 149. Alberto Burri: Courtesy Fondazione Palazzo Albizzini "Collezione Burri," Città di Castello, pages 27, 50, 66-67, and 71; Courtesy Museum of Fine Arts, Houston, page 62; Katya Kallsen, © 2004 President and Fellows of Harvard College, page 65; Tom Little, Courtesy Carnegie Museum of Art, Pittsburgh, pages 68-69. Marcel Duchamp: All works © 2005 Artists Rights Society (ARS), New York / ADAGP, Paris / Succession Marcel Duchamp. Courtesy the Marcel Duchamp Archives: pages 28, 31, 60, 159, 161, 178, 180, 181 and 183; Courtesy Barbara and Aaron Levine, pages 32-33; © Åsa Lundén Moderna Museet, pages 34 and 184; Courtesy National Gallery of Canada, Ottawa, pages 35, 37, 156 and 186; © Per-Anders Allsten Moderna Museet, page 36; Graydon Wood, Courtesy Philadelphia Museum of Art, pages 184, 190 and 191; Courtesy The Berardo Collection - Sintra Museum of Modern Art, page 187; Courtesy Philadelphia Museum of Art, page 195; Lucio Fontana: All works © Fondazione Lucio Fontana, Milan. Courtesy Darwin and Geri Reedy, page 21; Courtesy Fondazione Lucio Fontana, Milan, pages 72, 75, 76 and 163; Courtesy Maxine and Stuart Frankel, page 77. Robert Gober: All works © Robert Gober. Courtesy the artist, page 25; Geoffrey Clements, Courtesy the artist, pages 234 and 239; Douglas Parker, Courtesy the artist, page 237; Courtesy the artist and Matthew Marks Gallery, New York, page 238; Courtesy Ron and Ann Pizzuti, page 240; Ben Blackwell, Courtesy San Francisco Museum of Modern Art, page 241; Joshua White, Courtesy the artist, page 242; Russell Kaye, Courtesy the artist, pages 243 and 244-245. Felix Gonzalez-Torres: All works © The Felix Gonzalez-Torres Foundation, Courtesy Andrea Rosen Gallery, New York. Neil Goldstein, Courtesy Magasin 3, Stockholm Konsthall, pages 214 and 217; Stephen White, Courtesy Center for Curatorial Studies, Bard College, pages 218, 219, and 220-221. Eva Hesse: All works © The Estate of Eva Hesse, Hauser & Wirth Zürich London. Manfred Tischer, Düsseldorf, Courtesy The Estate of Eva Hesse, Hauser & Wirth Zürich London, page 8; Courtesy Hauser & Wirth, Zürich, pages 24, 118, 121, 123, 125, 126-127 and 129; Photograph © 1998 The Detroit Institute of Arts, pages 91 and 124; Ed Restle, Museum Wiesbaden, page 226. Jasper Johns: Art © Jasper Johns/ Licensed by VAGA, New York, NY. Courtesy the artist, page 26; Courtesy Philadelphia Museum of Art, page 110; Orcutt and Van Der Putten, Courtesy the artist, page 113; Dorothy Zeidman, Courtesy the artist, pages 114-115; Courtesy Sonnabend Collection, page 117. Yayoi Kusama: All works © Yayoi Kusama. Hal Reiff, Courtesy Yayoi Kusama Studio and Robert Miller Gallery, page 2; Tom Haartsen, Courtesy Becht Collection, Naarden, The Netherlands, pages 18 and 166; Courtesy Des Moines Art Center, page 169; Courtesy Hood Museum of Art, Dartmouth College, pages 170-171. Piero Manzoni: All works © 2005 Artists Rights Society (ARS), New York / SIAE, Rome. Orazio Bacci, Milan, Courtesy Archivio Opera Piero Manzoni, page 59; Courtesy Sperone Westwater, New York, page 78; Courtesy Michael Werner Gallery, New York and Cologne, page 81; Courtesy Constance Caplan, page 83; Attilio Maranzano, Milan, Courtesy Archivio Opera Piero Manzoni, pages 137 and 229. Allan McCollum: Courtesy the artist, pages 202, 205, 206, 207, and 208-209. Josiah McElheny: Courtesy the artist, Donald Young Gallery, Chicago and Andrea Rosen Gallery, New York, pages 252, 255, 256, and 257; Richard Nicol, Courtesy Henry Art Gallery, University of Washington, pages 262-263. Ugo Mulas: Copyright © Ugo Mulas Estate. All rights reserved, Courtesy Archivio Ugo Mulas, page 54. Bruce Nauman: All works © 2005 Bruce Nauman / Artists Rights Society (ARS), New York. Michael Tropea, Photography © Museum of Contemporary Art, Chicago, pages 150 and 153; James Isberner, Photography © Museum of Contemporary Art, Chicago, pages 154-155. Gabriel Orozco: Courtesy Marian Goodman Gallery, New York, pages 222, 246, 249, 250-251, 264, 268-269, 270, 271 and 272; Courtesy kurimanzutto, Mexico City, page 230. Robert Rauschenberg: Art © Robert Rauschenberg/ Licensed by VAGA, New York, NY. Courtesy the artist, pages 5, 96-96 and 102-103; Courtesy Sonnabend Collection, page 92; Eric Pollitzer, Courtesy the artist, page 95; Courtesy Ruth and Donald Saff, page 98; Dorothy Zeidman, Courtesy Jasper Johns, page 99; Dorothy Zeidman, Courtesy the artist, page 100. Auguste Rodin: Erich Lessing / Art Resource, NY, page 86. Cy Twombly: Courtesy the artist, page 104; Courtesy Robert Rauschenberg, page 107; Robert McKeever, Courtesy the Gagosian Gallery, New York, page 109. Julian Wasser: ©1963 Julian Wasser, All Rights Reserved, page 196. Rachel Whiteread: Courtesy the artist and Luhring Augustine, page 210. Courtesy the artist and Luhring Augustine, and Lee Stalsworth, Courtesy Hirshhorn Museum and Sculpture Garden, page 213. Bridgeman-Giraudon / Art Resource, NY, page 87.

Published in association with
PART OBJECT PART SCULPTURE

ORGANIZED BY
Wexner Center for the Arts
The Ohio State University
Columbus, Ohio

CURATOR
Helen Molesworth

ON VIEW
October 30, 2005 – February 26, 2006

Major support for *Part Object Part Sculpture* was generously provided by The Andy Warhol Foundation for the Visual Arts, Bill and Sheila Lambert, Agnes Gund and Daniel Shapiro, and The Trueman Family.

Significant contributions were also made by Mary G. and C. Robert Kidder, Joyce and Charles Shenk, Triumph International Speisshofer & Braun Kommanditgesellschaft, Altria Group Inc., Nimoy Foundation, The Judith Rothschild Foundation, and Nancy and David Gill.

Additional funding was provided by Constance R. Caplan, Greater Columbus Arts Council, National Endowment for the Arts, Art Alliance for Contemporary Glass, the Corporate Annual Fund of the Wexner Center Foundation, and Wexner Center members.

Preferred accommodations were provided by The Blackwell Inn.

CURATORIAL ASSISTANT
Megan Cavanaugh Novak

DESIGNERS
Lorraine Wild, Robert Ruehlman, and Hilary Greenbaum, Green Dragon Office, Los Angeles

EDITORS
Gloria Kury and Cherene Holland

PUBLISHED BY
Wexner Center for the Arts
The Ohio State University
1871 North High Street
Columbus, Ohio 43210–1393
Tel: +614–292–0330
Fax: +614–292–3369
www.wexarts.org

and

The Pennsylvania State University Press
820 North University Drive
USB 1, Suite C
University Park, Pennsylvania 16802–1003
www.psupress.org

Published with the assistance of the Getty Foundation.

Printed in China

LIBRARY OF CONGRESS CATALOGING-IN-PUBLICATION DATA
Part object part sculpture /
organized by Wexner Center for the Arts
The Ohio State University Columbus, Ohio;
Curator, Helen Molesworth. – 1st ed.
p. cm.
"On view October 30, 2005 – February 26, 2006." Includes bibliographical references and index.
ISBN 0–271–02855–6
1. Sculpture, Modern – 20th century – Exhibitions. 2. Duchamp, Marcel, 1887–1968 – Influence – Exhibitions. I. Molesworth, Helen Anne. II. Wexner Center for the Arts.

NB198.P35 2005
735'.23--dc22

2005021989

front cover Eva Hesse
Ringaround Arosie, 1965

back cover Marcel Duchamp
Air de Paris (Paris Air), 1919 / 1974